JOHN OF DAMASCUS,
First Apologist to the Muslims

JOHN OF DAMASCUS,
First Apologist to the Muslims

The Trinity and Christian Apologetics in the Early Islamic Period

DANIEL J. JANOSIK
Foreword by Peter G. Riddell

◤PICKWICK *Publications* • Eugene, Oregon

JOHN OF DAMASCUS, FIRST APOLOGIST TO THE MUSLIMS
The Trinity and Christian Apologetics in the Early Islamic Period

Copyright © 2016 Daniel J. Janosik. All rights reserved. Except for brief quotations in critical publications or reviews, no part of this book may be reproduced in any manner without prior written permission from the publisher. Write: Permissions, Wipf and Stock Publishers, 199 W. 8th Ave., Suite 3, Eugene, OR 97401.

Used by permission of Southern Evangelical Seminary, *Christian Apologetics Journal*:
Daniel Janosik, "The Development of the Trinity Through Controversy," *Christian Apologetics Journal*, Vol. 11, No. 1 (Spring 2013).
Daniel Janosik, "John of Damascus, First Apologist to the Muslims," *Christian Apologetics Journal*, Vol. 9, No. 1 (Spring 2011).

Used by permission of Melbourne School of Theology, The Centre for the Study of Islam and Other Faiths:
Daniel Janosik, "The Development of Early Islam According to the Neo-Revisionists," *Occasional Papers in the Study of Islam and Other Faiths*, No. 1 (July 2009), 13–24.

Pickwick Publications
An Imprint of Wipf and Stock Publishers
199 W. 8th Ave., Suite 3
Eugene, OR 97401

www.wipfandstock.com

PAPERBACK ISBN: 978-1-4982-8982-5
HARDCOVER ISBN: 978-1-4982-8984-9
EBOOK ISBN: 978-1-4982-8983-2

Cataloguing-in-Publication data:

Janosik, Daniel. |

John of Damascus, first apologist to the Muslims : An exploration of John of Damascus's use of his Trinitarian teachings in his apologetic approach to Muslims in the early period of Islam / Daniel Janosik.

Eugene, OR: Pickwick Publications, 2016 | Includes bibliographical references and index.

ISBN 978-1-4982-8982-5 (paperback) | ISBN 978-1-4982-8984-9 (hardcover) | ISBN 978-1-4982-8983-2 (ebook)

John of Damascus, Saint | Theology—History—Middle Ages, 600–1500 | Christianity and other religions—Islam.

BR1720 J36 2016 (paperback) | BR1720 (ebook)

Manufactured in the U.S.A.   11/07/16

I dedicate this book to the memory of Dr. William Larkin, Professor Emeritus, Columbia International University Seminary and School of Missions. Dr. Larkin was a scholar's scholar and an example to many, not only in his pursuit of knowledge, but also, to a greater extent, in his pursuit of his Lord and Savior, Jesus Christ. I am grateful for his wise counsel, instruction concerning Greek translations, many stimulating and instructive conversations, and most of all for his encouragement, prayers, and friendship.

Contents

List of Illustrations and Tables | ix
Foreword by Peter G Riddell | xi
Preface | xiii
Acknowledgments | xv
List of Abbreviations | xvi

1 The Development of the Trinity through Controversy | 1
2 John of Damascus: Controversies Regarding His Life and Work | 20
3 John's Islamic Context | 45
4 The Early Formation of Islam | 66
5 Theological Development of Islam | 79
6 Heresy of the Ishmaelites: Authenticity and Analysis | 90
7 Disputation between a Christian and a Saracen: Authenticity and Transmission | 115
8 Analysis of the Disputation between a Christian and a Saracen | 140
9 The Trinitarian Beliefs of John of Damascus | 170
10 The Development of John's Apologetic Approach | 199
11 The Apologetic Successors of John | 219
12 Concluding Thoughts | 249

Appendix A: Substantiated Historical "Markers" in the Life of John of Damascus | 255
Appendix B: Theological Development Chart | 259
Appendix C: Heresy of the Ishmaelites (Translation from Kotter's text) | 260
Appendix D: Disputation between a Christian and a Saracen | 269

Bibliography | 277
Index | 291

Illustrations and Tables

Possible Transmission of the Disputation | 117

Comparison Chart for the Transmission of the Manuscripts | 120

Comparison Chart for Kotter, section 5, lines 1–10 | 123

Possible transmission of the written dialogues and oral lectures of John | 137

Appendix A: Substantiated Historical "Markers"
        in the Life of John of Damascus | 255

Appendix B: Theological Development Chart | 259

Appendix C: Heresy of the Ishmaelites
        (Translation from Kotter's text) | 260

Appendix D: Disputation between a Christian and a Saracen | 269

Foreword

For readers who love history, this study of John of Damascus promises much. He is considered by the Roman Catholic Church as the last of the church fathers and, as such, his name is uttered in the same breath as the greatest names in early Christian history, including Tertullian, Augustine, Iraneaus and Clement of Alexandria. Together these men and the other church fathers succeeded in articulating Christian doctrine in all its complexity.

An engagement with John of Damascus represents a journey into a fascinating past. But this great man is far from being simply an artefact of history. The world that he lived in was dynamically changing. The great Western Roman Empire had given way to the Eastern Empire, centred on Byzantium, which had seen periods of greatness but was facing a mortal enemy in the form of the Islamic caliphate.

Indeed, John of Damascus was experiencing the challenge of Islam firsthand. The great Christian centre of Damascus had capitulated to the advancing Islamic armies 40 years before John's birth. Damascus had become the capital of the Islamic Umayyad dynasty, and John's own father held a high position in the bureaucracy serving the Caliph himself.

So although John is a key historical figure, he has a particular relevance for today's world. He felt called to develop sharply-honed apologetic tools to respond to the challenges to Christianity being posed by Muslim theologians. Dr Janosik rightly calls him the first apologist to the Muslims.

Today the Christian world is being similarly challenged by resurgent Islam. That challenge takes many forms: movement of populations, as also occurred in John's time; doctrinal challenges, as John experienced himself; and a quest for political supremacy through a growing Caliphate movement, which John witnessed in full flight.

So this study by Dr Daniel Janosik is extremely timely. Today the Islamic world is in turmoil, triggering substantial Muslim migrations into post-Christian Europe. This is a significant watershed moment in history, as was the period during which John of Damascus lived. In this book, Daniel Janosik has given John a voice in the present day through his analysis of John's life and works, including those of his writings of greatest relevance to Christian-Muslim relations.

Readers of this work will be equipped not only with insights into early Christian history but also with tools to respond to the challenge of Islam to the church today.

Professor Peter G Riddell
Melbourne
February 2016

Preface

John of Damascus was the first major theologian to confront early Islamic beliefs. His treatise, *Orthodox Faith*, a systemization of the Christian teachings from the first seven centuries, provided him with a basis for understanding the tenets of Christianity in contradistinction to Islam. His two works on Islam, the *Heresy of the Ishmaelites* and the *Disputation between a Christian and a Saracen*, were written in response to the religious and political pressure of this new form of monotheism, which John viewed as a Christian heresy. Through these works, which engaged Islam, John developed an apologetic model that presented Christianity as the one true faith. This model employed three steps: a statement of the heresies' tenets, an explanation of the heresies' errors, and finally a counter argument that used logical reasoning supported by Scripture. This apologetic approach was developed further by his successors.

This book explores in detail the way in which John of Damascus interacted apologetically with early Islamic beliefs. It re-assesses biographical facts about John and critically examines authenticity issues connected to his two works on Islam. Most importantly, this book seeks to present a clear theological exploration of John's doctrine of the Trinity, so that the reader can better understand his significant apologetic assessment of what he called the heretical views of the Ishmaelites.

The analysis of John's two works on Islam provides the modern reader with invaluable insight into the theological controversies of the eighth century as well as a critical contextualization of Islam's early development within its larger contemporary Christian community. Ultimately, these writings of John of Damascus on Islam —especially his explanation and defense of the Trinity—illustrate the historical and apologetical nature of the first arguments on the Trinity between a Christian theologian and the Muslims.

Daniel Janosik, PhD
March 2016

Acknowledgments

First and foremost, my thanks go to my wife, Ann, for her sacrifice of time in proofreading, her many helpful suggestions, her patience, and her steadfast encouragement to me throughout this research. I am also grateful to my daughter, Anna, for her encouragement and her wonderful suggestions of alternate words. In addition, the following people have made significant contributions to my research:

I also want to thank my Ph.D. supervisors, Tony Lane, former Director of Research and professor of Historical Theology at London School of Theology, and Professor Peter Riddell, former Director of the Centre for Islamic Studies and Christian-Muslim Relations at London School of Theology and now at Melbourne School of Theology, Melbourne, Australia, for their guidance, instruction, criticisms and constant encouragement. I would not have completed this book without their help.

Τῷ Θεῷ ἡ δόξα

Εἷς γὰρ ὄντως Θεὸς ὁ Θεὸς καὶ ὁ λόγος καὶ τὸ πνεῦμα αὐτοῦ.
John of Damascus (*Orthodox Faith*, I.8.221–22)

Abbreviations

AD	*Anno Domini*, "in the year of our Lord," the year according to the Christian Calendar
AH	*Anno Hijri*, "in the year of the Hijra," the year according to the Islamic Calendar
ANF	*Ante-Nicene Fathers.* 10 vols. Edited by Alexander Roberts and James Donaldson. Grand Rapids: Eerdmans, 1997.
DIS	*Disputation between a Christian and a Saracen* by John of Damascus. Critical Greek text in *Die Schriften Des Johannes Von Damaskos*, edited by Bonifatius Kotter, 4:427–38. New York: de Gruyter, 1981. English translation by the author (see Appendix D).
DIV	*On the Divine Images* by John of Damascus. In *Three Treatises on the Divine Images,* translated by Andrew Louth. Crestwood, NY: St. Vladimir's Seminary Press, 2003.
HER	*Heresy of the Ishmaelites* by John of Damascus. Critical Greek text from *Liber de Haeresibus [On Heresies]* in *Die Schriften Des Johannes Von Damaskos*, edited by Bonifatius Kotter, 4:60–67. New York: de Gruyter, 1981. English translation by the author (see Appendix C).
Jacobitas	*Contra Jacobitas* by John of Damascus. Critical Greek text in *Die Schriften Des Johannes Von amaskos*, edited by Bonifatius Kotter, 4:109–53. New York: de Gruyter, 1981. English translation by the author.
Kotter IV	Bonifatius Kotter. *Die Schriften Des Johannes Von Damaskos.* Vol. 4. New York: de Gruyter, 1981.
Lampe	G. W. H. Lampe, *A Patristic Greek Lexicon.* Oxford: Clarendon, 1961.

NPNF¹	*Nicene and Post-Nicene Fathers.* First Series. 14 vols. Edited by Philip Schaff. Grand Rapids: Eerdmans, 1997.
NPNF²	*Nicene and Post-Nicene Fathers.* Second Series. 14 vols. Edited by Philip Schaff and Henry Wace. Grand Rapids: Eerdmans, 1997.
OF	*Orthodox Faith* by John of Damascus. Part 3 of *The Fount of Knowledge* by John of Damascus. Translated by Frederic H. Chase. In *St. John of Damascus: Writings*, 165–406. Fathers of the Church 37. Washington, DC: Catholic University of America Press, 1958.
PG	*Patrologia Graeca.* Edited by J.-P. Migne. 162 vols. Paris, 1857–66.
Q.	*Qur'an.* Translated by 'Abdullah Yusuf Ali. *The Meaning of the Holy Qur'an.* Beltsville, MD: Amana, 1999.
S.	Sura (or Surah)—a chapter in the *Qur'an*.

1

The Development of the Trinity through Controversy

INTRODUCTION

John of Damascus, in his treatise *Heresy of the Ishmaelites*, called Muhammad a "false prophet" and referred to the religion that Muhammad started as the "forerunner of the Anti-Christ."[1] As one of the first major theologians to confront what he called a "heresy," John believed that it was his duty to protect believers from what he viewed to be false beliefs.[2] Therefore, he took it upon himself to summarize the preceding seven centuries of orthodox Christian faith in order to provide a theological foundation for Christians living among the Muslims. He also developed two works, the *Heresy of the*

---

1. John of Damascus, *Heresy of the Ishmaelites* (HER). The author's translation is from the critical text by Kotter, *Die Schriften Des Johannes Von Damaskos*, IV, lines 2 and 10, page 60. Future citations will employ the format of HER for the Heresy of the Ishmaelites followed by the lines in Kotter's arrangement, such as HER 2 and 10. The full translation of this work by the author is found in the Appendix.

2. Louth, *St. John Damascene*, 77. Griffith points out that Anastasios in the 690s, like John at a later time, also considered Islam a kind of Christian heresy: Griffith, *Shadow*, 31–32.

Ishmaelites and the *Disputation between a Christian and a Saracen*, in order to warn Christians of the dangers of the new beliefs,[3] to demonstrate the rational basis of Christianity, and to provide a model for refuting the challenges of Islam. In writing both doctrinal explanations and apologetic admonitions, John followed the pattern of theologians such as Origen and Augustine,[4] who responded to the pressing heresies of their day by articulating more precise explanations of the doctrines they were promoting as well as addressing perceived, and real, theological weaknesses. As George Williams writes in his preface to a book by Harold Brown on orthodoxy and heresy, "the clear truth of and about Jesus Christ and the only begotten Son among the Three Persons of the Trinity was gained only after centuries of theological debate and conciliar clarification and definitions."[5] It is often easier to explain what something is by showing what it is not. Thus, the Church Fathers were able to clarify and purify Christian doctrine as they contrasted it with the heretical views that threatened the existence of the early church.

Harold Brown explains the necessary relationship between heresy and orthodoxy when he writes,

> Heresy, as we said earlier, presupposes orthodoxy. And, curiously enough, it is heresy that offers us some of the best evidence for orthodoxy, for while heresy is often very explicit in the first centuries of Christianity, orthodoxy is often only implicit. If we hope, today, that the orthodoxy we believe is the "faith once delivered to the saints" (Jude v. 3), then it is necessary to assume that it is older than heresy. But heresy appears on the historical record earlier, and is better documented, than what most of the church came to call orthodoxy. How then can heresy be younger, orthodoxy more original? The answer is that orthodoxy was there from the beginning, and heresy reflected it. Sometimes one catches a glimpse of another person or object in a mirror or a lake before seeing the original. But the original preceded the reflection, and our perception of it. The same, we would argue, is true of orthodoxy—the original—and heresy—the reflection. The heresy we frequently see first, but orthodoxy preceded it.[6]

---

3. See Armour, *Islam, Christianity, and the West*, 41.

4. Origen would be represented with his theological work *De Principiis* and Augustine with his *City of God*, as well as their numerous writings against the heresies prominent in their day.

5. Brown, *Heresies*, xix.

6. Ibid., 4.

For Harold Brown, heresy was a response, or reaction to the orthodoxy that was there from the beginning but had yet to be articulated in a systematic and universally acceptable formulation. According to this view, the heresies forced the early theologians to define and develop the doctrine that reflected the truth in Scripture because otherwise false belief would prevail and sabotage the true faith. However, while it is evident that the defense against heresies brought greater doctrinal clarity to the orthodox position, the "received view" that orthodoxy predates heresy has become a highly controversial claim.[7]

In the 1960s, Walter Bauer argued that orthodoxy was simply the beliefs of those who were the winners, and therefore the heretical views may have once been orthodox views that simply lost out to the stronger factions.[8] More recently, theologians argue that Bauer's view is not supported very well by history.[9] According to Alister McGrath, it is not so much that there was an orthodox position and a heterodox position, but rather that there were competing positions which would reveal their adequacy in the test of time.[10] Those who were later named as heretics may have had the best of intentions, but their theological explanations were not faithful to Scripture and failed to adequately represent theological truth. Orthodoxy, then, developed as an "emergent phenomenon," a type of "proto-orthodoxy" that rose to the top and prevailed because it best reflected the truth of the Scriptures.[11] Wrong ideas had to be cast off or otherwise they would destroy the true faith, which, by the end of the fourth century, became synonymous with orthodoxy. As one writer describes the apologetic treatises against the distortions caused by heresy, he explains that,

> For the Church, this was a crisis of some urgency, because doctrine was not something incidental to Christian faith. It was essential. To believe in the Jesus of the Docetists or the Gnostics was to believe in a false messiah. Jesus Christ was true God and true man. False doctrine obscured and distorted these all important facts and so offered a vastly different person in the place of Jesus.[12]

---

7. McGrath, *Heresy*, 61–80.

8. Bauer, *Orthodoxy and Heresy*, xxi–xxv. Baur's influence is still seen in Pagels, *Gnostic Gospels*, xxxvi.

9. McGrath, *Heresy*, 81. See also Ehrman, *Lost Christianities*, 172–80.

10. Ibid., 62–72.

11. McGrath, *Heresy*, 79.

12. Aquilina, *The Fathers of The Church*, 20.

Heretics, however, were important in the whole process because their errors or exaggerations had to be addressed, and in working out the solutions, better ideas were developed and more precise language was created.[13] Also, the heretics were often more innovative, and their explanations were driven by a desire to make better sense of theological mysteries. As Harold Brown notes, "In a sense, the first heretics were the more sophisticated and more intellectual Christians. Their faith immediately sought understanding."[14] However, they were impatient with the slow process of testing and approving ideas that would best represent Scripture and often ended up distorting the early forms of Christian doctrine. Brown concludes that "Although the explanations proposed by the first heretics did not win acceptance from the church as a whole, they challenged it to produce better interpretations."[15] In the end, then, orthodox doctrine won out not because it was promoted by the victors, but because the orthodox explanations were more precise in their terminology, more logical in their teachings and more faithful to Scripture.

The Challenge of Apologetics

Throughout history, the church has met the challenges of heresy and cultural pressures by formulating creeds to define the orthodox and biblical stance of the church. It was essential, however, for the church to continually re-contextualize these doctrines and creeds through apologetic means, for each century would bring its own unique forms of heresy. For example, Athanasius was one who realized that innovation was necessary if the heretical claims of Arius were to be laid to rest by a more adequate orthodox solution.[16] Better explanations and more precise language were needed in order to express doctrinal integrity and develop a doctrinal formula that would be consistent with Scripture and *descriptive* of the true relationship between the unity of God and the distinctions within the three persons of the Trinity. As Athanasius dealt with the aberrant theology of Arius, he was able to retain the core of scriptural truth and wrap around it a contextual formula of the Trinity that rested on the incremental contributions of many

13. Lane remarked, "Heretics often provided a great service to the church. For example, Marcion rejected the Old Testament and the Gospels of Matthew, Mark, and John, thus forcing the church to define the New Testament canon. Arius, in denying the deity of Christ, made the church articulate the doctrine that became most crucial to Christianity." Lane, "Heresy In The Early Church," 2–3.

14. Brown, *Heresies*, 27–28.

15. Ibid., 28.

16. McGrath, *Heresy*, 66–67.

other theologians as they all sought to be clearer in their explanations and more precise in their use of terms. This doctrine was then crystallized into creeds, but these creeds would still need to be re-interpreted in future times and re-contextualized as new misunderstandings challenged orthodoxy. Otherwise, a fossilized creed was in danger of being distorted by a heterodox view and eventually subsumed by false doctrine. This is what occurred in the time of John of Damascus when Islam came to represent a challenge to the core doctrines of Christianity and to centuries of carefully constructed theology. In defending the orthodox position, John would need to summarize the doctrine of the Christian church up through the eighth century and then develop an appropriate apologetic that would defend as well as refute. This pattern was established in the early church as the Church Fathers hammered out the doctrine of the Trinity in the midst of heresies and other controversies. With this in mind, let us first go back and trace the development of the Trinity up until the time of John of Damascus. Then, when we study John's writings on Islam, especially his explanation and defense of the Trinity, we will gain a deeper appreciation of the historical and apologetical nature of the first arguments on the Trinity between a Christian theologian and the Muslims.

THE DEVELOPMENT OF THE TRINITY THROUGH CONTROVERSY

An overview of the first seven centuries of the development of the doctrine of the Trinity through controversy is important for a number of reasons. First, this study provides the foundation for exploring the relationship between theology and apologetics in the process of the formation of the doctrine of the Trinity, which John of Damascus will contribute to in his own response to the heresies of his day. Second, this overview provides points of comparison between the theologians who helped develop the doctrine of the Trinity and John's later summary of their ideas in his own writings. Third, understanding the pattern of how the earlier theologians dealt with heresies and being familiar with the arguments used will aid in a more accurate assessment of John's own arguments and analysis. Fourth, the earlier examples of how re-contextualization of the doctrine of the Trinity was necessary as time progressed and new heresies arose will illustrate the importance of John's work in re-contextualizing the doctrine of the Trinity in his defense of Christianity against Islam for his own time.

What is the role of controversy in the development of the doctrine of the Trinity? How was heresy used to spur on orthodoxy in regard to the

Trinity? What re-invented heterodoxical challenges needed to be contextualized with clearer language and updated interpretations? This brief study will document how various theologians countered specific heresies, how their struggles to "hammer out" better explanations led to the use of innovative language and greater clarity, and how, after they had formulated the doctrine of the Trinity in the Nicene Creed, they were faced with having to re-contextualize the doctrine as new and re-invented heresies arose over time to challenge the orthodox position. This overview will also explain how heresies tend to go to one extreme or the other. In regard to the Trinity, they tend to emphasize either the unity of God or the distinctions of the three persons. Only what became known as orthodoxy could balance the two extremes.

Early Church (33–100)

In the period of the Early Church the Apostles, especially Peter, John and Paul, defended the "faith that was once for all entrusted to the saints" (Jude 3) against various challenges. Believers were called "tritheists" because they were thought to worship three gods. They were threatened by Docetism,[17] a form of Gnosticism, which taught that Jesus was in reality a spiritual being, in the appearance of a man, and that he only appeared to suffer and die.[18] Finally, early Christians were slandered, persecuted, and martyred by the Roman Empire. Yet in the midst of these trials, they held fast to their faith, which was often expressed in simple creedal statements like "Jesus is Lord." They also recited the triadic formula, "in the name of the Father, and the Son, and the Holy Ghost," at baptisms, but this seemed to have been accepted without much introspection (Matthew 28:19).[19]

The first Christians understood that "Father, Son and Holy Spirit," somehow still related to "one God" though they had not worked out the relationship at this time. The relationship between the "one God and three persons" was accepted as something beyond the understanding, but still essential for belief. They knew, somehow, that the Father is God, the Son is God, the Holy Spirit is God; that the Son is not Father, the Holy Spirit is not the Son or the Father, and that there is only one God. Thus, the task of early Christians was to explain how the three persons, Father, Son and Holy Spirit, could all be called God and yet to maintain that there is only one God.

17. From the Greek δοκέω, "to seem."
18. See 1 John 4:2–3 and 1 Tim 6:20–21.
19. Letham, *Holy Trinity*, 89.

The Apostolic Fathers (100–150)

The Apostolic Fathers also faced Roman persecution, charges of polytheism, and an increase in Gnostic heresies. Gnosticism taught, among other things, a dualism that identified matter as evil and everything spiritual as good. Therefore, since matter was evil, the God who created the earth was also evil. Docetism, as stated above, was a heresy that derived from Gnosticism and taught that since Jesus was good he must have been only spiritual. Thus, he must have only appeared to be a man in a physical body and the "Christ Spirit" must have left him on the cross since, being spiritual, he could not die. This presented a problem to the Apostolic Fathers because a Christ who was not physical could not pay the penalty for physical man's sin. The challenge was to show that Christ physically suffered, died, and arose again from the dead as one who was fully human and not just a spirit.

Ignatius (30–107)

One of the first Apostolic Fathers to take up this challenge was Ignatius, the bishop of Antioch and a possible disciple of the apostle John. Ignatius frequently referred to Jesus as God and taught that the Son has been coexistent with the Father from before time. He also spoke out strongly against Docetic beliefs by emphasizing that Jesus truly came in the flesh and was not a merely a spiritual apparition.[20] In the epistle to the Magnesians, Ignatius made the claim that Jesus Christ was "with the Father before the beginning of time."[21] Thus, we have someone early in the second century, who was connected with the apostle John, clearly state that Jesus Christ was not merely a spiritual being, but rather came in the flesh to redeem the flesh. He was also with the Father before the beginning of time and was one of three who were worshiped as God.

Polycarp (69–155)

Polycarp was another Christian leader at this time who, in the face of Roman persecution, gave his life to proclaim the truth about God. Polycarp was the Bishop of Smyrna and also a disciple of the apostle John ("hearer of John,"). He was martyred in the Roman arena, but before his death he gave a clear triadic confession of God in letters to the Christians of Asia Minor.

---

20. Ignatius, *Epistle to the Trallians* 9; in Schaff, *The Creeds of Christendom*, 2:11–12.
21. *Epistle to the Magnesians* 6:1; ANF 1:61.

> O Lord God Almighty, *Father* of your beloved *Son* Jesus Christ
> ... I bless you because you have considered me worthy of this
> day and hour, that I might receive a place among the number
> of the martyrs ... to the resurrection to eternal life ... in the
> incorruptibility of the *Holy Spirit*."[22]

Clement of Rome (c. 96)

Clement, an early bishop of Rome (c. 96), and often termed the First Apostolic Father of the early church,[23] also repeatedly refers to the Father, Son and Holy Spirit in his writings. For example, he writes in his Epistle to the Corinthians, "Do we not have one *God and one Christ and one Spirit* of grace which was poured out upon us? And is there not one calling in Christ?"[24]

These references to the Father, Son and Holy Spirit were attempts to reaffirm what the Scriptures were stating, but they were also appeals to believers to recognize that their beliefs were often in sharp contrast to the heresies that were challenging the church. However, there was still confusion about the Father and the Son, and the Son and the Holy Spirit in the post-apostolic age. This was clarified more in the time of the Apologists of the second century.

Second- and Third-Century Apologists and Polemicists (AD 150–325)

The claims of Tritheism in the time of the apostles continued to be an issue on into the second century. As is often the case, some Christians swung to the opposite side and began promoting a modalistic view of God. While tritheism claims that there are three separate gods, modalism holds that the three divine persons were all incarnated in Christ, and therefore the Father died on the cross.[25] "Where tritheism sacrificed the vital identity of Father, Son, and Holy Spirit to their multiplicity, the opposite heresy of modalism took monotheism so rigidly that it sacrificed the multiplicity of the divine persons to their unity."[26] Roger Olson adds that, "almost inevitably, it seems,

---

22. *The Martyrdom of Polycarp* 14:1–2; ANF 1:42. Emphases throughout are my own.

23. "Clement of Rome, St.," s.v. Cross, ed., *Oxford Dictionary of the Christian Church*.

24. *1 Clement* 46:6; ANF 1:17.

25. This is known as patripassianism.

26. O'Collins, *Tripersonal God*, 86.

heresy erupts in the patristic period when people try to say too much, rather than too little."[27] Often it is easier to go to either extreme rather than remain in the center of biblical tension.[28] That is what happened with those who tried to explain the relationship between God's unity and the separate distinctions between the Father, Son and Holy Spirit. On the one hand, those who stressed plurality in the Godhead over unity could end up with a belief in three separate gods working together. This latter charge of tritheism led to Christians being condemned as polytheists.[29]

On the other hand, the modalists, like Sibellius and Praxeas, stressed unity over distinctions of persons. They argued that God can only have one nature, so he must have expressed that one nature interchangeably as Father, Son and Holy Spirit in his roles consecutively as Creator, Savior and Comforter. In this way there are not three persons, but rather one person with three different roles and corresponding names. However, this extreme also leads to a deficient understanding of the relationship between the one and the three.

Arius taught another view that became heretical because his strong emphasis on "the absolute unity of the monad . . . denied the possibility of any multiplicity in unity"[30] and led to a subordinate view of the Son. Arius' way of holding to a belief in one God was to identify the inherent oneness of God's nature with only the Father. Therefore, since the Son was a different person from the Father, he must be subordinate to the Father. At best, the Son was a lesser nature emanating from the Father and created at a point before the creation of the world as the Logos of God was transferred to a created body. With a presupposition that led him to believe that the Son could not have the same nature as the Father, there was no way that Arius could resolve this impasse.[31]

---

27. Olson and Hall, *The Trinity*, 27.

28. Robertson McQuilkin, president emeritus of Columbia International University, is well known for saying that "it is easier to go to a consistent extreme than remain in the center of biblical tension."

29. While working out the correct terminology between the Western and Eastern branches of the church leading up to the Council of Constantinople in 381, each side accused the other of "tritheism" or "polytheism" due to the misunderstanding of each other's preferred terms for "essence" and "persons." The Cappadocian Fathers were instrumental in clarifying this issue and settling the dispute.

30. Beisner, *God in Three Persons*, 113.

31. Some scholars, like Plantinga Jr., have argued that Arianism is also a form of tritheism because Arians believed that there were three separate beings that were worshiped. The Father was the only uncreated God, but because the Son was ontologically separated from the rest of creation, even though in their view he was the first created being, he was superior to the creation and should receive worship as a deity. The Holy

Only the orthodox view is able to solve this dilemma and remain at the "center of biblical tension." Both unity and distinction are emphasized when God is understood as having one nature (ousia) in three persons (hypostases). The three persons are equally God and the one God is equally represented in each of the three persons. This view not only explains the relationship between God's unity and each person's distinctiveness, but it also best represents the scriptural belief in only one God and yet the practice of worshiping the Father, Son and Holy Spirit.

Justin Martyr (110–65)

One of the most prominent and capable apologists during this period was Justin Martyr, a pagan-turned-philosopher-turned-apologist. Justin used his skill as a writer to refute the heretics and further the kingdom of Christ. Two of the heresies that he rejected in his writings were Gnostic dualism and Marcionism. Marcion was a Gnostic heretic who taught that there were two gods. He rejected the wrathful, imperfect "God of the Old Testament" as a vengeful god of war and taught that the spiritual Father revealed himself in Jesus Christ as the "spirit of salvation." Thus, since Marcion did not believe that God could die, Jesus could not have died on the cross. As a Docetist, he even denied that Jesus was truly incarnate.[32]

In response to Marcion, and in regard to Trinitarian issues, Justin began to clarify the relationship between the Father and the Son, promoting the divinity of Christ and also explaining that Christ has a distinct function in relation to the Father.[33] For example, in his Second Apology, Justin expresses his ideas concerning the relationship of Christ to God the Father when he says the Son "is with God and is begotten *before all creation*."[34]

Spirit was also seen as separate from creation and worthy of worship as well. Thus, since Arians worshiped and believed in three deities, even though they were not considered to be consubstantial or co-eternal, their beliefs should still be considered to be a form of tritheism. The problem with this view is that it rests on who is worthy to be worshiped rather than the nature of the personhood of the one God, which is the basis of the unity vs. plurality issue. See Plantinga Jr., "Social Trinity and Tritheism," 20.

32. Brown, *Heresies*, 60–66.
33. House, *Charts of Christian Theology And Doctrine*, 43.
34. *Second Apology* 6; ANF 1:190. "The Father of all has no name given him, since he is unbegotten. For a being who has a name imposed on him has an elder to give him that name. 'Father,' 'God,' 'Creator,' 'Lord,' and 'Master' are not names, but appellations derived from his benefits and works. His Son (who alone is properly called Son, the Word [Logos] who is with God *and is begotten before all creation*, when in the beginning God created and ordered all things through him) is called Christ because he was anointed."

Justin also "held that the Son, sharing in the essence (*ousia*) and mind of God, was/is truly divine."[35] However, in his concern to protect the absolute transcendence of the "Father of all things," Justin apparently, perhaps due to his Platonic background, interpreted the incarnation of the Logos as a subordinate role to the activity of the Father.[36] This view of Christ in the "second place" should not be interpreted as subordinationism in the Arian sense, however, since Justin accepted the full divinity of Christ, but his words still opened the door for later misinterpretation.[37]

Irenaeus (130–200)

Irenaeus was a Greek-speaking Christian from Asia Minor who claimed to be a student of Polycarp and served as bishop of Lyons in southern Gaul. In defense of the oneness of God against Gnosticism and Marcionism, Irenaeus laid the foundation for the doctrine of the Trinity. Otherwise, without an emphasis on the one nature of God, belief in the three persons could be viewed as teaching a type of polytheism.[38] In *Against Heresies*, Irenaeus recaps his arguments against the Gnostics and writes that "I proved also that there is one God, the Creator, and that He is not the fruit of any defect, nor is there anything either above Him, or after Him."[39] In regard to Marcion, Irenaeus charged that he "divides God into two and calls one God good and the other just. In so doing he destroys the divinity of both."[40] Instead of a dualistic theology, Irenaeus taught that there cannot be more than one case of deity, and yet this one God is manifested in three persons.[41]

In a number of ways Irenaeus seems to be ahead of his time. He rejected in advance the Arian heresy when he declared that the Son "did not

---

35. O'Collins, *Tripersonal God*, 90–91, 96.

36. *First Apology* 13; ANF 1:166–67. "We are not atheists, worshipping as we do the Maker of this universe . . . by the exercising of prayer and thanksgiving . . . Our teacher of these things is Jesus Christ . . . and we reasonably worship Him, having learned that He is the Son of the true God Himself, and holding Him in the second place, and the prophetic Spirit in the third, we will prove."

37. O'Collins, *Tripersonal God*, 90–96.

38. Brown, *Heresies*, 79.

39. *Against Heresies* 2.Preface.1; ANF 1:359.

40. *Against Heresies* 3.25.3; ANF 1:459.

41. *Against Heresies* 4.33.7; ANF 1:508. "In one God almighty, from whom are all things, . . . and in the Son of God, Jesus Christ our Lord, through whom are all things, and in the saving dispensations by which the Son of God became man; and in the Spirit of God, who in each generation publicly discloses among human beings the saving dispensations of the Father and the Son, as the Father wills."

begin to be; he existed always with the Father."[42] He stressed the oneness of God, and yet explained how the Father, Son and Holy Spirit worked in "union and harmony in creation, providence, and salvation, for they are in each other prior to creation."[43] Finally, Irenaeus rooted "his triadic view of God firmly in the Bible and in the history of salvation, in contrast to the philosophical speculation of his opponents." These matters connected the one God to his work of salvation within human history as Father, Son and Holy Spirit.[44]

During this time, there were others who contributed important components to the Trinitarian development. Around AD 181, Theophilus of Antioch was the first to use the term "Trinity" (or Τριάδος) in reference to the triune Godhead.[45] Theophilus was also one of the first to treat the Holy Spirit as distinct from the Logos.[46] In AD 160, Athenagoras, who wrote against the modalist Noetus, said that "although the Word is God's offspring, he never came into being. Rather, having been with God and in God eternally he issued forth at a point in time."[47] This reference to Christ, the Word of God, as not having a beginning was an important step in refuting the modalists, who did not accept separate persons in the Godhead. Also, around AD 190, Hippolytus, who also wrote against Noetus, after quoting part of John 1:1, strongly stated his case for three persons in the Godhead, in which "the Father is above all the Son is through all and the Holy Spirit . . . is in all."[48] Thus, by the end of the second century, there was already a strong sense of God as a Trinity of three persons who had different roles and still, somehow, made up only one God. Our next theologian, Tertullian, will continue to clarify these ideas as he defends the concept of the Trinity against heretics, but he will also contribute substantially to the vocabulary that will be so necessary in providing the precise language demanded by this very important doctrine of the church.

---

42. *Against Heresies* 3.18.1; ANF 1:446.

43. Letham, *Holy Trinity*, 96. This also precedes the concept of the perichoresis of the Trinity, or the indwelling of each person, which was explored later by Gregory Nazianzen and even later by John of Damascus.

44. Ibid., 96.

45. *Discourse to Autolycus* 2.15; ANF 2:101 (though the "Trinity" refers to God, and his Word and his Wisdom).

46. House, *Charts of Christian Theology and Doctrine*, 43.

47. *A Plea for the Christians* 12.20; ANF 2:133.

48. *Against the Heresy of One Noetus* 14; ANF 5:228.

Tertullian (160-220)

Tertullian was a layman and an apologist who is said to have had "one of the finest theological minds to appear in the Latin West."[49] He is known especially for his innovative Latin Trinitarian vocabulary, his development of the "one substance, three persons" formula and his staunch defense of God's oneness and uniqueness against Gnostic polytheists like Marcion as well as modalists like Praxeas. As an apologist, Tertullian, like others who followed after him, was forced to deal with increasing persecution and heresy by clarifying the biblical teaching concerning God the Father, Son and Holy Spirit and developing more precise language in which to express these core biblical truths.

In response to the monarchian heresies,[50] Tertullian was the first to assert clearly the tri-personality of God while maintaining substantial unity of the three persons. In his debate against the modalistic view of Praxeas, Tertullian argued that "the connection of the Father in the Son, the Son in the Paraclete, produces three coherent persons, who are yet distinct one from another. These three are one essence, not one person, as it is said, 'I and my Father are one,' in respect of unity of substance, not singularity of number."[51]

In his defense against the modalism of Praxeas, then, Tertullian developed a clearer explanation of how the unity of God can be reconciled to the plurality of the persons. In fact, we may notice that Tertullian is the first one to use the word *trinitas* (Trinity) in Latin in order to express the relationship of the Father, Son and Holy Spirit. Tertullian also coined the words *substantiae* (substance) for the nature of God, and *persona* (person) for the three distinct persons in the *trinitas* (Trinity) of the one God.[52] These are very important steps in the development of language that can be used to describe the intricacies of the Trinity.

---

49. Olson, *The Trinity*, 29. Letham says that he was a layman who was "once thought to be a lawyer" (Letham, *Holy Trinity*, 97).

50. At that time there were two forms of the monarchian heresy confronting the church. Dynamic monarchianism denied the true deity of Jesus Christ and portrayed Jesus as a man penetrated and gradually deified by the *dunamis* (power) of the Logos. This view does not believe that Jesus himself was God, but rather considered that Jesus was just a man indwelt by the "Christ Spirit." In other words, Jesus became the Christ at his baptism when he received this Christ Spirit or Christ Mind, which meant that he was "deified" but still not "deity." Modalistic monarchianism (modalism), which was defended by Praxeas, taught that there is one supreme monarch (i.e., one God or "one principle"—*mone arche*) who is one person revealing himself at different times in three modes, sometimes as Father, and other times as the Son or Holy Spirit.

51. *Against Praxeas* 25; ANF 3:621.

52. Letham, *Holy Trinity*, 98.

Origen (185–254)

As a theologian, educator and a priest, Origen wrote the first systematic theology of Christian beliefs, *On First Principles*, which was directed against modalism, adoptionism and Gnostic Docetism.[53] As with John of Damascus and his *Orthodox Faith*, this theological work was written so that Christians would understand the essential beliefs of their faith and not be persuaded to follow any of the competing heterodox views. Like other apologists before him, Origen seems to have developed his views on the Trinity in response to the heretical views of his time. For example, one of his most noteworthy ideas, the eternal generation of the Son by the Father, was constructed against the adoptionists who believed that Christ was merely a man who was adopted by God at his baptism. In response, Origen countered their belief that "there once was a time when He did not exist" with the view that the begetting of Jesus "is an eternal and ceaseless generation as radiance is generated from light."[54] It was also important for him to maintain that the divine substance of God could not be sub-divided between the persons of the Trinity.[55]

Not all of Origen's innovations, however, led to a stronger orthodox position in regard to the Trinity. For Origen, God was the First Principle, and Christ, the Logos, was subordinate to him. Ambiguity at this time in regard to the relationship between the Godhead meant that "stress on the subordination of the Son and the Spirit would lead to the denial of their deity (by the Arians and *pneumatomachii*), while the assertion of their deity in that context would foster allegations of tritheism (which Gregory of Nyssa would rebut.)"[56] Origen, however, maintained that the Son was not a created being. Thus, Beisner says that "whatever subordinationism there is in Origen is in function among the members of the Trinity, not in nature, and is purely voluntary on the part of the Son and the Spirit, not a necessity of their nature."[57] Origen's understanding of the subordinate role of the Son may have been orthodox, but his failure to keep the Son's eternal

---

53. Ibid., 102.
54. *De Principiis* 1.1.2; ANF 4:247.
55. *De Principiis* 4.1.28; ANF 4:376. Thus he writes, "For we do not say, as the heretics suppose, that some part of the substance of God was converted into the Son, or that the Son was procreated by the Father out of things non-existent, i.e., beyond His own substance, so that there once was a time when He did not exist; but, putting away all corporeal conceptions, we say that the Word and Wisdom was begotten out of the invisible and incorporeal without any corporeal feeling, as if it were an act of the will proceeding from the understanding."
56. Letham, *Holy Trinity*, 107.
57. Beisner, *God in Three Persons*, 73.

generation in biblical balance with his subordinate role to the Father may have enabled Arius to push the idea of Christ's subordination beyond an orthodox position.

FOURTH-CENTURY CHALLENGES

Arianism (319–36)

We now come to the major heresy of the fourth century, Arianism. The chief architect of this heresy, Arius, claimed that the Son was created by the Father before the creation of the world, and therefore stated that "there was a time when He was not."[58] Like the modalist monarchians, Arius emphasized the unity of God's essence, but unlike the modalists, Arius taught that the Son was distinct from the Father, though infinitely different.[59] Arius believed that the Logos of God was eternal, but the Son was not. Therefore, since the Son did not share the essential nature of God, he was "not equal . . . nor one in essence with him."[60] Thus, Arius pushed Origen's precarious balance between the eternal generation and the subordinate role of the Son to one of the extremes. This may be an example where clarity of theology would have precluded distortions which ultimately led to heretical conclusions. Due to his deficient view of the Son, Arius promoted a form of subordinationism that could accept that the Son was homoi-ousios (similar substance) with the Father, but not homo-ousios (same substance). Alexander, the Bishop of Alexandria, and others, recognized that this popular heretical position of Arius needed to be opposed, but after diplomatic entreaties proved fruitless the emperor Constantine called a council at Nicea in 325 to discuss the matter. Arius' intent may have been to make the relationship between the Father, Son and Holy Spirit easier for the common Christian to understand, but if his errant doctrine had not been confronted by the apologists of that time, Arianism could have destroyed the orthodox view of the Trinity.

Fortunately in *Athanasius* (295 –373), who served as an assistant to Alexander, and later as the Bishop of Alexandria, the orthodox position had a capable champion who rose to the crisis and responded to the heretical views. Athanasius asserted that the Son is of the same essence (homoousios) as the Father, i.e. He is fully God. He also argued that the Son existed eternally and was not created. Rather, the Son was "begotten" by "eternal

---

58. Alexander of Alexandria, *Depositio Arii* 2; NPNF[2] 4:70.
59. *Contra Arianos* 1.2.6; NPNF[2] 4:309.
60. *De Synodis, Councils of Ariminum and Seleucia* 2.15; NPNF[2] 4:457.

generation" from the essence of the Father.[61] Athanasius also pointed out that our salvation requires that the Son must be fully God. If he were only a created being, then he would not have been able to have redeemed man through his death on the cross.[62] Ultimately the council recognized that Athanasius' position was correct and condemned Arius' teaching. Arius was excommunicated from the church and exiled to Illyricum.

Nicene Creed (325)[63]

With the conclusion of the Council of Nicea, the church recognized that Scripture supported the belief that the Son is fully and completely God, "of one substance with the Father."[64] The response to Trinitarian heresies up through this time, especially the unorthodox teachings of Arius, led to the formulation of the Nicene Creed. This creed not only encapsulated the orthodox position, but it also provided the standard by which future errant beliefs would be judged. One writer commends the formulation of the Nicene Creed and concludes that "the fact that it was precise in its meaning, specific and unambiguous, made it especially useful in clearly differentiating between the orthodox party and the Arians."[65] However, because the various factions of the council were not fully agreed upon the terminology, further confusion developed in the aftermath due to ambiguous interpretations of *homoousios* and *hypostasis*.[66]

The Importance of the Right Language

There were three positions represented at the Council of Nicea. The Heteroousions (different substance) said that Jesus was a created being. The Homoiousions (similar substance) said that Jesus subsisted of a similar substance, and the Homoousians, represented by Athanasius, believed that the only way to uphold the deity of Christ was to consider the Son to be the same substance as the Father. By the end of the debate most were convinced by the Homoousians and all but two of the estimated 318 council members agreed that the Son was "one substance with the Father." However, within

---

61. *Contra Arianos* 1.5.14; NPNF² 4:314.
62. *On the Incarnation of the Word* 1–32; NPNF² 4:36.
63. Kelly, *Early Christian Doctrines*, 232.
64. Ibid.
65. White, *Forgotten Trinity*, 188.
66. See Letham, *Holy Trinity*, 118–26.

twenty years of Nicea, due to political persuasion and continued ignorance of the importance of precise terminology, Arians and semi-Arians gained prominent ecclesiastical seats throughout the empire. Arius himself was reinstated to his former position in Alexandria when he presented his version of the creed to Constantine and disguised his heretical interpretation behind ambiguous words. Some continued to say that the Son was *heteroousios* and others even claimed that the Son was *anomoios*, or "unlike the Father." Semi-Arians, who accepted the *homoiousian* position, were becoming prominent and attracting many to their side. What they could not gain through church councils they were winning through political means. In the midst of this controversy, some Christian theologians who used *homoousia* to refer to the essential nature of God thought the ones who used *homoiousia* denied the *unity* of the three persons, while the *homoiousians* charged the *homoousians* with denying the *distinctions* of the persons. The first misinterpretation would lead to tritheism and the second misinterpretation would support a modalistic view of God. Again, this demonstrates the tension between unity and distinction of persons. Fortunately, under the leadership of Athanasius at the synod of Alexandria in 362, who acknowledged that the meaning behind words was more important than the word itself,[67] both parties recognized that they essentially believed the same thing about the nature of the three persons in the Trinity and settled on *homoousia* as the best term. Beisner quips that this was a time when clear thinking "saved orthodoxy from a permanent split over vocabulary."[68] If anything, it underscored the importance of using clear, precise language.

However, there was still enough misunderstanding and mistrust that it required the brilliant minds of the three Cappadocian Fathers, Basil the Great, Gregory of Nyssa and Gregory of Nazianzus to crystallize the Nicene vocabulary by way of precise theological explanations. They emphasized the distinctives of the three persons of the Trinity while vigorously defending their unity: one essence in three persons (one *ousia* in three *hypostases*). Aided by the strong orthodoxy of the emperor Theodosius, who convened the Council of Constantinople in 381, the heresy of Arius was finally put to rest. The modified Nicene Creed of 381 rejected the Arian position and clearly affirms that the Son is one substance with the Father, eternal and

---

67. Letham, *Holy Trinity*, 125. See also Torrance, *Trinitarian Perspectives*, 15. Torrance suggests that Athanasius understood the need to fill the words *ousia* and *hypostasis* with new meaning. In the council Athanasius called in 362, he was able to bring about a "profound revision in the meaning of being," which was necessary in order to solidify agreement on the formula "One Being (*ousia*), Three Persons (*hypostases*)."

68. Beisner, *God In Three Persons*, 92.

begotten of the Father. These phrases were all specifically crafted to counter Arian heresy.

The Cappadocian Fathers also advanced the theological teaching on the Holy Spirit, which is reflected in the modified creed. Unfortunately, the phrase "filioque," describing the procession of the Holy Spirit from the Father *and the Son*, was inserted at the Synod of Toledo in 589 and gained widespread use in the Western churches. The rejection of this added terminology by the Eastern churches ultimately resulted in a schism between the Eastern and Western churches in AD 1054. This is another example of the importance of using precise language in theological explanations as well as maintaining the center of biblical tension.

RECONTEXTUALIZATION OF THE DOCTRINE OF THE TRINITY

Augustine (354–430)

Less than a generation after the doctrine of the Trinity was crystallized in a creed at the Council of Constantinople (381), the great scholar Augustine probably wrote his work, *On the Trinity* (400–420), as a response to the growing popularity of *homoian* Arians.[69] This work, which was, in part, an apologetic defense of Nicene theology against a "resurrected" form of Arianism, demonstrates the necessity of continually re-contextualizing doctrines and creeds through apologetic means, for each century will bring its own form of heresy. Thus, new cultural situations produce new or "resurrected" heresies which require new or updated explanations of doctrine. The truth does not change, but language and context do.

John of Damascus (675–749)

Almost three hundred years after Augustine, the task of writing a re-contextualized theology of the Trinity fell to John of Damascus. Following the model of Origen and Augustine, as a response to the growing hegemony of Islam in John's homeland, he took it upon himself to summarize the previous seven hundred years of Christian doctrine in order to provide a contextualized systematic theology for the persecuted Christians as well as to demonstrate how Christian beliefs were more logical than those of the invading Arabs. The first task was accomplished in his great theological

---

69. Letham, *Holy Trinity*, 185.

summary of Christian doctrine, the *Orthodox Faith*, and the second task was dealt with through his two apologetic treatises, the *Heresy of the Ishmaelites* and the *Disputation between a Christian and a Saracen*. John's work makes it apparent that both areas are necessary, for apologetics is employed to develop orthodox doctrine and then that doctrine is used to critique heterodoxical beliefs. John of Damascus was clearly a master of using apologetics to develop his theology and then defend that theology against heresy. Since doctrine must continually face re-contextualization, John's model of providing preparation, defense and refutation should be valuable for this generation as well as future ones.

2

John of Damascus
Controversies Regarding His Life and Work

INTRODUCTION

Who was John of Damascus and why is he significant? As a Christian theologian serving in a newly formed Arab empire, John stood between two worlds in conflict. His writings, and insight into early Islam, may have influenced the Christian apologetic approach with Islam for the next 300 years. His early testimony from an involved observer's viewpoint of the development of Islamic theology may assist the scholarly task of reconstructing the various political debates and responses to Christian-Muslim polemics.[1] In addition, his writings indicate that he knew about Muhammad and the scriptures of the Ishmaelites. These early reflections from a theologian's perspective provide documented evidence of the views Christians held in regard to Muhammad and the Qur'an. His treatises may also help us construct a timeline of events and ideas as they developed in the first 100 years of Islam.

The city of Damascus, where John grew up, was a Christian city conquered by the Arabs in A.D. 635.[2] Many thought that the marauding Arabs

---

1. See Pines, "Some Traits of Christian Theological Writing," 90–93, 105–25. See also Wolfson, *Philosophy of the Kalam*, 58–64.

2. Donner, *Early Islamic Conquests*, 130–32.

were a punishment from God for their unfaithfulness.[3] In A.D. 661 it became the center of the Umayyad Empire where John later served in a high position under the caliphs, as did his father and grandfather before him. From his view as a contemporary witness, together with his later years of studying and writing theological treatises, John was able to speak uniquely on the earliest controversies between Christianity and Islam. In regard to John's situation, J.W. Sweetman states "perhaps no individual Christian thinker is so important in a comparative study of Islamic and Christian theology as John of Damascus."[4] Of his influence on both the Christian and Islamic communities of his time Daniel Sahas writes,

> John of Damascus's short writings on Islam have had indeed a very long history, as well as a profound influence upon other Christian writers who dealt with or wrote about Islam. His exposition of Islam made Islam known to the Christian community and, therefore made interfaith "dialogue" part of the history and the development of Islam as well as of Christianity.[5]

John of Damascus, then, was a Christian theologian in dialogue with Islam. His first-hand testimony should provide an important historical link to the early development of Islam within a larger Christian community. Unfortunately, while his written works are well known, the biographical material that could help us contextualize historical details is at a minimum. The biographies of John are thought to be fairly late (200–300 years after his death) and of dubious quality. Florovsky says that "it is not easy to pick out what is authentic and indisputable,"[6] and Hoyland adds that "the information that would help us to form a proper assessment of his writings is either lacking or of doubtful veracity."[7] Andrew Louth emphasizes that the "hagiographical lives of John that survive are late and unreliable; his writings contain scarcely any personal clues; and references to him in other historical sources are sparse."[8] Father Martin Jugie, in his statement about what is factually known about John, summarizes that,

> St. John is a descendant of a distinguished Christian family of Damascus in Syria; he was a priest and monk at the Laura of St. Sabas near Jerusalem, he became a prominent figure in the

---

3. Kaegi, "Initial Byzantine Reactions to the Arab Conquest," 139–49.
4. Sweetman, *Islam and Christian Theology*, 63.
5. Sahas, *John of Damascus on Islam Revisited*, 114.
6. Florovsky, *Byzantine Fathers*, 254.
7. Hoyland, *Seeing Islam*, 480.
8. Louth, *St. John Damascene*, 3.

iconoclastic controversy, as a preacher, he enjoyed a far-reaching reputation, and has left us numerous scholarly works which witness to his encyclopedic erudition. All other data must rest on conjectures.[9]

Actually, though, there are a number of other biographical pieces of information that can be put together to form a verifiable picture of this important "Christian in the court of the Caliph." One thing that a number of the early biographies did not do was to sort out what was factual and what was probably apocryphal. This work will attempt to categorize the life of John along the following three divisions:

I. Substantiated historical evidence

II. Logical conclusions based on writings from that time

    a. Internal evidence

    b. External evidence

III. Traditional biographical information on John

Hopefully, then, we will be able to piece the information together so that we have a more integrated picture of his birth, death, and education; his involvement in the Caliphate; his knowledge of Islam and the Qur'an; and finally his writings (especially in relation to the development of Islam and the Qur'an).

First, we will determine what we can say factually about John of Damascus from historical sources as well as his own writings (see Appendix A). The traditional accounts (especially information from the *Vita* on John of Damascus) will then help "flesh out" some of the details so that, together with the more substantiated material, we may connect more of the pieces of the puzzle and gain a clearer picture of his life, work and influence.

SUBSTANTIATED HISTORICAL EVIDENCE[10]

Birth and Death

The year of John's birth is very important because it is tied to who he may have known and what he may have witnessed. Most scholars place John's

---

9. See Tsirpanlis, *Anthropology of Saint John of Damascus*, 8.

10. See Appendix A: Substantiated Historical "Markers" in the Life of John of Damascus

birth in either 674 or 675,[11] but Sahas suggests that his birth may have been as early as 652,[12] allowing for a friendship with Yazid I, who was born in 644 and served as the caliph between 680–83.[13] However, this seems to be based on a statement by Lammens which claimed that a "young son of Sergius, named John"[14] was a friend of the caliph Yazid (680–83), when an Arabic source states only that it was the caliph's "freedman Sarjun the Christian"[15] who was present, meaning the father of John.[16] If Robert Hoyland is correct in his assessment that it is John's father who was a friend of the caliph Yazid I around 680 (when John would have been only about 5 years old), then the year 675 for John's birth is still the best choice compared with any earlier dates.[17]

The traditional date of his death is December 4, 749,[18] and Sahas adds that "there is no compelling reason to dispute this date."[19] The *terminus post quem* for John's death would be 743 when he supposedly dedicated his theological masterpiece, *De Fide Orthodoxa*, to his friend Cosmas Melodus, a fellow monk and friend of John from the monastery at St. Sabas, who was installed as the Bishop of Maiuma in 743.[20] There is a possible problem with this date, however, from Hoyland's perspective, in that the dedication date

---

11. Sahas, *John of Damascus on Islam. Revisited*, 106. Hoyland, *Seeing Islam*, 482.

12. Sahas derives this year by adding twelve years, the age of John when his tutor, Cosmas, was redeemed by John's father, and then subtracting the twelve years from a year mentioned by Theophanes, 664, when many people from Sicily were captured as slaves and brought to Damascus. Sahas, *John of Damascus on Islam*, 39. Other dates given are 655–60 (Nasrallah, *Saint Jean de Damas*, 58); Bonifatius Kotter suggests 650 (in Louth, *St. John Damascene*, 5), as does Karl-Heinz Uthemann (*Life of Saint John of Damascus in German*, 2). There was even one source that stated that John was born "only five years after the death of Mohammed," which would be AD 637! (*Butler's Lives of the Saints*, 36).

13. Sahas, *John of Damascus on Islam*, 38–39. Sahas is summarizing the view of Nasrallah, St. *Jean De Damas*, 58: "Il est établi que Jean fut le commensal et le compagnon de l'héritier de Mu'awaia Ier, Yazid, et du poète Ahtal."

14. Sahas, *John of Damascus on Islam*, 39. See note 1: "une jeune fils de Sergius, appelé Jean..."

15. Hoyland, *Seeing Islam*, 482. See note 92 where another writer, Aghani Isfahani, states that it is "Sarjun, freedman [*mawla*] of Mu'awiya," the previous Caliph.

16. Ibid., 482.

17. Ibid.

18. Chase, *St. John of Damascus: Writings*, xviin32. See also, Simmons, *Fathers and Doctors of the Church*, 96.

19. Sahas, *John of Damascus on Islam. Revisited*, 107, though Sahas was implying the year only and not the day and month.

20. Chase, *St. John of Damascus: Writings*, xvi and 3 (preface from *The Fount of Knowledge*).

was not part of the text, but rather part of a "secondary addition" in the lemma, and a later copy of the document from an eleventh-centuryGeorgian translation did not have the date attached at all.[21] Nonetheless, Frederic Chase relates that it can be said with a degree of certainty that "John and Cosmas were fellow monks and friends and that John composed his *Fount of Knowledge* at the request of Cosmas when this latter had become Bishop of Maiuma,"[22] and the earliest that this could have been accomplished was in 743 when Cosmas was installed. Therefore, John had to still be alive in A.D. 743. On the other side, the *terminus ante quem* of 754 for John's death has been assumed based on his anathematization by the synod of Hieria (east of Chalcedon) in that same year.[23] Though the general consensus seems to be that this marked John's death, we cannot surmise that he must have been dead before 754 when he was anathematized *in the past tense* by the Iconoclastic Council,[24] because, as Hoyland points out, the word καθεῖλεν may simply mean "deposed" or "degraded," and not necessarily "dead."[25] Thus, John may have been living through that time, as some have speculated (for some put his age at death over 100 years). Still, Andrew Louth concludes that the construction of the phrase suggested that John, as well as the other two who were being anathematized, were all dead by 754.[26]

The specific year of 749 or 750 for John's death primarily comes from the deduction of several researchers (such as Vailhe and Chase)[27] who note that the early ninth-century biography of St. Stephen the Sabaite states that Stephen was the nephew of John and came to the monastery where John was living in the year 735 when his father Theodore, the brother of John, was exiled.[28] According to the biography, he stayed for 15 years and left in the year 749 or 750, apparently because of the death of his uncle.[29] This would

21. Hoyland, *Seeing Islam*, 483n97.

22. Chase, *St. John of Damascus: Writings*, xvii.

23. Though some place the anathematization in 753 rather than 754 (see Chase, *St. John of Damascus: Writings*, xvii, for example).

24. Chase, *St. John of Damascus: Writings*, xvii.

25. Sahas, *John of Damascus on Islam*, 47. See also Tsirpanlis, *Anthropology of Saint John of Damascus*, 11–12. The actual phrase was "Ἡ τριὰς τοὺς τρεῖς καθεῖλεν" (Mansi, *Collectio*, XIII, 356; in Sahas, *John of Damascus on Islam*, 4n2).

26. Louth, *St. John Damascene*, 7.

27. Chase, *St. John of Damascus: Writings*, xvii. Simeon Vailhé, "Date de la mort de Jean Damascène," Echos d'Orient, IX (1906), 28–30, cited in Sahas, *John of Damascus on Islam*, 48n1.

28. Turtledove, *Chronicle of Theophanes*, 102.

29. Sahas (*John of Damascus on Islam*, 48) notes that Stephen's biographer states that he died in 794 at the age of 69. Therefore he was born around 725 and entered the monastery at the age of 10 in AD 735.

put John's death specifically in 749 or 750.³⁰ However, Hoyland believes that Vailhe and others have "wrongfully assumed" that St. Stephen the Sabaite referred to Stephen ibn Mansur al-Dimashqi, who was the son of Theodore and the nephew of John of Damascus.³¹ Sahas also cautions us that Stephen's departure does not necessarily warrant John's death at that time, and he acknowledges some of the same doubts that Hoyland has. However, Sahas points out that Leontius, the biographer of Stephen, and the one who ties Stephen together with John, makes no reference to John after the departure of Stephen in the year 749/750, thus giving a credible end to John's life.³² Ultimately, though the supporting details for John's death, as well as for his birth, are suspect, even Sahas has concluded, after carefully weighing the historical information, that there is no compelling reason to reject the year of John's death as 749 or 750.³³ Also, the date of 675 for his birth is still the best validated year according to the sources that we have.³⁴ Thus, John's life would have spanned a total of about 75 years between 675—750 and would have included familiarity with the following Umayyad Caliphs: Mu'awiyah I (661–80), Yazid I (680-83), Mu'awiyah II (683), Marwan I (684), 'Abd al-Malik (685-705), al-Walid I (705-15), and possibly up through Sulayman ibn Abd al-Malik (715-17) and Umar II (717-20).³⁵

Prominence of his family's religious and public resources

John of Damascus' grandfather, Mansur ibn Sarjun, was the financial governor³⁶ of Damascus when the Arabs besieged the city in 635. After six months he apparently capitulated to the Arab leader, Khalid b. al-Walid, and surrendered the city after receiving favorable conditions of surrender.³⁷ Later, in the year 661, Mansur was promoted to the highest position in the caliphate, under Mu'awiya I (661–80).³⁸ Apparently he was the

---

30. Chase, *St. John of Damascus: Writings*, xvii. See also Sahas, *John of Damascus on Islam*, 48.

31. Hoyland, *Seeing Islam*, 482n95.

32. Sahas, *John of Damascus on Islam*, 48.

33. Sahas, *John of Damascus on Islam. Revisited*, 107. Sahas, *John of Damascus on Islam*, 48. Florovsky, *Byzantine Fathers*, 254.

34. Sahas, *John of Damascus on Islam. Revisited*, 106.

35. Warraq, *Quest for the Historical Muhammad*, 550.

36. Hoyland, *Seeing Islam*, 480.

37. Sahas, *John of Damascus on Islam*, 17-19.

38. Ibid., 26.

chief financial officer for the city, also known as the general "logothetes" (λογοθέτης),[39] a position which implied the collection of land taxes, which would have involved the local Christians (since at that time the Arabs could not hold land personally).[40] This position seems to have been passed down through family lines, for John's father, Sargun b. Mansur (or Sergius), inherited the position and then passed it on to John during the caliphate of 'Abd al-Malik (685–705),[41] who apparently was a good friend of John's father.[42] It is also important to note that Sahas indicates that John may have attained a higher position than his father—that of personal secretary to the caliph, though he would have continued with the financial responsibilities that his father left to him. Sahas identifies the position as πρωτοσύμβουλος, or head advisor,[43] or as Phillip Schaff suggests, "chief councilor." Schaff also states that the term is often interpreted as "vizier," but that office did not yet exist.[44]

John's family was probably Semitic, and "Mansur" most likely means "victorious,"[45] though other renderings are "ransomed,"[46] or "saved."[47] John was known to the Arabs as Mansur ibn Sarjun, which was the same as his grandfather's name (though in his later life it was Yuhanna b. Mansur b. Sarjun).[48] Sahas, Louth, and Chase[49] all point out that John's surname is Arabic, but Le Coz says that "his family was without doubt of Syrian origin."[50] Both aspects could be true, for if his family ancestry were indeed Syrian, his grandfather could have been given an Arabic name when the Arabs

---

39. "Originally, logothetes were accountants. As Byzantine bureaucracy evolved and many late-Roman offices disappeared during the crises of the seventh and eighth centuries, logothetes began to fill their functions, and the title came to mean 'minister.'" Turtledove, *Chronicle of Theophanes*, 212.

40. Sahas, *John of Damascus on Islam*, 26–27, see esp. n4.

41. Ibid., 26–29.

42. Theophanes attests to this: (Annus Mundi 6183 (Sept 1, 691—Aug 31, 692): "Abd al-Malik also sent orders to rebuild the temple at Mecca. He wanted to take way pillars from holy Gethsemane, but Sergios the son of Mansur (a Christian who was public finance minister and was very friendly with Abd al-Malik) and his co-leader of the Palestinian Christians, Patricius (surnamed Klausus), asked him not to do this, but to persuade Justinian through their request to send other columns in place of these. This was done." Turtledove, *Chronicle of Theophanes*, 64.

43. Sahas, *John of Damascus on Islam*, 42.

44. Schaff, *History of the Christian Church*, 627.

45. Chase, *St. John of Damascus: Writings*, ix.

46. Schaff, *History of the Christian Church*, 627.

47. Sahas, *John of Damascus on Islam*, 5.

48. Ibid., 105.

49. Ibid. Louth, *St. John Damascene*, 6. Chase, *St. John of Damascus: Writings*, ix.

50. Le Coz, *Jean Damascène*, 43 ("sa famille était sans doute d'origine syrienne").

took over the government. Whatever the case, the Mansur family seems to have been respected by both the Christians and the Arabs alike, and they were known for their "piety and attachment to the Orthodox faith."[51] However, this favor did not remove the stain of history. Even though two later members of the family, Sergius I (842–58) and Elias III (878–907), became esteemed patriarchs of Jerusalem, the Mansur family name still carried with it the scar of that one member who had surrendered the city to the enemy.[52] This resentment may have built up over time as the effects of the Pact of Umar were felt more deeply. This Pact of Umar is supposed to have been the terms of peace offered to the Syrians when they were conquered by the Saracens in 635, though it could have been from a later time when Saracens had a greater hold over their empire.[53] Some of the obligations imposed upon the Christians were that they had to pay a poll tax, also known as a *dhimmi* tax, or jizyah, (which was not imposed upon Saracens), they could not build new churches or repair old ones if they were in Arab quarters, they could not proselytize Muslims or convert anyone to their beliefs (though there was no prohibition against anyone who wanted to embrace the religion of the Saracens), and they had to show preferential treatment to the Saracens such as standing in their presence and offering their seats when Saracens wished to sit.[54] It is easy to see how this "second-class citizenship" could wear thin after a while, and blame could be channeled to anyone involved in capitulation to such humiliating terms.

To those outside of the Arab-dominated world, John was known by his Christian name and place of origin: John of Damascus or John Damascene.[55] He was also known as a "presbyter and monk,"[56] and one of the greatest writers of theology, poetry and hymns in the Eastern Orthodox Church.[57] Theophanes (758–817), a Byzantine Chronicler, referred to John of Damascus as the one "who has well been called 'Chrysorrhoas' because

---

51. Sahas, *John of Damascus on Islam*, 29–30. Theophanes also refers to John's father as ἀνὴρ Χριστιανικώτατος, or a "devout Christian man." Theophanes, 6183 (AD 691–92) in Turtledove, *Chronicle of Theophanes*, 64.

52. Sahas, *John of Damascus on Islam*, 30–31. Also, Nasrallah, *Saint Jean De Damas*, 58.

53. The pact may have originated with Umar around AD 637, but the document we have by that name is probably from the ninth century (see following note).

54. *Pact of Umar*, probably from the ninth century, Medieval Sourcebook, January 1996, http://sourcebooks.fordham.edu/halsall/source/pact-umar.asp. Accessed, August 15, 2016

55. Sahas, *John of Damascus on Islam. Revisited*, 105.

56. Turtledove, *Chronicle of Theophanes*, 100.

57. Louth, *St. John Damascene*, 13.

of the golden grace of the Spirit that is reflected in his speech."[58] His facility with Greek verse and prose demonstrates that he had some type of classical education, and people writing about John three centuries later were still amazed at the breadth of his grasp of not only theological matters, but also of math, science and philosophy. On the other hand, Andrew Louth seems to believe that this should not have been so uncommon for a young man growing up in a prosperous Christian family which had been thoroughly influenced by the Hellenistic world which was so prevalent before the Arab invasion.[59] Frederic Chase says that his understanding of classical Greek philosophy and science is amply demonstrated in his first portion of the *Fount of Knowledge*, which is known as the *Dialectica*, for it not only provides the "first example of a manual of philosophy especially composed as an aid to the study of theology," but it "has remained to the present day indispensable for a proper understanding of Greek theology."[60] Chase also concludes that John's writings are "sufficient to show that his traditional reputation as an eloquent, learned, and devout preacher is fully justified."[61]

John probably succeeded his father as the chief financial officer of the Umayyad Empire during the reign of Abd al-Malik (685–705).[62] Though the Arabic sources used by Hoyland state that John's father left office around A.D.700, allegedly because the caliph imposed a rule that only Arabic speakers could hold a high office, they do not mention that John served under Abd al-Malik, and therefore cast suspicions on John's actual service under the caliph.[63] This story, however, is one of several anecdotal explanations for the policy change that took place in the first half of the eighth century when Greek was replaced by Arabic as the official language of the bureaucracy. There are two problems with trying to use this gradual movement with the idea that John's father was removed from office during the last part of Abd al-Malik's reign. The first problem is that it is very possible that the senior Mansur knew Arabic well since he had functioned in a high position under the Arab rule for many years and early sources have John's father

---

58. PG 94:108.841A. Chase adds that the term "Chrysorrhoas" can be translated "golden-flowing" and probably refers to the name of the river that ran through Damascus (Chase, *St. John of Damascus: Writings*, xiv–xv). Louth gives a slightly different rendition of Theophanes's words relating that Theophanes called him "John Chrysorrhoas ('flowing with gold'), 'because of the golden gleam of spiritual grace that bloomed both in his discourse and in his life.'" (Louth, *St. John Damascene*, 6).

59. Louth, *St. John Damascene*, 19.

60. Chase, *St. John of Damascus: Writings*, xxviii.

61. Ibid., xv.

62. Sahas, *John of Damascus on Islam. Revisited*, 106.

63. Hoyland, *Seeing Islam*, 481.

conversing with the caliph on several occasions.[64] The other problem is that a number of sources suggest that Greek was still used in the bureaucracy of the Umayyad Empire until most of the positions were filled by Arabs, which wasn't until almost the end of their rule in 750.[65] If this is accurate, then it is unlikely that ibn Mansur, John's father, was pushed out of office, which would have precluded his son from inheriting the position. Sahas also maintains that Christian sources, as well as Muslim ones, support the fact of John's service in the caliphate.[66] Sahas writes that John's father may have died between 691 and 695, since he is mentioned in the chronicle by Theophanes in relation to an event that took place in 691 and presupposed the death of Emperor Justinian II, which took place in 695.[67] If we use as our markers Sahas' date of 695 and Hoyland's date of 700, we can at least make a strong supposition that John's father died between the years of 695 and 700 and John assumed his father's position toward the latter part of Abd al-Malik's reign. The report by the Seventh Ecumenical Council of 787 also strongly conveys the view that John had a financial position in the caliphate since they likened him to the apostle Matthew, who had been a tax collector before he followed Jesus. The report reads as follows:

> John, who is insultingly called Mansour by all, abandoned all, emulating the evangelist Matthew, and followed Christ, considering the shame of Christ as a richness superior to the treasures which are in Arabia. He chose rather to suffer with the people of God than to enjoy the temporary pleasure of sin.[68]

Though it may be difficult to give a precise beginning and ending date for John's role as an administrator in the caliphate, there is really no reason to doubt that John served in the same office as his father and grandfather before him.[69]

---

64. Sahas, *John of Damascus on Islam*, 46.

65. Ibid.,

66. Sahas, *John of Damascus on Islam*, 41–42. Nasrallah (*Saint Jean De Damas*, 35) gives references from Al-Ṭabari (*Annales* 2.837), Ibn ʿAbd Rabbihi (*Al ʿIqd* 2.332; 5.162, 163; 4.225), al-Masudi (*Kitab al Tanbih* 398), Ibn Assaker (*Tarikh* 6.71), Michael the Syrian (*Chronique* 2.477), and Theophanes, *Chronoq.*, ad. Ann. 6182, 559).

67. Sahas, *John of Damascus on Islam*, 42.

68. Hoyland, *Seeing Islam*, 481–82.

69. See Sahas, *John of Damascus on Islam. Revisited*, 106; and Chase, *St. John of Damascus: Writings*, xii.

Retirement from Public Office

In time, John resigned from his post in the Umayyad government and retired to a monastery near Jerusalem, perhaps St. Sabas. Two questions that enter in here are "why did he leave his prominent position" and "when did this take place"? In the early stages of the Arab takeover of Syria, the Arabs were more tolerant than even the Byzantine emperor Heraclius,[70] and they usually retained the existing administrative structure as well as the official Greek language.[71] After all, the Arabs were not used to ruling the more sophisticated lands that they conquered and they did not have enough educated followers to assume the responsibilities needed to keep the government working smoothly. In time, however, the Arab rulers began to replace their Christian administrators with fellow Arabs and demanded that Arabic be used instead of Greek.

Theophanes records, however, that some things still required the use of Greek, so some Christians were still needed in the government.[72] Andrew Louth believes that John probably resigned from his governmental post as early as 706 during the time of Walid I when this changeover from Greek to Arabic was taking place.[73] However, this should not have been a problem for John since Sahas states that there is good reason to believe that he knew Arabic.[74] Raymond Le Coz also supports this view when he argues that if John had not been well-versed in Arabic, then he would not have retained his post in the reign of al-Walid (705–15) because of the Arabization that took place at that time.[75] Thus, Le Coz argues that John probably resigned his position in the Caliphate during the time of Umar II, who was particularly intolerant of having Christians in his administration.[76] Ernest Simmons concurs with this, and adds that the Caliph Umar "even refused them [Christians] the right to hold public office."[77] John then made his way

---

70. During the Persian victories of 611–20.

71. Sahas, *John of Damascus on Islam*, 25.

72. Turtledove, *Chronicle of Theophanes*, 73. "In this year (707–8) Walid . . . stopped the use of Greek in the public record books of the departments, ordering them to be written in Arabic instead: that is, except for numbers . . . Because of this their scribes are Christians even to the present day."

73. Louth, *St. John Damascene*, 6.

74. Sahas, *John of Damascus on Islam*, 45–46.

75. Le Coz, *Jean Damascène*, 52. On the other hand, Griffith believes that John left office and became a monk near the beginning of al-Walid's caliphate. See Griffith, "John of Damascus and The Church In Syria," paragraph 26.

76. Le Coz, *Jean Damascène*, 54.

77. Simmons, *Fathers and Doctors of the Church*, 91.

to the monastery at St. Sabas near Jerusalem[78] where he did most, if not all, of his writing.[79] Other scholars document his entry into the monastery as early as 715, at the end of al-Walid's reign.[80] Phillip Schaff even has John becoming a monk in the Convent of St. Sabas in the year 730,[81] perhaps because the first time Theophanes refers to John in his *Chronographia* it is the year 730 and he places John (the son of Mansur) as a "priest and monk" in "Syrian Damascus."[82] The most likely scenario is that he made the transition from palace to cell in time to become a priest and take up his pen against the iconoclasts in 726.[83] Thus, since Umar II was so intolerant of Christians serving in administrative posts, even if they knew Arabic, it is likely that John remained through the reign of Walid I (706–15) and entered the monastic life around the year 716.

Monastery Life and Writings

It is assumed that John entered the Monastery of St. Sabas near Jerusalem since John mentions being close to the patriarch of Jerusalem (presumably John V, 706–35) and often preached in the Church of the Holy Sepulcher in Jerusalem.[84] However, John does not mention the monastery of St. Sabas in any of his writings, and Hoyland maintains that John's absence from a list of "luminaries" who lived there during the eighth century mitigates against St. Sabas as his place of residence.[85] In fact, the earliest connection made between John and St. Sabas is in one of the tenth-century *vitas* composed by a later John, Patriarch of Jerusalem (John VII, 964–66).[86] However, lists can be incomplete and designed for purposes other than what researchers are using them for, and most biographers still accept St. Sabas as John's resi-

78. Le Coz, *Jean Damascene*, 54.
79. Sahas, *John of Damascus on Islam*, 51.
80. Chase, *St. John of Damascus: Writings*, xii.
81. Schaff, *History of the Christian Church*, 627.
82. Turtledove, *Chronicle of Theophanes*, 100. "In Syrian Damascus the priest and monk John Chrysorrhoas (the son of Mansur), an excellent teacher, shone in his life and his words."
83. The year that Leo III published his first edict against icons (see Chase, *St. John of Damascus: Writings*, xii). Nasrallah strongly suggests that due to the intolerance and hostility to Christians beginning in the reign of Abd al-Malik, and especially under his successors, John must have retired earlier than the traditional dates between 718 and 720, during the reign of Umar II. Nasrallah, *Saint Jean De Damas*, 72–73, 81–82.
84. Chase, *St. John of Damascus: Writings*, xii, xv. Louth, *St. John Damascene*, 6.
85. Hoyland, *Seeing Islam*, 483.
86. Louth, *St. John Damascene*, 6.

dence.[87] Even Hoyland accepts the possibility that the extract of the *Life* of St. John the Eremopolite gives credible witness to the fact that both Cosmas and John of Damascus were received into the monastery at St. Sabas at the hands of the same abbot named Nicodemus sometime in the eighth century.[88] Also, Frederic Chase states that "one may still see the cell of St. John of Damascus where he lived and wrote," and also his burial site at St. Sabas.[89]

Recently, Marie-French Auzépy has called into question this traditional view that John of Damascus had retired to the Great Laura at Mar Saba (founded in 487) to live and to write.[90] Her suppositions are derived mainly from her research on two works concerning the monastery in the eighth century, the *Vita of Stephen the Sabaite* (725–94), written by Leontius of Damascus between 807–21 and the *Passion of the Twenty Sabaite Martyrs*.[91] Her main argument rests on the premise that in the *Vita of Stephen the Sabaite*, Stephen does not mention John of Damascus in his list of important members living in the monastery during the eighth century. Her reasoning seems to be that if John of Damascus were such an important figure in such a rich and powerful establishment, then his reputation would have warranted mention in a book reflecting on the great luminaries of the monastery. Yet, the two texts are silent in regard to John of Damascus. She goes on to infer that John was either not a monk at Mar Saba or the two texts did not consider him to be of much importance. However, her conclusions rest solely on an argument from silence.

One reason Leontius may not have mentioned John of Damascus in Stephen's list of important Sabaites is that the purpose of the hagiography may not have been so much to honor specific members of the monastery, but rather to promote Chalcedonian Christianity itself. As Sidney Griffith writes in relation to the *Life of Theodore of Edessa*, "The real heroes of the piece are the monastery of Mar Saba, the see of Jerusalem, with its holy places, and the desert monks, who are presented as the guarantors of Christian orthodoxy in the Islamic milieu."[92] This may explain why *Stephen the Sabaite's* list of important luminaries who brought renown to the monastery were miracle-workers and martyrs rather than scholars, though there were a number of important scholars present at Mar Saba in the eighth century.

---

87. Sahas, *John of Damascus on Islam*, 38; Chase, *St. John of Damascus: Writings*, xii, xv; Le Coz, *Jean Damascene*, 55.

88. Hoyland, *Seeing Islam*, 111.

89. Chase, *St. John of Damascus: Writings*, xvii. See also PG 94:485–86.

90. Auzépy, "De La Palestine a Constantinople," 183–218.

91. Ibid., 184–85.

92. Griffith, "The Life of Theodore of Edessa," 147.

At one point in her argument, Auzépy writes that Stephen could not have been an admirer of John, because when Stephen promoted a role model for his disciples, he recommended that they strive to be like two prestigious monks who were known for their miracles rather than someone who wrote doctrine, liturgy and hymns, like John.[93] However, this may simply have revealed Stephen's preference for miracle workers, at least in the context of his own life as a miracle worker.[94] If this is the case, then Auzépy's argument from silence loses its significance.

In another attempt to explain the possible silence regarding John's absence from the list, Andrew Louth proposes that John of Damascus may have resided at another monastery situated near Jerusalem, rather than at Mar Saba. He refers to a tenth-century manuscript[95] of John's first sermon on the Dormitian that contains a phrase, "της παλαιας λαύρας" ("of the Old Laura"), which refers to the monastery of St. Chariton (founded 275), which is also located near Jerusalem.[96] Is it possible that John lived and wrote in a different Chalcedonian monastery which was known for promoting Maximus the Confessor, whom John of Damascus seemed to emulate? However, there are several reasons why the Old Laura of Chariton would not fit John's location as well as the Great Laura of Mar Saba. First of all, even though it is known that Chariton was a monastery where the monks produced copies of manuscripts and translated works from Greek to Arabic, the monastery consisted mostly of a series of seven caves where the monks lived and worked. It probably did not contain an extensive library as was

---

93. Auzépy, "De La Palestine a Constantinople," 191. This would not make much sense if Stephen were the nephew of John of Damascus and actually came to the monastery at a young age to live there and learn from his famous uncle. Indeed, if Stephen were in fact John's nephew, then he most certainly would have named John as one of the famous monks at Mar Saba in the eighth century—if his purpose had been to simply name the celebrities rather than the miracle workers and the martyrs. See Sahas, *John of Damascus on Islam*, 48. See also Turtledove, *Chronicle of Theophanes*, 102; and Hoyland, *Seeing Islam*, 480n85.

94. Griffith holds up Leontius's *Vita of Stephen* as an example of how the lives of miracle workers were often used to promote other causes: "In this same milieu other saints' lives also appeared, which had as their purpose the commendation of the central institutions of the "Melkite" community in the world of Islam, such as the monasticism of the Judaean desert, particularly the monastery of Mar Saba, and the centrality of the patriarchate of Jerusalem for the rule of faith." See Griffith, "The Life of Theodore of Edessa," 148. On the other hand, it would seem logical that laying claim to a scholar of John's ability and reputation would also promote the monastery, and yet he is not mentioned.

95. gr. 2081– Vatican collection

96. Louth, "St. John Damascene: Preacher and Poet," 249. See also Louth, "John of Damascus and the Making of the Byzantine Theological Synthesis," 301.

housed at Mar Saba.[97] For such a scholar as John of Damascus, it is likely he would have wanted to locate as near as possible to the best library available. As Nasrallah notes in his assessment of John's writings, they contained 738 citations found in 258 works by 48 different authors.[98] This would have necessitated a well-stocked library, which Chariton did not seem to have. In addition, Patrich notes that even in the time of Cyril of Scythopolis (ca. 555), "the library of the Great Laura was the largest and most developed of those in all the monasteries" around Jerusalem.[99] Also, as far as the heading of the sermon on the *Dormition* containing a reference to the Old Laura, it could simply indicate that John had written this particular sermon while visiting Chariton. He was known for preaching and teaching fellow Melkite monks, so it would not be unusual to find him doing some of his sermon preparation in another monastery.

John of Damascus was first and foremost a scholar. He was not a miracle worker and he was not martyred. This may be the reason why he was not on Stephen's list of Sabaite celebrities. As a scholar, it seems more likely that he would have desired to live at Mar Saba in order to have access to the best library in the area. Tradition has also strongly linked him to the Great Laura rather than the Old Laura. In addition, he could have easily written and studied at other monasteries, such as Chariton, while teaching, preaching and researching. We know he served in Jerusalem at the church of the Sepulcher and he was also friends with the Patriarch.[100] These were all sources for more resources for his research. Therefore, it makes more sense of the evidence to place John's residence at Mar Saba with travels to Jerusalem and beyond for purposes of preaching, teaching and research.

While we may not have direct evidence, outside the tenth-century *vitae* on John of Damascus, that he ever lived at the Monastery of St. Sabas, it is pretty certain that he was ordained as a priest and took the monastic name of John.[101] Theophanes, who died in 818, calls John "priest and monk" in his chronicle of the year 730,[102] and Florovsky states that his ordination must have been before 734 since even John alludes to his ordination at the

---

97. Tzaferis, "Early Christian Monasticism," 319.

98. Nasrallah, *Saint Jean De Damas*, 95.

99. Patrich, *Sabas, Leader of Palestinian Monasticism*, 191. In reference to Nasrallah's figures, Patrich adds that "this gives some idea not only of the scope of his scholarship but also of the content of the Laura's library in this later period, although the library of the patriarch of Jerusalem was available for him as well." 191n16. See also Peristeris, "Literary And Scribal Activities," 172–73.

100. Louth, "St. John Damascene: Preacher and Poet," 247.

101. Louth, *St. John Damascene*, 6.

102. Turtledove, *Chronicle of Theophanes*, 100.

hands of his mentor, John V, who died in 735.¹⁰³ Chase, on the other hand, ascertains that it must have been by the year 726,¹⁰⁴ probably because it is likely that John wrote his first letter against the iconoclasts in 726, and it carried the authority of a priest.

LOGICAL CONCLUSIONS BASED ON WRITINGS FROM THAT TIME

Internal and External Evidence from John's Writings

Andrew Louth expands on some of the other aspects of John's life that can be ascertained from internal and external evidence from John's writings. For example, John was of the Melkite tradition and therefore was a supporter of the Orthodoxy of the Byzantine king (which in Syrian is *malka*).¹⁰⁵ In the title of one of John's homilies he is described as a Presbyter (priest) of the Holy resurrection of Christ our God, which may refer to the Church of the Holy Sepulcher in Jerusalem,¹⁰⁶ which was also known as the Church of the Anastasis (resurrection). In this context, Eustratiades even goes so far as to identify John as the "sacred preacher of the Church of Anastasis."¹⁰⁷ If it is the case that John preached at this church in Jerusalem, then it may have been the venue for the writing of his liturgical poetry and homilies, for which he is well known.¹⁰⁸ Under the year 743, Theophanes writes that John delivered a sermon in praise of Peter of Maiuma, who was martyred for blaspheming Muhammad. It is the second time that Theophanes refers to John as "Chrysorrhoas," which means "golden flowing," and praises him because the "brilliant grace of the Spirit gleams golden in him, both in his words and in his life."¹⁰⁹ Indeed, John is probably best known for his writings, which fell into three categories: theological exposition and defense of the Orthodox faith, sermons and homilies, and liturgical poetry and hymnody.¹¹⁰ His work in theology, *De Fide Orthodoxa*, for example, was considered a type of *summa theologica*¹¹¹ and has become a standard for the

103. Florovsky, *Byzantine Fathers*, 254.
104. Chase, *St. John of Damascus: Writings*, xii.
105. Louth, *St. John Damascene*, 12
106. Ibid., 6.
107. Ibid.
108. Ibid.
109. Turtledove, *Chronicle of Theophanes*, 107.
110. Louth, *St. John Damascene*, 9.
111. Sahas, *John of Damascus on Islam*, 53. The purpose of John's theological

Eastern Orthodox Church. He was also one of the "greatest liturgical poets," and some of his hymns are still used today, and his poetry still graces the pages of Orthodox liturgy.[112]

Writings on Iconoclasm

The works that he was best known for in his lifetime were the three treatises against the iconoclastic Emperor Leo III. The first was written shortly after Leo's first condemnation of icons in 726, and the other two were written around 730, when Leo deposed Germanos, the Patriarch of Constantinople, who opposed him.[113] Living under Arab rule and outside the realm of the Emperor, John had more freedom to be bold in his "anathema" against Leo. The clear logic and force of John's arguments became widely known throughout the eastern world and even today are considered "such a complete defense of the veneration of sacred images based upon Scripture, tradition, and reason" that it would be hard to add anything to it.[114] This voice from the unreachable Saracen lands angered the Iconoclast emperors to such a degree that in 754 at the Iconoclastic council held in Hieria near Constantinople, John received three anathemas against him while Germanos, the former Patriarch of Constantinople, and George of Cyprus only received one each. It is revealing that Leo's son, Constantine V, Copronymus (741–75) referred to John by his Arabic name, and in one of the anathemas he not only changed the name "Mansur" to "Manzer" so that in its Hebrew form it became a vulgar term, but he also condemned him for having "Saracen sentiments!"[115] He was also anathematized for being a "worshiper of images and writer of falsehood," as well as being an "insulter of Christ and traitor to the Empire."[116] Then the words, "the Trinity has brought them down all three," bring finality to the series of anathemas.[117] Fortunately for John, the

---

compilation may have been to provide a summary of Christian theology from the previous seven centuries in order to provide Christians under the rule of Islam with a basis for their beliefs as well as an understanding of doctrines in contradistinction to Islamic theology so that Christians would stand firm and not convert to Islam. See also Schaff, *History of the Christian Church*, 588, 635.

112. Ibid., 13.

113. Chase, *St. John of Damascus: Writings*, xii–xiii. Louth, *Three Treatises on the Divine Images*, 10.

114. Ibid., xiii.

115. Ibid., xiii–xiv.

116. Chase, *St. John of Damascus: Writings*, xiv. See also Sahas, *John of Damascus on Islam*, 3–7.

117. Chase, *St. John of Damascus: Writings*, xiv. Sahas translates the phrase, "H

iconoclasts lost their support and in the 2nd Council of Nicaea (the Seventh Ecumenical Council of 787) John was exonerated and restored. It is interesting to note that the council used a parallel construction in its rehabilitation of John, so instead of the phrase "the Trinity had deposed the three," (Η τριὰς τοὺς τρεῖς καθεῖλεν), they use the phrase, "the Trinity had glorified the three," (Η τριὰς τοὺς τρεῖς ἐδόξασεν).[118] From that time through today his writings have influenced many people, and his hymns and liturgical poems are still used throughout the Eastern Orthodox world.

Simply a "Priest and Monk"

As Robert Hoyland concluded his summary of John's life, he raised the question about the scarcity of factual information. He muses that it may be as Theophanes says and that John "was simply a 'priest and monk,' a reclusive man who, however, reached out far with his pen."[119] Hopefully, the material presented above reveals a more extensive historical view of this "reclusive man" as well as the changing world that he experienced. As we turn to the more apocryphal stories of John, we should note that the basis of the story is often built around some of the historical details that we outline above. There may be an exaggeration of the events, but, as is often the case with legends, there is a skeleton of fact beneath the flesh of embellishment which may help give us a more complete picture of John's life.

TRADITIONAL BIOGRAPHICAL INFORMATION ON JOHN

The Greek *Vita* of St. John Damascene is attributed to John of Jerusalem—either John VI ((838–42), John VII (964–66 or 969) or John VIII (1106–56). Louth favors the latter because of an eleventh-century Arabic *vita* discovered recently.[120] John the Patriarch's *vita* was apparently a Greek translation from an earlier Arabic one, thought to have been written by Michael, a monk and priest who lived in Antioch and escaped the sentence of slavery when the Seldjuk Sultan Sulaiman ibn Kutulmis forced the city to surrender. This was on a Wednesday, December 4, 1084, the feast day of St. John

---

τριὰς τοὺς τρεῖς καθεῖλεν," as "The Trinity has deposed these three." Sahas, *John of Damascus on Islam*, 4n2.

118. Tsirpanlis, *Anthropology of Saint John of Damascus*, 11–12.

119. Hoyland, *Seeing Islam*, 484.

120. Louth, *St. John Damascene*, 16n2.

of Damascus. In his gratitude, Michael committed himself to find out all that he could about John. When he was told that there were no biographies, either in Greek or Arabic, Michael took it upon himself to write one. Apparently there were few authentic sources that he could locate, so he ended up putting together stories, legends and scraps of information from contemporary Fathers.[121] Daniel Sahas, however, favors John VII (964–66 or 969) and bases his conclusion on the existence of an earlier Arabic vita, possibly from as early as 808.[122] Sahas also explains that the "Michael story" is from a codex dated only from 1646, and based on other information he concludes that the rest of the *vita* ascribed to Michael is actually from an earlier Arabic work written before the tenth century.[123] For instance, due to the mention of the vita of St. Stephen written in 808,[124] Sahas states that the *terminus post quem* of the Arabic *vita* should be this date. He also brings to light that an early Greek palimpsest codex pushes the date before the tenth century. He then favors John VII (964–66 or 969) over the earlier John VI (838–42) as the Patriarch who translated the earlier Arabic text and therefore gives his *terminus ante quem* at 969.[125] If this is the case, then there is possibly only 60 years between the earliest *vita* (808) and John's death (749), which would give us a stronger connection with actual events that transpired in his life.

Robert Hoyland, however, cautions that the *vita* can only be used in a limited sense since the "information that would help us to form a proper assessment of his writings is either lacking or of doubtful veracity."[126] Frederic Chase also notes that there are a number of problems with this short biography which he complains is "bombastic and poorly written," and is, he feels, also "quite unreliable."[127]

What can we learn from the *vita*? Following is a summary of the major events outlined in the *vita* according to the Greek translation.[128] Following

121. Tsirpanlis, *The Anthropology of saint John of Damascus*, 6.

122. Sahas, *John of Damascus on Islam*, 32.

123. Ibid.

124. Auzépy, "De La Palestine a Constantinople," 184–85.

125. Sahas, *John of Damascus on Islam*, 34–35. Sahas never really gives a reason for choosing John VII over John VI and says that the question is still open to further investigation.

126. Hoyland, *Seeing Islam*, 480. His full statement is that "despite the enormously important role he played in the struggle against iconoclasm, we know very little about the life of John of Damascus, and the information that would help us to form a proper assessment of his writings is either lacking or of doubtful veracity."

127. Chase, *St. John of Damascus: Writings*, vi.

128. PG 94:429–90. See also, Chase, *St. John of Damascus: Writings*, vi–x. Louth, *St. John Damascene*, 15–21. Sahas, *John of Damascus on Islam*, 32–48. Le Coz, *Jean Damascene*, 41–58. Schaff, *History of the Christian Church*, 628–29.

this summary is a more detailed assessment of the vita and its possible use in reconstructing a more accurate biography of John of Damascus.

Part I: John's Prominence in the Arab Government

The *Vita* states that John came from a prominent Christian family.[129] The *Vita* also relates the story of a monk from Calabria (or Sicily), named Cosmas, who had been captured and enslaved by the Arabs, and who was freed by John's father and became John's tutor, as well as the tutor of another adopted son named Cosmas.[130] After Cosmas has taught John all he knows, he asks permission to retire to the monastery at St. Sabas to resume his monastic life—and permission is granted.[131] After John's father dies, John is made the first councilor (or protosymboulos) under the Caliph (?), perhaps Abd al-Malik (685–705).[132]

Part II: The Controversy over Icons and His Miraculous Healing

In 726 the Byzantine Emperor Leo III banned the use of icons and John wrote three treatises against this mandate from the safety of the Arab-held lands (726–30).[133] Enraged, and yet powerless to harm John directly, the Emperor sends forged letters that implicate John in a treasonous plot against the Caliph.[134] The Caliph orders John's right hand amputated as punishment for his disloyalty and has the hand put on public display.[135] John begs to have his hand returned to him so that he can bury it, and the Caliph relents.[136]

Miraculously, after John prays to the Mother of God, his hand is restored as he sleeps.[137] The next day the Caliph sees John with his restored hand (suture marks and all) and ascertains that John must be innocent of the charges and offers him a promotion.[138] John has had enough of government work, however, and retires to the monastery at St. Sabas, located near

---

129. PG 94:436–37.
130. Ibid., 440–41.
131. Ibid., 449.
132. Ibid.
133. Ibid., 452.
134. Ibid., 453.
135. Ibid., 456.
136. Ibid., 457.
137. Ibid.
138. Ibid., 460.

Jerusalem.¹³⁹ Before he can do this, however, he must defend himself in a duel.¹⁴⁰ John gives away his wealth, tours the holy places around Jerusalem and settles into the monastery at St. Sabas with his adopted brother, Cosmas.¹⁴¹

Part III: His Early Struggle in the Monastery at St. Sabas

John's fame precedes him, and as he enters the monastery at St. Sabas there is no one who feels qualified to undertake his training.¹⁴² Finally one of the older, stricter monks takes it upon himself to receive John into his cell and train the young theologian.¹⁴³ This is difficult for John because the older monk forbids him to write and sets about trying to teach John humility by sending him back to the city of Damascus, where he was well known, to sell baskets for exorbitant amounts. This task, however, turns out to be in John's favor, for instead of being ridiculed one of his former servants has pity on him and pays the high price for the baskets.¹⁴⁴ In time one of his fellow monks comes to him and begs him to write some funeral poetry for a relative who has just died. After some persuasion John relents and writes a poem for his bereaved friend. When the older monk hears about this he turns John out of his cell in anger. The other monks finally persuade the elder monk to relent and take John back in, and in time he agrees upon the condition that John would clean out the latrines in the monastery with his bare hands. John cheerfully accepts this humiliating task.¹⁴⁵ Shortly after this, the Virgin Mary supposedly appears to the older monk one night and tells him that John will one day play a significant part in the destiny of the church and that he should be allowed to write.¹⁴⁶ Thankfully, the ban is lifted and John is allowed to spend his days in writing, and in time great treatises on theology as well as beautiful poetry flow from his pen.¹⁴⁷

139. Ibid., 461.
140. Ibid., 460.
141. Ibid., 461.
142. Ibid., 464.
143. Ibid., 465.
144. Ibid., 468.
145. Ibid., 469.
146. Ibid., 473.
147. Ibid., 476–77.

The Truth beyond the Mirror

Andrew Louth also recognizes the shortcomings of the *"Vita,"* but he concedes that "even if the Greek *vita* is worthless as a historical source for the life of John, it is not without interest."[148] What he means by this statement is that even if it only acts as a mirror to reflect what future generations "recall" of John's life, it may not be strictly historical but it may nonetheless be "informative."[149] For example, there is the question as to how John gained his profound education? The Calabrian monk offers a possible explanation, though, as Louth points out, John could have been an astute student in a time when Hellenistic learning was still flourishing in the Middle East in the seventh century.[150] In regard to the emperor Leo's revenge, the story of the forged letter and the miraculously restored hand illustrates not only how Leo could have responded, but it raises John's stature in the eyes of his later followers. Also, there is a particular icon of the Mother of God with three hands called *Theotokos Ticherousis* which may have come from this story or, perhaps, inspired the story.[151] Also, Louth explains that the story of his struggles at the monastery could have been a reflection of the (false) beliefs of some people that monks had been opposed to liturgical hymns and singing.[152] Finally, John's exoneration and permission to write, indeed, even a supernatural authentication of John's gift, could be a reflection of the author's recognition of John's renown of liturgical poetry.[153] So, if we allow the *vita* to become an open window through which we can view the "historical landscape of John's life," what kind of information do we find reflected there?[154]

The High Quality of His Education:

First of all, we can learn some things about John's educational development from this *vita*. According to the biography, John's father desired a good education for his son, and upon hearing of a newly enslaved monk from Calabria (in Sicily), named Cosmas, he asks the Caliph, who would have been 'Abd al-Malik, for his release. Facing possible death, Cosmas' greater

---

148. Louth, *St. John Damascene*, 16.
149. Ibid., 16–17.
150. Ibid., 19.
151. Ibid.
152. Ibid., 20.
153. Ibid.
154. Ibid., 16.

distress was that he would have no one to pass on his great knowledge that he had acquired during his life. Because John's father and the Caliph were on friendly terms, the monk was released to the Mansurs and became John's tutor. Supposedly there is another Cosmas[155] who is said to be John's adopted brother, and the two of them benefited greatly from the teaching of the monk. After teaching John all he knew of Greek, philosophy, science, mathematics and theology,[156] Cosmas asked to be released so he could go back to the monastic life. Of course this was granted to him. In this story the mirror reveals that John had developed a keen knowledge in a number of fields, such as philosophy, science and theology, and the fruit of his education was well known centuries later and made manifest through his writings. The Sicilian teacher, Cosmas, may never have existed, but the story still illustrates the phenomenal intellectual talents of John, and it also provides an explanation for John's great theological understanding, for a learned monk would be able to give him a love for theology that would not necessarily be present in a classical education.

The *vita* also claims that after John's father died, John was invited by the Caliph to become his "first councilor," or "vizier." John may not have attained that level of responsibility in the Caliph's court, but even the Acts of the Seventh Ecumenical Council of 787 recognized that John held an important financial post in the Caliphate government, probably the same as his father and grandfather before him.[157]

The *vita* continues on with a story of how John was framed for treason by Leo III, against whom John had written his anti-Iconoclastic treatises, and the Caliph ordered John's right hand to be cut off. After the hand was "miraculously" restored by the Virgin Mary during the night, the Caliph then proclaimed John innocent. John had had enough of politics, however, and resigned his post in order to retreat to the monastery. Surely much of this part of the *vita* can be put aside as legend, especially the "miraculous" restoration of his severed hand,[158] but often ancient hagiography can reflect reality. In John's case, for example, his anti-iconoclastic writings against Leo

---

155. Traditionally this other Cosmas went off to the St. Sabas monastery with John later on and is identified as the Cosmas who becomes the Bishop of Maiuma, to whom John later dedicates his great theological treatise the *Fount of Knowledge* in AD 743.

156. Simmons, *Fathers and Doctors of the Church*, 90, states that Cosmas taught John "grammar, logic, arithmetic, geometry, and theology."

157. Hoyland, *Seeing Islam*, 481.

158. In fact, there is good evidence that John was already at St. Sabas by 726 when the Iconoclastic controversy broke out (cf. Tolan, *Saracens*, 51; Chase, *St. John of Damascus: Writings*, ix, xii, xiii; Louth, *St. John Damascene*, 7, 17, 19).

III were recognized for their sound arguments in his day as well as for generations afterward.[159]

The story of his early days in the Monastery at St. Sabas also provides a mirror into John's life. According to the *vita*, monastic life in the beginning was not easy for John, for apparently, because of his great learning, there were no older monks who wanted to supervise his training. Finally one of the elders, or spiritual fathers, relented, but gave John a course of strict discipline which did not allow for writing or the study of secular subjects. In time, though, after John had demonstrated his humility, and after some of the other monks, who had witnessed John's gift of writing, encouraged his mentor to allow John to write liturgical poetry, the older monk finally gave his approval and John's pen began to flow with liturgical songs, as well as with sermons and theological treatises.[160] While it is difficult to validate that John was Abused by an older monk and restricted from writing when he first entered the monastery, the story does help us fill in some other details about when John may have left Damascus for the monastic life and where he may have actually resided. As we have discussed above in the more factual section, there is good reason to believe that John resigned from his governmental position around the year 715 when Umar II became the new caliph and began to impose stricter regulations on who would be able to serve in the administrative posts. John may have traveled to the monastery outside of Jerusalem at that time. However, Theophanes places John in Damascus around the year 730, embroiled in writing his defense of icons against the iconoclasts.[161] Then, when we put this together with an eighth-century inscription referring to Peter, the Patriarch of Damascus (who died in 743), as "John's bishop," we may be able to see how the *vita* demonstrates that John may have become a monk while still in Damascus and after he left public office.[162] It also assumes a later entry into St. Sabas, perhaps after the publication of his three letters against the iconoclasts. This would explain the monks' difficulty in finding an appropriate mentor for one of such fame. It would also explain the older monk's perception that there was a "need" for John to learn humility. Likewise, it would provide the backdrop for the drama and intrigue under Leo III. If John were still in Damascus when the letters were being circulated, then his friends may have suggested that he retire to a more "remote" monastery out of the reach of Leo and the Arab

159. Louth, *St. John Damascene*, 19.

160. PG 94:429–90. See also, Louth, *St. John Damascene*, 15–19; and Chase, *St. John of Damascus: Writings*, vi–ix.

161. Turtledove, *Chronicle of Theophanes*, 100.

162. Louth, *St. John Damascene*, 8.

government. The monastery at St. Sabas would be an ideal location for that strategic retreat. Other events would then fall into place. For example, we know that John was ordained as a priest by John the Patriarch of Jerusalem before his death in 735, so if John of Damascus entered around 730 as a monk from another monastery, his ordination in the remaining years of the Patriarch would not pose a problem. There is also a reference to John's friendship with John the Patriarch in one of his works that gives us a rare glimpse into his personal world.[163] We may not be able to put together a complete year by year biography of John, but together with the better substantiated facts and the glimpses from the *vita*, we at least have more than a mere reflection in a distant mirror of historical events, and when we take a look at his writings, we will also have a glimpse into his very soul.

CONCLUSION

The biographical material on John of Damascus may be minimal, but through the substantiated historical evidence, together with the logical conclusions based on the internal and external evidence of writings during that time, as well as the hagiographical information on John's life, education and accomplishments, it can be established that John was employed in a key position as chief financial officer in the Umayyad Empire, served as a priest and monk in the Melkite tradition, and was responsible for writing at least two treatises on Islam as well as significant doctrinal and liturgical works for the church. In the following chapters, an overview of the historical and theological development of Islam in its first 100 years will be filtered through the writings of John of Damascus in order to see what can be learned from the pen of this "simple priest and monk."

---

163. Ibid., 6.

3

John's Islamic Context

INTRODUCTION

Robert Hoyland notes that "John of Damascus was particularly important as a source for Byzantine and Western Christian views of Muhammad, being the first to speak of Muhammad's revelation and legislation, portrayal of Christ, carnal vision of Paradise, his many wives and his instruction by a monk."[1] In reality, John not only gives us information about Muhammad, but he also provides an important window into the early developments of Islam, the Qur'an and the nature of eighth-century theological disputes.

The traditional view, drawing on Muslim sources,[2] provides many details of the life and teachings of Muhammad[3] and recounts thousands of Muhammad's sayings collected in what is known as the *Hadith*.[4] This view also holds that the Qur'an was canonized in perfect Arabic[5] within twenty

---

1. Hoyland, "The Earliest Christian Writings on Muhammad," 276n2.

2. Al-Ṭabari, *The History of Al-Ṭabari*; Al-Baladhuri, *The Origins of the Islamic State*; Ibn Ishaq, *The Life of Muhammad*.

3. Earliest extant written account is early ninth century (two hundred years after the fact); see Karl-Heinz Ohlig, and Gerd-R. Puin, *The Hidden Origins of Islam*, 7–10.

4. Ninth century (two hundred years after). See, for example, Al-Bukhari, Abu 'Abd Allah Muhammad ibn Isma'il, *The Translation of the Meanings of Sahih al-Bukha'ri*.

5. Earliest copy is late eighth century (one hundred and sixty years after); there are some possible fragments from Sana'a, Yemen, dated preliminarily to the early eighth century by Gerd Puin (personal conversation). See Puin, "Observations on Early Qur'an Manuscripts in San'a," 739–46; and also Saeed, *The Qur'an: An Introduction*, 110.

years of the prophet's death and relates detailed accounts of battles and lists of the people involved.[6] Yet, none of these things can be validated to the seventh century when they allegedly occurred because they were not written down until almost 150–200 years later.[7]

The Traditional View concerning Muhammad, Islam and the Qur'an is accepted by most Muslims and also by a number of Western scholars, such as John Esposito and Karen Armstrong.[8] Many other Western scholars, however, point to the paucity of sources for the Traditional View, and raise more questions than answers.[9] Some, like Arthur Jeffery, conclude that after reviewing the traditional account of the development of the Qur'an, "very little examination is needed to reveal the fact that this account is largely fictitious. Nothing is more certain than that when the Prophet died there was no collected, arranged, collated body of revelations."[10] This regular absence of documentary evidence, not only in relation to the Qur'an but also in regard to the life and teaching of Muhammad and the early religious beliefs of his followers, has created a number of possible scenarios; for where there is a lack of evidence, there is an abundance of speculation. One scholar, Fred Donner, describes four categories or approaches that researchers have come up with in order to interpret the evidence that is available.[11]

DONNER'S FOUR CATEGORIES CONCERNING THE DEVELOPMENT OF ISLAM

Donner's four categories concerning the development of Islam are the Descriptive Approach, the Source-critical Approach, the Traditional-critical Approach and the Skeptical Approach. The Descriptive Approach essentially accepts the "traditional picture of Islamic origins presented by the Muslim sources."[12] This approach was founded upon three main assumptions about the sources. First, that the Qur'an contained factual information

---

6. Earliest Islamic documents are from the eighth century (over one hundred years after the fact).

7. Gilchrist, *Jam' Al-Qur'an*, 147. See also Ohlig, *The Hidden Origins of Islam*, 7–10; Donner, *Narratives of Islamic Origins*, 20; Wansbrough, *Quranic Studies*, xv; and Nevo and Koren, *Crossroads to Islam*, 11.

8. Esposito, *Islam: The Straight Path*; Armstrong, *Islam: A Short History*.

9. Hoyland, "New Documentary Texts and the Early Islamic State," 1–4; Nevo and Koren, *Crossroads to Islam*, 5–12; and Berkey, *Formation of Islam*, 57–58.

10. Jeffery, "Materials for the History of the Text of the Koran, 116. (Jeffery's article was first published in 1937.)

11. Donner, *Narratives of Islamic Origins*, 5–31.

12. Ibid., 5.

about Muhammad and his teachings. Second, that the Muslim chronicles, written almost 150 to 200 years after the death of Muhammad, were reliable for reconstructing an accurate picture of "what really happened," and third, that the Hadith were separate from the historical accounts of the chronicles and could be treated as a distinct religious literature helpful for developing religious piety rather than determining historical reliability.[13] Donner comments that writing from this view is appealing, and often applauded by the Muslims, but the reliability of the narratives unravels under the scrutiny of historical and philological analysis.[14] Donner concludes that "numerous instances of glaring contradictions among different sources, or of logical and chronological absurdity, implausibility, or patent sectarian or political bias" marginalized this approach as outdated and historically unacceptable.[15] It is also interesting to note that John of Damascus, writing over 100 years after Muhammad's death, makes no mention of Hadith material in his writings on Islam, nor does he seem to be aware of any chronological factors, though he is cognizant of some of the writings of Muhammad and some of the claims of the Ishmaelites.

The Source-critical Approach, begun in the mid-nineteenth century by Julius Wellhausen and others, attempted to use source-criticism, as it had been applied to the Bible, in order to resolve "patent contradictions" and "logical absurdities in the sources."[16] Donner outlines four assumptions for this view. First, it was assumed that much of the early historical material could be considered reliable, but it was intermixed with unreliable material that had been corrupted by inaccurate oral transmission, tribal biases and polemics. A second assumption was that non-Muslim sources, especially in Syriac and Greek, could provide corroboration of the reliability of evidence mentioned in the Arabic narratives. The third assumption was that the Hadith material was essentially non-historical and therefore unreliable for any accurate reconstruction of Islamic history. Finally, the fourth assumption was that the Quranic text itself has been accepted without any firm documentary evidence.[17] Donner's overall assessment of the source-critical approach is that it provided good insight and guidelines for the interpretation of the Qur'an and other written sources in regard to Muslim beliefs as well as politics, and it allowed for a more accurate arrangement of material so that interdependencies and relationships could be ascertained. The main

13. Ibid., 5–6.
14. Ibid., 7–8.
15. Ibid., 8–9.
16. Ibid., 9.
17. Ibid., 9–10.

limitation, however, is that, while scholars could gain a better understanding of how Muslims in the third century AH viewed their first-century origins, they would not be able to verify those views since there were no Muslim documents from that period. In other words, this approach works well for written documents, but fails to promote historical and philological confidence in the absence of first-century written sources. When we compare this view with the writings of John of Damascus on Islam, who did write at the end of the Islamic first century, we are reminded that he also considered the writings of Muhammad to contain "absurdities" and the message to be motivated by a polemical agenda. In addition, He wrote that some of the practices were based on pagan rituals and erroneous theological interpretations.

The Tradition-Critical Approach, inaugurated by Ignaz Goldziher's study of the Hadith in 1890, accepted the idea that the sacred literature of Muslims, the Qur'an, the Hadith and the Sira, contained a "kernel of historical fact," but they argued that much of the tradition evolved over time and "shows the impact of political, theological, social, and other issues that were important not at the time of the event the accounts are supposedly describing (e.g. the life of the Prophet), but only at some time during the long period when the tradition was being transmitted, first orally and later in increasingly rigid written form."[18] In doing his research, Goldziher discovered that many of the Hadiths that he was using to reconstruct early events in the life of Muhammad were actually forgeries. In time he questioned the whole corpus of hadiths as well as the *isnads*, which traced the transmission of the hadiths and gave them their authority.[19] This also led to other questions about the way that Muslim scholars evaluated their own traditions and interpretations. Ultimately, Donner points out, those in the Tradition-Critical approach rejected the "documentary hypothesis" of the strictly source-critical approach and claimed that while many of the early accounts from the Muslims may be spurious from a historical point of view, there is still a reasonable belief that with careful analysis and comparison of sources that the original account may be determined, or at least the earliest extant version can be recovered.[20] One of the obvious difficulties with maintaining this position is that there are no Islamic documentary sources that recorded these early events.[21] At best, there are oral accounts that were written down

18. Ibid., 15.

19. Ibid., 14.

20. Ibid., 15–16. Note: Donner, in his desire to determine the "kernel of truth" in the early Islamic conquests (see Donner, *Early Islamic Conquests*), would probably place himself in this camp. (This was verified in a private conversation with Donner.)

21. Earliest written Arabic sources are from the Abbasid period, which began in

perhaps starting in the middle of the eighth century, but the bulk of them are from the ninth century. Without written documentation, how can these events be verified? This is why the works of John of Damascus on Islam are so important for us today. As a devout Christian, John lived in the midst of the Islamic stronghold and witnessed the events as they unfolded. If anyone can verify the state of Islam in the early eighth century, it is certainly John of Damascus.

This lack of written documentation on the part of the Muslims is the basis of the argument of the fourth group that Donner deals with, those who hold to a Skeptical or Revisionist Approach. While these scholars may accept the notion of the tradition-critics that the origins of Islam are the result of an evolution of oral traditions, they reject the idea that any "kernel" of historical information has remained intact so that the "real story" of Islam could be reconstructed. After all, they would say, if the Hadith with their isnads were forgeries, then why would the so-called historical accounts not merit the same conclusion since they can also be shown to follow a similar isnadic transmission? Also, the earliest written documents to give evidence to these sayings in the first place date from almost 200 years after Muhammad's death.[22]

Donner states that there are generally three assumptions put forth by the Skeptics: First, the Qur'an was derived from a number of sources external to Islam, perhaps even including Syriac Christian liturgy and Jewish Commentary,[23] and the Qur'an itself was not canonized until late in the second century AH. Therefore, it cannot be used to give an accurate picture of the origins of Islam or the role of Muhammad. Second, the narratives of Islamic origins should be understood from a bias of "salvation history." In other words, it is not possible at this time to retrieve the "kernel" of historical information because whatever facts survived would be inextricably woven into the fabric of later polemical interpretation. Third, the narratives concerning the life of Muhammad are derived from Sirat literature that tried to explain the Qur'an through exegetical extrapolations and second-century interpretations. Therefore, they cannot be used to determine historic events that took place in the first century of Islam or provide a basis for the legal tradition developed from the Hadith because the connection to Muhammad may only be illusory and certainly not adduced from any

---

751.

22. Donner, *Narratives of Islamic Origins*, 20.

23. See chap. 4 of the present work: the author's specific additions of possible sources based on material cited by Luxenberg, Firestone, and Nevo.

historical documents.[24] In other words, the Revisionists are saying that the Hadith were derived from early commentaries on the Qur'an, beginning sometime in the latter half of the eighth century, as believers tried to make sense of various passages in the Qur'an, and then "this material was used to write the 'history' of the Prophet's life, and to explain the Quranic text in a second layer of exegetical activity."[25] Regarding this historiographical approach by early Muslims which draws one body of literature (the Hadith) from another (the Qur'an) in order to redact a third (the life of Muhammad), Patricia Crone claims that much of the material is merely comprised of "residues of religious arguments" and in the end, "the bulk of it is debris of an obliterated past."[26] Even Donner gives credit to the Skeptics when he states that "the skeptical approach derives plausibility from years of source-critical and tradition-critical research that has conclusively demonstrated the existence in Islamic tradition of a heavy overlay of pious legend and the influence of manipulations, distortions, and fabrications of all kinds."[27] In the end, the skeptics take it a step further and argue that the kernel of historical "truth" may never be recoverable since it is built on "only successive layers of repeatedly reshaped and redacted material."[28] Donner, however, is not willing to go this far in his critique of the Islamic sources and concludes that the Revisionist view does not adequately assess the complex historical developments and societal paradigm shifts that took place in the first 100 years of Islam. However, when we examine the writings of John of Damascus, we notice a number of correlative areas shared with the Revisionists. First of all, John's recognition of some writings of Muhammad with different titles reveals his familiarity with some parts of the Quranic text, and his inference that they comprise different writings rather than one book mitigates against a fully canonized Qur'an by the mid-eighth century, which corresponds with what the Revisionist purport. Secondly, much like the Revisionists, his staunch defense of the Trinity and the deity of Christ against the clear doctrinal attacks of Quranic statements attest to his recognition of the nature of polemical interpretation on the part of the Muslims. Lastly, John's limited knowledge of Muhammad may infer that biographical information was scarce even in the mid-eighth century, perhaps revealing the lack of Sirat literature and the Hadith. However, this may support the

---

24. Donner, *Narratives of Islamic Origins*, 23.

25 Ibid., 24–25. Donner is referring to the assessment of Burton in his book *The Collection of the Qur'an*.

26. Crone, *Slaves on Horses*, 9–10.

27. Donner, *Narratives of Islamic Origins*, 25.

28. Ibid., 25.

Revisionist's view that much of the life of Muhammad was redacted from the Qur'an, which, in turn, was used to develop the Hadith.

AN ALTERNATIVE VIEW OF THE DEVELOPMENT OF ISLAM

While Donner's Revisionist view seems to correspond best with the mid-eighth-century writings of John of Damascus, there are still historical and theological perspectives that do not match up. Perhaps this is because one of the main problems with Donner's four views is that they are basically nineteenth- and twentieth-century interpretations of eighth- and ninth-century reconstructions. Is there a more "scientific history" that will interpret and reconstruct the events according to data that corresponds to the seventh and early eighth centuries, such as archaeological, epigraphic and numismatic evidence? Gary Habermas, one of the world's authorities on the historicity of the resurrection of Jesus Christ, posits that if history is the "occurrence of past events, as well as the recording and interpreting of them," and if we want to obtain the most objective data possible, then we need to "ascertain as nearly as possible those facts that best fit the data." In regard to early Islam, we should choose our interpretation according to that which best fits the evidence and that which provides the "most probable conclusion." In other words, when dealing with the evidence, whether it is documentary, archaeological, epigraphic or numismatic material or eyewitness reports, the "results should conform to all known data and provide the most comprehensive and probable judgment on the issues." It should also be defensible based on the most "factual data available." In this way, historical investigation takes on the role of a "scientific study" of the events and historians are able to use their evidentially-based tools in a fashion much like forensic scientists who seek to reconstruct a past event based on the best data and the most probable conclusions.[29] The British historian G.R. Elton seems to agree with this view and adds that historical events are independent and have a real existence outside of the interpretations of modern observers, and, therefore, when the evidence for the events increases, the likelihood of constructing a more feasible understanding of the event also increases. Thus, history can be 'scientifically' studied, he says, and with more accurate evidence the historian will be able to provide a more probable explanation of the events.[30] This is very much what the Revisionists[31] attempted in the

---

29. Habermas, *The Historical Jesus*, 259–74.
30. Elton and Evans, *The Practice of History*, 46–60.
31. John Wansbrough, Patricia Crone, Michael Cook, Andrew Rippin and G. W.

1970s and the 1980s. Donner may have pointed out the weakness of the lack of documents to promote the Revisionist views, but their use of other evidence has revolutionized recent Islamic studies.[32]

In addition to the Revisionists, we now have a host of scholars, whom I call the "Neo-Revisionists,"[33] who have corrected some of the shortcomings of the Revisionists and bring to bear a much more scientifically accurate interpretation of the first two centuries of Islam based on a higher level of investigative research using a type of historical forensics. In the end, their view may not be the most plausible one for a reconstruction of the history of early Islam, but it is certainly interesting and revolutionary, and deserves to be held up against the testimony of the seventh-century non-Muslim accounts as well as the eighth-century testimony of John of Damascus.

THE NEO-REVISIONIST VIEW

From the Neo-Revisionist school we get a very different picture of the development of Muhammad, the Qur'an and the religion of Islam. Jeremy Johns, of Oxford University, believes that one of the reasons for this difference is due to the problematic character of the Islamic literary sources. Johns writes,

> If our goal is to comprehend the way in which Muslims of the late 2nd/8th and 3rd/9th third/ninth centuries understood the origins of their society, then we are very well off indeed. But if our aim is to find out 'what really happened'—i.e., to develop reliably documented answers to modern questions about the earliest decades of Islamic societies — then we are in trouble.[34]

The problem, of course, is that there is an almost total lack of any contemporary sources from the Islamic side until late in the eighth century, almost 150 years after the death of Muhammad.[35] The earliest written ac-

---

Hawting.

32. Forensic evidence such as archaeological sites, epigraphic and numismatic material and seventh-century non-Muslim eyewitness written accounts.

33. Robert Hoyland, Yehuda Nevo, Jeremy Johns, Sidney Griffith, Reuven Firestone, Christoph Luxenberg, Gerd-R Puin, Karl-Heinz Ohlig, and Kevin Van Bladel. Please note: Robert Hoyland is difficult to categorize in any of these views, but through a private conversation with Hoyland he agreed that, based on his way of dealing with the evidence, I could put him in this category, though he would dispute the conclusions of some of the others in this list.

34. Johns, "Archaeology and the History of Early Islam," 412.

35. Donner, *Narratives of Islamic Origins*, 1–5. Donner also mentions that from the late eighth century there are "copious literary sources in Arabic that purport, at least, to tell us much about this earliest phase of Islamic history. These include chronicles,

count dealing with the life of Muhammad, for example, is the biography by Ibn Ishaq, supposedly written before 767, but only appearing as a recension in Ibn Hisham's biography written in the early ninth century.[36] This "paucity of material evidence" from the earliest decades of Islam makes it extremely difficult to ascertain anything about Islamic origins from Muslim sources.[37] Thus, outside of some archaeological and epigraphic information, knowledge about the prophet Muhammad, the first four Caliphs and the development of the Qur'an is "undocumented" according to modern historical research methods.[38] Johns points out that there is a "late crystallization of a fluid oral tradition" represented by the "copious" written Arabic narratives of the late eighth century, but they could not be considered to be what he calls "scientific history" unless they can be corroborated by earlier external non-Muslim evidence.[39] As an archaeologist, Nevo suggests that there are three things that tell a better story than written accounts, since they avoid the inherent bias of the writer: rock inscriptions, archaeological sites and coins.[40] Even then, the archaeological, epigraphical, and numismatic evidence left by the Arabs differs greatly from their later Traditional Account, which Nevo advises "needs to be radically reinterpreted or discarded altogether as *historical fact*."[41] Like Jeremy Johns, Nevo cautions that

> Non-contemporary literary sources are, in our opinion, inadmissible as historical evidence. If one has no source of knowledge of the 7th century except texts written in the 9th century or later, one cannot know anything about the 7th century: one

---

poems, collections of Hadith (sayings) attributed to the Prophet or his Companions, epistles on theological issues, collections of *adab* (belles-lettres), and other materials, in addition to the text of the Qur'an itself. It is mainly on the testimony of these literary sources that the outlines of Islamic origins have been sketched, by both traditional Muslim and by modern scholars." It is important to note, however, that these documents are from the late eighth century on, and may not have existed before that time.

36. Berkey, *Formation of Islam*, 57. Crone says that this is like "*reconstructing* the origins of Christianity on the basis of the writings of Clement or Justin Martyr in a recension by Origen." Crone, *Slaves on Horses*, 202n10.

37. Hoyland, "New Documentary Texts and the Early Islamic State," 395. See also Bright, "The Great Koran Con Trick," 1–4; Nevo and Koren, *Crossroads to Islam*, 5–12; and Berkey, *Formation of Islam*, 57–8. Berkey even quotes G. R. Hawting, who says that "none of the Islamic texts available to us yet existed," meaning that the texts that purport to give the definitive history of Muhammad, the Qur'an and the rise of Islam were not written until two centuries after the events.

38. Donner, *Narratives of Islamic Origins*, 3.

39. Johns, "Archaeology and the History of Early Islam," 412.

40. Nevo and Koren, *Crossroads to Islam*, 8–9.

41. Ibid., 8, 11; italics in the original.

can only know what people in the 9th century or later believed about the 7th.[42]

LITERATURE THAT MAY CONVEY HISTORY

This is perhaps why Patricia Crone believes that the best thing to do is to "to step outside the Islamic tradition altogether and start again,"[43] for if "it was the storytellers who created the tradition" in the first place, then how will we know which stories to accept and which ones to discard?[44] Robert Hoyland agrees and further suggests that a study of non-Muslim evidence pertaining to the seventh century may be able to give us the insight needed to piece together the puzzle of early Islam.[45] Hoyland argues that these non-Muslim literary sources from the first one hundred years of Islam, corroborated by the archaeological, epigraphic and numismatic evidence, may "tell us more than skeptics allow for."[46] Hoyland recounts, for example, that early Christian writers, from the late seventh and early eighth centuries, indicate that Muhammad, or at least the one who was recognized as the leader of the Arabs, was known variously as a military leader, a trader, a king, a monotheist revivalist, a lawgiver and a prophet.[47] These are very specific terms that argue for a specific person fulfilling these roles. We must proceed with caution, however, for while these testimonies give evidence for an historical person, the accounts are often biased by religious influences and some of the documents that recount these eyewitness reports are later copies that may have been altered due to political or religious motives.[48] With this caution in mind, the few non-Muslim writers from the seventh century do seem to give evidence of cult-like religious practices and a controversial leader. In addition, it is evident from these sources that the invading *mu'minun*,

---

42. Nevo and Koren, *Crossroads to Islam*, 9.

43. Crone and Cook, *Hagarism*, 3.

44. Crone, *Meccan Trade*, 225.

45. Hoyland, *Seeing Islam*, 546. It is interesting to note that Hoyland was a student of Patricia Crone. It is very much like a puzzle: we don't have all the pieces; sometimes the pieces seem to change shape; also, some that seem to fit in one place are later understood to fit better elsewhere; instead of being two-dimensional, the full puzzle is three-dimensional because it involves views from Christians, Jews, and Arabs of that time, and views from the present trying to interpret it all.

46. Hoyland, "New Documentary Texts and the Early Islamic State," 395–96.

47. Hoyland, "The Earliest Christian Writings on Muhammad," 277–78.

48. It is also curious that any Muslim evidence on Muhammad is conspicuously absent until the time of 'Abd al-Malik, almost 60 years after Muhammad's death.

or "believers," did in fact have a monotheistic faith with distinctive values in opposition to the beliefs of the Christians. They were iconoclastic and they prayed toward the ka'ba, which they considered the "house of God." They also sacrificed before the ka'ba, worshiped a sacred stone and conducted their worship in specific places called "masjid." A few, like Sebeos (c. 660), referred to Muhammad[49] as a "guide" and "instructor" who urged his followers to obey the law that was revealed to him by God. Sebeos also wrote that Muhammad "legislated that they were not to eat carrion, not to drink wine, not to speak falsehoods, and not to commit adultery."[50] This is similar to John's list of Saracen customs and practices at the end of *Heresy of the Ishmaelites*, where he mentions the practice of circumcision of men and women, orders not to observe the Sabbath, orders not to be baptized, orders not to eat certain forbidden food, and orders not to drink any wine.[51] Furthermore, these sources recognized that although the Arab muhajirun held Jerusalem in honor, they were hostile to the cross and denied that Christ was the Son of God.[52] Thus, even though we do not have seventh-century accounts of Muhammad from Muslim writers, we do have indications from non-Muslims that Muhammad not only existed, but was responsible for ushering in a new belief system with laws, practices and beliefs that not only motivated the Arab invaders, but also unified them under a new vision. Writing almost eighty years later, John of Damascus also considered Muhammad to be an historical figure, but he called Muhammad a "false prophet" and he called the religion of his followers a "heresy." He also ridiculed the so-called writings that came down to Muhammad from heaven. Did John receive his information from seventh-century non-Muslim accounts? Was he privy to documentary sources that no longer exist, both Muslim and Christian, or was he subject to the same influences as those around him? Tracing the development of Muhammad, as well as possible sources for the Qur'an and other early Islamic writings, may help us better understand the eighth-century context from which John of Damascus wrote his critiques on Islam. In addition, the earlier written accounts by non-Muslim eyewitnesses may be able to provide more of the background that is necessary in

---

49. There were only three writers who referred to Muhammad by name—Thomas the Presbyter (c. 640), Sebeos (c. 660), and the Chronicler of Khuzistan (c. 660). The others either referred to an anonymous Arab leader or the name of Muhammad was redacted back into the document at a later time in a later copy. See Hoyland, *Seeing Islam*, 549.

50 Sebeos, *Armenian History*, 96.

51. HER 153–56.

52. Hoyland, *Seeing Islam*, 549–50.

order to best understand John's context. It is to these accounts that we now turn our attention.

TESTIMONY OF THE NON-MUSLIM SOURCES

When the Arabs began conquering the cities of the Middle East, non-Muslim eyewitnesses believed that their attackers were a punishment from God for their own spiritual rebellion or for sins committed by other rival Christian groups. Walter Kaegi examines a number of these eyewitness accounts. He writes that Sophronius believed the Arab invasion was divine punishment for Christian sin: "Because of countless sins and very serious faults" (139); Anastasias perceived the Arab conquest was a divine retribution for Christian sins, also, especially the fault of Emperor Constans for his persecution of the Orthodox Church (143); Sebeos blamed Christians themselves: "for we have merited it, for we have sinned against the Lord" (146); Pseudo-Methodius was another who believed it was "because of the lawlessness of the Christians" (143); and John of Nikiu, who was a Monophysite, said that it was due to divine anger against the errors of the Chalcedonian Christians (148).[53] A number of the witnesses testified not only to the brutality of the invading forces, but also to their godless nature.[54] Others, however, testified that while some in the marauding forces were pagan, others seemed to espouse a type of monotheism that incorporated definite Jewish overtones mixed with an amalgamation of Arab traditions and anti-Christian beliefs.[55] Most of the Byzantine inhabitants seemed to expect that the invaders would be beaten back by a reinforcement of the Byzantine army, but after that hope faded a bewilderment set in as they determined to make the best of the situation. The invading forces called themselves *muhajirun*, "emigrants," or *mu'minun*, the "believers." Yet, exactly what they believed in was not readily apparent. Most of the Syrian Christians knew the Arab conquerors as "Saracens," "Hagarenes," or "Ishmaelites," all of which have religious associations.[56] Even 100 years after John of Damascus' grandfather had surrendered the city of Damascus to the enemy forces, John was still referring to the Arabs with these same terms, though he only used the appellations

53. Kaegi, "Initial Byzantine Reactions to the Arab Conquest," 139–49. See also Saadi, "Nascent Islam," 219.

54. Sophronius's Christmas sermon for AD 634; Latin text, PG 87:3205, lines 48ff. See Nevo and Koren, *Crossroads to Islam*, 105.

55. *Homily on the Child Saints of Babylon*, 36. See Hoyland, *Seeing Islam*, 121. This view of a type of monotheism is also found in the dialogue of the Patriarch John of Sedreh and the Emir developed in Nevo and Koren, *Crossroads to Islam*, 224, 228.

56. Berkey, *Formation of Islam*, 73–74.

given by the Christians. Through the title of John's treatise, the "*Heresy of the Ishmaelites*," we can ascertain that John accepted the religious nature of the Arabs, but he also still considered their beliefs to be an aberration from true Christianity. In fact, John went so far as to call Muhammad a "false prophet" and the religion of the Ishmaelites the religion of the "anti-Christ." He even blamed Muhammad's false theological views on his encounter with an Arian monk.[57]

Like John, early witnesses provide a window into the development of the "heresy of the Ishmaelites" as well as examples of the responses of the various Christian groups displaced by the conquest. These non-Muslim "voices" are very significant, not only in that they give us a literary connection back to the beginning of the conquest in the 630s, but also because they provide an outsider's critical view of the events and developments in the religion that has become Islam. These sources may not be as abundant as the Muslim sources dated from the late eighth century, but, they are eyewitness accounts, and, as Nevo points out, they "reflect the period in light of a completely different wavelength and from a different angle."[58] As with any literary sources, however, Nevo warns us that there are problems and shortcomings associated with the texts, besides the normal dating and authenticity tests. The primary shortcoming is that these sources were religious in nature rather than historical. They were comprised of sermons, religious moralizing, apocalyptic literature, letters from church officials and even polemical responses to the perceived heresies of the Arabs. The purpose of the documents was not necessarily the recording of historical events, but rather the promotion of a particular religious view. Thus, "even when the source is apparently factual, reading history from it can be hazardous," since it may be dealing with theological disputes between rival Christian sects or it may contain biases based on particular theological interpretations.[59] Therefore, Nevo believes that there are several questions that need to be asked of the non-Muslim texts in order to determine the actual historical nature of the events. First, what is the factual content that can be extracted from the source, minus its particular bias? Second, are the events describing things that have taken place in the past, during the time of the writer, or still to take place in the future (such as in apocalyptic literature)? Third, which theological perspective is being promoted (since it will act as a filter for the events described)? For example, Sophronius, Patriarch of Jerusalem, recorded in his Christmas sermon of 634 that the reason the Arabs blocked the Christ-

---

57. HER 2, 11, 12.
58. Nevo and Koren, *Crossroads to Islam*, 103.
59. Ibid., 103.

mas procession to Bethlehem that year was due to the many "sins and gravest errors" committed by the people of God, and therefore they were "unfit" to make their annual pilgrimage to the holy site.[60] From this sermon we can ascertain that the Arabs were in control of the area in the year 634 and they had limited the access to the town of Bethlehem. However, when Sophronius refers to the conquerors as "vengeful and God-hating Saracens,"[61] who carried a "blood-loving blade,"[62] he was not only saying that they were prone to violence, but he was also strongly indicating that they were not religious. Yet, in 639 Sophronius gives an account of the "godless Saracens" entering Jerusalem and building a place "intended for their prayer called a mosque (*midzgitha*)."[63] How "godless" could they be, though, if they rushed in to establish a place of prayer as soon as they had control of the city? This account reveals how the bias of the author can misconstrue factual events due to a religious agenda, which is a caution we need to heed as we proceed.

One of the earliest non-Muslim sources is the anti-Jewish tract, *Doctrina Jacobi nuper baptizati*, set around the year 634. It mentions that "a false prophet has appeared among the Saracens . . . and is proclaiming the advent of the anointed one who is to come."[64] This leader is also supposed to have had the keys to paradise and to have come with the sword and the chariot. Nevo does not believe this describes the Muhammad[65] that we know in the traditional sense since he does not proclaim that "the hour is nigh," but rather proclaims the coming of the anointed one and is said to have the keys to paradise (something that is not mentioned in any of the traditional accounts). Nevo also believes that the message was probably in Aramaic, or something that people north of Arabia would be familiar with, rather than Arabic, which they would not have paid heed to.[66] Crone and Cook believe, on the other hand, that this could be an earlier reference to an actual historical account of Muhammad which would run contrary to the traditional account since it occurs two years after his death in 632.[67] Thus,

---

60. Sophronius's Christmas sermon for AD 634; Latin text, PG 87:3205, lines 48ff. See Nevo and Koren, *Crossroads to Islam*, 105; as well as Tolan, *Saracens: Islam in the Medieval European Imagination*, 41–43.

61. Sophronius, *Holy Baptism*, 166–67. See Hoyland, *Islam as Others Saw It*, 72.

62. Sophronius, *Christmas Sermon*, 515. See Hoyland, *Islam as Others Saw It*, 71.

63. Sophronius, *Pratum spiritual*, 100–102. See Hoyland, *Islam as Others Saw It*, 71.

64. *Doctrina Jacobi* 5.16, 209. See Hoyland, *Islam as Others Saw It*, 57.

65. Note that the name Muhammad is not used in this document. The reference is only to a "false prophet."

66. Nevo and Koren, *Crossroads to Islam*, 208–9.

67. Crone and Cook, *Hagarism*, 4. Crone also says that this reference to Muhammad may have come from "a stratum of belief older than the Islamic tradition itself."

Muhammad, in their view, would have "led the invading Arabs, proclaimed the advent of the Messiah, and claimed to hold the keys of paradise."[68] In the end, Nevo cautions us, the prophet that is described would be more out of a Judeo-Christian background than an Arab one, and therefore could be just a reference to a passing prophet of the times. Nevo also reminds us that the prophet of the *Doctrina Jacobi* is not named, and it is only by inference that Crone and others adopt the name of "Muhammad." Indeed, the "prophet" could have been the leader of the Saracens at that time, either Abu Bakr or Uthman, or another Ishmaelite prophet who was raised up by God to conquer the Byzantines and restore the land.[69] It could even have been a reference to a prophet in the rabbinic apocalyptic tradition.

About that same time, Thomas the Presbyter (wr. ca. 640), writing in Syriac, relates how the Arabs invaded and conquered Syria in 635–36, even killing a number of monks when they stormed the monasteries.[70] He is also, apparently, the first one to mention Muhammad by name. Thomas says there was a "battle between the Romans and the Arabs of Muhammad (*tayyaye d-Mhmt*) in Palestine twelve miles east of Gaza."[71] The reference to Muhammad, however, may have been inserted in a later copy of this document, as was commonplace at this time;[72] but if it originally did refer to Muhammad by name, then we would have documentary evidence of the existence of Muhammad as early as AD 640, the time of the completion of Thomas' chronicle. There is also a mention of the Arabs of Muhammad (Muhmd) on the fly-leaf of a sixth-century Syriac manuscript of the Gospels, scribbled in Arabic. Hoyland believes that it is post-636, but a definitive date is impossible to give due to the fragmentary nature of the page. The phrase "we saw" may indicate that it was an eyewitness account of a battle that took place in 636, but even Donner advises caution due to the fragmentary nature and indeterminate date.[73]

One of the dangers in using literary sources to determine actual history is that the documents can be changed later on when they are copied or

---

68. Nevo and Koren, *Crossroads to Islam*, 209.

69. Ibid., 210.

70. Apparently the monasteries of Qedar and Bnata (Thomas the Presbyter, *Chronicle*, 148).

71. Thomas the Presbyter, *Chronicle*, 147. See Hoyland, *Islam as Others Saw It*, 120. See also Griffith, *Shadow*, 25.

72. See the material on John of Nikiu later in this chapter.

73. Donner, *Early Islamic Conquest*, 144. See Hoyland, *Islam as Others Saw It*, 116. "In January the people of Homs took the word for their lives and many villages were ravaged by the killing of the Arabs of Muhammad (Muhmd) and many people were slain and taken prisoner from Galilee as far as Beth. . ."

translated into a different language. For example, Nevo argues that a sermon on the Feast of the Epiphany (636 or 637) by Sophronius could have been embellished with a long list of Arab atrocities by a later transcriber who knew the Traditional Account.

> We have no information on the date of the manuscript or its transmission history, but suggest that either the entire section was tacked on to Sophronius' sermon at a later date, or that his initial rhetorical question, "Why do barbarian raids abound?" was considerably embellished by a later transcriber who knew the Traditional Account and therefore "knew" better than Sophronius what the prophesied "abomination of desolation" entailed.[74]

Words could have been added to the sermon or changed by later translators, and in this way the Traditional Account could have been "read back" into Sophronius' account. Since the earliest copy that we have of this sermon is from the sixteenth century, this scenario is certainly possible.[75]

Another barrier to accurately assessing the literary sources is that modern critics may be reading the Traditional Account back into the words of these early witnesses. Nevo uses Sophronius' Christmas sermon of 634 to illustrate this point. Sophronius would have certainly mentioned the religion of the "invaders" as *Islam* if he had been aware that the term referred to them at this time. He did not mention Muhammad at all, and, as Kaegi points out, "in his view, the Arabs were simply terrible, godless invaders without any religious impulse."[76] Yet, some modern critics are reading the Traditional Account back into the words of Sophronius, and other writers, in order to promote a view that Islam was present from the beginning of the conquest. For example, in the quote above by Kaegi, he added the word "invaders" to Sophronius' description of the "godless Saracens." This is because Kaegi, like other modern critics, apparently believes that many of the invading tribesmen had only recently converted from paganism to Islam and therefore were imperfect followers of Muhammad. However, Nevo argues that "if the Arabs of whom Sophronius complained were still pagan, and Muhammad yet unknown, the fact that Sophronius mentioned neither their Prophet nor their religion ceases to require explanation."[77] In other words, we need to be aware that when a document mentions "Muhammad"

---

74. Nevo and Koren, *Crossroads to Islam*, 121.

75. Ibid., 120.

76. Kaegi, "Initial Byzantine Reactions to the Arab Conquest," 140. See also Nevo and Koren, *Crossroads to Islam*, 212.

77. Nevo and Koren, *Crossroads to Islam*, 212–13.

or "Islam" or the "Qur'an," the original words may have been something like "Saracen prophet," "religion of the Ishmaelites" or simply "writings" or "scriptures."

A good example of this substitution may be found in the *Chronicle* of John of Nikiu, written in Egypt around 690.[78] John refers many times to the "Muslims" and even mentions the "detestable doctrine of the beast, that is, Muhammad."[79] However, since the earliest text that we have is a 1602 Ethiopic translation from an earlier Arabic translation from the original Greek and Coptic, there is no way to verify that the original word was "Muslim" instead of "Saracen" or "Ishmaelite," which were also used in the chronicle.[80] It would also have been easy to insert the word "Muhammad" in reference to the "doctrine of the beast." Nevo argues that the John of Nikiu text suffered tampering and distortion, since the term "Muslim" does not occur elsewhere in Christian texts until AD 775.[81] Hoyland also says that the term was probably "Saracen" or "Arab" in the original Coptic. Moreover, he suspects that the use of "Muhammad" in respect to the "beast" is also a later gloss.[82]

If these early non-Muslim texts are so problematic, what can we ascertain from them? One thing we can pick up from a number of the early documents is that the Arabs espoused a form of a transitional, monotheistic religion similar to the forms of Judaism and Christianity found in that area. For example, the *Homily on the Child Saints of Babylon*, written sometime in the 640s, referred to the Saracens as religious yet barbaric. They would boast about their fasts and prayer, but were also regarded as "oppressors" who "massacre and lead into captivity the sons of men."[83] Their religious activities were present, apparently, but not very efficacious. From the discussion between the Patriarch John of Sedreh and an Arab governor referred to as the "Emir," which took place around 644, we can determine that though the Emir was religious, following a basic monotheism with Jewish-Christian associations, he was not a Muslim and he did not mention Muhammad, Islam nor the Qur'an.[84]

---

78. *John of Nikiu: Chronicle*.

79. *John of Nikiu: Chronicle* 121.5. See also Nevo and Koren, *Crossroads to Islam*, 233.

80. See Nevo and Koren, *Crossroads to Islam*, 233–34.

81. Ibid., 235n82.

82. Hoyland, *Seeing Islam*, 156.

83. *Homily on the Child Saints of Babylon*, 36. See Hoyland, *Seeing Islam*, 121.

84. Nevo and Koren, *Crossroads to Islam*, 224, 228. See also Saadi, "Nascent Islam," 219–20.

A number of non-Muslim writers in the 650s and 660s, such as Sebeos, the bishop of the Bagratunis,[85] and the Chronicler of Khuzistan, provided outside sources regarding many of the battles between the Byzantines and the Arabs. The Chronicle of Khuzistan even records another possible reference to the leadership of Muhammad (*mhmd*).[86] In the last decades of the seventh century, men like John bar Penkaye (wr. 687) offer a more positive account of the Arab rule. John writes, for example, that in the time of Mu'awiyah justice and peace flourished, as well as freedom for the Christians to worship. He even presents Muhammad as a "guide," a "teacher," and a "legislator," for those who follow him as their prophet.[87] This would fit in well with what we know of the rise of 'Abd al-Malik during this time and his proclamation of Muhammad as the prophet in the year 691. In the time of 'Abd al-Malik, however, Christians began to turn their attention from recording the events of the conquests to engaging in theological and apologetic responses to the challenges of the Arabs. Sidney Griffith even states that it may have been 'Abd al-Malik's campaign to launch the new "hegemony of Islam" that precipitated the defensive, apologetic undertaking that characterized the first half of the eighth century and led up to John of Damascus and his treatise on the "Heresy of the Ishmaelite."[88] As early as 700, Anastasios of Sinai referred to "false notions of the Arabs" in regard to developing theological ideas. He seems to be aware of Quranic terms and had conversations with Arabs about doctrine, but he "makes no explicit reference to Muhammad, the Qur'an or to Islam."[89] In his book, *Hodegos*, he says that Christians were engaging in religious controversy with religious Arabs in his day, especially in regard to the Arab condemnation of anyone who says, "Two gods" or that God could have carnally begotten a son.[90] These were topics that John of Damascus dealt with several decades later. In fact, like John of Damascus, Anastasios believed that the Arab religion was a heresy.[91]

Another writer from around the turn of the century, a Syrian Orthodox bishop named Jacob of Edessa (d. 708), was aware of Arab religious

---

85. Hoyland, *Seeing Islam*, 124–31.

86. Ibid., 185–88.

87. Ibid., 194–200. See also, Hoyland, "Earliest Christian Writings on Muhammad," 277–97. Note: John bar Penkaye does not use the word "prophet" in regard to Muhammad.

88. Griffith, *Shadow*, 32.

89. Ibid., 28.

90. Ibid., 29.

91. Ibid., 30–31.

beliefs that were monotheistic, but neither Christian nor Jewish. The Arabs,[92] according to Jacob, acknowledged that Jesus was the Messiah, unlike the Jews, but they did not accept Jesus as the son of God. He also recognized that they called Jesus the Word of God as well as admitted that Jesus was the Spirit of God, though without seeming to realize the significance of these roles.[93] This material was also familiar to John of Damascus and used in his critique of Islam written several decades later. It is significant, however, that although Jacob of Edessa seemed to be aware of these Quranic ideas and Islamic teachings during the time of 'Abd al-Malik's reign, he did not mention the Qur'an or the religion of Islam.

Finally, there is a purported letter from Leo III to Umar II (717-20) which details information about Islam and may be an earlier work than that of John of Damascus, but the authenticity of the letter is disputed and still unresolved. The earliest form we have is an Armenian translation from the late eighth century and this differs greatly from a later Latin version (the original version being presumably in Greek). Schacht dates the document no earlier than mid-second century A.H., or some thirty years after John of Damascus wrote *De Haeresibus*.[94]

Leo, who is reported to have known both Greek and Arabic, may still be able to give us a theological "snapshot" of the mid-eighth century. Curiously, Leo only knows the Qur'an by the name of "Furqan"[95] and refers to it as a book of God that he believes was really written by Umar, Ali and Salman the Persian, presumably in the earlier decades.

> You admit that we say that it [the Gospel] was written by God
> ... as you pretend for your Furqan, although we know that it
> was Umar [i.e., the second caliph], Abu Turab [i.e., Ali] and
> Salman the Persian, who composed that.[96]

However, he is aware of some of its main teachings, and seems to focus on the material found in Surahs 2-5, which, interestingly enough, are

---

92. Patricia Crone refers to the Arabs as "Mahgraye," a Syriac term for emigrants, in her translation of Jacob, and Robert Hoyland translates the term as "Muslim." Crone and Cook, *Hagarism*, 11-12. Hoyland, *Seeing Islam*, 166-67.

93. Griffith, *Shadow*, 31-32. See also Crone and Cook, *Hagarism*, 11-12; Hoyland, *Seeing Islam*, 166-67. Similarities to these statements can be found in the Qur'an in surah 4:171.

94. Schacht, *The Origins of Muhammadan Jurisprudence*, 4-5.

95. Another name for the Qur'an used in the second century AH. See Nevo and Koren, *Crossroads to Islam*, 240.

96. Ibid., 240.

the same ones that John of Damascus was familiar with.[97] These surahs are also concerned with legal issues facing the young empire. This makes more sense when we realize that Leo never refers to Muhammad as a prophet, but rather relegates him to the position of "legislator," or "Head" of the Saracen religion. Thus, Leo's perception of Islam and of its leader in the middle of the eighth century seems to be focused on the political realm rather than the spiritual one. John of Damascus, on the other hand, in his assessment of these same surahs, and around the same time, emphasized the spiritual implications of the civil procedures, such as when he questioned their strong reliance on witnesses for any property dealings yet held their prophet to a different standard:

> On the one hand, you take wives and possess property and donkeys and everything else through witnesses; yet, on the other hand, you accept your faith and your scriptures unwitnessed. For the one who has handed down this scripture to you has no verification from any source, nor is there any prior witness to him known.[98]

CONCLUSION

Based on the best historical information at hand, did John of Damascus accurately portray Muhammad, the Qur'an, and the early Islamic theological disputes? When we consider that the earliest biography of Muhammad written by Muslims was in the late eighth century, or even the early ninth century, and the earliest date that Muslims even mention the name "Muhammad" is around AD 691, then what we have from the Muslim side are ninth-century writers relating what they believe happened in the seventh century. On the other hand, the non-Muslim written descriptions of Muhammad and the early conquests by the Arabs provide a valuable source for understanding the history of Muhammad's time. They also corroborate the writings of other contemporary writers such as John of Damascus, who added theological insights to the historical ones. According to these documents, the invading Arabs espoused a form of a transitional, monotheistic religion similar to the forms of Judaism and Christianity found in the area. Some of these non-Muslim writers mention Muhammad as a prophet, guide, teacher, legislator, and even king, decades before any Muslims record

---

97. These Surahs were some of the last ones said to have been written (in the so-called Medinan period).

98. HER 56–60.

his name. Even though the earliest extant copies of some of these documents are several centuries later, allowing the name of Muhammad to have been redacted back into the copies, these documents at least attest to the fact that there was a religious Arab leader in the early part of the seventh century who preached a form of monotheism and motivated his fellow countrymen to migrate north. In the early part of the eighth century, John of Damascus also seemed to accept the historicity of Muhammad, but referred to him as a false prophet. John also viewed the "coercive" religion that Muhammad started as a heresy of Christianity.[99] The other non-Muslim voices from the seventh and eighth centuries seem to bear witness to the same things.

In addition, when we evaluate the evidence for what Nevo calls the development of an "intermediate monotheism," many of the conclusions dovetail with John's observations.[100] The view from the non-Muslim sources provides only a portion of the picture. However, when it is put together with the forensic evidence, represented in archaeological, numismatic and epigraphic research provided by the Neo-Revisionists, a more detailed "snapshot" of John's context is revealed. We have looked at the non-Muslim sources—now we need to turn to what the forensic evidence, represented in archaeological, numismatic and epigraphic research, reveals about John's context.

99. HER 1, 11.
100. Nevo and Koren, *Crossroads to Islam*, 195–99.

4

The Early Formation of Islam

INTRODUCTION

In light of the scarcity of primary sources for the seventh century, and therefore piecing together the events according to the "media" available to us from that time, Jonathan Berkey concludes that Islam emerged slowly and probably did not begin as anything more than a monotheistic religion of the Arabs shaped through a process of dialogue with Judaism and Christianity.[1] Patricia Crone also argues for a gradual evolution of Islamic institutions as the early Arab community carried out an "exodus" (*hijra*) from their homeland to the newly established garrison cities in the conquered lands.[2] This *hijra* may have been fueled by the promise of a new Arab state based on "conquest, rape and pillage,"[3] or it may have been a people movement aided by the withdrawal of the Byzantine forces and the discontinuation of subsidies to the *foederati* for guarding the borders.[4] Hoyland notes that papyri and inscriptions refer to a certain date given for the *hijra*, AD 622, but they

---

1. Berkey, *Formation of Islam*, 7, 57.
2. See Crone and Cook, *Hagarism*, 9, and Hoyland, Seeing Islam, 547–48.
3. Bright, "The Great Koran Con Trick," 3, referring to Patricia Crone's assessment in Meccan Trade and the Rise of Islam.
4. Nevo and Koren, *Crossroads to Islam*, 89–98. The foederati were Arab allies of the Byzantine forces who were paid a subsidy to guard the border lands. When the subsidies were paid, they acted as protectors of the empire. However, when the subsidies stopped, the disgruntled soldiers often took out their frustrations by attacking their former employers.

The Early Formation of Islam 67

do not explain the nature of the inauguration of this movement.[5] Crone believes that this *hijra* was an exodus taken by the "muhajirun," or those who were on the exodus to a promised land, but she also concludes that this *hijra* was not from Mecca to Medina, as in the Traditional Account, but rather from Medina to the promised land of Israel.[6] She bases her conclusions on the fact that the term "muhajirun" corresponds to the Syriac term "Mahgraye," or those who take part in a hijra, or exodus. The corresponding Greek term, "Magaritai" appears in a papyrus as early as 642, and the Syriac term, "Mahgraye," also appears around that time. Crone writes that there are two notions involved in the use of the term, one linking the Arabs to the "Mahgraye" as descendents of Abraham and Hagar, and therefore also called "Hagarenes," but also ascribing to these same Arabs a term describing their participation in an "exodus" or "hijra," and therefore known as the "muhajirun," or those who take part in the hijra.[7] The significance of this use of the term is to demonstrate that the Islamic religion did not rise "full blown" until much later, perhaps in the time of Abd al-Malik. Therefore, the use of the terms "Muslim," "Islamic," or "Islam" would be inappropriate in the mid-seventh century. Indeed, the first recorded use of the term "Islam" is the inscription in the Dome of the Rock, dated around 691–692,[8] while the first recorded use of the term "Muslim" by a believer is AD 741,[9] and AD 775 for a non-Muslim.[10] The preferred term used by the early Muslims was "*mu'minun*," or believer, and is found 32 times in the Constitution of Medina,[11] though most of the seventh-century-century non-Muslim witnesses of the Arab conquests would not attribute any religious appellations

5. Hoyland, *Seeing Islam*, 547–48. In fact, the attachment of the hijra to Muhammad and his escape to Medina is part of the late eighth-century traditional literary account.

6. Crone and Cook, *Hagarism*, 9.

7. Crone and Cook, *Hagarism*, 8–9. Also see Warraq, "Introduction," in *The Origins of the Koran*, 29–30; and Saadi, "Nascent Islam," 218. Saadi even says, "The unprecedented name, Mhaggraye, is provocative because it provides the greatest evidence for their self-identification as immigrants (muhajirun in Arabic). In other words, the name Immigrants (muhajirun) implies that the Arabs had arrived to stake a claim on, occupy, and then inherit the land. The Syriac writers, reporting and repeating what they were hearing rather than inventing a historical event, merely Syriacized this native Arabic name."

8. Crone and Cook, *Hagarism*, 8–9.

9. Hoyland, "The Content and Context of Early Arabic," 78.

10. Nevo and Koren, *Crossroads to Islam*, 235n82. Also Hoyland, *Seeing Islam*, 156. John of Damascus only used the terms "Ishmaelite," "Hagarene," or "Saracen," and this was in the middle of the eighth century.

11. Hoyland, *Seeing Islam*, 548. It should be noted that the existence of the Constitution of Medina cannot be verified until the ninth century, since it is first mentioned in Ibn Isḥaq's Sirat.

to the "godless Saracens" that they encountered.¹² At this point some may want to point out that the term "Moslem" is used 98 times in the chronicle of John of Nikiu, for example, which is said to have been written around 690. However, the earliest copy of John's chronicle is from a 1602 Ethiopic translation of an earlier Arabic translation which, like the original Greek and Coptic manuscript, is lost.¹³ Therefore, it would have been very easy to have replaced the original terms like "Ishmaelite," or "Saracen," or "Mahgraye" with the term "Muslim," even though the latter term probably had not come into common usage until the late eighth century.¹⁴ This practice of substitution was apparently often used,¹⁵ and is quite natural, for we also tend to refer to the "Muslims" in the time of Muhammad when the historical data tells us that the term was probably not used until 140 years later.

THE EARLY FORMATION OF ISLAM ACCORDING TO THE NEO-REVISIONISTS

What can we say, then, about the early development of Islam? On the one hand, the earlier skeptics led by Wansbrough and Crone, want to postulate, in the absence of documentary evidence, that "Mecca was not Muhammad's birthplace or the Hijaz Islam's home, that the Quran was not compiled in the seventh century or written in Arabic, and even that Muhammad and the Arab conquests were a later invention."¹⁶ On the other hand, Hoyland argues that Islamic practices, which can be traced through the early non-Muslim sources and documentary evidence, are present early on. There is a new calendar dated from AD 622, the Muhajirun appear, written Arabic is used and their ruler is called the commander of the believers and serves a god named "Allah."¹⁷ Jeremy Johns adds that coins, building inscriptions, tombstones and traveler's graffiti can be used to trace out the early growth and development of a new religious community.¹⁸ Hoyland concludes that there is enough evidence to "infer that the newcomers did possess a distinctive

---

12. Hoyland, *Seeing Islam*, 71. This quote is from Sophronius, who wrote around AD 634.

13. Ibid., 152.

14. See Nevo and Koren, *Crossroads to Islam*, 134, especially note 118, where Nevo says that "Hoyland (1997) consistently translates mhaggare as 'Muslim' in order to differentiate it from tayyaye, which he translates 'Arab.'"

15. Nevo and Koren, *Crossroads to Islam*, 7.

16. Hoyland, "New Documentary Texts," 403–4.

17. Ibid., 396.

18. Johns, "Archaeology," 414.

cult."¹⁹ Indeed, it is significant that the Christians in the seventh and early eighth centuries did not consider the religious beliefs of the Arabs to be a different religion altogether, but rather they viewed it as more of a cult or a heresy of Christianity. This is exactly what John of Damascus (c.675–c.750) concludes in the middle of the eighth century.²⁰ His portrayal of Islam is that of an outgrowth of the pernicious Christian heresy, Arianism, and his apologetic approach is designed to help Christians deal with Muhammad as a "false prophet" and the false beliefs of the Ishmaelites whom he says will usher in the "anti-Christ."²¹

Muhammad and the "Full Light of History"

Was knowledge of the prophet Muhammad (570–632) present from the mid- seventh century, or did it gradually evolve along with the religion? A British Muslim writer, Ziauddin Sardar, proudly pronounced that "The Life of Mohammad is known as the Sira and was lived in the full light of history."²² Even in John's time, however, the first *sira* by Ibn Isḥaq had not yet been written. It is possible, since Ibn Isḥaq died in 767, that some other written stories were already circulating about Muhammad during John's life time. These were later collected by writers like Ibn Hisham (d. 833), who states that he incorporated a recension of Ibn Isḥaq's biography in his own book. These are, however, all over 130 years after the death of Muhammad. Also, if Muhammad lived in the "full light of history," why do we have virtually nothing from Muslim sources pertaining to Muhammad before the time of Caliph Abd al-Malik (r. 685–705), nearly 70 years after the death of Muhammad? This is one of the central problem areas raised by the Neo-Revisionists.

Some Neo-Revisionists, like Yehuda Nevo, even doubt whether Muhammad was an actual historic figure, for he can only be traced back historically to around 72/691 when his name appears on a coin minted by Abd al-Malik.²³ Nevo also believes that the "very few passing references to

19. Hoyland, "New Documentary Texts," 404.
20. Berkey, *Formation of Islam*, 74, 93.
21. HER 2 and 11.
22. Bright, "The Great Koran Con Trick," 1–2.
23. Nevo, as well as Hoyland, believe the earlier numismatic reference to a Muhammad as prophet, in 687, probably refers to the governor of Azerbaijan, Muhammad ibn Marwan, or to a religious prophet at that time, Muhammad Ibn al-Hanafiyyah, who was also known as the "mahdi." Nevo also points out that Bashear argues that "many events in the life of the Prophet reported in the Muslim sources are in fact retrojections into the past of later incidents, e.g., some from the life of the mid-to-late-seventh-century

him in earlier literary sources should be regarded as later interpolations by copiers who knew the Traditional Account."[24] In other words, it is difficult to explain how the central figure in a wildly successful religious conquest could avoid the "full light of history" until the time he is needed as a focal point in a religion that is also the basis for the government.

On the other hand, Michael Cook concludes that the non-Muslim sources give enough of a picture of the first 70 years to indicate that Muhammad not only existed, but that he was a leader in a movement that started around AD 622.[25] Even Patricia Crone, who once said that Muhammad did not exist as an historical figure, has changed her mind enough to say that "Mohammad is clearly an individual who changed the course of history," but she also points out that "we do not know how much of the Islamic tradition about him is true."[26] Part of the problem is that the biographies, as well as the other literary material written about Muhammad by Muslims in the late eighth and ninth centuries, were mostly constructed from the only literary source that may have existed, at least in part, before the end of the seventh century, which was the Qur'an. In the next section we will consider the development of the Qur'an, but suffice it to say at this point, that if the earliest biographical literature on Muhammad were derived from exegetical explanations of the obscure narratives in the Qur'an, and then parts of the Qur'an were written in order to give a "history" to a new religious movement, then how do we get at any "kernel of truth," much less an understanding of which events were played out under the "full light of history"?

Hoyland also finds it very curious that, aside from the early non-Muslim sources, "before AH 72 the archaeological record is strangely silent about Islam," as well as Muhammad and the Qur'an.[27] In fact, it really is not until 691 that we have a firm archaeological attestation to Muhammad on a coin minted by Abd al-Malik, as well as the inscription bearing Muhammad's name in the Dome of the Rock. Hoyland offers that "it is of course true that only with the passage of time does a man become a hero and a book authoritative,"[28] but that does not account for the abrupt way that Muhammad suddenly "appears" on the Arab scene. Is it possible, then, that

---

"prophet" Muhammad ibn al-Hanafiyyah." See Nevo and Koren, *Crossroads to Islam*, 6; and Hoyland, *Seeing Islam*, 550n24.

24. Nevo and Koren, *Crossroads to Islam*, 10–11.

25. Warraq, "Introduction," 27.

26. Robinson, *Cambridge Illustrated History of the Islamic World*, 10. See also Crone, "What Do We Actually Know about Muhammad?"

27. Hoyland, *Seeing Islam*, 549–50.

28. Ibid.

Abd al-Malik utilized Muhammad as a "propaganda weapon"[29] in his bid to make his new government more legitimate through an appeal to a religion, a prophet and a scripture?

By the time John of Damascus was writing about Muhammad in the 730s, Muhammad was considered to be an historical figure,[30] but how much of his image of Muhammad had been created by the narratives that were probably circulating at that time[31] as well as the strong propaganda that had been in place at least from the time of Abd al-Malik? John called Muhammad a "false prophet" and he called the religion of his followers a "heresy." He also ridiculed the so-called writings that came down to Muhammad from heaven. How closely does John's view of Muhammad corroborate with the evidence assembled by the neo-revisionists? Is it possible to reconstruct the first 100 years of Islam from a distance of 1400 years?

THE FORMATION OF INTERMEDIATE MONOTHEISM

As John of Damascus demonstrated in his writings against what he saw as a heresy of Christianity, there was a need to prepare Christians to defend their beliefs against the new religious doctrine that was assailing the Christian church throughout the Middle East. Leading up to John's time, some neo-Revisionist scholars propose that there was an intermediate monotheism forming from an amalgamation of Jewish and Christian influences. Over time, because of heretical and unorthodox Monophysite, Nestorian and Arian beliefs, which were further influenced by Rabbinic Judaism, this monotheistic movement incorporated a strong animosity for fundamental Christian doctrine, such as the deity of Christ and the Trinity.[32] Others found that Islam "was in essence a tribal conspiracy against the Byzantine and Persian empires with deep roots in Judaism, and that Arabs and Jews were allies in these conquering communities."[33] They would claim that a stronger rabbinic Jewish element pushed the agenda at first, but, after the conquests started up, for some reason the Jews were also marginalized and in time vilified in later writings even more than the Christians. Some even argue that

---

29. Hoyland, "New Documentary Texts," 396–97.
30. Warraq, "Koranic Criticism."
31. Hoyland mentions a papyrus from the late Umayyad period that contains some biographical material on the prophet. See Hoyland, *Seeing Islam*, 545. He also says that the earliest theological writing is not documented before AD 718 (546).
32. Nevo and Koren, *Crossroads to Islam*, 10. See also Berkey, *Formation of Islam*, 61.
33. Bright, "The Great Koran Con Trick," 2.

it was the Arab religion that developed the most as it came in contact with the more defined social, cultural and religious institutions of the conquered territory.[34] Berkey even argues that Islam is not understandable outside the influence of Judaism and Christianity.[35] Indeed, neo-Revisionists claim that it is from these two religious influences that Islam derived a good deal of its religious ideas and the vocabulary with which it was able to communicate to the inhabitants of the conquered lands.[36] Berkey also indicates that there was a general understanding in the first fifty years that Islam was merely a continuation of Judaism. One example given is that when the Dome of the Rock was built people saw it as a rebuilding of the ancient Temple.[37] Even Ibn Warraq relates that Wansbrough "argued that Islam emerged only when it came into contact with and under the influence of Rabbinic Judaism."[38] Certainly each culture influenced the other, but since Muhammad was not identified by the Muslims until AD 691 and the religion was not defined theologically and scripturally until the end of the eighth century, some of the Neo-Revisionists, such as Yehuda Nevo, prefer to call the developing religion an intermediate monotheism.[39]

While supporting some aspects of Nevo's "intermediate monotheism," Robert Hoyland questions Nevo's interpretation of seventh-century rock inscriptions to support claims of a Judeo-Christian basis for Islam. Hoyland posits that "to say that 'the inscriptions lack typical Islamic expressions' or 'exhibit indeterminate monotheism' just because they do not mention Muhammad is to misconstrue Islam, which is not primarily Muhammadanism, but rather subordination to an omnipotent and unique God. So the very common formula *la ilaha illa Allah wahdahu la sharika lahu*,[40] though not incompatible with Judaism or Christianity, can nevertheless be said to be specifically Islamic."[41] Hoyland then gives three reasons for the significance of these early inscriptions: They are in Arabic, they are in the same Kufic script, and they "draw upon a common stock of words and phrases."[42] As an example, Hoyland then shows how the phrase "forgive him his former

34. Berkey, *Formation of Islam*, 75.
35. Ibid., 65.
36. Ibid., 68.
37. Ibid., 74.
38. Warraq, "Introduction," 24. Warraq cites R. Stephen Humphreys, who adds, "that Islamic doctrine generally, and even the figure of Muhammad, were molded on Rabbinic Jewish prototypes." See Humphreys, *Islamic History*, 84.
39. Nevo and Koren, *Crossroads to Islam*, 207–8.
40. "There is no God but God, and He has no partners."
41. Hoyland, "The Content and Context of Early Arabic Inscriptions," 86.
42. Ibid., 83–84.

The Early Formation of Islam 73

and his latter sins" is found as early as AD 683 in southwest Iraq and then throughout the Middle East for the next two centuries.[43] However, we have the same phenomena today with a phrase such as "rest in peace" (RIP). It has been used throughout the world. Ubiquity does not necessarily denote distinctiveness. Even when he relates that the primary source upon which early Arabic inscriptions draw upon is the Qur'an, he overlooks the possibility that the many variations and "eclectic blend[s] of words and phrases taken from different verses of the Qur'an"[44] may also suggest pre-Quranic sayings or verses from other sources, such as Christian Syriac liturgy or Jewish Targums.[45] Certainly there was a tremendous mix of political and religious contrasts taking place at this time. Douglas Pratt suggests that "into this context there erupted a brash and bold new religious movement, apparently proclaiming the same monotheism but vehemently eschewing the Christocentrism of the faith into whose territories and communities its early expansion made dramatic inroads."[46] The Traditional View claims that Muhammad and the Qur'an were responsible for this tremendous upheaval, and many Western scholars have accepted this picture as a factual representation of the events at the close of the seventh century. On the other hand, Nevo, who says that neither the traditional view of the Muslims nor the Western view is correct, offers up a third interpretation. He says that

> In the third decade of the seventh century Arab tribesmen took possession of the eastern provinces of the Byzantine Empire. This would appear to be no mean feat, and the obvious question is, why did they win? The classical Muslim literature portrays a series of pitched battles against the forces of a mighty power, and ascribes the Arab success to their newfound faith. They won, in short, because God was on their side. The current Western version suggests that the Arabs won because the Byzantine Empire had been weakened and impoverished, first by Justinian's partially successful but exhausting attempts to regain the western provinces and then by the Persian wars of the early seventh century. Heraclius conquered the Persians but was left in no state to withstand the Arabs ... Archaeological work over the past decade and a half, together with evidence from literary sources, suggests that neither of these views is accurate.[47]

---

43. Ibid., 84.
44. Ibid., 82.
45. See Firestone, *Journeys in Holy Lands*, 11–21.
46. Pratt, *Challenge of Islam*, 102.
47. Nevo and Koren, *Crossroads to Islam*, 17.

Nevo goes on to say that the Byzantine leaders had already decided to pull out of the Arabian lands and to not defend them militarily, but rather to transfer the control to Arab tribes which had become allies during the long occupation. This worked for a while, but problems came when the Byzantine government decided to cut off the subsidies to these allies. Without the needed income, the reluctant allies began to look for other sources of income. Some turned back to raiding other Arab tribes. In time they became more unified, perhaps under Muhammad and his new ideas, and they decided that the greater riches were to be found in the lands to the north where the Byzantine armies had pulled out and the cities were left defenseless. Thus, the Arab sweep of the middle decades of the seventh century were not defined by large armies clashing over the fate of the land, but rather by a type of emigration, or exodus (also known as hajj or even hijra), accompanied by local skirmishes and occasional raiding parties.[48] In this way, most of the towns and cities of Syria and Iraq were "conquered" when they surrendered to the advance parties of Arab *Maghazi* warriors[49] seeking easy booty and taxes. Even the great city of Damascus was handed over peacefully when John of Damascus' grandfather, Mansur ibn Sarjun, who was the mayor of the city, surrendered to the Arabs without a fight. The new rulers continued allowing the Byzantine administrators to run the country though, since the Arabs were unfamiliar with the task of running such a government. They even preferred to live in their "garrison towns" and remain aloof from the main operations of the cities, as long as they received the benefit of the taxes. In time this changed, especially under the leadership of 'Abd al-Malik, and by the middle of the eighth century most of the important administrative roles were in the hands of the Arabs or converts to Islam.[50]

During this time in the second half of the seventh century, when the Arabs kept to themselves in garrison towns and only carried on raids from these central points, Nevo concludes that the intermediate monotheism was mostly practiced by the elite. The Arab masses were still mostly pagan and their forces were mixed with Christian, Persian and other foreign soldiers (who were mostly out for the booty or had been captured and forced to fight as slaves). In areas where the majority was made up of Arabs, the prior citizens were often forced to adopt the religion of the invaders. Nevo states, however, that the reason "was not missionary zeal on the part of the invading Arabs, but a political decision to encourage assimilation of all Arabs, old

---

48. Crone and Cook, *Hagarism*, 9.
49. Maghazi refers to military campaigns.
50. Nevo and Koren, *Crossroads to Islam*, 17.

and new, into a uniform population."[51] The emphasis seems to be on the fact that the general "religion" of the Arabs was a form of paganism, not of an early form of Islam.[52] This was not true in regard to the elite, "who for political reasons had accepted a form of monotheism."[53] Eventually, through the leadership of Mu'awiya and 'Abd al-Malik, this intermediate monotheism developed into the all-encompassing religion of Islam.

According to some of the Neo-Revisionists, Mu'awiya (661–680) was the first bona-fide Arab leader and caliph, and it was under his leadership that the Arabs were first unified. Then, through concerted efforts, they solidified their control over the land that they conquered.[54] Mu'awiya is the first Arab leader to appear on a coin bearing his name with the appellation "*amir al-mu'minin*" (commander of the believers) on one side and the phrase "bism Allah" (In the name of Allah) on the reverse.[55] The striking of a coin is usually a political statement demonstrating political control or the advent of a new regime, but it is questionable as to whether Mu'uwiya's reign was anything other than a "loose confederation of Arab tribes" or "politically independent communities of *mu'minun* (believers)."[56] Jeremy Johns argues that "a centralized administrative and fiscal apparatus is absent under Mu'awiya, and is first introduced under 'Abd al-Malik and his successors."[57] Hoyland counters Jeremy John's idea that there was only a loose tribal organization before 'Abd al-Malik, but his evidence is mostly the striking of coins.[58]

Under Mu'awiya Muhammad and the Qur'an are not mentioned, even as nascent religious views. This is not from a lack of power under Mu'awiya, but perhaps due to the very nature of the religion at that time.[59] The real question is, even if Mu'awiya had a powerful centralized government in

51. Ibid., 220–21.

52. Ibid., 219–20.

53. Ibid.

54. This means that the first four caliphs (Abu Bakr, Umar, Uthman, and Ali), known by the traditionalists as the rightly-guided caliphs, may have either been minor historical leaders or mostly made up in later eighth- and ninth-century writings (which is when they are first mentioned in the literature). See Nevo and Koren, *Crossroads to Islam*, 96.

55. Johns, "Archaeology," 418.

56. Hoyland, "New Documentary Texts," 398. See also Johns, "Archaeology," 418.

57. Johns, "Archaeology," 422.

58. Hoyland, "New Documentary Texts," 399. The striking of coins was often a sign of political control, but even rebel groups were known to strike coins proclaiming their power (such as with the rebel caliph, Ibn al-Zubayr, who beat 'Abd al-Malik to the punch by proclaiming Muhammad as the prophet three years before).

59. Ibid., 403.

place, why is there no mention at all of Muhammad, the Qur'an or the religion of Islam? It is clear from the non-Muslim sources that some type of Arab cult was in place during the time of Mu'awiya; and it is also clear from the archaeological sources that it was not publicly proclaimed until the rule of 'Abd al-Malik.[60] What could possibly account for such an oversight? Perhaps the reason is that Islam was not yet a developed religion, separate from Christianity and Judaism, but rather an amalgamation of various beliefs that were beginning to be defined under Mu'awiya and 'Abd al-Malik. This may be why the Arabs were called *mu'minun* (believers) without a mention as to what they believed.[61] This may also be why John of Damascus, almost 50 years later, still considered the beliefs of the Ishmaelites to represent a heresy of Christianity rather than a religion distinct from his own faith.

It All Starts with 'Abd al-Malik

Why, then, are the proclamations by Arabs concerning Islam and Muhammad absent before the last decade of the seventh century? Jeremy Johns believes that it is because there was no centralized government and no Muslim state before 'Abd al-Malik.[62] Under Mu'awiya, life went on as usual—the administrations were still for the most part left intact under the Byzantine administrators and the "believers" were mostly in garrison towns. This could have been, as Johns points out, because Mu'awiya still did not have control over all the tribes of Arabia. This apparently changed under 'Abd al-Malik (685–705). Once 'Abd al-Malik established firm control over the region and squelched the rebellions of rival leaders, such as Ibn al-Zubayr, it is possible he would have realized that in order to have a credible government in the midst of the other monotheistic faiths, he needed a formulized religion, a scripture and a prophet. Indeed, Hoyland picks up on this and concludes that "it was pressure from rebel factions that induced 'Abd al-Malik to proclaim Islam publicly as the ideological basis of the Arab state."[63] This gave him the opportunity to rally the forces around him and bring unity in the midst of strife. Hoyland even says that it stole the thunder from his opponents, strengthened his own legitimacy and allowed him and his successors to style themselves as "God's deputies on earth with the right and responsibility to determine matters of religion."[64] The earliest declarations

---

60. See Hoyland, *Seeing Islam*, 554.
61. See Donner, *Muhammad and the Believers*.
62. Johns, "Archaeology," 418.
63. Hoyland, "New Documentary Texts," 397.
64. Hoyland, *Seeing Islam*, 553.

of Islam, for example, are found during the time of 'Abd al-Malik, but not beforehand.[65] These coins, documents and monumental inscriptions give testimony to a government claiming divine authority, religious writings that proclaim dominion over all other religions, and a prophet who claims to be the "seal" of all prophets.

According to this view, the minting of coins under 'Abd al-Malik was used to solidify his position as "Commander of the believers"[66] and to also produce a new Arab identity. His coins were inscribed with the words, "*bism Allah la ilaha illa Allah wahdahu Muhammad rasul Allah*," or "In the name of God, there is no god but God alone, Muhammad is the messenger of God."[67] However, the coins from 691 up through 699 still had images of the caliph. After that time there were only words. His later epigraphic coin with the bold proclamation that "Allah was the only God and Muhammad was his prophet" not only encapsulated the core beliefs of the new religion, but it also became the "model for Islamic coinage for the next half millennium."[68]

The construction of the Dome of the Rock begun in the year 692 also solidified Abd al-Malik's position and gave a voice to the movement.[69] According to the neo-Revisionist view, this mosque, built on the former site of the Jerusalem Temple, not only provided a worship center for the intermediate monotheism which was now breaking free from its Jewish and Christian roots, but it was also a strong symbolic act to demonstrate that a new religion had mounted the former and had claimed victory. Berkey mentions that the Dome of the Rock "marks an important stage in the crystallization of a distinctly Islamic identity," even though it "incorporates much in the way of Byzantine architectural motifs, and was in fact built with the help of Byzantine craftsmen."[70] The inscriptions emblazoned on the walls represent the earliest compilation of Quranic-like verses, and together with the adoption of Muhammad as the prophet, this physical edifice signaled the formation of a new state religion.[71]

Is it possible that the scenario of the development of an intermediate monotheism, as outlined above, is the most comprehensive and probable

65. Johns, "Archaeology," 416.
66. 'Abd al-Malik was the first one to call himself Khalifat Allah (Caliph of Allah)
67. Johns, "Archaeology," 426, 430.
68. Johns, "Archaeology," 431.
69. Berkey, *Formation of Islam*, 81. See also Nevo and Koren, *Crossroads to Islam*, 231.
70. Berkey, *Formation of Islam*, 62.
71. Nevo and Koren, *Crossroads to Islam*, 231. See also Hoyland, "New Documentary Texts," 396. The term "Qur'anic-like" is used since the verses are variants of what is in the Qur'an. Therefore, they may represent an earlier form of the verses.

judgment on the issues? After all, this view seems to coincide with many of the seventh-century non-Muslim eyewitness accounts. It is also supported by the archaeological, epigraphic and numismatic evidence from that time period. Furthermore, it fits with John's assessment of Muhammad, the incomplete nature of the scriptures and the heretical nature of the religion. How, then, do these things help us understand John better? Does the forensic evidence presented by the Neo-Revisionists dovetail with John's own assessment? Are the eyewitness accounts from the seventh and early eighth centuries echoed in John's own eyewitness account from his position in the Umayyad court? And, finally, how does John's own understanding help us understand early Islam better? Does his trained theological intellect allow us to take a "snapshot" of Islam in the middle of the eighth century from which we will then be able to connect even more pieces of the puzzle? *What do we see of Islam through the Eyes of John?*

Now that we have explored possible explanations for the formation of Islam based on various forms of evidence, let us now consider another important area for providing context, which is the development of Islamic theology.

5

Theological Development of Islam

INTRODUCTION

If in regard to the development of the doctrine of the Trinity, controversy between factions forced greater clarification of language, more precise use of logic, and greater articulation of orthodox teaching, why would this not be a possibility in the development of Islamic theology as well? The early Muslims wrestled with issues regarding faith versus works, free will versus predestination, and the uncreated nature of the Qur'an. These doctrines were not hammered out in a vacuum, but rather in the midst of a predominantly Christian milieu. Just as apologetics was used to forge Christian doctrines such as the Trinity, evidence suggests it was also employed in the development of the early Islamic doctrines. As Christians and Jews critiqued the Qur'an and argued against Muslim theological viewpoints, Muslim scholars devised ways to counter their opponent's beliefs and strengthen their own views. Muslim theologians also had to suppress heretical ideas within their own fold. From this crucible of controversy, "orthodox" Muslim theology was forged and defended. What were the factors involved in the internal and external political and theological struggles? How did they shape Islamic theology? How did this "heresy of the Ishmaelites"[1] force Christian

---

1. This is the way John of Damascus and other Christian in the early eighth century viewed the developing Islamic religion. Because of many similarities and historical connections, they did not view it as a foreign religion; because of many key differences, they could not view it as anything other than a heresy of Christianity or Judaism.

theologians like John of Damascus to re-contextualize doctrinal issues that were under fire such as the Trinity and the deity of Christ?

EARLY DEVELOPMENT OF ISLAMIC THEOLOGY[2]

Caesar Farah illustrates how the different views in early Islamic theology made a standard belief system very difficult to establish:

> Qadarites, for instance, stressed the doctrine of free will, while the Jabrites denied it; the Sifatites argued for the eternal nature of the attributes of God, while the Mu'tazilites denied they were eternal; the Murji'ites stressed that human actions must not be subject to human judgment, while their opponents, the Wa'dites, insisted on the condemnation of man in this life, before the Day of Judgment; the Kharijites played down the importance of the role of secular leadership, i.e., the caliphate which they considered merely a human institution, while the Shi'ites went so far as to consider their imam as divine.[3]

All of these controversies revolved around three early disputes. The first dispute involved the Murji'ites claiming that faith alone was sufficient for salvation while the Kharijites argued that faith without works signified that the person was also devoid of true faith and was therefore to be condemned as an infidel. The second dispute focused on the question of whether man had free will before God or whether his whole life was predestinated. The Qadarites, and later the Mu'tazilites, held fast against the traditionalists[4] and the Jabrites for almost 200 years, even though popular sentiment remained with the traditionalists, whose position won out in the end. The third major

---

2. See Appendix B: *Theological Development Chart* for an overview.

3. Farah, *Islam: Beliefs and Observances*, 207.

4. Traditionalism has to do with Muslims who follow the received traditions found in the Qur'an and in the life and words of Muhammad. In the early centuries of Islam, the traditionalists became associated with a school founded by Abu al-Hasan al-Ash'ari (early tenth century). The traditionalists used speculative theology (*kalam*) to defend their faith, but in time they rejected the more extreme rationalism of the Mu'tazilites and held to a belief in predestination and the uncreated nature of the Qur'an. In time traditionalism became associated with orthodox Islamic faith. In this way it is similar to the Traditionists (*ahl al-hadith*, literally "people of tradition") who typically hold revelation through the Qur'an and the actions and sayings of Muhammad as the final word in all disputes. Pratt writes that the Traditionists were "those who were keen to preserve and promote the Traditions of the Prophet of Islam and so Islam itself. The task of the Traditionists, collectively speaking, was to produce the parameters of Muslim orthodoxy, so far as it could then be determined." See Pratt, *Challenge of Islam*, 45–48, 51, 149.

dispute involved the controversy over whether the Qur'an, as the Word of God, was uncreated, since it involved God's speech, or whether it was created, since an uncreated entity outside of God would imply that the unity of God could not be maintained.[5] In the end, the Ash'arites won popular favor by formulating a compromise position only to later reject the very pathway of reason that brought about the compromise, and again everything was subordinated under the rigors of a revelation that could not be questioned.[6]

Disputation One: Faith versus Works

The earliest theological issue facing Islam took place in the late seventh century and dealt with the relationship of faith to works. The Kharijites equated faith with works. They insisted that in regard to the relationship between faith and works, "there could be no compromise, no middle ground. A Muslim was either rigorously observant, a true believer, or not a Muslim at all."[7] True believers were those who did the right things and unbelievers were those who did not, or those who compromised. This view came to a head during the time of Uthman, Mu'awiyah and Ali, who compromised their beliefs, according to the Kharijites, and therefore were no longer believers and had to be resisted. During the battle of Siffin in 657, Mu'awiyah, a relative of Uthman, called for arbitration with Ali's forces. This was mainly employed as a delaying tactic, but Ali's acceptance was seen as weakness and his forces split into loyalists and mutineers, who became known as the Kharijites or Secessionists. The Kharijites believed that Uthman had acted wrongly because of his nepotism, that Mu'awiyah had sinned by rebelling against the rightful successor to Uthman, and that Ali had committed a grave sin (*kabirah*) by accepting the arbitration. Therefore, the Kharijites no longer supported Ali as caliph. In their developing theology they argued that a man who had committed a grave sin called into question his very status as a true Muslim. Thus, the strictness of the observance of this belief was such that if the caliph himself committed a grave sin or departed from the true path, then even he should be deposed or killed. (One Kharijite follower carried out this injunction by assassinating Ali in 661, paving the way for the Umayyad takeover through Mu'awiyah). This rigid definition of orthodoxy soon equated true belief in Islam with absolute obedience, and entrance into Paradise became dependent on actions rather than faith.[8]

---

5. Goldziher, *Introduction to Islamic Theology and Law*, 97.
6. See Reilly, *The Closing of the Muslim Mind*, 11–39.
7. Esposito, *Islam: The Straight Path*, 69.
8. Fakhry, *A Short Introduction to Islamic Philosophy*, 11–13.

The group that opposed the Kharijite position was known as the Murji'a, or Murji'ites, and they believed that faith alone saved a person. The name refers to "those who defer," and it was given to them because they deferred final judgment to God, who was the only one who could ultimately decide who would be saved on the Last Day.[9] They emphasized that right belief was entirely a matter of "inner assent," rather than "external performance or practice" and consisted of knowing, loving and submitting to God.[10] Thus, a true believer would be able to enter Paradise based on his faith in God rather than on whether he was obedient to the end. On the other hand, the Kharijites said that if a sinner died unrepentant then he would not be able to escape hell, even if he believed in God and the prophet. Of course, the Kharijites would say that this person could not be a believer "in the true sense" because otherwise he would not remain unrepentant.[11] Abu Hanifa, one of the Murji'ites, developed a middle way where he said that faith was with the tongue and heart and works needed to follow faith.[12] Due to the extremism of the Kharijites, the majority of the *ulama* were drawn to the more moderate position of the Murji'ites, and even the rulers were positively inclined toward the theology of the Murji'ites since these theologians refused to condemn sinners and left the final judgment up to God. This theological openness also fit in well with a socio-political debate taking place at that time which involved whether man had the free will to act toward securing his salvation or whether all his thoughts and actions were already predestined by God. This spirit of inquiry began to develop into what Fakhry has called the "first articulate theological movement in Islam."[13]

Disputation Two: Predestination versus Free Will

At the end of the seventh century a very important theological question was being asked in regard to the rule of the Umayyads, which had a definite political overtone, and this was whether the Umayyad leaders were predestined by God to rule. The Qadarites were at the forefront of this discussion, and though their ideas were generally accepted at first, they began to cause quite a political stir. Goldziher notes that the theology of determinism (predestination) can be traced back to this time in Damascus, which was

9. Goldziher, *Introduction to Islamic Theology and Law*, 74.
10. Fakhry, *A Short Introduction to Islamic Philosophy*, 13.
11. Macdonald, *Development of Muslim Theology*, 126.
12. Ibid.
13. Fakhry, *A Short Introduction to Islamic Philosophy*, 16. See also Goldziher, *Introduction to Islamic Theology and Law*, 82.

also the center of the debate on man's *qadar*, or power. Essentially, in the Qadarite position, man determines his own fate or *khalaq al-af'al*. This was set against the blind compulsion of the Jabriya, who followed the majority of the Kharijites and believed in *jabr*, or predestination.[14] The Qadarites believed that man must have free will and responsibility over his actions. Otherwise, if God were to determine everything that happens in a person's life, then he would also be responsible for the evil deeds that are committed and ultimately accountable for the fate of that person. If a man sins and it is pre-determined by God, how then can God hold him responsible for that action on Judgment Day?

On the other hand, the testimony of the Qur'an mandates that God predestined all things because it assumes the eventual development of the Arab people and an Arabic language as well as specific references to the life of Muhammad and the unique problems he was facing in early seventh-century Arabia. If the Qur'an were from all eternity, then these things would have to unfold as they were revealed to Muhammad, meaning that God had predestined the Arab people and all the events recorded in the Qur'an. If believers were free to choose otherwise then God would be seen to be less than almighty, for they might choose to reject the revealed path and negate the mandates of the Qur'an. However, as the Qadarites pointed out, if all actions were predestined by God then He was also responsible for all the evil things that men did. If man had free will then he had responsibility for his own actions. More importantly, the Qadarite emphasis on free will had political ramifications. At that time the Umayyad Caliphs taught that God had predestined their rule over the people and so they could safely do as they pleased. If, as the Kharijites believed, the grave sins of the caliphs negated their right to rule, then they should be ousted. However, if God had foreordained their position and circumstances, then whatever they did should be accepted as the will of God.[15] For the Umayyad court, then, it was expedient to promote the view of predestination because it gave legitimacy to their already unpopular rule. They argued that God put them in control, so it was God who determined their actions, even if those actions were cruel and unjustified.[16]

At first the Qadarite beliefs were deemed heretical because belief in predestination was so strong. The Umayyad leaders were also afraid that widespread belief in free will would undermine their control. Men like Ma'bad al-Juhani (d. 699), the founder of the Qadari movement, challenged

---

14. Goldziher, *Introduction to Islamic Theology and Law*, 80–82.
15. Stewart, *Unfolding Islam*, 159–60.
16. Goldziher, *Introduction to Islamic Theology and Law*, 83–84.

the injustices of the Umayyad court by claiming that it was not God's will that caused the caliph and his followers to do evil works, but their own free will to choose those sinful actions. This challenge was not acceptable and Ma'bad al-Juhani was ordered to be executed by 'Abd al-Malik in 699 for his doctrine.[17]

The Rise of the Mu'tazilites

Ignaz Godziher writes that the Mu'tazila, or "those who separate themselves" were the first to apply reason to their view of God's justice in man's freedom of will. The founder is said to have been Wasil ibn Ata (d. 748), an ascetic and a disciple of al-Hasan al-Basri (d. 728), one of the leaders of the Qadarite movement, from which the Mu'tazilites originated.[18] Some have traced the origin of the Mu'tazilites back to Wasil's compromise view, which taught that the grave sinner was neither a believer nor a non-believer, but rather just a grave sinner "to whom the sanctions against apostates or infidels do not apply."[19] This led to a reaffirmation of the Qadarite position on free will and the Mu'tazilites soon found themselves entrenched against strong believers in predestination, such as Jahm Ibn Safwan (d. 745). Safwan taught that *jabr*, or strict predestination, would not allow men the capacity for power (*qadr*) to counter the absolute power of God, for, in their estimation, that would limit God's power and make Him less than all-powerful.[20] On the other hand, the Mu'tazilites believed that God's divine justice required human free will and responsibility, for otherwise God would be solely responsible for all acts of evil and injustice.[21] The Mu'tazilites further believed that reason demanded that God could not be blamed for doing what is evil, and they claimed that God could only command what is right and prohibit what is wrong.[22]

Eventually this conflict split the theological camps into two diametrically opposed positions: free will, or *qadr*, on one side and predestination, or *jabr*, on the other. This division was so central that Fakhry even says that

17. Macdonald, *Development of Muslim Theology*, 127–29; Farah, *Islam: Beliefs and Observances*, 208; Wensinck, *Muslim Creed*, 52.

18. Goldziher, *Introduction to Islamic Theology and Law*, 86; see also Wensinck, *Muslim Creed*, 52.

19. Fakhry, "Philosophy and Theology," 279. See also Fakhry, *A Short Introduction to Islamic Philosophy*, 15, and Esposito, *Islam: The Straight Path*, 70.

20. Fakhry, "Philosophy and Theology," 15.

21. Macdonald, *Development of Muslim Theology*, 135.

22. Fakhry, *A Short Introduction to Islamic Philosophy*, 16.

"almost all subsequent theological developments would take the form of variations on, or a synthesis of, these two antithetical positions."[23]

The Mu'tazila were known for criticizing popular beliefs, especially in the areas of superstition, such as the belief in the bridge *sirat*, or the hair-thin bridge that was as sharp as a razor in order to foil those who were destined to hell. They also argued against the image of the scales where people had to outweigh their bad works with more good works in order to make it into heaven. The Mu'tazilites saw all of these beliefs as unworthy of God. Above all they wanted to develop a belief in a God who was transcendent but who was also involved in the lives of people because of his divine justice. In their defense of God's justice and man's responsibility, they were similar to the Qadarites. However, in time the Mu'tazilites went several steps beyond the Qadarite position because they insisted that due to his justice, God is obligated to do all that he can for man. In due course, their consistency in this position led them to build up the model of the free man, but, according to their critics, it also obligated God so that in the end he became less free than the creatures he had created.[24]

With the support of Caliph Ma'mun (813–33), the Mu'tazilite position became the official doctrine of the early Islamic empire in the ninth century, during the beginning of the Abbasid period in Baghdad. Over time, Ma'mun attempted to force the theological position of the Mu'tazilites onto the general population, who generally rejected the idea of free will and held fast to their belief in God's pre-determined rule of their lives. Even the scholars who opposed the Mu'tazilite doctrine were forced out of their positions, tortured or even executed in what was known as a type of inquisition procedure called the *mihna*. This lasted for about two decades and then the persecution was relaxed and other schools of *Kalam* which placed more reliance on revealed knowledge than on human reason came forward, and soon the Mu'tazilite position was sidelined.[25]

Disputation Three: Created Word (Qur'an) versus Uncreated Word (Qur'an)

From the early eighth century on into the Abbasid period, the Qur'an was popularly believed to be uncreated.[26] The rationale behind this was that

23. Ibid., 15–16.

24. Goldziher, *Introduction to Islamic Theology and Law*, 86.

25. Feener, *Islam in World Cultures*, 18; see also Esposito, *Islam: The Straight Path*, 71.

26. Esposito, *Islam: The Straight Path*, 69–70.

God's speech is first of all as eternal as any of his other attributes, such as his power or his knowledge. Since the Qur'an is his revelation to man through the act of speaking, then the Qur'an itself must be eternal like God himself, and therefore uncreated. The Mu'tazilites, on the other hand, viewed the act of God "speaking" as another anthropomorphism that would ultimately destroy the unity of God. If the Qur'an existed apart from God, then there would be two eternal entities rather than one. The unity of God would be compromised and negated.[27]

In support of their belief in God's unity, the Mu'tazilites agreed with their opponents, the Jahmites, and regarded God's attributes as inseparable from his essence. In other words, God is powerful because divine power is part of His very essence. It is the same for his knowledge, life and will, which are some of the seven essential attributes that the Mu'tazilites acknowledged. On the other hand, their opponents contended that God's eternal attributes were distinct from his essence. The Mu'tazilites saw this as inconsistent with the unity of God since it would create a "plurality of eternal entities." The traditionalists, however, in their determination that the Qur'an had to be uncreated, accused the Mu'tazilites of denying that God had any attributes at all. For example, F.E. Peters notes that Ibn Khaldun (d. 1406), a later historian and critic of the Mu'tazilites, accused them of denying that God could have any attributes because any attribute would jeopardize the sense of God's unity, since it would be considered as additional to his essence. This, according to Ibn Khaldun, led to the Mu'tazilite denial of God's hearing, speech, vision, power, knowledge, life and even to the denial of God's possession of volition, which ultimately led to the denial of God's ability to predestinate.[28] In actuality, however, Ibn Khaldun did not seem to understand the Mu'tazilite position at all, for the Mu'tazilite insistence on identifying God's attributes with his essence upheld God's unity rather than dismissed it, for otherwise God's attributes would be considered separate deities themselves. Therefore, through reason, as well as revelation, the Mu'tazilites decided that the Qur'an had to be created, since it would challenge the sense of unity and oneness of God if the Qur'an were also eternal and separate from God. Unfortunately, though, even with the later Ash'arite synthesis, the Mu'tazilite intention to safeguard the unity of God was subsumed by the conviction that the Qur'an, "as the embodiment of divine speech (*kalam Allah*) was uncreated and eternal."[29]

---

27. Goldziher, *Introduction to Islamic Theology and Law*, 97.

28. Peters, *A Reader on Classical Islam*, 360, in regard to a critique of Mu'tazilite viewpoint by Ibn Khaldun.

29. Fakhry, *A Short Introduction to Islamic Philosophy*, 18–20.

Throughout the eighth century the Mu'tazilites were persecuted as heretics for their belief in a created Qur'an.[30] In truth, however, the Mu'tazilites taught that the Qur'an is the "created word of God, who is its uncreated source."[31] This meant, among other things, that the teaching of the Qur'an as the actual speech or Word of God resulted in a belief in two deities, which would itself be a heresy.[32]

Caesar Farah notes that the belief in the uncreated Word of God, one of the central doctrines in Christian theology, "was perhaps behind the Muslim Traditionist's insistence on the Qur'an, the word of God, being by similar reasoning also uncreated. These Muslim theologians could have been influenced by St. John of Damascus."[33] Indeed, in his two works on Islam, the *Heresy of the Ishmaelites* and the *Disputation between a Christian and a Saracen*, John challenged the Saracens on the issue of the uncreated Word of God. John, however, was referring to Jesus Christ, the Logos of God, as the Word of God and the Spirit of God, rather than the Qur'an. The Qur'an itself, however, identified Christ as God's Word and Spirit,[34] and John used that knowledge in his favor. He argued that God could not have existed from eternity without his Word and Spirit, therefore concluding that if Jesus were the Word and Spirit of God then he must also be as eternal as God; and since there is only one God, then Jesus must also be that one God.[35] Tritton admires the logical development of John's argument and reasons that John's use of the meaning of Logos as the uncreated Word of God "may well have provoked the doctrine of the uncreated Koran."[36]

---

30. Farah, *Islam: Beliefs and Observances*, 209.

31. Esposito, *Islam: The Straight Path*, 71.

32. Ibid., 71.

33. Farah, *Islam: Beliefs and Observances*, 209. See also Watt, *Islamic Philosophy and Theology*, 44. Here the reference to the "traditionists" would also seem to apply to the earlier use of "traditionalists" since the traditionalists at this time were the ones who promoted the belief that the Qur'an was uncreated, a position that the traditionalists, who were keen to preserve and promote the Traditions of the Prophet of Islam, later found in the Hadith, recognized was dependent on the Qur'an being uncreated. This also demonstrates that the two terms, "traditionists" and "traditionalists," were often used similarly if not synonymously.

34. Surah 3:45; Surah 4:171.

35. DIS 6.1–11.

36. Tritton, *Muslim Theology*, 56.

The Fall of the Mu'tazilites and the Rise of the Ash'arites

In the ninth century, under the caliphate of al-Ma'mun, the Mu'tazilites finally "gained reprieve and official support."[37] Over time, however, the Mu'tazilites pushed their rational consistency too far and sparked a violent theological battle by devising an explanation that the revelation given to a prophet was not the actual voice of God, but rather a "speech created by God" that corresponded to the Word and will of God.[38] Even the inquisition under the caliph al-Ma'mun could not suppress the rejection of this Mu'tazilite view, and the reaction of the people brought a strong reversal to this position. Proponents of the uncreated Qur'an began advocating that not only was the revelation given to Muhammad the uncreated Word of God, but that also the written word between the covers of a book and even the recited words of the Qur'an by Muslims in their daily prayers was to be regarded as God's speech and therefore eternal.[39] Taken to an extreme, the very Qur'an would be worshipped as another "god," which, of course, would be heretical. Thus, in the end, it seemed that the most reasonable position was dismissed and replaced by one that rejected reason, and though some scholars would continue espousing the Mu'tazilite doctrine, it became marginalized and lost its appeal.

The view that eventually asserted itself was the Ash'arite school of theology founded by Abu al-Hasan Ali al-Ash'ari (d. 935), who rose out of the Mu'tazilite camp. He emphasized that human reason was not enough to determine the role of God in man's affairs and taught that God's power and will transcended man's categories and therefore His nature could not be understood.[40] However, he did not give up fully on the ability of man to use reason. Instead Al-Ash'ari "undertook a synthesis of contending positions. He staked a middle ground between the extremes of ibn Hanbal's literalism and the Mu'tazilite's logical rationalism."[41] He reaffirmed God's role in creation as transcendent, and re-asserted the doctrines of God's omnipotence as well as the uncreatedness of the Qur'an, but he balanced this with the belief that God also decreed that people would be accountable for their own actions. The key idea that won over the masses was that while he promoted the use of reason and logic, he still held that they were subordinate to revelation. This middle view became quite popular, and by the eleventh century had

---

37. Farah, *Islam: Beliefs and Observances*, 209.
38. Goldziher, *Introduction to Islamic Theology and Law*, 98.
39. Ibid., 99.
40. This deals with the doctrine of "bi-la kayf," or the teaching that since God was beyond understanding some things had to be accepted without "asking how."
41. Esposito, *Islam: The Straight Path*, 73.

attracted many followers[42] and became one of the predominant views for Muslims of that time, and later for the dominant school of Sunni theology.[43]

In time the Ash'arites proposed a middle way which would preserve a belief in an uncreated Qur'an, but would also alleviate the problems mitigated by a belief that every utterance of the Qur'an was an eternal utterance of God. Al-Ash'ari advanced the idea that God's speech is eternal, but only in a spiritual sense and as one of the attributes of God. When God's revelation came down upon the prophets, they received a representation of this speech, not the utterance of God itself. In the end, however, al-Ash'ari rejected his earlier Mu'tazilite views and remained close to the traditionalist view and maintained that even the written copies of the Qur'an, as well as the recited verses, were all copies of the eternal Qur'an which was preserved on a tablet in heaven and they were all "identical with the heavenly original; what is true of the original is true of those spatial and temporal manifestations that ostensibly come into being through a human agency."[44] For the next 1,000 years the Ash'arite position became the basis of orthodox Sunni theology, and many famous Muslim thinkers laid the foundation of the subsequent theological discussions that are still taking place today.

CONCLUSION

From the beginning, Islam had a deep distrust of anything having to do with reason, and in the end, any theology or philosophy that raised reason above the Qur'an was rejected.[45] Therefore, while some of the early Muslim theologians were prepared to apply the features of philosophy to the realm of religion through the means of reason, as time passed more Muslim thinkers turned away from the fruits of reason and held fast to the rigors of revelation. However, it was in the hotbed of the early theological controversies that this "heresy of the Ishmaelites" forced Christian theologians like John of Damascus to re-contextualize doctrinal issues that were under fire such as the Trinity and the deity of Christ. It is to these apologetic works that we now turn.

---

42. Some of the most famous were al-Baghdadi (d. 1037), al-Juwayni (d. 1086), Abu Hamid al-Ghazali (1058–1111), al-Shahrastani (d. 1153), and Fakhr al-Razi (d. 1209)—Majid Fakhry, *Philosophy and Theology*, 281.

43. Esposito, *Islam: The Straight Path*, 72–73.

44. Goldziher, *Introduction to Islamic Theology and Law*, 99.

45. Ibid., 3.

6

Heresy of the Ishmaelites
Authenticity and Analysis

INTRODUCTION

Throughout history, the church has met the challenges of heresy and cultural pressure by formulating creeds to define the orthodox and biblical stance of the church. It has been essential, however, for the church to continually re-contextualize these doctrines and creeds through apologetic means, for each century has brought its own unique forms of heresy. As with the development of the doctrine of the Trinity, better explanations and more precise language were needed in order to express doctrinal integrity and develop a doctrinal formula that would be consistent with Scripture and *descriptive* of the true relationship between the unity of God and the distinctions within the three persons of the Trinity. As the first Christian theologians dealt with the aberrant theology of Trinitarian heresies, they were able to retain the core of scriptural truth and wrap around it a contextual formula of the Trinity that rested on the incremental contributions of many other theologians as they all sought to be clearer in their explanations and more precise in their use of terms. This doctrine was then crystallized into creeds, but these creeds would still need to be re-interpreted in future times and re-contextualized as new misunderstandings challenged orthodoxy. Otherwise, a fossilized creed was in danger of being distorted by a heterodox view and eventually subsumed by false doctrine. This is what occurred in the time of John of Damascus when Islam came to represent a challenge to the core doctrines of Christianity and to centuries of carefully constructed theology. In defending the orthodox position, John needed to summarize the doctrine of the Christian church up through the eighth century and then develop an appropriate apologetic that would defend as well as refute. In this section, the writings of John of Damascus on Islam will be utilized, especially his explanation and defense of the Trinity, to foster a deeper understanding of the historical and apologetical nature of the first arguments on the Trinity between a Christian theologian and the Muslims.

John's work in re-contextualizing the doctrine of the Trinity in his defense of Christianity against Islam was significant for his own time, and it also had far reaching effects on his successors. He summarized Christian doctrine systematically for his day based on prior work done by theologians who were also apologists. He was also the first major theologian to engage in a written apologetic with Islam through two works specifically crafted to defend Christianity against what he referred to as the "heresy of the Ishmaelites."[1] John's teaching on the Trinity revealed the standard of orthodoxy at this stage of the church's development. Together with his critique of Islam, John's works can therefore show how Trinitarian doctrine developed through previous councils and theological writings up through the time of these new challenges facing the church.

John Tolan, in his chapter on *Early Eastern Christian Reactions to Islam*, notes that the body of John's extant writings numbers over 1500 pages, and yet only about 12 of those pages deal directly with Islam.[2] This page count may be misleading, however, since most of the 100 heresies John recorded were short paragraph descriptions, while his treatment of the *Heresy of the Ishmaelites* was much longer. In addition, it is likely that most of what John wrote, especially apologetically, would have been written with Islam in mind.[3] The importance of this material is underscored by Tolan when he proposes that these "dozen pages on Islam provide a key glimpse at the formation of an apologetic Christian response to Islam, and they were to be read and reread by scores of later Christian writers as they attempted to come to terms with Islam."[4] The text focused on by this study is part of John's *Fount of Knowledge*, which he dedicated to Cosmas, the newly installed Bishop of

---

1. Louth, *St. John Damascene*, 77. See also Saperstein, "Encounters with Islam."

2. Tolan, *Saracens*, 51. It is possible, however, that he wrote most of his works with Islam in mind (see chap. 9).

3. See chap. 9.

4. Tolan, *Saracens*, 51.

Maiuma, in A.D. 743.[5] It is divided into three major sections: *The Philosophical Chapters*, *On Heresies*, and the *Orthodox Faith*.[6] The *Philosophical Chapters*, also known as the *Dialectica*, consist of SIXTY-EIGHT chapters, and give a philosophical and rational basis to John's theological tome. Much of the logic is borrowed from Greek philosophy and demonstrates John's training in this field of knowledge. The 100 chapters which make up the third part, *De Fide Orthodoxa*, are often referred to as the first "*summa theologica*" of the church.[7] These chapters systematically summarize the orthodox conclusions of the key theologians who lived before John. Indeed, John humbly states at the beginning of his work that he will add nothing of his own, but rather "shall gather together into one those things which have been worked out by the most eminent of teachers and make a compendium of them."[8] It is his desire that the truth demonstrated in this section would "destroy deceit and put falsehood to flight."[9] The falsehood that John is referring to is found in the middle part, called "On Heresies," (*De Haeresibus*) and it is the part that concerns us now. Although ninety-seven chapters can be traced back to earlier sources, especially eighty chapters from Epiphanius, (who was bishop of Salamis in Cyprus at the end of the fourth century),[10] the last three are probably written by John.[11] The particular heresy that we will now turn to is titled the *Heresy of the Ishmaelites*.

---

5. Chase, *St. John of Damascus: Writings*, 3, though Louth disputes this date and concludes that with the scant information we have, we will have to hold the date as questionable (cf., Louth, *St. John Damascene*, 33).

6. The *Dialectica*, *de Haeresibus* and *De Fide Orthodoxa*.

7. Sahas, *John of Damascus on Islam*, 53. See also Chase, *St. John of Damascus: Writings*, xxvi, where Chase states that John of Damascus's *Fount of Knowledge* "is the first real *Summa Theologica*."

8. Chase, *St. John of Damascus: Writings*, 6.

9. Ibid.

10. Louth, *St. John Damascene*, 56. Chase adds that while the "first eighty are taken verbatim from the *Panarion* of St. Epiphanius," they are "not, however, from the main text of the *Panarion*, but from the summaries which precede each of its seven parts and serve as tables of contents." Chase, *St. John of Damascus: Writings*, xxix.

11. Chase, *St. John of Damascus: Writings*, xxxi. Chase refers to the chapters on the *Ishmaelites, the Iconoclasts and the Aposchistae*, a "sect which rejected the sacraments and the priesthood."

THE HERESY OF THE ISHMAELITES: AUTHORSHIP AND AUTHENTICITY OF THE WORK

If John's treatise, *Heresy of the Ishmaelites*, were not written by John, and were, perhaps, from a later period, then we would not be able to make any definitive statements from this text about the nature of the Muslim belief system in the first half of the eighth century or, indeed, about the first one hundred years after the death of Muhammad in the year A.D. 632. However, if the work is authentic, then there are some critical assessments we can make about Islam, Muhammad and the Qur'an that may differ greatly from the information that has been passed down to us from the Muslim sources, which date from the middle of the eighth century at the earliest.[12] Thus, we should have an earlier eyewitness account from the pen of John than even the early Muslim *Siras* and *Hadith*. Andrew Louth stresses the importance of John's work by saying that "if these two works [referring also to the *Disputation between a Christian and a Saracen*] are indeed by John Damascene (or even if their arguments can be traced back to him), they constitute the earliest explicit discussions of Islam by a Christian theologian."[13] Pim Valkenberg goes so far as to say that "since this text is one of the earliest Christian reflections on this new phenomenon and for a long time certainly the most influential one, John of Damascus may be seen as 'the real founder of the Christian tradition' concerning Islam."[14] Robert Hoyland concurs with Louth and Valkenberg and adds that if the chapter on Islam is "genuinely by John of Damascus, it represents the earliest Greek polemical writing against Islam,"[15] thus making John the "first" apologist to the Muslims.[16]

There are two things to consider in regard to John's authorship of the chapter on Islam and the authenticity of his work. The first deals with

12. Gilchrist, *Muhammad and the Religion of Islam*, 225. Cf. Leites, "Sira and the Question of Tradition," 49. Both authors are referring to the earliest Sira, or biography, of Muhammad.

13. Louth, *St. John Damascene*, 77.

14. Valkenberg, *Sharing Lights on the Way to God*, 74.

15. Hoyland, *Seeing Islam*, 485.

16. This is not to say that John was the first to use apologetics against the Muslims. As was noted in chapter 3 under the section titled "Testimony of the Non-Muslim Sources," there were a number of eyewitnesses who gave testimony to the treatment of Christians at the hands of the Muslims, such as Sophronius (ca. 640), Thomas the Presbyter (ca. 640), Sebeos (660s), John bar Penkaye (687), and John of Nikiu (690), as well as some who engaged in debates, such as the monk at Bet Hale (717) and Leo III (720). However, John was the first one who engaged in a substantive and systematic written apologetic with Islam, based on his own well-developed theological synthesis of Christian doctrine. This is further evidenced by the number of successors who followed John's apologetic approach in the following centuries.

whether he even wrote the section on 100 heresies, which included the chapter on Islam, and the second deals specifically with his authorship of the chapter on Islam. We will first consider John's authorship of *De Haeresibus* as a whole. One of the reasons that his authorship of *De Haeresibus* is considered problematic is that some of the early manuscripts of the *Fount of Knowledge* do not contain the section on the heresies, and others place the section on heresies at the end, as if it were a later addition.[17] However, in John's preface to his *Fount of Knowledge*, he stated that he would provide a section between the *Dialectica* and the *De Fide Orthodoxa* consisting of the various heresies that Christians have faced:

> Then, next, after this, I shall set forth in order the absurdities of the heresies hated of God, so that by recognizing the lie we may more closely follow the truth.[18]

Clearly this indicates that John intended to have the section on heresies situated before the section on the orthodox faith so that he could provide a contrasting view for what he believed would be the superior beliefs found in true Christianity. Therefore, those copies that either excluded the section on heresies, or placed it at the end of the collection, were not congruent with the original intent of the author.

Andrew Louth has his own theory as to how these discrepancies can be explained. In trying to put the pieces of the puzzle together, Louth believes that the structure of John's *Fount of Knowledge* (or *Pege Gnoseos*) developed over time. Since a number of the early renditions of the *Fount of Knowledge* only contain the *Dialectica* and the *De Fide Orthodoxa*, which follows the standard pattern of one hundred and fifty chapters (such as what is present in the earlier *Doctrina Patrum*, or The Teaching of the Fathers), and since there are some early manuscripts that attach the section on heresies at the end, Louth conjectures that John may have written the *Dialectica* and the *De Fide Orthodoxa* at an earlier time in his life (perhaps in the 720s or 730s) and then decided to include them in a longer, three part work later on. It was at this time that John would have written the preface which mentions that the work would be in three parts with the section on the heresies in the middle. This could have taken place around 743, which is indicated in the preface, or it could have been written between that time and his death, around 750, since Louth indicates that John never finished revising the first section on dialectics. For Louth this would tie up some of the loose ends, such as the appearance of *De Haeresibus* as chapter 34 in a manuscript of the *Doctrina*

---

17. Sahas, *John of Damascus on Islam*, 55.
18. OF Preface.

Patrum, as well as being tagged on to the end of some of the manuscripts of the *Dialectica* and *De Fide Orthodoxa*. However, even if there were different stages involved in John's "masterpiece," it does not in any way negate the fact that he wrote all three sections and merely put them together in an early and late form, with the latter, three-part format outlined in his preface.[19] Finally, we can rest our case on the basis of the critical edition of John's work by Bonifatius Kotter, since he has verified that the earliest copies of the *Fount of Knowledge* not only contain the section on *De Haeresibus*, but also place it between the *Dialectica* and *De Fide Orthodoxa*, just as John had outlined in the preface.[20]

We will now consider the chapter on Islam itself and whether John actually wrote it or whether it was penned by a later author. The authenticity of the "Heresy of the Ishmaelites" has been considered problematic because the best known version of *De Haeresibus*, published in Migne's *Patrologia Graeca* (PG), consisted of 103 chapters instead of one hundred ("Heresy of the Ishmaelites" was listed as number 101). Andrew Louth argues that these chapters would conform to the monastic literary genre of that time and be comprised of "a century of 100 chapters."[21] Bonifatius Kotter, in a new critical edition of John's writings, counters Migne's view that there were 103 heresies and reveals that the original was composed of one hundred chapters with the one entitled "Heresy of the Ishmaelites" as the final one.[22] This conclusion is based somewhat on an early manuscript from the ninth or tenth century which concludes the 100 chapters with the chapter on Islam.[23] In his critical edition of John's work, Kotter says that "Heresy 100" may have been written as a separate work by John and then attached to an earlier collection (such as Epiphanius' *Panarion*).[24] He also says that the use of one hundred chapters followed the common practice of trying to complete a "century" of chapters. Thus, John may have pulled together the earlier heresies from other sources and then rounded them off with some things that

---

19. Louth, *St. John Damascene*, 31–35.

20. Kotter IV, 4. He bases this on the ninth/tenth-century *MS Moscow Synod* and two early *florilegium* from the eighth century, which include the chapter on "Heresy of the Ishmaelites."

21. Louth, *St. John Damascene*, 59.

22. Kotter IV, 4.

23. Louth, *St. John Damascene*, 76.

24. See McGinn, *The Doctors of the Church*, 97: "The first eighty are copied from the Panarion, a fourth-century anti-heretical book of Epiphanius of Salamis, though John adds important material on the heresy of Messaians (chap. 80). The final chapters, though they may not be by John, contain new material on a number of heresies, especially the Ishmaelites (i.e., Muslims) and the Iconoclasts."

he had already written. Of great significance is Kotter's conclusion that the *De Haerisibus*, including chapter 100 on the Ishmaelites, is contained in a ninth/tenth-century manuscript (gr 315 or the MS Moscow Synod).[25] Robert Hoyland reinforces this conclusion by adding that there is a *florilegium* that includes the first two paragraphs of John's work, and it is dated even earlier than the ninth century.[26] In contrast, Daniel Sahas, writing in 1972, details the objections of Armand Abel, who argues that the "Heresy of the Ishmaelites" was the first part of a work by the twelfth-thirteenth century Byzantine writer, Nicetas Acominatus.[27] One of the main problems in Abel's argument, however, is that the objections he raised as to why John could not have been the author are actually dealing with material that was later *added* to the earlier original account.[28] Thus, even Sahas concludes at the end of his discussion that

> What can be said at this point with certainty is that this text was already known a few decades after the writing of the *Fount of Knowledge*, which is an attested work of John of Damascus, and that it has been attributed to him since then. This seems sufficient justification for us to discuss chapter 101 as John of Damascus' work.[29]

Raymond Le Coz concurs with Sahas in his assessment of Abel's argument, and also points out that the first part of the *Thesaurus* by Acominatus (the part that should properly be attributed to John), portrays the monk who helps Mahmed (Muhammad) as an anonymous Arian monk, rather than the monk "Bahira," who is first mentioned in Ibn Ishaq's Sirat, written after John's death.[30] Thus, since the writer of the first part of the Thesaurus (presumably John) is unaware of the later tradition, which views the monk as Nestorian rather than Arian, this can be seen as another piece of internal evidence for an early date for the first part of the work.[31] It can also be used as evidence that Acominatus incorporated this earlier work by John into his

---

25. Kotter IV, 4.
26. Hoyland, *Seeing Islam*, 485.
27. Book 20 of the *Thesaurus Orthodoxae Fidei*.
28. Sahas, *John of Damascus on Islam*, 63–66. C.f. Le Coz, *Jean Damascene*, 186–89.
29. Sahas, *John of Damascus on Islam*, 66. Chapter 101 here actually refers to Kotter's chapter 100.
30. Guillaume, *The Life of Muhammad*, 79–81. Guillaume relates that while Ibn Ishaq wrote before AH 151/AD 768, his work came down through Ibn Hisham, who died in AH 218/AD 835.
31. Sahas, *John of Damascus on Islam*, 73n5.

later elaboration.[32] Finally, in consideration of Kotter's conclusions in regard to his manuscript studies, the consensus of scholars at this time is that the treatise titled "Heresy of the Ishmaelites," and listed as the one hundredth chapter in a series of heresies collected as well as authored by John of Damascus in his larger work called the *Fount of Knowledge*, is indeed authored by John of Damascus. The significance for us, then, is that we can now use the text in order to determine not only what an informed Christian would have known about Islam in the first half of the eighth century, but also what arguments were being used against the Muslims by the Christians. We will now look at his work in six sections.

CONTENT OF THE HERESY OF THE ISHMAELITES

Origins of the Saracen religion

In the first section of chapter 100, John refers to the "coercive religion of the Ishmaelites," which is the "forerunner of the Antichrist."[33] Having used strong words in his description of the religion of the Ishmaelites, it is curious that John refers to them as a "heresy" of Christianity rather than a false religion. Daniel Sahas cautions that "the word 'heresy' in John of Damascus needs to be understood in a much broader sense than it is used today, as a deviation from mainstream orthodoxy."[34] This is because John includes twenty "heresies," which he calls the "mothers of heresies," at the beginning of his list of one hundred,[35] even though they are pre-Christian belief systems. Hoyland adds that "evidently, then, the term simply signifies an erroneous belief or a false doctrine."[36] For John, Christianity is seen as the truth and the standard by which all other religions or cults should be judged. Whenever a religion proclaims something that is contrary to the Bible or a distortion of its truth, it is then deemed to be "heretical."[37] Sahas concludes,

---

32. Le Coz, *Jean Damascene*, 191–93. Cf. Sahas, *John of Damascus on Islam*, 73n2.

33. HER 1–2—the author's translation of Kotter's critical edition of John's *Heresy of the Ishmaelites*.

34. Sahas, "John of Damascus. Revisited," 112.

35. Chase, *St. John of Damascus: Writings*, 111. The first four "parents and archetypes of all heresies" are listed as Barbarism, Scythism, Hellenism, and Judaism.

36. Hoyland, *Seeing Islam*, 485.

37. Traditionally, heresy refers to false doctrine and a heretic is one who believes and teaches what is contrary to the orthodox beliefs of the Church. It is significant that John of Damascus used this term in reference to the teachings of Islam, since in his time a heresy would have been false teaching against the established doctrine of the Christian church. However, John did not view the beliefs of the Ishmaelites as a

then, that "the heresies are heresies insofar as they can be contrasted to Christianity. They are discussed in reference to Christianity, not independently of it; thus, the justification of treating Islam as a heresy, too."[38] That may be the case. However, we also need to remember that at that time there were no references to a universal religion called Islam, but rather that the conquering people group, referred to as Ishmaelites, Saracens or Hagarenes, espoused beliefs and traditions that seemed to be distorted extractions from the two major religions in the area, Judaism and Christianity. It may be that during the first half of the eighth century the religion that was to become Islam was still in its formative process, and the rules, the traditions and the Qur'an may still have been developing as the Arabs absorbed more and more land, money and power. Thus, Islam was not very distinct from Christianity in the time of John of Damascus and it is only in the latter half of the eighth century, when the earliest biographies on Muhammad were being written and the first *hadiths*[39] were being penned, that the finalization of the Qur'an was also taking place and the distinctions were becoming sharper and more defined, both in a theological and a cultural sense. For example, in this first section of his treatise John refers to the Arabs by three titles: "Hagarenes," "Ishmaelites" and "Saracens."[40] The term "Hagarene," of course, comes from the belief that the Arabs descended from Abraham's son Ishmael, whose mother was Hagar. The term Ishmaelite would also connect them to Abraham, who is also the ancestral father for the Jews and the Christians. Yet these two terms, in and of themselves, do not make a connection to the universal religion of Islam. Even the term "Saracens," a favorite term for the Arabs at that time, again only provides a familial kinship with other descendents of

---

separate religion, such as Manichaeism or even Judaism, but rather as a competing system of doctrines within a Christian context that claimed to be true yet were contrary to the orthodox teachings of Christianity.

38. Sahas, "John of Damascus. Revisited," 112. See also McEnhill and Newlands, *Fifty Key Christian Thinkers*, 156: "In a manner later to be followed by Adolf Harnack, John controversially viewed Islam as a Christian heresy. John, of course, had lived among Muslims and experienced Islam as the dominant culture and this may account for his fiercely polemical approach to it. He saw in the advent of Islam a forerunner of the Anti-Christ, and he considered Muhammad to be a false prophet who had a very confused and superficial knowledge of the Bible and who was influenced by an Arian monk."

39. Hadiths are the purported "sayings of Muhammad" that were used to formulate the law code of Islam. The earliest collection is from *al-Bukhari* in the ninth century. Therefore, it can only be inferred that some of these sayings originated around the time of John of Damascus.

40. The name "Muslim" does not appear at all in this chapter on the "Heresy of the Ishmaelites."

Abraham.⁴¹ The actual origin of the term is unknown,⁴² but John portrays it as coming from the verses in Scripture (Gen. 16:8; 21:10) where Sarah sends Hagar and Ishmael away empty; so John plays on the verb κενοι ("to cast away") which together with Sarah (Σάρρα) would give us the word Σάρρα-κενοι, or "Saracens."⁴³ Whatever the case, Andrew Louth believes that John's etymologies still only "identify Islam as the religion of the Arabs, which is historically sound for the Umayyad period, though contrary to the portrayal of Islam in the Qur'an as a universal religion."⁴⁴ It is important to note that John was probably writing this in the early 740s, so it is likely that the religion that became Islam was not yet seen as distinctive enough to be called anything more than a distant relative of Judaism, or, in John's eyes, a strange admixture of twisted, erroneous beliefs coming from both Judaism and Christianity—in other words, a heresy.⁴⁵ John even alludes to a time when the Saracens once worshiped idols in Arabia, apparently referring to Aphrodite and the morning star. In pre-Islamic times the Arabs apparently worshiped the morning star as Al-Uzza, one of their three main goddesses or "daughters of Allah." Reference to the three goddesses is found in the Qur'an in surah 53:19-20, along with the names of the other two, Al-Lat and Manat. In John's treatise, Aphrodite is referred to twice, once near the beginning and once toward the end. Both times she is linked with the Arab word Khabar (Greek, Χαβάρ),⁴⁶ which John says means "great." He then reminds his readers that the Saracens remained idolaters up until the time of Heraclius, when there appeared a false prophet named "Mamed" (Μάμεδ), or Muhammad, who developed the new "heresy."⁴⁷

Muhammad

In this next section, John indicates that this "false prophet," Mamed, only knew the Old Testament and New Testament superficially and probably learned aspects of his heresy from an Arian monk.⁴⁸ It is interesting to note

---

41. Sahas, *John of Damascus on Islam*, 70–71.

42. Some have suggested that the term possibly comes from the Arabic word, شرقيين (*sharqiyyin*), which means "from the East." See also Louth, *St. John Damascene*, p. 78.

43. HER 4–5.

44. Louth, *St. John Damascene*, 78.

45. Sahas, "John of Damascus, Revisited," 112–14. Here Sahas has some good comments on John's usage of "heresy."

46. HER 8, 93.

47. Louth, *St. John Damascene*, 78.

48. HER 11–13.

that John does not refer to the monk as the Nestorian monk named Bahira, who is mentioned in Ibn Ishaq's Sirat at a later time.[49] This would indicate, perhaps, that John is unaware of any tradition of Muhammad traveling to Syria and meeting a monk who claimed to recognize the sign of a prophet in Muhammad.[50] However, since he does mention the involvement of a monk, this could indicate an earlier rendition of the story before it took on the Nestorian persuasion and the monk was given a name. As with the comparison of early and late *hadiths*, when a story contains more specific references to people or events, it is usually an indication that the story has been embellished through the passage of time and the earliest version is the more correct one. Also, in linking Muhammad to Arianism, John perhaps is indicating that he recognizes the essence of the Muslim objection to Christianity, since Arianism denies that Jesus Christ is consubstantial with the Father, making Jesus only a created being, much as the Muslims argued that God could not have any associates.[51] If this is the case, is it possible that what became Islam grew out of a partial mixture of the Arian heresy and other Semitic influences? This could also explain John's tendency to call it a heresy rather than a false religion.

John also finds fault with Muhammad's "rumor" that the scriptures that he gave to his people were brought down from heaven without witnesses, even though other ordinary acts such as marriage and buying property required witnesses. The real travesty, according to John, was that Muhammad then expected his followers to obey the pronouncements which, in John's estimation, were worthy only of "laughter."[52] This knowledge of the transmission of the teachings of Muhammad from heaven, however, reveals that in the time of John there was at least recognition of the existence of some type of scriptures that the Arabs collected and followed. In the last section, the actual surahs that John may be citing will be explored.

One of the most important features may be what is actually *missing* from John's overview. He does not seem to have any historical awareness of the life of Muhammad— where he was from, his struggle in Mecca, his departure to Medina, the early formation of the Muslim community or even the many raids on the local caravans—anything that would give any indication as to what kind of person Muhammad was. Even though Muhammad

---

49. Guillaume, *The Life of Muhammad*, 79–81; Leites, "Sira and the Question of Tradition," 49. Ibn Ishaq lived between 85–151 AH (AD 707–67), but probably finished his biography shortly before his death, almost 20 years after John's death (AD 749–50).

50. Chase, *St. John of Damascus: Writings*, 153n101. This would also argue for an earlier date for the composition of chapter 100.

51. Sahas, "John of Damascus. Revisited," 108. See Qur'an 5:73.

52. HER 16.

is mentioned by name only four times in the Qur'an, these are stories that should have been in circulation at that time, since Ibn Ishaq (d.767), the first biographer of Muhammad, would have been collecting information on Muhammad from a number of John's contemporaries. Did John consider these historical matters as merely inconsequential or was he just ignorant of them? Were any of these stories in circulation during his lifetime or were they waiting to be "birthed" through the pen of Ibn Ishaq and others who followed?[53] It is also interesting to note that John did not seem to be aware of any arguments for Muhammad's prophethood based on stories of miracles that Muhammad performed, such as his miraculous night journey on the back of a winged horse to the city of Jerusalem. John merely mentions that the Saracens should seek witnesses to verify the so-called revelations of their prophet. Since these references to Muhammad's miracles were used in Christian-Muslim dialogues in the later eighth century and through the ninth century, this may be another indication for a mid- eighth century authorship of this treatise.

Muhammad's Teaching on Christ

John also detects that the core of the false belief is the Saracen portrayal of one God without any associations. At this point John seems to be referring to surah 112:1 and 3, or the Suraht al-Ikhlas,[54] which says, according to John, "that there is one God, creator of all things, who has neither been begotten nor has begotten."[55] It is interesting to note that John has the order reversed here from the way that it is found in the Qur'an. Is he using a different source or is he reciting from memory, or is he just trying to recollect what he has heard from the Saracens? He also may be alluding to Surah 4:171,[56] and perhaps Surah 19:16–30[57] when he refers to the Saracen belief

53. It is important to note that we only have Ibn Ishaq's abridged biography through the redaction of Hisham, who wrote in the ninth century. Therefore, we really cannot confirm the belief that there existed an earlier biography before Hisham.

54. Yusuf Ali, *The Meaning of The Holy Qur'an*, 112:1 "Say: He is Allah, the One and Only;" 112:3 "He begetteth not, nor is He begotten."

55. HER 17–18.

56. Q. 4:171 "O People of the Book! Commit no excesses in your religion: nor say of Allah aught but the truth. Christ Jesus the son of Mary was (no more than) a Messenger of Allah, and His Word, which He bestowed on Mary and a Spirit proceeding from Him: so believe in Allah and His Messengers. Say not 'Trinity': desist: it will be better for you: for Allah is one God: glory be to him: (far exalted is He) above having a son. To him belong all things in the heavens and on earth."

57. Srah 19:16–30, and perhaps, Surah 3:45. John even records the error of the Qur'an when it states that Mary, the mother of Jesus is the sister of Moses and Aaron!

that "Christ was the Word of God and his Spirit, but only a creature and a servant, and that he was born without seed from Mary, the sister of Moses and Aaron."[58] Or, on the other hand, John may be referring to Surah 4:156–58[59] when he relates that Jesus, without human father, was born a prophet, and that the "Jews unlawfully wanted to crucify him, but after arresting him they only crucified his shadow; for, he says, the Christ was not crucified nor did he die, for God, took him up to himself into heaven because he loved him."[60] In Heaven, Jesus denies telling people that he was the Son of God, as well as God Himself,[61] which is similar to the dialogue found in Surah 5:116ff.[62] This understanding shows that John had knowledge of at least portions of the Qur'an around AD 743. It is also important to note that he would have been referencing an Arabic version, since the earliest Greek translation post-dated him.[63]

In this treatise, it is almost as if John is trying to develop an apologetic against this new threat to Christianity by demonstrating, on the one hand, how inadequate the theological positions of this new religion are when countered by the truth of Christianity, and, on the other hand, how utterly foolish are some of the things that are recorded by Muhammad, their so-called prophet. In regard to this last statement, John writes that Muhammad "spread rumors that a book had been sent down to him from heaven by God," but the "heretical pronouncements inscribed in his book" were only "worthy of laughter."[64]

In John's first counter-argument, he deals with the three main objections the Saracens have to Christianity: belief in the Trinity, belief in the deity of Jesus Christ, and belief that Jesus really did die on the cross and then rose triumphantly from the dead. Realistically speaking, these are

---

(Surah 19:28).

58. HER 18–20.

59. Q. 4:157 "That they said (in boast), "We killed Christ Jesus the son of Mary, the Messenger of Allah"— but they killed him not, nor crucified him, but so it was made to appear to them, and those who differ therein are full of doubts, with no (certain) knowledge, but only conjecture to follow, for of a surety they killed him not—" 4:158 "Nay, Allah raised him up unto Himself;"

60. HER 22–25.

61. HER 25–27.

62. Q. 5:116 "And behold! Allah will say: "O Jesus the son of Mary! didst thou say unto men, "Worship me and my mother as gods in derogation of Allah?" He will say: "Glory to Thee! never could I say what I had no right (to say). Had I said such a thing, Thou wouldst indeed have known it. Thou knowest what is in my heart, though I know not what is in Thine. For Thou knowest in full all that is hidden."

63. Louth, *St. John Damascene*, 80.

64. HER 15–16.

the cardinal doctrines of the church. The Saracens taught, however, that God could not be a Trinity since He has "neither been begotten, nor has begotten."[65] Although they admitted that "Christ is the Word of God and his Spirit,"[66] they believed that the greatest sin, which they referred to as "shirk," was to associate God with a created being. Therefore, since they believed that Christ was only a created being, it was "shirk" to say that he was also in the very nature, God. The conclusion that Jesus died on the cross was also problematic, for an admission to an actual crucifixion would open the door to the understanding that Christ therefore died for our sins (which only God could do).

In the next counter-argument, John ridicules the Saracen story of Jesus denying his deity before God when he arrives in heaven. According to the story, God questions Jesus after he is miraculously swept into heaven to avoid the crucifixion and says, "O Jesus, did you say that 'I am the Son of God and God'?"[67] Of course, according to the story, Jesus vehemently denies that he ever said such a thing and assures God that it was a lie told by those who had turned away from God and the truth. This must have been something that the Saracens brought up in their arguments, and rather than counter their beliefs with a review of the applicable passages in the Bible, John merely sweeps it aside as a saying that is only "worthy of laughter."[68]

In the area of prophethood, John confronts the Saracens' argument that Muhammad is a true prophet of God and therefore should be heeded. According to the Bible that both the Jews and the Christians use, there are strict conditions for prophets of God. Deuteronomy 18:17–22, for example, deals with the sign of a prophet and states that if a so-called prophet says that something will take place and "it does not take place," then he is a false prophet. The Qur'an does not give any indications that Muhammad ever dealt with this type of prophecy. Muslims would say, however, that Muhammad is a prophet because he was given the recitation known as the Qur'an. John makes the point that if Muhammad were a true prophet, then he should have agreed with all the earlier prophets, as well as Moses, who foretold the coming of Christ. They not only foretold his coming, but they would have agreed with the view that "Christ is God, and the Son of God," and that he would be "crucified, and die, and rise again, and that he will be the judge of the living and the dead."[69] These beliefs, however, were denied by Muham-

---

65. HER 17–18.
66. HER 18.
67. HER 26–27.
68. HER 32–33.
69. HER 39–41.

mad. When John asks why their prophet did not come in this way and with this knowledge they only shrug and say "God does as he pleases."[70]

John's Critique of Muhammad's Teaching

In this next section John criticizes Muhammad's claim of receiving the scriptures[71] while he was asleep and without any witnesses.[72] This struck John as specious since the Saracens required witnesses for many other transactions, such as marriages and acquiring property. In regard to this he says,

> On the one hand, you take wives and possess property and donkeys and everything else through witnesses; yet, on the other hand, you accept your faith and your scriptures unwitnessed. For the one who has handed down this scripture to you has no verification from any source, nor is there any prior witness to him known. Furthermore, he received this while asleep![73]

John chides the Saracens for requiring witnesses for almost everything else, from marrying a woman to buying an animal to acquiring property,[74] but for the most important thing in their lives, their relationship with God, they did not require witnesses to verify the writings of Muhammad. Even more than that, they accepted that what he said was revealed to him in his sleep. Therefore, John ridicules them for accepting the revelation which he says may have only been a dream.[75]

John also criticizes Muhammad's teaching on Jesus Christ and His relationship with God, the Father. According to the religion of Muhammad, Christians are called "Associators" for ascribing a partner or son to God. John, in turn, calls them "Mutilators" for tearing apart the Trinity, for he reasons that if God's Word and Spirit are taken away from Him, then He is less than God. Indeed, if there were a time when God did not have his Word or his Spirit, John argues, then God would have been incomplete. If God then attached himself to the Word and the Spirit, something would have been added to him and therefore he would have been changed. However,

---

70. HER 45–46.

71. Greek, γραφή, ("writings," or "scriptures"); the term "Qur'an" is not used in John's writings.

72. HER 46–48.

73. HER 58–60.

74. Surah 2:282.

75. He even quotes a proverb that may have been by Plato, "you are spinning me dreams" to make his point.

change is something that only a creature can experience, not the Creator. Thus, in order for God to have always been the Creator rather than a created being, he must have always had his Word and his Spirit, which necessitates the eternal nature of his Word, Jesus Christ.

The Saracens said that Christians were "associators" (ἑταιριαστάς),[76] because they introduced "in addition to God a partner by saying that Christ is the son of God and God."[77] Today, the worst sin that anyone can commit in Islam, referred to as "shirk," is to associate one of God's creatures with God Himself. For Muslims this denigrates God. John may not have been aware of the full extent of *shirk* in his time, but he still counters the misrepresentation of the Son of God by reminding the Saracens that their book claims that "Christ is Word and Spirit of God."[78] Therefore, since God's Word and His Spirit cannot be separated from Him, then Christ must also be God, for otherwise they are mutilating Him by tearing Him apart! Mark Beaumont feels that this was a good move by John for

> Denial of this argument by Muslims would result in an inadequate understanding of the nature of God, so that the Christian can say; 'if, on the other hand, this is outside of God, then God, according to you is without word and without spirit.' In John's logic, since Muslims wish to deny that Christ is God they have to accept that the word and spirit are split off from God as a result of the appearing of Christ. Christians can drive the point home; 'thus trying to avoid making associates to God, you have mutilated him.'[79]

Indeed, John counters their accusation of the Christians being "associators" by accusing the Saracens of being "mutilators" or *koptae* (from *koptas*—κόπτας).[80]

His next objection is that Christians are said to be idolaters by the Ishmaelites because Christians venerate the cross, so John inquires how the Ishmaelites may escape the charge of idolatry since they kiss and rub themselves against the stone in the Ka'ba after the example set by Muhammad himself.[81] John ridicules their actions by relating how some Saracens even believed that the stone was the place where Abraham had sex with Hagar,

---

76. In Arabic, *mushrikun*, or those who commit "shirk" by associating a partner with God.

77. HER 61–62.

78. HER 69–70.

79. Beaumont, *Christology in Dialogue With Muslims*, 15.

80. HER 76–77.

81. HER 78–80.

and others said it was where he tied up his camel when he was about to sacrifice Isaac. If this were true, John says, the Saracens should feel ashamed of venerating the stone rather than take pride in their misguided devotion. He also indicates that the stone was probably once the head of a statue of Aphrodite, which was used in previous pagan worship of the goddess.[82] In contrast to these objectionable practices of the Ishmaelites, John states that it is much better to show reverence to the "Cross of Christ through which the power of demons and the deception of the devil have been destroyed."[83]

John also criticizes the Ishmaelites for locating Abraham's sacrifice of Isaac in Arabia rather than Jerusalem since the former would not offer the abundance of trees for easy retrieval of the needed wood. In addition, the writings of Muhammad mention camels while the biblical account mentions only donkeys. These discrepancies only increased John's disdain for the account of the Ishmaelites. In all these arguments John is either trying to demonstrate what he considers the superiority of Christianity or the foolishness of the religion of Muhammad, more for the sake of boosting belief in Christianity in the eyes of his Christian readers than for offering detailed arguments against the new "heresy," though he is interested in countering their false beliefs.

The Qur'an and the Surahs Used

In this fifth section, John refers to the "scriptures" of the Ishmaelites and the doctrines of Muhammad, especially as they are related in four surahs.[84] In fact, he refers primarily to three Medinan Surahs:[85] Surah 4: *The Women (al-Nisa)*; Surah 5: *The Table (al-Ma'idah)*; Surah 2: *The Heifer (al-Baqarah)*; and a surah that is not in the Qur'an: *The She-Camel* (though there are allusions to this story in other Surahs).[86]

---

82. Before the time of Muhammad, Aphrodite was called Al-Uzzah by the Arabs. She is one of the three "daughters of Allah" mentioned in the Qur'an (53:19–20). John also indicates that traces of an engraving are visible on the stone even in his day, which begs the question of how knowledge of this would have come to him.

83. HER 90–91.

84. It is important to remember that John uses the Greek term γραφή ("writings") and does not mention the words "Islam," "Qur'an," or "surah," which may indicate that the words were not in use during his lifetime.

85. The Qur'an was allegedly revealed in two cities, Mecca and Medina, which represent different phases in the "revelations" given to Muhammad.

86. HER 95–148. Similar parts to the story of the camel are found in surahs 7, 11, 17, 26, 54, 91.

In the book John identifies as "The Woman,"[87] he presents his description in a way that emphasizes the foolishness of the practices involved. First of all he deals with polygamy, which he says is allowed, but only for the man. The husband is allowed up to four wives, and he may also have "one thousand concubines." However, the woman can only have one husband. Clearly John is trying to show the lasciviousness of these religious beliefs. He brings up the example of Zayd (Muhammad's adopted son-in-law), divorcing his wife, Zaynab (who is not mentioned by name), so that Muhammad could satisfy his lust and marry her. Interestingly, John's story of Zayd and his divorce is more detailed than what is found in the Qur'an.[88] Could it have been a story circulating around and then later written down by Ibn Ishaq? Or could it have been an actual rendition by Ibn Ishaq that John had chanced upon? John also seems to delight in demonstrating how ridiculous it is for Muhammad to reason that it is fine for a man to divorce his wife, but that if he wants to marry her again he must wait until she has married and been divorced by another. It is also important to note that John accuses Muhammad of committing adultery with Zayd's wife before he made a law making it legal (or actually God granting special conditions to Muhammad). John then alludes to even more immorality that is too obscene for him to mention and then moves on to the next point of ridicule.[89]

The *Camel of God* is not a separate surah in the Qur'an, though parts of the story are found in several surahs. John elaborates in the telling of this story so that he can bring about the pinnacle point of his exposé of foolishness to his readers. Yehuda Nevo even reminds his readers that this

87. The actual name of the surah is pluralized, *Al-Nisa*—"*The Women.*"

88. The Qur'an indicates that it was Allah's will for Muhammad to marry his adopted son's wife after she had been divorced in order that "there may be no difficulty to the believers in marriage with the wives of their adopted sons." (Q. 33.37) The Quranic account mentions Zayd, Muhammad's adopted son, but it does not mention Zayd's wife, Zaynab, who was supposedly Muhammad's first cousin. In John's account he indicates that Muhammad had fallen in love with Zayd's beautiful wife and told Zayd, who was only named as a comrade, and not as Muhammad's adopted son-in-law, that Allah had commanded Zayd to divorce his wife and then for Muhammad to marry Zayd's former wife. It is interesting to note that this account is found in surah 33 and not surah 4 which John has been alluding to. Does this indicate that these things were all in the book called "The Woman" at one time, or that John is simply pulling material from different places in the Qur'an? Was he reading from a written source or was he writing from memory of what he had heard?

89. John quotes Muhammad as saying "till the land which God has given you, and beautify it. And do this and in this manner," which may be referring to verses such as Q. 2:223 which says, "your wives are as a tilth ["the plowing of land in preparation for growing crops"] unto you; so approach your tilth when or how ye will." This is an obvious reference to overtly sexual behavior where the man has complete dominion over the woman and the woman is seen as merely a sexual object.

story is not in the Qur'an, though there are references to it in surah 7:73, 77 and 91:13-14. Nevo also mentions that John devotes more attention to this account than any other canonical surah, specifically for the purpose of ridicule.

In this tale John narrates the story of a camel from God that drank a whole river and then could not pass between two mountains. Since the water was gone, the she-camel offered her milk to the people looking for water, but they were wicked people and after a time they killed her. However, one of her offspring, a small she-camel, survived, and John makes jest of her situation. He asks the Saracens a series of questions about where the camel may have come from and who gave it birth, since apparently the camel is "without father, without mother, without genealogy."[90] Either John is alluding to a biblical character such as Melchizidek, (Heb. 7:3) or he is trying to bring out the irrationality of the story. He relates that the smaller camel is taken up to Paradise by God and he uses this situation to ridicule their view of Paradise, for if the camel is in paradise then she may drink up the river of water, one of the "three" rivers that he says are present there (water, milk and wine). However, the Qur'an mentions a fourth river of honey (Q. 47:15). Also, John implies that if all the water is gone and they end up drinking out of the river of wine, without water to dilute it, then they will become drunk, fall asleep and miss out on the pleasures of Paradise. However, the Qur'an states that the river of wine will not intoxicate anyone (Q. 37:47).[91] At the end of the story, he says that the camel has run ahead of the Saracens and has entered into the souls of donkeys! John then implies that their destiny will be the same if they continue to follow the foolish words of their "prophet."[92]

John then makes brief mention of two more surahs, *The Table* and *The Cow*. As far as the reference to *The Table* is concerned, John is accurate in what the surah says—"Christ requested a table from God and it was given to him."[93] However, the Qur'an suggests that this "miracle" from God was to provide food for the followers of Jesus, and this provision was the true meaning of the Last Supper, not the biblical idea that Jesus was instituting a core belief that he was going to give his "body" and "blood" in exchange for the eternal lives of his followers. This surah is one of the longest ones in the Qur'an and provides many of the laws for Muslim society, such as what to eat, how to live, what to do about thieves and non-believers as well as a number of injunctions against Christians and Jews that abrogate some of the

---

90. HER 124–25.
91. It is possible that this view of non-intoxicating wine came after John's life.
92. HER 146–48.
93. HER 149–51.

earlier Meccan surahs. For example, Surah 5:51 admonishes Muslims not to take "Jews and the Christians for your friends and protectors," whereas surahs said to be written at an earlier date encouraged the Muslims to seek out "people of the book" for answers to their theological questions, in a way that showed respect and friendship toward Jews and especially Christians.[94] Surah 5 also has verses such as ayah 33 which rails against those who refuse to follow Allah and his messenger:

> The punishment of those who wage war against Allah and His Messenger, and strive with might and main for mischief through the land is: execution, or crucifixion, or the cutting off of hands and feet from opposite sides, or exile from the land: that is their disgrace in this world, and a heavy punishment is theirs in the Hereafter.

There are also a number of passages that counter any belief that Jesus is God, such as ayah 72 which starts out "They do blaspheme who say: 'Allah is Christ the son of Mary.'" In this surah there is a very conscious effort to persuade the reader that this core belief in Christianity is incorrect and misleading. It seems strange, then, that John does not comment on some of these passages that contradict his beliefs. Was he really aware of all that is contained in the surah as we now have it, or was he only aware of some of the major issues that he brings up earlier that may be found in this surah? It may just be a matter that the brevity of his treatise limited what he could cover. On the other hand, a lack of information on the part of an involved and generally informed scholar may also indicate that he was familiar with only a portion of the Quranic material.

Lastly he mentions the second surah, the surah of The Cow, but apparently believes that he has already provided enough foolish sayings and declines any comment on the surah other than to state that it is also full of foolish sayings. Yehuda Nevo notes that John's lack of knowledge in regard to passages in the Qur'an is very revealing:

> The text of the De Haeresibus reveals that John was familiar with many Arab traditions, and part but not all of the Qur'an. In our opinion, it supports Meyendorff's conclusions that John knew

---

94. Yusuf Ali, Qur'an 5:82 "Strongest among men in enmity to the Believers wilt thou find the Jews and Pagans; and nearest among them in love to the Believers wilt thou find those who say, we are Christians: because amongst these are men devoted to learning and men who have renounced the world, and they are not arrogant." Qur'an 4:136 "O ye who believe! Believe in Allah and His Messenger, and the scripture which He hath sent to His Messenger and the scripture which He sent to those before (him)" [Jews and Christians].

only the surahs he paraphrased (nos. 2–5), plus some locutions which also appear in the Qur'an but probably antedate it. Sahas's attempt to show that he had a detailed knowledge of the whole Qur'an are somewhat far-fetched, and do not refute the supposition that what John actually knew were some of the stories and ideas on which the Qur'an was also based, or from which it was compiled. The most interesting aspect of John's account, to us, is that he relates to the Qur'anic material as separate 'books,' not as one book, and that he presents a story called 'The Camel of God' as one of these books.[95]

It is interesting that the four surahs he is somewhat familiar with are all from the so-called "Medinan" period, which was considered to be revealed to Muhammad in the later period of his life when he was living in Medina. It is also curious that John limits his critique of the Ishmaelite religion to these particular sources. This could mean that Nevo and Meyendorff are correct in their assessment that John only knew some of the surahs as well as a limited number of stories concerning Muhammad that were circulating at that time. However, John spent at least the first forty years of his life in the midst of the Saracen stronghold. It is only logical to conclude that he must have been well informed in regard to the prevailing writings and doctrines of the Saracens. Therefore, the limited selection of surahs and stories may simply be explained by John not having access to a Qur'an in the monastery and therefore relying on his memory of discussions that he may have had while a civil servant in Damascus. It could also indicate that, while there may have been much more that he could say, he may have felt that he made his point and it would be unnecessary to go on. It certainly would have been helpful for us today if he would have written more on these subjects.

Practices of the Saracens

John's *Heresy of the Ishmaelites* closes with a list of Muslim customs and practices,[96] such as the circumcision of men and women, orders not to observe the Sabbath, orders not to be baptized, contradictory orders to eat certain forbidden foods and to abstain from other foods that were permissible, and absolute orders not to drink any wine. John does not comment on these practices, but he may have selected them in order to show polemically how each practice is contrary to the truth of Christian teaching. For example, in the Bible circumcision was instituted as a sign of God's cov-

---

95. Nevo and Koren, *Crossroads to Islam*, 238.
96. HER 153–56.

enant to Abraham and demonstrated to the surrounding people that the descendents of Abraham were set apart from the world for God's blessings and purposes. It was only commanded for males. Therefore, the practice of circumcision for the Saracens, which included both males and females, negated the connection to God's covenant with Abraham and merely made it a barbaric practice with no spiritual context. The orders not to observe the Sabbath and not to be baptized were easily understood to be directly against the practice of worship on Sunday for Christians and Jews on Saturday. The Saracen leaders, in other words, were forcing their followers to turn away from the established days of worship and replace Christianity and Judaism with another belief system that required a different day of worship. John may have considered the religion of the Ishmaelites to only be a heresy of Christianity rather than a fully separate religion, but he was keenly aware of how these counter-practices would lead to a further rejection of Christian doctrines and a replacement of all the Christian practices.

The Saracen practice of eating foods forbidden by Jews and Christians may have mostly targeted the Jewish dietary regulations since Christ had given Peter (and, therefore, Christians) approval to eat anything. A shift in eating habits could be construed as an attack on every day common practices that would eventually separate people groups more definitively than even some spiritual disciplines. The abstinence from foods that were permissible is a curious dictate, unless it would include practices such as the partaking of the bread in the communion service, which no doubt would have been shunned by the Saracen. This action would have further alienated the Saracen from the Christian. This may also have been on John's mind when he concluded this list with the total abstinence from wine, for wine was used in the central focus of the Mass and represented the very sacrifice of the Lord Jesus Christ. However, the Saracens did not believe that Jesus died on the cross as a sacrifice for our sins and therefore they would find the Lord's Supper abhorrent to their own beliefs. Surely there were other more practical reasons that the Saracens abstained from drinking wine, but John may have also realized that this early rejection of Christian practices, such as taking bread and wine in the communion service, would lead to other major rejections of Christian doctrine. It is very possible that he had witnessed a number of these paradigm shifts taking place in his life both in his role as civil servant in the court of the Caliph and also from his distant observation post in the desert outside of Jerusalem, and therefore desired that his Christian readers would also be aware of the dangers these Saracen practices represented.

WHAT DOES JOHN KNOW ABOUT ISLAM?

At the end of his detailed examination of John's *Heresy of the Ishmaelites*, Daniel Sahas summarizes what John knows about Islam:

> He presents the facts about Islam in an orderly and systematic way, although not at all complimentary; he demonstrates an accurate knowledge of the religion, perhaps higher than the one that an average Muslim could possess; he is aware of the cardinal doctrines and concepts in Islam, especially those which are of an immediate interest to a Christian; he knows well his sources and he is at home with the Muslim mentality.[97]

Others concur with Sahas in regard to John's expert knowledge of this area. Hoyland contends that John is well informed about the "Islam" of his day.

> This composition exerted great influence upon the language, tone and content of subsequent Byzantine polemic against Islam. The subjects of Christology, Muhammad's prophet hood and scripture, worship of the cross and Muslim licentiousness, as evidenced by the story of Zayd and the description of paradise were all to feature time and time again and to be presented in the same hostile fashion. But though unsympathetic, the author is well informed.[98]

Andrew Louth also believes that John has a fairly accurate picture of early Islam, for

> He dates Muhammad correctly, and knows about the revelations that came to form the Qur'an; he seems to know of the Qur'an as a book, and knows certain of the surahs, though he appears to be mistaken about 'the Camel of God,' though much of the story he relates is authentic enough; his summary of Muslim teaching, especially as it affects Christian beliefs, is accurate; and his account of the charges Muslims make against Christians is precisely what one would expect, though John's replies seem to reveal some misunderstanding of Muslim practice.[99]

If these experts in their fields are correct, then John's assessment in his *Heresy of the Ishmaelites* demonstrates a fairly accurate knowledge of the religion and the founder, and reveals that he is aware of some of the main

---

97. Sahas, *John of Damascus on Islam*, 95.
98. Hoyland, *Seeing Islam*, 488.
99. Louth, *St. John Damascene*, 80.

Heresy of the Ishmaelites 113

doctrines of the religion, especially in regard to Christ. He also knows some of the Surahs which must have been available in some form at that time. However, there are also a number of traditions and practices that he is not aware of, such as the Nestorian monk, Bahira, and he has misunderstandings on some things that should have been known by a scholar in those times, especially one living in the presence of the Caliph. It may be that John was writing from his memory of conversations with Muslims and therefore did not have readily available a copy of the Qur'an, which had not been translated into Greek until after John's death, or it may have been that there was so much to write about that he needed to be selective. Whatever the case, John's critique of Islam indicates that he did not have a high regard for the beliefs of the Ishmaelites, nor for their scriptures.

As a result of this study, it is tempting to agree with Andrew Louth when he says that he is "tempted to go further" down the pathway and look at an idea that has been advanced by scholars such as Patricia Crone and Michael Cook, which gives a different account of the growth and development of early Islam.[100] According to this idea,

> Islam was not fully formed by the time of the death of Muhammad in 632, but was, in part, a reaction to the success of the Arab conquest of the Middle East in the 630s and 640s. From a movement inspired by apocalyptic Judaism, emerging Islam distinguished and separated itself from Judaism, and found its identity in the revelations made to Muhammad. The development of the religion took some decades, and only towards the end of the seventh century did something recognizable as Islam emerge. John's account, if written about the turn of the century, would fit with such a picture. The clear sense of Islam as a (pseudo-) prophetic religion, focusing on the unity and transcendence of God, John's understanding of Islam as finding its identity in Ishmael (as opposed to Isaac), his rather fluid awareness of the scriptural status of the revelations made to Muhammad (awareness of written traditions, most, but not all, of which were soon to find their place in the 'book,' the Qur'an): all this fits such a picture.[101]

While Andrew Louth concludes, "but here is not the place to pursue this topic any further," this is exactly where future research involving John's first-hand account needs to pick up the pursuit. John's picture of Islam in the early eighth century coincides with a number of details from the

---

100. See Crone and Cook, *Hagarism*.
101. Louth, *St. John Damascene*, 80–81.

twentieth-century neo-revisionist view of the development of early Islam. This may be coincidental, or it may indicate that John's account may help us better contextualize a twenty-first-century understanding of an eighth-century dilemma.

Almost 1300 years ago John of Damascus first developed his apologetic approach to Islam. The first step in this approach was to fully understand the Saracen beliefs. The next step provided an explanation as to how the Christian Scriptures and doctrine countered those beliefs. He also provided a re-contextualized rationale for disputed doctrines such as the Trinity and the deity of Christ. As a result of his initiative, John led the way in developing an apologetic that was used for centuries after he died.

7

Disputation between a Christian and a Saracen

Authenticity and Transmission

INTRODUCTION

While the *Heresy of the Ishmaelites* addressed the theological dangers of the new Arab religion in a treatise that revealed its heretical nature, another document, the *Disputation between a Saracen and a Christian*, was probably intended as a training manual for Christian apologetics. It was primarily written to Christians so that they would be able to answer the theological questions that the Saracens were raising.[1] It was also meant to bolster the beliefs of Christians so that they would not succumb to the theological demands of the new Arab regime which was already applying considerable political and economical pressure to accept the new religio-political policies. Sahas confirms that "the *Disputatio* is a kind of manual for a dialectic confrontation of a Christian with a Muslim. This short treatise is a valuable source of information about the earliest stage of Muslim-Christian dialogue, of the development of Muslim theology and the theological inquiries and divisions inside the Muslim community."[2] The *Disputation* was first writ-

---

1. Cf. Pratt, *Challenge of Islam*, 103–4. This also shows that if the author is indeed John, then he was familiar with the issues that were currently being debated in the middle of the eighth century.

2. Sahas, *John of Damascus on Islam*, 121.

ten in Greek and then translated into Arabic and then later into Latin.[3] It has been ascribed to John of Damascus, but others say that it was probably written by one of John's disciples, Theodore Abu Qurra. If it were indeed written by John, then it would have provided a powerful tool to accompany his treatise on early Islam, the *Heresy of the Ishmaelites*. Also, if John is the author of the *Disputation*, then it would have solidified his position of influence for centuries after his death, since this dialogue provided the pattern for apologetic approaches with Islam for hundreds of years afterward. In fact, Colin Chapman says of John that

> His writings had a considerable influence on later generations of Christians. Some of his arguments (for example, proving the divinity of Christ from the titles "Word" and "spirit" given to Jesus in the Qur'an, and suggesting that Muhammad could not have been a prophet because his coming was not foretold in the Bible and he did not work miracles) became widely accepted in Christian apologetics.[4]

Also, as Andrew Louth has reminded us, "If these two works are indeed by John Damascene (or even if their arguments can be traced back to him), they constitute the earliest explicit discussion of Islam by a Christian theologian."[5] Though there is a use of *reductio ad absurdum* arguments at times, the dialogues reveal that the author is a balanced polemicist since they do not have the negative or aggressive tone that was to emerge in later centuries. They demonstrate the mind and heart of a theologian who was concerned that Christians would be prepared to defend their beliefs against the insurgent religious ideas that attempted to overthrow the truths of Christianity. One commentator even goes so far as to say that such work "may be one of the earliest instances of Christian theology offering its help to other believers without any ulterior motive."[6]

AUTHENTICITY, DATING, AND AUTHORSHIP ISSUES

With the *Disputation*, as with the *Heresy of the Ishmaelites*, it is very important to know whether John of Damascus is the original author, for it would

---

3. Kotter IV, 421. Note 5 indicates that Beck and Hoeck consider that the Greek version was present before the Arabic one.
4. Chapman, *Cross and Crescent*, 65.
5. Louth, *St. John Damascene*, 77.
6. Gaudeul, *Encounters & Clashes*, 30. The "other believers" refers to monotheists outside of Christianity.

demonstrate not only that he was aware of the intellectual and theological issues that were being discussed and debated by the Christians and Saracens at that time, but also that he may have been responsible for training early Christian apologists and even framing some of the Christian-Saracen theological debates that developed in the mid-eighth century. Therefore, we would then be able to utilize what he knew in order to gain a more precise picture of the contemporary stage of development of Islamic theology and perhaps even explore whether the Qur'an had yet been finalized or was still in the process of becoming canonized.

In an attempt to examine the complex issues involved in determining the authenticity and authorship of the text, the chart below has been developed in order to trace the possible transmission routes of the *Disputation*.[7]

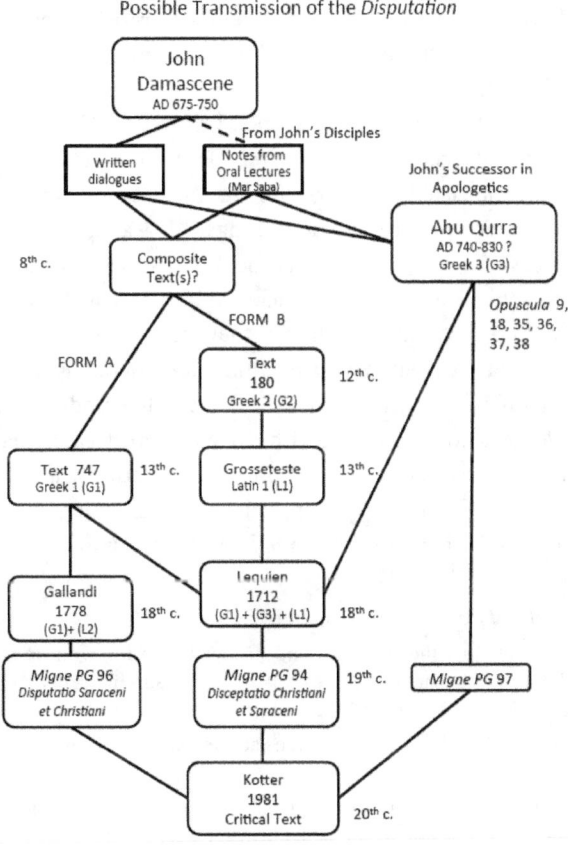

Possible Transmission of the *Disputation*

---

7. The chart was assembled through a comparison of Kotter IV, 421–38; Sahas, *John of Damascus on Islam*, 99–102; Louth, *St. John Damascene*, 81–83; Le Coz, *Jean Damascene*, 199–203; PG 94:1585–89; PG 96:1336–48; PG 97:1588–96.

Sahas points out two different problems that must be addressed in regard to the question of authenticity. The first problem regards the question of who authored the work, and the second problem involves the two different forms of the text.[8] These problems exist because there are two editions of the *Disputation* that have come down to us.[9] One is a Latin translation with Greek fragments juxtaposed next to the Latin, which was edited by Lequien and published in 1712 (MPG 94). This was probably from the Latin translation made by Grosseteste (ca. 1170–1253) in the thirteenth century, with section headings added in 1546. It is titled in Lequien's edition as the *Disceptatio Christiani et Saraceni*. In his introduction, Lequien remarks that his edition uses an older Latin translation from a Greek text which was subsequently lost.[10] Therefore, it is possible that Lequien used a portion of the dialogues from Theodore Abu Qurra's works (especially sections 35, 36 and 38) as well as *opusculum* 18, which includes the phrase "διὰ φωνῆς Ἰωάννου Δαμασκηνοῦ"or "through the voice of John of Damascus," in order to give context to the Latin translation.[11]

Another edition, published in 1788, was from a Greek manuscript[12] from the thirteenth century that Andrea Gallandi, a patristic scholar, reproduced and translated into Latin for his 14-volume reference work on smaller and lesser known patristic writings.[13] It was included in Migne's 1860 edition as PG 96: 1336–58 under the title *Disputatio Saraceni et Christiani*. Since Lequien's edition is also included in Migne with a different title, this has caused confusion as to whether they were two completely different works, but we shall see that these two editions are essentially the same work, albeit with a different transmission history and a slightly different sequence of topics. Perhaps we can view this history as two streams that diverged from the same source and now have come back together again.[14]

One of the difficulties in tracing out the transmission routes is determining the source of the earliest Greek text for the two editions we have

---

8. Sahas, *John of Damascus on Islam*, 100.

9. Hoyland says that the "text is found in inverted order, with numerous variations," but Kotter shows that there are really two main strains in the manuscript history. Hoyland, *Seeing Islam*, 489; Kotter IV, 420–23.

10. PG 94:1585/1586. "nec recenti translatione, cujus Graecum textum obtinere non potui."

11. PG 94:1585/1586. "Caeterum magnam ejus partem expiscari mihi licuit ex dialogis Theodori Abucarae, qui ut suum 18, quem subjiciemus, ita et alios διὰ φωνῆς, ex ore Joannis nostri excepit."

12. Kotter IV, 423. This refers to text 747 in Kotter's manuscript chart.

13. Schlager, "Andrea Gallandi."

14. See the chart on the possible transmission development on the previous page.

today. Daniel Sahas believes that Galland's[15] Greek text (from the thirteenth century) corresponds to the Greek portions in Lequien's edition.[16] Kotter, on the other hand, agrees with Lequien and states that the Greek text of MPG 94 (Form B from Lequien, which was added to his Latin text) is from Theodore Abu Qurra's *Opuscula*, which is reproduced in MPG 97.[17] If Kotter is right, this verifies that Lequien took part of Abu Qurra's Greek text and added it to the Latin text that he had.[18] If Sahas is right, then how would Abu Qurra's *Opuscula*, which Kotter dates back to the end of the eighth century, fit into the transmission issues, especially since Galland's Greek text matches closely with Abu Qurra's work (sections 35, 36 and 38)? It may be that Galland's thirteenth-century Greek text used Abu Qurra plus another text, conceivably original sections from John of Damascus. Another possibility is that Galland's version is an arrangement of sections originally written by John of Damascus and later used by Abu Qurra in his material against the Saracens. In order to determine the answer to this dilemma, it may be helpful to view a chart that compares the various transmissions.

15. Andrea Gallandi is referred to as "Galland" by Sahas, Kotter, Le Coz, and others.
16. Sahas, *John of Damascus on Islam*, 99.
17. Kotter IV, 421n6.
18. Ibid., 421.

Comparison Chart for the transmission of the Manuscripts[19]

Kotter (pp. 420–26) – with titles from Kotter	Galland PG 96: 1336–48	Lequien PG 94: 1585	Abū Qurra PG 97: 1588–96
1. The omnipotence of God, the cause of good and evil, the freedom of the human will, the justice of God, Creation and generation, Godly providence and predestination	1 (1336 B1—1340 B 11)	L7* (7–9 compressed in Lequien—1590 B 6)—K1 *The "L" refers to the section divisions in Lequien, which were originally added in 1546 to Grosseteste's translation. The "K" refers to Kotter's divisions.	*Opusculum* 35 (1588 A1)
2. Baptism before Christ's appearance on earth	2 (1340 B12)	Missing	*Opusculum* 35 (1589 C 6)
3. God's providential and permissive will	3 (1340 C 13)	(1594 B 11)	*Opusculum* 35 (1592 A 1) (and part of Op. 9, 1529 A 1–7)
4. God's providential and permissive will	4 (1341 B 10)	Missing	*Opusculum* 35 (1592 B 4)
5. Christ as the Word and Spirit of God	5 (1341 C 4)	L1 (1586 A 1)—K5	*Opusculum* 35 (1592 B 8)
6. The Word (λόγος) versus the words (λογια ῥήματα) of God	6 (1344 A 3)	L2 (1587 A 9)—K6	*Opusculum* 36 (1592 C 10)
7. The sending of God's word to mankind in the Incarnation, the doctrine of two natures of Christ,	7 (1344 C 5)	L3 (1587 D 1)—K7	Missing
8. The sending of God's word to mankind in the Incarnation, the doctrine of two natures of Christ,	8 (1345 A 4)	L4 (1589, 4)—K8	Missing
9. the death of the Theotokos	9 (1345 B 6)	L5 (1590 A 9)—K9	*Opusculum* 37 (1593 B 12)

19. The basis of this chart is from Kotter IV, 420–26, and the author's re-examination and comparison of the texts in Migne (PG 94, PG 96, and PG 97).

10. Creation and the secondary causes after Creation week	10 (1345 B 14)	L6 1590 A 9)—K10	Opusculum 37 (1593 C 2)
11. The relationship of the baptized (Jesus Christ) to the baptizer (John the Baptist)	11 (1345 C 13)	L8 (1594 D 7)—K11	Opusculum 38 (1594 D 3)
		Lequien added a section by Theodore Abū Qurra (*opusculum* 18) on the "refutations against the Saracens" which includes the phrase "διὰ φωνῆς Ἰωάννου Δαμασκηνοῦ"or "through the voice of John of Damascus" (1596 B 2—1597 C 6)	

By studying the chart above we can see that one major difference between Galland's edition and Lequien's lies in the arrangement of the material. Kotter divides up the *Disputation* into 11 sections and labels them as we see in the first column.[20]

Using the three main divisions of the *Disputation*, as advanced by Sahas, we can see that Lequien's version starts with Kotter's section (5), the nature of Christ as the Word of God, which is followed by a dialogue concerning the cause of good and evil (1) and ends with the discussion of the relationship between John the Baptist and Jesus (11).[21] Galland's version starts with the dialogue on good and evil (1), continues with the question as to whether Christ is the Word of God (5), and ends with the same issue about John the Baptist and Jesus (11).[22] Galland's edition also consists of the three units found in Abu Qurra's *opuscula* which are numbered 35, 36, and 38. *Opusculum* 35 deals with the source of good and evil (1) through Christ as the Word of God (5). *Opusculum* 36 deals with the Word and the words of God (6), and *opusculum* 38 deals with the relationship between Jesus and John the Baptist (11).[23] The question that this raises is whether

20. Kotter IV, 422.

21. We are using the three main divisions of the *Disputation*, as advanced by Sahas, *John of Damascus on Islam*, 99n3, with the division numbers put together by Kotter IV, 422, for our comparison.

22. Sahas, *John of Damascus on Islam*, 99.

23. PG 97:1588–96. Sahas also includes opuscula 9 and 37; see Sahas, *John of Damascus on Islam*, 101.

the *Disputation* was originally composed by John and then later adapted by Abu Qurra or whether Abu Qurra is the sole author of the *Disputation* and it has been erroneously attributed to John of Damascus.[24] As we have shown above, however, the *Disputation* transmitted by Galland coincides with the sections of Abu Qurra's writings as they are found in Migne's *PG* (the former in 96:1336–48 and the latter in 97:1588–96). Abu Qurra, in turn, attributes the original content to his mentor John. However, the section that refers to being transmitted "orally" from John of Damascus is one of at least seven separate sections (*opusculum* 18, PG 94:1596 compared to *opuscula* 9, 35, 36, 37 and 38), and is only found at the end of Lequien's edition. Therefore Sahas concludes that "these indications seem to suggest that the text published by Galland is an edition of short treatises written by John of Damascus and utilized by Abu Qurra who incorporated them as *opuscula* 9, 35, 36, 37 and 38 in his collection of short essays on Islam."[25]

When another comparison chart is consulted, however, it appears that there is more of an overlap between Galland's text and Abu Qurra's *opuscula* as they meet together in the Greek fragments used in Lequien's edition, and this may reveal a more accurate picture of the transmission of the various manuscripts.

In the chart below, the left column represents the critical text constructed by Bonifatius Kotter and the author's English translation. The second column is from the thirteenth-century Greek text, reproduced by Galland in 1778, which coincides with the divisions made by Kotter. The third column is from Lequien's 1712 Latin edition, which utilizes Grosseteste's thirteenth-century Latin translation and Greek portions from a different source, since the Greek source for Grosseteste's version is missing. The fourth column is a matching section from Abu Qurra's refutations against the Saracens, found in *opusculum* 35. The beginning of section 5 in Kotter's critical text has been selected since it poses the very significant question, "Who do you say the Christ is?" Also, as noted above, both Galland and Abu Qurra follow the same order, with this question in the middle of their transmissions, but Lequien's edition places this question at the very beginning, which tends to skew the rest of the order.

It may be interesting to speculate as to why Lequien starts here, though, since the question about Christ's deity is the central question in regard to Christianity, it may be more useful to ask why the other texts did not start with this question. However, since the manuscript of Abu Qurra's text is older, it is safer to say that the original order probably coincided more with

---

24. Sahas, *John of Damascus on Islam*, 100.
25. Ibid., 101.

Disputation between a Christian and a Saracen 123

his transmission rather than with Lequien's, and this seems to be Kotter's conclusion as well, since his chosen order coincides with Abu Qurra and with Galland.

Comparison Chart for Kotter, section 5, lines 1–10

Kotter, section 5[A]	Galland PG96: 1341	Lequien[B] PG 94: 1585	Abū Qurra PG 97: 1591
Ἐὰν ἐρωτηθῇς ὑπὸ Σαρακηνοῦ λέγοντος· Τί λέγεις εἶναι τὸν Χριστόν; (ll. 1–2) If you will be asked by a Saracen, "What do you say the Christ is?"[C]	Ἐὰν ἐρωτηθῇς[D] παρὰ[E] Σαρακηνοῦ λέγοντος· Τί λέγεις εἶναι τὸν Χριστόν;	Ἐρωτηθεῖς παρὰ Σαρακηνοῦ, Τί λέγεις τὸν Χριστόν;	Βαρβ. Τί λέγεις εἶναι τὸν Χριστόν;
	Latin: Si interrogeris, Saraceno dicente; Quem ais esse Christum? If you will be asked by a Saracen this question: Who do you say the Christ is?	Latin: Si interroga[e]ris a Saraceno: Quid dicis Christum? If you will be asked by a Saracen this question: Who do you say the Christ is?	Latin: Barb. Quem dicis esse Christum? Barbarian: "Who do you say the Christ is?"
εἰπὲ αὐτῷ Λόγον θεοῦ, μηδὲν ἐν τούτῳ νομίζων ἁμαρτάνειν, ἐπεὶ καὶ λόγος λέγεται παρὰ τῇ γραφῇ καὶ σοφία καὶ βραχίων καὶ δύναμις θεοῦ καὶ ἄλλα πολλὰ τοιαῦτα· πολυώνυμος γάρ ἐστιν. (ll. 2–4) say to him, "Word of God." And do not suppose that you commit a sin, because in the Scripture he is called Word and wisdom and arm and power of God and many other similar things, for he has many names.	εἰπὲ αὐτῷ·Λόγον θεοῦ, μηδὲν ἐν τούτῳ νομίζων ἁμαρτάνειν, ἐπειδὴ καὶ λόγος λέγεται παρὰ τῇ γραφῇ, καὶ σοφία καὶ βραχίων, καὶ δύναμις θεοῦ καὶ ἄλλα πολλὰ τοιαῦτα· πολυώνυμος γάρ ἐστιν.	καὶ βραχίων θεοῦ, καὶ δύναμις καὶ ἄλλα μθρία.	Χριστ. Λόγον θεοῦ, σοφίαν θεοῦ, Υἱὸν θεοῦ, βραχίονα θεοῦ, δύναμιν, καὶ ἄλλα μθρία.
	Latin: Et sapientia et brachium et virtus Dei, et alia id genus multa. And wisdom and arm and strength (goodness) of God, and many other of that sort	Latin: Et brachium Dei, et potentia Dei, et multa talia. And the arm of God, and the power of God, and many such [things]	Latin: Brachium Dei, virtutem et alia innumera. Arm of God, virtue [Gk. power] and innumerable others

Παρὰ τῇ γραφῇ μου πνεῦμα καὶ λόγος θεοῦ λέγεται ὁ Χριστός. (line 8) "In my Scripture Christ is called Spirit and Word of God."	Παρὰ τῇ γραφῇ μου πνεῦμα καὶ λόγος θεοῦ λέγεται ὁ Χριστός.	πνεῦμα καὶ λόγος θεοῦ λέγεται	Βαρβ. Πνεῦμα καὶ λόγον θεοῦ λέγεται
	Latin: A Scriptura mea Spiritus et Verbum Dei dicitur Christus. In my Scripture Christ is called Spirit and Word of God.	Latin: A Scriptura mea Spiritus et Verbum Dei dicitar. In my Scripture he is called Spirit and Word of God.	Latin: Barb. Christum dico esse Spiritum et Verbum Dei. I say Christ is Spirit and Word of God.

A. DIS 5.1–10.

B. The Greek text in Lequien's section is fragmentary and from an unknown Greek manuscript. It may be from an earlier manuscript than either Galland's text or even Abu Qurra's, though Kotter seems to favor Galland's text over Lequien's as the earliest representative. These three fragments represent the corresponding portion matching Kotter's lines 1–8.

C. The English text is the author's translation from Kotter's Greek critical text and the Latin sections in Migne. The pertinent phrases that correspond to Lequien's fragmented text have been highlighted.

D. This is different from the format of sections 1–4 and 9–11, which follow a normal dialogue pattern. Here section 5 (as well as 6–8) begins with Ἐὰν, and together with ἐρωτηθῇς translates as "*if* you will be asked." However, section one begins with Ἐρωτηθεὶς ὁ Χριστιανὸς, which translates as "*when* the Christian was asked."

E. Found in manuscript 747 from the thirteenth century and used by Galland.

Another anomaly to note is that section 5 begins a different style in Galland's version. Sections 1–4 are in a normal dialogue structure with dialogue tags to mark when the Christian or the Saracen have their parts. Section 5, however, begins with a subjunctive clause, "If you will be asked by a Saracen this question," rather than a dialogue tag, such as "Saracen: Who do you say is the Christ?" It is constructed more like a lecture rather than a dialogue. This may indicate that the original Greek manuscript was a record of a lecture John gave to his disciples, and then later was included in Galland's Greek source. Lequien's edition also follows this same style in the Latin portion, though the Latin is somewhat different from the Latin in Galland's own translation. The matching Greek text from Abu Qurra is the only one that retains a dialogical structure throughout. If his original material were from John of Damascus, however, why would Abu Qurra not have the lecture style rather than a dialogical style? Were the Greek texts that Lequien used from a different source or a shared one? Looking more carefully at the sources may provide further clues on how to answer these questions.

Since Galland's edition and Abu Qurra's dialogue are the prime texts used to make up Kotter's critical text, we can assume that they are closer to the original Greek text. As mentioned above, Lequien took the Latin translation by Grosseteste and juxtaposed Greek "markers" next to some of the Latin text. Lequien stated that he did not have the Greek text that was used for the translation, so apparently he brought in text from other sources.[26] Sahas identifies Galland's edition as the major source and Kotter names Abu Qurra. In comparing just Galland and Abu Qurra we can identify many similarities, even though Abu Qurra's text uses a dialogue format throughout, even in section 5 represented above, while Galland has some extensive monologues. When we compare these two Greek texts with Lequien's Greek fragments, there are some peculiar associations. In the first section (lines 1–2) Galland's text is the same as Kotter's except for replacing ὑπὸ with παρὰ. Lequien's Greek text follows Galland's more than Abu Qurra's, but this is not always the case, as we shall explore at a later point.

Galland also introduces his question in the subjunctive case using ἐὰν (if) with the 2nd person Aorist passive subjunctive verb, ἐρωτηθῇς. On the other hand, Lequien uses a participle, ἐρωτηθεῖς, which can be understood in a subjunctive sense, so that both Galland's and Lequien's phrase can be translated into English as "if you will be asked." It is important to note that Lequien did not take his Greek directly from Galland. Nor did he borrow it from Abu Qurra, since Abu Qurra uses a direct dialogue format in the present tense without any reference to the verb ἐρωτάω. Therefore, we can at least say that Lequien did not take his Greek text directly from either Galland or Abu Qurra. Did he borrow some from both; did he have access to another text that was a composite of Galland's text and Abu Qurra's text, combined with other independent manuscript material; or did he have another source that was extant in the time of Abu Qurra, from which Abu Qurra developed his own dialogue and from which the major strains, Form A and Form B, later developed?

Considering the next phrase, which refers to the "arm and power of God," it can again be noted that Lequien seems to have taken a large portion of his Greek text from Galland, but he uses the word μυρία (myriad), which is in Abu Qurra's text, rather than πολλὰ τοιαῦτα, which Galland utilizes. Again, why would there be an "intrusion" of a word from Abu Qurra's dialogue if Lequien were strictly using Galland's Greek text, unless he was either making a composite text from these other sources or he was referring

---

26. PG94:1585/1586. Lequien's introduction included this phrase: "nec recenti translatione, cujus Graecum textum obtinere non potui."

to another earlier text that reflects knowledge of Abu Qurra's differences?[27] This leads to the conclusion that there may have been an earlier version, which was also available to Abu Qurra at the end of the eighth century, that pre-dated Galland's use of a thirteenth-century text. This manuscript, therefore, could have been the original one written by John of Damascus, or at least the lecture notes taken down by one of his disciples; then Abu Qurra, who had access to the manuscript and the lecture notes at the Mar Saba monastery, could have later used this material in his own dialogue. It is possible that Theodore Abu Qurra was a direct disciple of John of Damascus, but most scholars date his life from around A.D. 740 to 830.[28] Therefore, it is more reliable to say that Abu Qurra, who probably came to the monastery at Mar Saba from Mesopotamia after John's death, was the prime successor to John's apologetic legacy rather than his direct disciple.[29]

Disputes on the Dating of the *Disputation*

Before answering this puzzle concerning the disputes on the dates, a review of some of the difficulties of dating the original manuscript according to other researchers should be helpful. Le Coz says that there are three possibilities for the dating of the *Disputation between the Saracen and the Christian*. The first possibility is that the writings of Abu Qurra precede the *Disputation*, but Kotter shows that this is not likely due to the internal

---

27. However, since the more complex forms are usually simplified in later copies rather than the opposite occurring, it is possible that the phrase πολλὰ τοιαῦτα in Galland's text may have preceded the less complex μυρία which is used in both Lequien's fragmentary text and Abu Qurra's dialogue.

28. W. G. Greenslade (740–820); David Kerr (740–820); Debbie Schlussel (740–825); Adam Francisco (c. 750–820); Sidney Griffith (750–820); Mark Beaumont (c. 750–c. 829); Herman Teule (755–830).

29. Recently this has been disputed by Lamoreaux, who claims that Theodore Abu Qurra was not present at Mar Saba and therefore could not have received oral instruction from John or from John's disciples. Lamoreaux also claims that another version of Abu Qurra's *opusculum* 18, which Lequien introduced with the phrase διὰ φωνῆς Ἰωάννου Δαμασκηνοῦ, should actually read "through the voice of John the Deacon" and represents an account of the latter's summary of some of the debates he witnessed by Theodore Abu Qurra. However, even if this particular work (*opusculum* 18) is not related to John of Damascus, the content of the other sections of the *Disputation* ascribed to John of Damascus and transcribed by Theodore Abu Qurra, reveal strong similarities and a keen understanding of theology, both Christian and early Islamic, so that the internal evidence of the work points to John of Damascus. (Notice in figure 6.4 that *opusculum* 18 has a separate line and is not included in the transmission of the *Disputation*.) See Lamoreaux, *Theodore Abu Qurrah*, xii, xiii, and also the discussion in chapter 10 of this book.

inconsistencies that would result from this scenario. The second possibility is that the *Disputation* inspired Abu Qurra, and that therefore he included a part or the whole in his own rendition. This is likely, as has been noted above, but not easy to verify. The third possibility, according to Le Coz, is that both John's version and Abu Qurra's version are more ancient than the dialogue that we have now. This would mean that someone else, perhaps in the thirteenth century, utilized both John's material and Abu Qurra's dialogues and is responsible for the present ideas represented in the *Disputation*. Kotter, however, narrows the date to the end of the eighth century and the beginning of the ninth century, which was the time that Abu Qurra lived and wrote. Thus, it is possible, and even logical to accept Abu Qurra's statement that the document was written by John and later transmitted by Abu Qurra himself.[30]

Andrew Louth points out that some critics dispute an earlier origin for the dialogues and establish the time of the writing in the thirteenth century because they were ascribed to John at that time by Robert Grosseteste, who translated them into Latin. In one of his footnotes, however, Kotter explains his belief that although Grosseteste may have been the one responsible for later editions referring to John as the author of the *Disputatio*, it does not necessarily mean that the work has a thirteenth-century origin. In fact, the confusion may have been a result of the way that Grosseteste both put the Heresy of John together with the *Disputatio* and attached John's initials to the latter. This may have been an oversight by Grosseteste, but Kotter takes the connection between the two documents even further by concluding that "the writing under consideration may be attributed to the same author because at the end of H 100 there is also a similar way of dealing with the Saracen."[31] It would be natural, then, for both of the documents to be combined together under one author. If the *Disputation* were from the twelfth or thirteenth century, however, then it could not have been written by John of Damascus, and it could not have the authority and value of being a first-hand account of the development of Islam in the middle of the eighth century. Four centuries later, Islam would have been well established and the arguments found in the *Disputation* would have lost their historical significance. Louth refutes this late date, however, by reiterating that Theodore Abu Qurra, John's successor, wrote in the late eighth century and early ninth century, so the original material, even if it were not written by John, could not have been from the twelfth or thirteenth centuries. Moreover, if the *Disputation* was recorded by Abu Qurra, or another monk at the monastery,

---

30. Le Coz, *Jean Damascene*, 200.
31. Kotter IV, 420n2.

from an earlier oral account of John's, then we can ascribe the original ideas developed in the dialogues to John himself.[32] However, while Andrew Louth and Raymond Le Coz accept this scenario, others do not.

Disputes on the Authorship of the *Disputation*

In his article, *Byzantine Views of Islam*, John Meyendorff deals with four works on Islam connected with the name of John of Damascus. He accepts John's authorship of the chapter on the "Heresy of the Ishmaelites" in the greater work called the *Fount of Knowledge*, but he believes that most of the 100 heresies catalogued by John were based on a fifth-century work by St. Epiphanius of Cyprus. In regard to *A Dialogue between a Saracen and a Christian*, he claims that the two main transmissions by Galland and Lequien are actually transmissions of Abu Qurrah's work rather than John's because, according to Myendorff, the manuscripts of Galland and Lequien are "in reverse order" and inconsistent with "the Damascene's manuscript tradition." However, this is quite misleading since Abu Qurrah's dialogue was separate from the other two transmissions. It better indicates Abu Qurrah's own rendition of the material that he derived from John's lectures and written dialogues. It is also not true that Galland's edition is in the reverse order, since Kotter in his critical edition follows the same order as Galland. Nor was Lequien's edition in the reverse order. Though Lequien begins in the middle and the beginning is attached to the end, the sections are arranged in the same relative sequence of Galland's work and Kotter's edition.[33] Rather than the *Dialogue* being a "compilation of Abu-Qurra's writings, attributed to John of Damascus by later scribes," as Meyendorff suggests, the evidence supports the initial authorship of John and a later re-working of the sections by others. It is interesting to note that Meyendorff even states that the "real author" of the third work on Islam, the dialogue that Lequien includes in his edition as Opuscula 18 of Abu Qurrah, is "obviously Abu-Qurra" even though Abu Qurrah writes that he received the material from John διὰ φωνῆς, or «according to the oral teaching» of John. Meyendorff bases this on independent manuscripts of the dialogue that do not include the preface ascribing the work to oral material derived from John of Damascus. However, as we have seen with the convoluted way that the manuscript of the *Dialogue* has been transmitted to us, it is easy to understand how works can be passed on in different forms.[34]

32. Louth, *St. John Damascene*, 76–77.
33. Please refer to charts.
34. Meyendorff, "Byzantine Views of Islam," 16–17.

Yehuda Nevo, a Jewish archaeologist and writer, concurs with John Meyendor *De Haeresibus*, but allocates the authorship of the *Disputatio* to Abu Qurra because the nature of some of the issues raised in the dialogues coincided with issues that were not discussed until the second half of the eighth century, after John's death.[35] Robert Hoyland also comes to this conclusion, but his reasons are based on authenticity issues and the various structures of the document, rather than on content issues. He does not consider the *Disputation* as a work that would come from the pen of a theologian since there was no overall plan for the dialogue and there seemed to be a number of variants, and he says that the different order of the variants sometimes led to a "number of incomprehensible passages." Due to these inconsistencies, Hoyland concludes that although the teachings could have come from John of Damascus himself, the form that we have now is a composite and therefore could not have come directly from John.[36] Martin Jugie also argues that a written original by John may never have existed, but only a composite derived from his oral deliveries combined with a collection of smaller separate sections of his arguments.[37] While this may account for the variety of transmissions, it does not explain the development of the present text. Also, as Kotter has already mentioned, the topics that are discussed are almost without exception controversial points of early Islamic theology, so the author of the dialogue would have most certainly been involved in the early discussion of these issues.[38] We have also shown that the variants can easily be cleared up as two main forms of a composite text composed of John's writings and oral teachings with slightly different sequences. The nature of the resulting form, then, may have more to do with how some of the editors, such as Lequien, have "cobbled" together some of the sections, but that does not negate the original text coming from John's hand or voice.

Another researcher, A.T. Khoury, does not even accept that Abu Qurra is directly responsible for all the material that is ascribed to him in *opuscula* 35–38 (PG 97 1588–92), which would make the connection between Abu Qurra and John of Damascus even less defensible. He reasons that three of the *opuscula* attributed to Abu Qurra must be from some other source since they do not mention Abu Qurra's name as the interlocutor of the Saracens

---

35. Nevo and Koren, *Crossroads to Islam*, 236.

36. Hoyland, *Seeing Islam*, 489.

37. Jugie, "St. Jean Damascène," 701. See also, Cameron, "Jean Damascène: Ecrits sur l'Islam," 368.

38. Kotter IV, 422.

as other *opuscula* do.[39] However, if Abu Qurra is fashioning these dialogues after his notes taken from John's lectures, then he probably would use the same format that John used, i.e., the use of the terms "Saracen" and "Christian" rather than his own name, which he apparently used in his own later dialogues.[40]

The real question that still arises in the midst of these criticisms is whether John is the author of the *Disputation*, or whether it is a collection of dialogues written by John's successor, Abu Qurra, and credited erroneously to John.[41] A.T. Khoury at least concedes that even if the *Disputation* is not by John, it still deals with theological issues that occupied Arab thought in the eighth century.[42] Andrew Louth also does not seem to accept the direct authorship of the *Disputations* by John, though he is open to the original document/ideas coming from John. Thus, he concludes that "even though the Dispute between a Saracen and a Christian, in its present form, is unlikely to be by John, it is appropriate to discuss it here, for it concerns issues that were live in the Damascene's time, issues to which he certainly devoted attention."[43]

There is a possible way to put all of these views together and show that John was the primary person responsible for these ideas which influenced apologetic approaches with Muslims for centuries to follow. As some have argued, the *Disputation* may not have been directly "written" by John, but perhaps he orally communicated the dialogues to some of his disciples and successors, such as Theodore Abu Qurra, who then recorded and developed the arguments.[44]

Daniel Sahas shows that in Lequien's Latin edition there is an additional section almost two columns long that is apparently written by Theodore Abu Qurra but attributed to John *ex ore*, or διὰ φωνῆς, which translates «through the voice,» or «orally.»[45] Therefore, it is reasonable to assume that one of John's disciples had taken notes of John giving a lecture on these matters, and then these were passed down to Abu Qurra. This would very much be like a student today reconstructing his professor's arguments from the notes taken in class. A further question we could ask is whether the rest

---

39. See *opusculum* 18, PG 94:1596–97.
40. Sahas, *John of Damascus on Islam*, 101. See especially note 1.
41. Ibid., 100.
42. Khoury, *Les theologiens byzantius et l'Islam*, 71.
43. Louth, *St. John Damascene*, 81.
44. Le Coz, *Jean Damascène*, 202. "La controverse entre un Musulman et un Chrétien n'aurait donc pas été composée directement ni révisée par Jean Damascène, et M. Jugie pense qu'elle est le résumé de leçons orales."
45. Sahas, *John of Damascus on Islam*, 99.

of the dialogue is due to the same form of transmission, or whether it was actually written down by John and later incorporated together with the sections that were "orally" passed down.

Andrew Louth gives support for the idea that at least part of the *Disputation* was taken from oral notes given by John. He indicates that the first part of the *Disputation*, (Sarac. 1–4), and the last part (Sarac. 11), are consistent with a proper disputation (The Christian speaks and then the Saracen replies), but that the middle section (Sarac. 5–10) alters the format by making the exchange between the Christian and the Saracen more colloquial and didactic ('If the Saracen were to ask you, saying ... then you should'), which would be more consistent with a lecture or a training session. This would then support the view that the middle section of the *Disputation* (in Kotter's critical edition) was adapted from notes taken from John's teaching.[46] Daniel Sahas also concludes that John was involved in the final product that has been passed down. "The fact, also, that the *Disputatio* is found among the *Opuscula* of Abu Qurra, a student and an admirer of John of Damascus, leaves little doubt that John of Damascus is not unrelated to this treatise. Even if the text in its present form does not come from his own hand, its content is a product of his thought."[47]

Bonifatius Kotter also asserts that the central ideas are from John, but for different reasons than cited above by Sahas. Le Coz explains that Kotter, in his critical edition, judges that the *Disputatio* at least puts forth the integral ideas that are found elsewhere in his writings, especially in *De Haeresibus*. Thus, if John had not directly written the dialogue, his influence is seen throughout.[48] Actually, showing a consistent flow of thought between John's *De Haeresibus* and the *Disputation between a Saracen and a Christian* should support the thesis that John was involved in the latter work. Sahas, for one, confirms that the subject matter discussed in the *Disputation* is also found in the chapter on the "Heresy of the Ishmaelites" in *De Haeresibus*, which he points out has been attributed to John.[49] Le Coz also says that the theological ideas presented in the *Disputation between the Saracen and the Christian* are the same as the theological ideas found in John's other works. This again would at least provide a link between the two works.[50]

46. Louth, *St. John Damascene*, 77.
47. Sahas, *John of Damascus on Islam*, 102.
48. Le Coz, *Jean Damascène*, 203. "S'il n'est donc pas possible d'affirmer que Jean en est le rédacteur définitif, il est cependant légitime de considérer ce texte au moins comme un héritage de l'enseignement du Damascène, et, à ce titre, de le retenir comme partie intégrante de ses œuvres, ainsi que l'a juge B. Kotter dans son édition critique."
49. Sahas, *John of Damascus on Islam*, 101.
50. Le Coz, *Jean Damascène*, 202. "Enfin, dans ce même chapitre v nous avons pu

For example, there are similar phrases used in the "Heresy of the Ishmaelites" and the *Disputation*. In the *Heresy*, John responds to the Saracen accusation that Christians wrongly associate Christ with God. John suggests that Christians challenge the Saracens on their understanding of Jesus as the Word and Spirit of God, for the Saracens accept that "Christ is Word and Spirit of God."[51] He then points out that if Christ is the Word and Spirit of God then the Saracens should acknowledge that he must also be "God as well"[52] since they would otherwise be "mutilators" for tearing God's Word and Spirit from Him.[53] In the *Disputation* the author points out that if the Saracen asks the Christian: "What do you say that Christ is?" then the Christian should reply that he is the "Word of God."[54] This is so that the Christian may then pressure the Saracen to admit that in their scripture as well, Christ is called "Spirit and Word of God." Then, just as John did in the *Heresy*, the author of the *Disputation* corners the Saracen by asking him if "before God created the Spirit and the Word, did He have neither Spirit nor Word."[55] The intent is the same in both the *Heresy* and the *Disputation*: to force the Saracen to admit that Christ must be God if he is truly God's Word and Spirit. The reaction of the Saracen to this challenge, as represented in the *Disputation*, may be another way to give support to John's authorship of both documents, for the Saracen feels such shame at his inability to answer the question in his own favor that the author gloats that "he will flee" from the Christian for lack of an answer.[56] This is very similar to John's treatment of the Saracen interlocutor in *Heresy of the Ishmaelites*, for in that document, too, the Saracen is at a loss to give an appropriate answer. One time in the *Heresy*, John writes that the Saracen is "surprised and at a loss"[57] as to what to say in regard to the Christian's reasoning ability. Another time John chides them for remaining "silent because of shame"[58] in their inability to answer questions about their use of witnesses for marriage and routine transactions, but failing to demand any witnesses to their leader's claim of receiving their scriptures directly from God while asleep. A third instance

---

mettre en évidence que le contenu doctrinal de la *Controverse entre un Musulman et un Chrétien* se trouvait toujours en parfaite conformité avec l'enseignement théologique transmis par Jean Damascène dans l'ensemble de son œuvre."

51. HER 70–71. (Also, Surah 3:45, 5:110).
52. Ibid., 73–74.
53. Beaumont, *Christology in Dialogue with Muslims*, 14–15.
54. DIS 5.1–2
55. Ibid., 5.18.
56. Ibid., 5.19.
57. HER 36.
58. Ibid., 54.

Disputation between a Christian and a Saracen   133

of this mocking technique is when "they are indeed ashamed"[59] for making statements about Abraham's sacrifice of Isaac that are not reasonable in a location such as Arabia, where they claim the incident transpired, rather than in Jerusalem. From these instances we should be able to see that the author of the *Disputation*, if not John himself, employed some of the same literary and apologetic techniques as John.

There is another pattern that may tie these two documents together. Sahas shows how John would follow a formal presentation of a heretical belief with a more informal elaboration of the ideas developed in a dialogue form. For example, his short treatise on Manichaeans (Heresy 66) was followed by a longer *Dialogus Contra Manichaeos*, and the statement of the beliefs of the Monophysites (*Heresy* 83) was followed by the work *Contra Jacobitas*, which further developed his ideas.[60] Thus, the chapter on *Heresy of the Ishmaelites* may be John's introduction to the new religion of the Saracens and the *Disputation* may be his elaboration of the main topics previously addressed, especially in regard to the problem of good and evil and the belief that Christ is the Word and Spirit of God. Kotter also recognizes the importance of these particular subjects and the connections that are implied, for he states that

> The topics that are mentioned are almost without exception controversial points of early Islamic theology. The author of the dialogues is therefore very well-acquainted with Islam, and from the contents of our manuscript could be equated with John of Damascus, as far as we already know him from *Heresy* 100.[61]

Another comparison of texts reveals a theological connection that may tie the writer of the *Disputation* to one of John's known works. In section 8 of the *Disputation*, the Christian is explaining to the Saracen how the two natures of Christ could be represented in one person. He uses fairly deep theological concepts when he states,

> You should know also that Christ is said to have two natures but one hypostasis. For the pre-eternal Word of God is one, even after he assumed the hypostatic body, personally but not

---

59. Ibid., 87.
60. Sahas, *John of Damascus on Islam*, 102.
61. Kotter IV, 422. "Die angesprochenen Themen sind fast ausnahmslos Kontroverspunkte der frühislamischen Theologie. Der Verfasser des Dialogs ist somit sehr wohl mit dem Islam vertraut und könnte vom Inhalt unserer Schrift her gut mit JD gleichgesetzt werden, soweit wir ihn schon von H 100 her kennen."

physically, *for a fourth person has not been added to the Trinity after the ineffable union with the flesh.*[62] (emphasis added)

This is very similar to John's exposition in chapter 8 of book 3 in his theological masterpiece, *Orthodox Faith*, which is clearly John's own work. In this section, he is also dealing with the hypostatic union found in the two natures of Christ. He makes his case for the two natures being united without confusion in the perfect God-man, and concludes by stressing that though there are two natures in Christ, he is still one. He emphasizes this point by saying,

> Thus, *I do not add a fourth person to the Trinity*—God forbid!— but I do confess the Person of the Word of God and of his flesh to be one. For, even after the Incarnation of the Word, the Trinity remained Trinity.[63] (emphasis added)

It is interesting to note that the main phrases that include a reference to a "fourth person" are almost exactly alike. In the *Disputation*, the Greek reads, "οὐ γὰρ προσετέθη τῇ Τριάδι τέταρτον πρόσωπον,"[64] while John writes in his *Orthodox Faith*, "οὐ γὰρ τέταρτον παρεντίθημι πρόσωπον ἐν τῇ Τριάδι."[65] While the verbs may be different, they both refer to the idea of "adding" another person to the Triune God, which the author in both cases refutes. The use of a similar phrase as well as the similarly constructed theological explanation may provide another piece of the puzzle with which the original forms of the *Disputation* may be constructed. Is there a way for all these pieces to fit together?

CONCLUSION

Since Bonifatius Kotter collected all the manuscripts of the *Disputation*, as well as of the *Heresy*, and then constructed the authoritative critical text of both of these documents, it would be advantageous to use his assessment as a means to bring the various ideas presented above to some concluding assertions based on the evidence at hand. In his introduction to the critical

---

62. DIS 8.8–11.

63. OF 3.8, p. 285. Although the phrase, "the holy Trinity does not add a fourth person as an appendage" is found in an edict by emperor Justinian, the time and location of the phrase used in the *Disputation* provide a much stronger link to John of Damascus than anyone else. Justinian, *Confessio fidei*, quoted in Grillmeier, *Christ in Christian Tradition*, 487n39.

64. DIS 8.11.

65. OF 3.8, p. 285.

text of the *Disputatio Christiani et Saraceni*, Kotter states that he does not believe that the authorship of the dialogue can be firmly ascertained through the manuscript evidence alone. One of the primary reasons for this is that there are a number of variants by which the manuscripts have come to us, and only one of them indicates an author, a Grammatikos Sisinnios (twelfth century), who is relatively unknown and seems to have added parts of the *Disputatio* to John's *Heresy of the Ishmaelites*. In all the other manuscripts, it is clear that the *Disputatio* is separate from *Heresy 100*, (which is also known as the *Heresy of the Ishmaelites*). A number of the other manuscripts, however, do add John's treatise on the Ishmaelites as a separate document, as if it were an appendix, and even ascribe it to John of Damascus by way of the initials "J.D." Still, Kotter does not accept this as evidence that the *Disputatio* itself was written by John, at least in the form that we have, and concludes, therefore, that "the way this transmission has come to us does not allow us to attribute the *Disputation* directly to John of Damascus."[66]

In the second paragraph of his introduction to the *Disputatio*, Kotter explains that there are great similarities between the *Disputatio* and the *Opuscula* of Theodore Abu Qurra, which is recorded as a different document in Migne (94 for the *Disputatio* and 97 for Abu Qurra). Kotter suggests that there are two possibilities for these similarities: both manuscripts are from the same source or one comes from the other. He goes on to say that the first postulation may be correct, but the manuscript trail does not give enough evidence to support that claim. He also doubts that the second option is viable because "internal reasons" do not allow for this possibility.[67] He then gives a third possibility, which he dubs a "subordinate position," but in the end seems to make the best sense of the various manuscripts. In one of the *opuscula* of Theodore Abu Qurra, the one known as Op. 18, there is a phrase attached to the name of John of Damascus which opens up a viable alternate pathway for the manuscripts. The phrase attached to John's name is διὰ φωνῆς, which means «through the voice» or «speaking,» or even «orally,» indicating that a disciple of John of Damascus could very well have written down the basis of the *Disputatio* while listening to John give a lecture or series of "dialogue" applications to illustrate the points of his lecture. Thus, the original ideas would have come from John and then would have been transmitted through the notes of one of his disciples to Abu Qurra and then into the final form that we have today. This is not very different from what we have with the four Gospels which were transmitted

---

66. Kotter IV, 420. "Von der Überlieferung her berechtigt also nichts, die Disputatio dem JD zuzuschreiben."

67. Some of these differences were illustrated in the diagram.

through the words of Jesus' disciples through secondary scribes, such as "Peter's gospel" transmitted through Mark. Kotter therefore concludes that "If one wants to take this subordinate position, even though it is not specifically confirmed, it is quite possible that the author of our *Disputatio* could be John of Damascus."[68]

In conclusion, according to Kotter, Sahas, Louth, Le Coz, and others, the evidence suggests that it is at least possible to say that John is responsible for the ideas and the format of the *Disputation*, and someone else, perhaps Theodore Abu Qurra, is responsible for the final transmission. However, in comparing Abu Qurra's text with that of Galland's and Lequien's, we can conclude that there were also written dialogues utilized by Abu Qurra which likely came from the hand of John himself. In fact, sections 1–4 and 11 may be from the written dialogues of John, which Sahas says are preserved in Galland's Greek text, and sections 5–10 may be from John's oral arguments that were passed on down to Abu Qurra through John's disciples. Therefore, it seems warranted to say that the final form of the *Disputation* that we have today was derived from actual written dialogues of John of Damascus as well as orally transmitted dialogues that were collected into a "composite" text. It is likely that this composite was later transmitted through two different versions, Form A and Form B, as well as an independent version that was edited by his successor Theodore Abu Qurra.

The chart below has been constructed in order to better explain a possible transmission of the documents that not only represents the content of the various editions, but also supports the feasibility of a direct line back to John's authorship of these dialogues.

---

68. Kotter IV, 421. "διὰ φωνῆς geschrieben ist, also nach einem Lehrvortrag des JD. Will man dieses Abhängigkeitsverhältnis, zwar nicht ausdrücklich bestätigt, auch auf die für die Disputatio einschlägigen Abhandlungen ausdehnen, wäre JD alsAutor für unser Streitgespräch sehr wohl möglich."

Disputation between a Christian and a Saracen 137

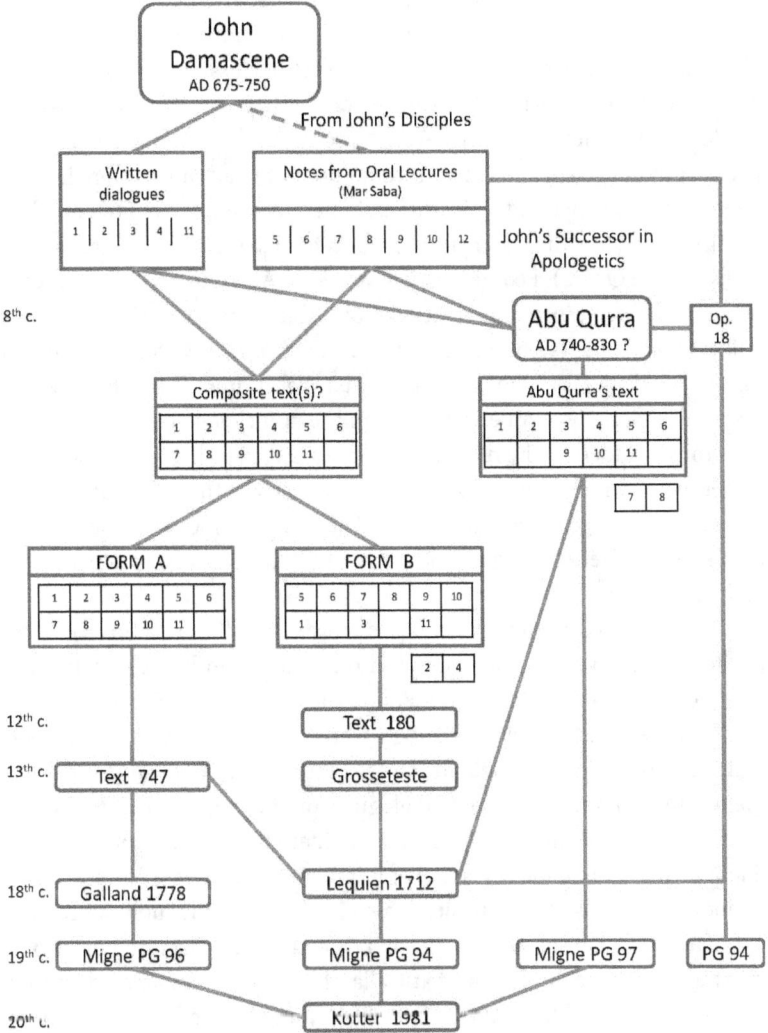

In all, there are twelve sections that have come down to us. It is possible that there were even more sections, but these are the only ones that are represented in the documents that we have on hand. Sections 1–4 and 11 are written in a formal dialogical style, with a Christian alternating with a Saracen, and the Christian usually answering the question raised by the Saracen (who is sometimes referred to as a "barbarian" or a "Hagarene" in Abu Qurra's rendition). This style is retained in both Form A and Form B.[69] Sections 5–10 all have a "lecture" style which begins with a subjunctive

---

69. Remember that Abu Qurra only uses a dialogical style for his edition, even

"if" statement and concludes with a "then" statement that seeks to answer the question. Section 12 refers to Abu Qurra's short dialogue, known as *opusculum* 18, which elaborates on the brief discussion in section eleven regarding who is greater, the baptizer or the baptized. This discussion is not found in either Form A or Form B, so if there is a composite text that led to both of these strains then it would not have had this section. Lequien includes this segment after the discussion concerning the baptizer and the baptized, which is the same ending found in Galland's text (minus section 12 from Abu Qurra). Lequien may have added Abu Qurra's *Op.* 18 since he was already including some material from Abu Qurra's text (PG 97), which includes *opuscula* 35, 36, 37 and 38, but not *Op.* 18 (PG 94). Lequien apparently had access to *Op.* 18 and realized that it fit well with the previous material, especially as an elaboration on the point made in section 11, and therefore included it. The real significance of *Op.* 18 is that it uses the phrase "διὰ φωνῆς," which implies that Abu Qurra received the information orally from John. Or, since Abu Qurra arrived at Mar Saba monastery after John's death, he may be referring to notes taken of John's lectures by other priests at the monastery.

The reason that Abu Qurra could not be the editor of a possible composite of John's written dialogues and the notes from his oral lectures (at least for what has become Form A and Form B) is that Abu Qurra's *opuscula* is transmitted completely as a dialogue without any "if . . . then" statements, which are found in both Galland's and Lequien's editions. If Abu Qurra were the original compiler, then only dialogue would be represented in the later manuscripts, since it would be less likely that later editors would take the dialogue format and change some of it into an "if . . . then" format. Also, as we look at the possible composite, which I believe includes both John's written dialogues represented in sections 1–4 and 11 and "lecture notes" from his students, we can ascertain that Galland has all 11 sections represented. He even has the dialogue section in the beginning (sections 1–4, 11) and the "if . . . then" format (sections 5–10) in the latter portion, which Kotter has determined to be the most likely arrangement. Lequien represents the same two formats with the same sections, but he puts the material in a different order and does not have sections 2 and 4. He also adds Abu Qurra's *Op.* 18 to the end of his edition, even though it is not found in the earlier versions of Form A or Form B.

Another indication that Abu Qurra was probably not the compiler of the composite (for A and B) is that his text lacks section 7 and 8. If he

---

when representing sections 5,6,9 and 10 which are in the "if . . . then" style in the other editions of Galland (Form A) and Lequien (Form B).

constructed the composite from the material he found in the monastery, then it would be less likely that he would leave two sections out of his own dialogue and then add them to a composite. It is more likely that he received his information independently of the composite, and since he lived so close to the time of John's writing, it is very possible that he received his sources directly from John's work at the monastery—his written dialogues, as well as the notes from lectures that John gave to his students. *Opusculum* 18 may have come from some of the material that he would have had access to at the monastery that others living at a later time would not. In the same way, the two main transmissions of the *Disputation* that have come down to us, which we have referred to as Form A and Form B, may have come from a composite, or several composites, made up from John's actual written dialogues as well as lecture material that he gave to his disciples. If this is an accurate assessment, then we can place these dialogues back to the fourth decade of the eighth century, which not only means that they could have come directly from the hand and the mind of John of Damascus, but it gives us a more accurate description of what the theological arguments between the Christians and the Saracens consisted of in the middle of the eighth century.

This assessment is further supported by the analysis of the *Disputation*, for the topics discussed were the same topics that were being explored by the Saracens in the mid-eighth century. It is to this analysis that we will now turn.

8

Analysis of the Disputation between a Christian and a Saracen

INTRODUCTION

If the *Disputation between a Christian and a Saracen* were indeed written by John of Damascus in the first half of the eighth century from the vantage point of a Christian in the service of the highest governmental leaders in the Umayyad Empire, then the analysis of his writings should provide a knowledgeable contemporary account of events and beliefs. In fact, if these dialogues were written by John of Damascus, then we should expect that he, as a major theologian of the time, would know the background of the theological controversies that were taking place. Moreover, it is likely that he discussed first-hand these theological issues with Muslims of the mid-eighth century. If he were the author of the *Orthodox Faith*, which most scholars attest to, then he would be more than capable of understanding the intricacies of Christian doctrine and explaining these issues to his fellow Christians through popular level dialogues. In addition, similar arguments found in the *Disputation* and John's *Orthodox Faith* may provide evidence that one author wrote both works.[1] Hopefully, then, once the *Disputation between a Christian and a Saracen* is analyzed, John's authorship should

---

1. Similar arguments may also point to a teacher authoring one work and his student authoring the other, or neither being written in original form by John but both being written by later students.

Analysis of the Disputation between a Christian and a Saracen

be further substantiated and his insight into early Islam should provide a meaningful contribution to the knowledge of that time.

ANALYSIS OF THE CONTENT

Le Coz divides the content of the *Disputation between a Christian and a Saracen* into two main themes: The first division revolves around man's free will in relationship to God's absolute power (K 1–4, 10). The second deals with various aspects of Christology (K 5–9, 11).[2] These divisions will be adapted in this chapter, and, in addition, each division will be placed within Kotter's arrangement of eleven sections and the pertinent translation from the Greek will be presented for analysis. Comparisons between John of Damascus' *Orthodox Faith*, as well as contemporary Islamic theology, will be made with his dialogues in order to determine similar themes and possible connections. The speaker tags are in bold print in order to make their identification easier.

Section 1a: The omnipotence of God and the cause of evil[3] (Kotter 1)[4]

> When the Christian was asked by the *Saracen*, "Who do you say is the cause of good as well as of evil?"
>
> The *Christian*: "We say that God alone is the author of all that is good, but not of evil."
>
> The *Saracen* asked in response: "Who do you say is the cause of evil?"
>
> The *Christian*: "Obviously the devil, who has perverted the truth by choice, and we humans."
>
> *Saracen*: "Because of what?"
>
> *Christian*: "Because of our own free will."[5]

---

2. Le Coz, *Jean Damascene*, 135.

3. The titles used in this analysis are gleaned from Sahas and Le Coz, with some of the author's own additions and clarifications.

4. Kotter IV, 427–38.

5. DIS 1.1–6 (section 1, lines 1–6). The translation from Kotter's critical Greek text is by the author. The complete selected translation is found in the Appendix. The English translation for John of Damascus's *Orthodox Faith* (OF) is from Chase, *St. John of Damascus*.

When the Saracen asks the Christian what causes good and evil, the Christian answers that it is the Devil and man following the negative aspects of free will. Le Coz writes that the response of the Christian in the dialogue is exactly what Byzantine Christians would say in regard to the dilemma the Saracens faced when they tried to reconcile God's absolute power with the free will of man.[6] For example, John wrote in his *Orthodox Faith* that "God is not the author of evil."[7] Indeed, John goes on to say that sin "is an invention of the free will of the Devil," and though the Devil was made good he became evil because he freely chose to follow what was evil instead of what was good.[8] These statements by John coincide with the response of the Christian in the dialogue, who agrees that evil comes from the Devil as well as from fallen humans.

In the *Disputation*, it has also been noted that John's confession of a single God could have been a refutation of the dualistic beliefs of the Manichaeans,[9] who shared some beliefs with the Muslims, especially the denial of the death of Jesus Christ.[10] The Manichaeans were dualists who did not believe in an omnipotent power of good, but rather that there were two realms which were in constant battle with one another, the realm of light and the realm of darkness.[11] This battle played itself out in the drama of human nature, with the realm of light manifested in all that was good in the soul, and the body manifesting the realm of darkness. Le Coz notes that there was a revival in Manichaeism during the time of John.[12] Therefore, due to the Manichaean view of dualism and the presence of similar Manichaean ideas in early Islam, John may have realized the danger to orthodox Christianity in regard to the Saracen view on the origin of evil. Andrew Louth supports this assessment when he recalls that the doctrine of providence, which is a significant concern in John's *Dialogue against the Manichees*, is also one of the principal concerns in the "intellectual climate of early Islam," of which, Louth says, "John seems to have been thoroughly aware."[13]

---

6. Le Coz, *Jean Damascene*, 136.
7. OF 4.19–23, esp. p. 384.
8. OF, p. 387.
9. Thomas, *Syrian Christians Under Islam*, 37.
10. Daniel, *Islam and the West*, 210.
11. Chase, *St. John of Damascus*, 127.
12. Le Coz, *Jean Damascene*, 136.
13. Louth, *St. John Damascene*, 82.

In John's treatises against the Manichaeans, the *Disputation with a Manichaean*[14] and *Dialogue against the Manichaeans*,[15] he discusses in dialogue form the nature of God, the problem of evil and the reconciliation of God's foreknowledge with man's free will.[16] These are the same issues that he brought up with the Saracen in the first half of the *Disputation between a Christian and a Saracen*. The Christian in the *Disputation* is emphasizing to the Saracen that God gave men the ability to choose between good and evil. However, the choice is limited to the areas of morality and of faith. The Christian points out that while God is the source of all that is good, He cannot be blamed for that which is evil, for evil comes when men reject the morality of God and turn away from God in unbelief. The Kharijites in early Islam proposed that it was necessary that God was responsible for both good and evil, for otherwise man would have the power to counter God's will, and this was interpreted as limiting God's power. This *qadr*, or power, is addressed in the next section.

Section 1b: Man's Power (Kotter 1)

Saracen: "What then? Do you have free will to do anything you wish?"

Christian: "God has created me free in regard to only two things."

Saracen: "What are they?"

Christian: "Doing what is evil and doing what is good. Accordingly, if I do wrong, the law of God punishes me, but if I do what is good, I do not fear the law. Instead, I am rewarded by God and by his mercy. In the same way, before the first man, the devil had been created with his own free will by God, but he sinned, and God expelled him from his proper state."[17]

Here the Saracen asks the Christian if he has power, or free will (αὐτεξούσιος),[18] to do whatever he wishes.[19] The Christian replies that he

---

14. PG 96:1319–36; Kotter IV, 19–67.
15. PG 94:1505–84. Kotter IV, 351–98.
16. Chase, *St. John of Damascus*, xix.
17. DIS 1.7–15.
18. It seems that αὐτεξούσιος has more the sense of "power" in the New Testament, but in Patristic Greek it has more of the sense of "free will." See Lampe, 266.
19 Sahas, *John of Damascus on Islam*, 105. Sahas says that this term may have been borrowed from John by the Qadarites, though their emphasis was more on a counter to the absolute predestination of God espoused by the Jabarites, rather than on John's

has free will to do two things, either power to do good, and please God, or power to do evil and be rejected by God. Here the Christian seems to be relating power to free will. The Qadarites of that time believed, like John, that man was responsible for his own evil, unlike the Jabarites who believed that since God is all powerful He must also be the author of evil.[20]

One of the main questions disputed in the early eighth century dealt with the authority of the caliph. The Qadarites believed the caliph should be held responsible for his actions, and the Jabarites taught that the authority of the caliph was simply an expression of the will of God. The caliphs favored the Jabarite position since it supported their actions, and they persecuted the Qadarite leaders, especially Ma'bad Al-Juhani (d. 699) and, later, Gaylan of Damascus (d. 743), who were both killed for their opposition.[21] During the reign of Yazid III (744), however, the doctrine of free will for humans became the official policy.[22] This decision may have been heavily influenced, though, by the fact that his predecessor, Walid II (743–44), was assassinated by a Qadarite. If this action had been God's will rather than the free will of the assassin, then it would mean that the caliph had been murdered at God's command. It was more politically convenient to believe that the assassin acted on his own volition.

Le Coz wonders whether John of Damascus, as well as other Christians living at the time, may have had influence in regard to this major change in policy. Though some, like Van Ess, believe that the debate concerning predestination and free will, and its outcome, was solely based on the Qur'an,[23] M.S. Seale and others confirm the influence of Christians on the debate.[24] In fact, Le Coz notes that Al-Juhani, the founder of the Qadarite movement, had once been a disciple of an Iraqi Christian, and Gaylan had been a Christian convert to Islam. Indeed, Le Coz suggests that the Christian influence on the discussion of *qadr* (power) may have even brought about the development of the science of *Kalam* in Islam, which influenced theological discussions for the next two centuries.[25]

---

emphasis on the involvement of the deliberation of man in the act. This may demonstrate John's influence on the theology developing at that time.

20. Sahas, *John of Damascus on Islam*, 105–6. See also Fakhry, *A Short Introduction To Islamic Philosophy*, 15–16.

21. Fakhry, *A Short Introduction to Islamic Philosophy*, 2.

22. Le Coz, *Jean Damascene*, 142.

23. Van Ess, "Kadariyya," 368–72.

24. Seale, *Muslim Theology*, 27–29.

25. Le Coz, *Jean Damascene*, 143.

Section 1c: Justice of God (Kotter 1)

> *Christian*: "If, as you say, good and evil come from God, then God is unfair; but he is not. Indeed, if God had commanded the adulterer to fornicate, the thief to steal and the murderer to kill, as you say, then these men deserve honor for their obedience to his will."[26]

The Saracen, according to the Christian, wants to say that both good and evil are from God. The Christian argues that if evil, such as fornication, theft and murder, is by the will of God, then these actions should be praised rather than condemned. However, since the law of the Saracens condemns these acts, they do not believe that evil is from God, for otherwise they should not be condemned for the acts about which they had no choice. Many Saracens, such as the Jabarites, apparently believed that God had to be in control of everything, even of evil, otherwise He would not be all-powerful. John uses his argument to reveal a God who does not command his followers to do evil, but rather encourages them, through their own free will, to act in a praiseworthy manner.

We see this critique carried out further in an examination of God's justice involving the Qadarite opposition to the Jabarites, who argued that "God is the cause of everything, both good and evil."[27] The Qadarites, on the other hand, tried to explain that man possessed power, or *qadr*, over his own actions and therefore man, rather than God, was responsible for evil in the world. In contra-distinction, John teaches that while God's direct creative role is over, He still works His will through the lives of His followers and through the laws He set up in nature. This would allow for a belief in an omnipotent God (Jabarite emphasis) who also established true free will (Qadarite emphasis) for his followers. For example, in *De Fide Orthodoxa* John writes that "all things which God makes He makes good, but each one becomes good or evil by his own choice."[28] In regard to God's goodness and justice John states that He is not only "good" and "just,"[29] but that He is the "source of goodness and justice,"[30] and because of His justice He took on flesh and became man and died in our place to fulfill the justice required by God for our transgressions.[31] On the other hand, while the Qur'an refers to

---

26. DIS 1.20–24.
27. Louth, *St. John Damascene*, 82.
28. OF 4.21, p. 387.
29. Ibid., 1.2, p. 167.
30. Ibid., 1.8, p. 176.
31. Ibid., 3.1, pp. 268–69.

Allah as *Al-'Adil*, or "the just God," John argues that the Saracen God could not be very just if He pre-determines all actions of people, both good and evil, and then punishes people eternally for their transgressions. This was the core inconsistency of the Jabarite position that the Qadarites, and later the Mu'tazilites, tried to resolve.

In the dialogue, the Saracen is concerned with emphasizing the omnipotence of God and the Christian with emphasizing the justice of God. This latter position was taken up by the Mu'tazilites, who stressed the justice of God, and denied that He was responsible for evil. Evidence suggests that the Mu'tazilites further developed the earlier Qadarite concept of free will through the influence of Greek thought and Christian doctrine, as well as internal theological struggles.[32] In time the Mu'tazilites developed a position that sought to preserve God's justice and unity in a way that would hold the individual person responsible for his own actions, but yet reserve the final judgment for an omnipotent God. It is noteworthy that Sahas remarks that since John, or the author of the *Disputation*, is cognizant of the controversies present in mid-eighth-century Islamic theology, and addresses them as present controversies, he must have been "contemporary to the pioneers of the Mu'tazilite movement."[33]

Section 1d: "Creation" and/or "Generation," (Kotter 1)

> And the *Saracen*: "Who," he says, "forms the infants in the wombs of the women?" (The Saracens present this difficult objection because they want to prove that God is the cause of evil. For if I reply by saying, "God forms the infants in the wombs of the women," the Saracen will say, "Behold, God is cooperating with the fornicator and the adulterer.")
>
> The *Christian* responds to this: "We find nowhere in Scripture where it says that God formed or created anything after the first week of the creation of the world ... For God created the heavens and the earth and the universe in six days, and the seventh day he rested from all the work he had started doing, as the Scriptures witness to me."[34]

The Saracen tries to trip up the Christian by asking who forms the infant in the womb; for if God creates the human fetus in the womb of a

32. Fakhry, *A Short Introduction to Islamic Philosophy*, 1–5.
33. Sahas, *John of Damascus on Islam*, 107.
34. DIS 1.28–35; 1.61–63.

Analysis of the Disputation between a Christian and a Saracen 147

woman who has become pregnant due to infidelity, then God is complicit in the sin. The Christian, however, responds by explaining that God set the natural world in motion through creation, and from that point it is the responsibility of man to live righteously so that the offspring of a man and a woman, born by natural means, can be a blessing rather than a curse.

The central question that is really being asked here by the Saracen is "Where does man come from?" It is very much related to the issue of God's sovereignty because it not only deals with the capacity of free will in man, but it also defines the extent of God's participation in the formation of each human born, from Adam and Eve to the present age. The Saracen view was that God is involved in every phase in the process of man's origin, starting from the "drop of fluid" created by God,[35] through the formation of the "clot" or the embryo, which is fashioned by God,[36] to the final formation of the male or female infant.[37] It was very important for the early Muslims to demonstrate that God was sovereign over every aspect of a person's life, from conception to death, for otherwise God's sovereignty would be jeopardized.

Le Coz states that John understands perfectly the teaching in the Qur'an on this subject, and claims that it is contrary to the Bible, for not only does he emphasize that God finished his creative acts on the 7th day, but he also illustrates this point by referring to the genealogies in Genesis which mention that the sons are born from their fathers and not from God.[38] In other words, John differentiates between "creation" and "generation" and claims that while creation is God's role, procreation is the role of man and part of the natural process.[39]

Again, this supports a view of the *Disputation* as contemporaneous with the development of the Muslim theology of free will, for the author of this dialogue understood the debate between the Qadarites and Mu'tazilites, (who would tend to agree with John on this issue), and the Jabarites and the traditionalists, (who would argue that God must be in control of all phases of life or else He could not be a sovereign God).[40]

---

35. Q. 23:13, 14
36. Q. 22:5
37. Q. 23:13, 14
38. Le Coz, *Jean Damascene*, 150. See also DIS 1.70.

39. See also OF 2.30, pp. 264–65, where John states, "Now, the first forming is called 'creation,' not 'begetting.' Creation is the first forming by God, whereas begetting is the succession of one from another made necessary by the sentence of death resulting from the fall."

40. Sahas, *John of Damascus on Islam*, 104–5.

Section 1e: God's Foreknowledge of Man's Destiny (Kotter 1)

And the *Saracen*: "How is it that God said to Jeremiah, 'Before I formed you in the womb I knew you, and while in the womb I sanctified you?'"

The *Christian*: "Since Adam onwards, God gave to every man the power to engender life in the womb. For Adam, having the power to engender life in the womb became the father of Seth, and Seth of Enosh, and every man engenders sons who in turn engender sons until this present time."[41]

In this exchange, The Saracen brings up the issue of Jeremiah, who proclaimed that God "formed [him] in the womb."[42] The intent is to imply that the Christian Scriptures also reveal that God predestines human actions, even from the womb. John acknowledges that God foreknows the birth of every man, but he denies that God necessarily predestines all things since God honors the freedom of action and will in man.

In book 2, chapter 30 of *De Fide Orthodoxa*, John notes that God's foreknowledge is not the same as His predetermined will, for while "God foreknows all things He does not necessarily predestine them all." John goes on to say,

> Thus, He foreknows the things that depend upon us, but He does not predestine them—because neither does He will evil to be done nor does He force virtue. And so, predestination is the result of the divine command made with foreknowledge. Those things which do not depend upon us, however, He predestines in accordance with His foreknowledge. For, through His foreknowledge, He has already decided all things beforehand in accordance with His goodness and justice.[43]

Using a similar argument as the Christian in the *Disputation*, John denies that God's foreknowledge is equivalent to his predestination simply because He has foreknowledge of the outcome, for God does not "force virtue" nor does He "will evil to be done." In other words, God may know the outcome of every situation, but because He also honors the free agency of humans, He will not interfere in order to predetermine a person's action or a choice even if it is contrary to His divine will. God's will is fulfilled in spite of man's freedom to choose contrary to that will, because God's foreknowledge

---

41. DIS 1.64–70.
42. Jer 1:5
43. OF 2.30, pp. 263–64.

Analysis of the Disputation between a Christian and a Saracen   149

operates in "accordance with His goodness and justice." As Daniel Sahas frames it, though John "stressed the fact that God foreknows all things, he denied that He predestines all things. Predestination has to do only with those things which are not dependent upon man's power, and not with those which depend upon him."[44] This view demonstrated by John, as well as the Christian in the *Disputation*, allows for the sovereignty of God to work in such a way that God's will is always fulfilled, and yet man is able to exercise his own free will in such a way that he also retains his dignity as one who is made in the image of God. Such a concept, however, made little sense within a Saracen framework.

Section 1f: Baptism and the Will of God (Kotter 2)

> And the *opponent*: "But was there baptism before Christ, for Jeremiah was born before Christ?"
>
> The *Christian*: "There was, according to the testimony of the holy apostle, some who were baptized in the cloud and others in the sea. And the Lord said in the gospels, 'He who is not born of the water and the Spirit will not enter the kingdom of heaven.' Therefore, Abraham, Isaac, Jacob, and all the other saints who preceded Christ and have entered the kingdom of heaven have been baptized before, since, according to the testimony of Christ, if they had not been baptized, they would not have been saved... Therefore, we proclaim that all who were and are saved through baptism, were or are saved by the grace of God."[45]

In one sense, it is strange for the Saracen to bring up Jeremiah in his questions since that particular prophet is not mentioned in the Qur'an. However, this may be a segment where John is fabricating the dialogue in order to teach Christians a deeper understanding of their faith in contrast to the Saracen beliefs. For example, in the previous section the Christian refers to John 1:12–13 to emphasize that a person is saved not by their own will or effort, but by the power of God. This affirms the sovereignty of God, but it also upholds the free will of man, for the verse begins with the words "to all those who received him," which implies a choice on the part of man.

In *De Fide Orthodoxa*,[46] John elaborates on what we find here in the *Disputation*. First of all, he assures Christians that there is "one baptism

---

44. Sahas, *John of Damascus on Islam*, 111.
45. DIS 2.1–12.
46. OF 4. 9, p. 343.

unto remission of sins and life everlasting. For baptism shows the death of the Lord."[47] He also alludes to John 3:5 in both *De Fide Orthodoxa* and the *Disputation*, which states that unless the Christian is "born of water and the Spirit, he will not enter the kingdom of God."[48] This seems to emphasize both man's part in salvation ("born of water"—the act of baptism), and God's part (by the Spirit). Again, this would counter the Saracen understanding of the place of man and God in Salvation. Indeed, without an understanding of the grace of God, it would be difficult, if not impossible, for Saracens to fathom the meaning of salvation.

One of the more obscure phrases used in the *Disputation* actually answers the question posed by the Saracen. In I Corinthians 10:2, the Apostle Paul writes that the people of Israel were all "baptized into Moses in the cloud and in the sea." This referred to the Israelites being united under Moses' leadership in the Exodus just as Christians are united in their baptism into Christ. In *De Fide Orthodoxa*, John writes that the "cloud is a symbol of the Spirit, while the sea is a symbol of the water."[49] Besides providing another correlation between the author of the *Disputation* and the author of *De Fide Orthodoxa*, this reference, as well as the other references used, seems to be illustrating the idea that baptism is a spiritual event that mysteriously brings together the sovereign will of God with the free will of man. In other words, it is through baptism that the foreknowledge of God is realized in the free agency of men.

Section 1g: God's Providential and Permissive Will (Kotter 3 and 4)

> The *Saracen*: "In your opinion, is the one who does the will of his God good or evil?"
>
> The *Christian*, sensing a trap, said: "I know what you are getting at."
>
> The *Saracen*: "Explain it to me."
>
> The *Christian*: "You want to ask me: 'Did Christ suffer willingly or unwillingly?' So that if I say to you, 'He suffered willingly,' then you will say to me, 'go and bow down before the Jews, for they have done the will of your God.'"

---

47. Rom 6:3
48. OF 4.9, p. 345.
49. Ibid., 4.9, p. 346.

Analysis of the Disputation between a Christian and a Saracen 151

> The *Saracen* admits, "That is what I wanted to tell you. If you can answer me, do it."
>
> The *Christian*: "What you call 'will,' I call 'tolerance' and 'patience.'"
>
> The *Saracen*: "How can you demonstrate that?"[50]

This is where John seems to persuade the Saracen that it is because of God's tolerance and patience that He allows man to sin, rather than man sinning because God wills it. The Saracen says that man is bound to do the will of God. The Christian, however, in explaining his view, draws a distinction between God's "will" and His "tolerance," or perhaps better, His "permissive will." John establishes a distinction between what God wants and what he allows. He wants what is good, but he allows evil. John even makes the point in *De Fide Orthodoxa* that sometimes God uses evil in order to bring about "conversion and salvation," which is a greater good, but he refutes the idea that God is the "author of evil."[51] Sahas adds that "for John of Damascus, God wills only the good deeds while He tolerates the evil ones because of man's freedom of will and his own power."[52]

In this section of the dialogue the Saracen ends up agreeing with the Christian that God does not want man to "steal or commit adultery" because it is against His will; yet he also agrees that God will allow these evil acts to occur because of his "forbearance" or "patience," and because He respects man's free will. This view may suggest that the Saracen portrayed here followed the Qadarite position since the Qadarites were the ones who promoted a belief in the free will of man. It may also represent John's success in convincing some of the Saracens that reason dictated that man's free will within God's sovereignty was not only possible but desirable. On the other hand, the Jabarites held the extreme view of predestination that taught that all of man's actions, both good and evil, were under the compulsion of God. In the end, their position was the one that most Muslims accepted, and the one that became foundational to Sunni doctrine. We now move into the second major controversy between Christians and Saracens, the concept of the Word of God.

---

50. DIS 3.1–9.
51. OF 4.19, p. 384.
52. Sahas, *John of Damascus on Islam*, 112.

Section 2a: Christ and the Word of God (Kotter 5)

If you will be asked by a *Saracen*, "What[53] do you say the Christ is?" *say* to him, "Word of God." And do not suppose that you commit a sin, because in the Scripture he is called Word and wisdom and arm and power of God and many other similar things, for he has many names. And *you* also return the question to him and ask "What is Christ called in your Scripture?" If he tries to avoid this question and wants to question you on another subject, do not answer him before he has answered your question. *He* will be compelled to answer you, "In my Scripture Christ is called Spirit and Word of God." And then *ask* him again, "According to your Scripture, are the Spirit of God and the Word said to be uncreated or created?" If *he* says they are uncreated, *tell* him: "Behold, you agree with me, for that which is not created by someone must be God who creates!" If he is actually bold enough to say that they are created, say to him, "And who created the Spirit and the Word of God?" And if, out of perplexity, *he* tells you that God created them, *say* to him: "a little before you were saying that they are uncreated, and just now you are saying that God created them. Well, if I told you the same thing, *you* would have said to me, 'You have destroyed your testimony, and whatever you say from now on, I will not believe you.' Nevertheless, I will ask you this, 'Before God created the Spirit and the Word did he have neither Spirit nor Word?'" And *he* will flee from you, having nothing to say in answer to you. For those who say such things among the Saracens are regarded as heretics and are rejected and detested by other Saracens. And if you want to denounce him to other Saracens he will be very much afraid of you.[54]

In this section, the author of the Disputation changes from the formal dialogue style and chooses a more conversational style, beginning with a subjunctive clause, "if you will be asked by a Saracen," rather than his preceding use of the dialogue tags, *Saracen*: and *Christian*:. As stated earlier, this construction may indicate that the original Greek manuscript for this section was a record of John's lecture given to his disciples and then incorporated into later collections. In this presentation, using a didactic lesson format, John seeks to present possible scenarios to Christians so that

---

53. Ibid., 113n1. Sahas notes that the use of the interrogative pronoun in the neutral gender, instead of the masculine "whom" do you say, indicates that the focus is on the nature of Christ as the "Word of God" rather than the person of Christ.

54. DIS 5.1–22.

Analysis of the Disputation between a Christian and a Saracen 153

they would be better able to answer their interlocutors. The author has the Saracen begin with the most important question in Christianity, "What do you say that Christ is?" One would think Peter's answer would still be the best one: "You are the Christ, the Son of the Living God (Matthew 16:16)." However, as Sahas points out, the form of the interrogative pronoun translates better as "what" rather than "who," which indicates that the focus of the conversation is on the nature of Christ rather than the person of Christ.[55] Therefore, John advocates that the Christian reply to the Saracen that Christ is the "Word of God." This is because, when pressed, John says the Saracen will admit that in the Saracen's scripture, Christ is called "Spirit and Word of God."[56] For the Christian, however, the "Word of God" refers to Christ, the eternal λόγος, while, for the Saracen, the "Word of God" usually refers to the Qur'an, which Muslims believe to contain the perfect message of God. Perhaps this is why John illustrates the perplexity that a Saracen may have when asked whether the Word is created or uncreated. For the orthodox Saracen believer at that time the proper answer would be "uncreated," because they believed that the Qur'an was eternal. However, in the dialogue, the Christian is demonstrating to the Saracen that even their scriptures affirm that Christ is the Word of God. Therefore, if Christ is the Word of God, and the Word of God is uncreated, then Christ must also be uncreated; and not only that, but if he is uncreated then he must also be God because only God is the uncreated one.[57] The Saracen is trapped! Therefore, when the Saracen changes his answer and says that the Word of God is created, perhaps having in mind Christ as the Word of God rather than the Qur'an, the Christian springs the second "trap" and points out that if God created the Spirit and the Word, then how could he have had his Spirit and Word before they were created? Not only is the Saracen perplexed, caught between the Word referring to Christ on the one hand and the Qur'an on the other, but he also realizes that his answers are contradictory and therefore he "flees" from the Christian. The author then remarks that this Saracen must be a heretic because he admitted that the Word was "created," which in the time of John was the persecuted view.[58] This is the same argument that John uses

---

55. Sahas, *John of Damascus on Islam*, 113n1.

56. Q. 4:169, 171.

57. OF 3.8, p. 169. John writes in *Orthodox Faith* that "consequently, things which are changeable must definitely be created. Created beings have certainly been created by something. But the creator must be uncreated, for, if he has been created, then he has certainly been created by someone else—and so on until we arrive at something which has not been created. Therefore, the creator is an uncreated and entirely unchangeable being. And what else would that be but God?"

58. Sahas, *John of Damascus on Islam*, 114. Sahas is probably referring to the

in the *Heresy of the Ishmaelites*, where he concludes that if God does not always have his Word and Spirit then He has been "mutilated," and therefore unworthy of being God.[59] In the *Heresy*, when the Saracen heretic hears this logical pronouncement, he apparently understands the errors of his logic and flees the scene, much like the Saracen in the *Disputation between a Christian and a Saracen*.

It is likely that John had actual conversations with Saracens in regard to the nature of the Word, and therefore was familiar with their arguments in determining the distinction between the Word referring to Christ or the Qur'an. The confusion may very well have centered on the concept of the λόγος, or the "Word" of God. The concept of the Word is central to Christianity and it was central in John's teaching. In *De Fide Orthodoxa*, he writes that "God is not without a Word," and "there never was a time when God the Word was not."[60] He also testifies that "the son of God was not brought from nothing into being," but "He was always with the Father, being begotten of Him eternally and without beginning."[61]

The concept of the Logos, or Word, developed from the early Greek philosophers, such as Plato, Aristotle and Zeno (the founder of Stoicism), who identified the Logos as God and creator or, alternatively, as the essence of man's soul.[62] The Stoics described the Logos as "God, nature, or the soul of the universe" who, as the active principle, "permeates reality as mind or consciousness pervades the body."[63] Philo, a first-century Jewish philosopher, was enamored with Plato, and understood the Logos as an intermediary between God and the universe with the double role of both "God's agent in creation," and the "means by which the mind apprehends God."[64] Later the early Christian apologists blended some of these concepts together and sifted them through the Bible where Jesus was called the "Word of God" who was in the beginning with God and "was God" Himself. The Word, as Jesus Christ, also came down from heaven, "became flesh," and "dwelt among" men (John 1:1, 1:14). The synthesis of these early Christians promoted the idea that "as pre-existent, Christ was the Father's thought or mind, and that, as manifested in creation and revelation, He was

---

Jahmites and the Mu'tazilites.
 59. HER 76–77.
 60. OF 1.6, p. 174.
 61. OF 1.8, p. 178.
 62. Kelly, *Early Christian Doctrines*, 18–20.
 63. Ibid., 18.
 64. Ibid., 10.

Analysis of the Disputation between a Christian and a Saracen 155

its extrapolation or expression."[65] By the eighth century this foundational doctrine for Christianity was well established throughout Christendom. In the development of early Islamic theology it was evident that Jesus Christ as the Word of God could not be reconciled with the belief that the Qur'an was the Word of God, but it is likely that the Saracen view was primarily a reaction to the primacy of the deity of Christ inherent in the concept of Jesus as the "Word of God." It is very possible, then, that John of Damascus' role in this debate was significant. In fact, Sahas writes that "it is generally held that the doctrine of the Logos—a long debated issue in the Christian church—played a formative role in the doctrine of the Qur'an."[66]

Sahas argues that the Greek text has erroneously copied the word "uncreated" instead of "created," for he cannot make sense of the use of "uncreated" in this context.[67] However, in Kotter's critical text, which includes several additional lines that Sahas' text does not contain, it is clear that John was referring first to the orthodox position (with reference to "uncreated"), and then, secondly, to the heretical position (with reference to "created"). The point was still to show that the only logical understanding of the Word of God was in the uncreated sense, which would mean that Jesus Christ, as the Logos and the only Word of God, must be God Himself.

This dialogue shows that John was aware of some of the internal theological struggles taking place among the Saracens.[68] In the dialogue, when the Christian asks the Saracen his second question, "According to your scripture, are the Spirit of God and the Word said to be uncreated or created,"[69] he is probably referring to the Jahmite and Mu'tazilite controversies of the early eighth century.[70] The orthodox view of that time was that the Qur'an was uncreated, but the Mu'tazilites realized that a belief in the Qur'an as the "uncreated speech of God" could pose a problem in regard to the unity of God, which was known as "al-tawhid" and was the most important tenet of their teaching.[71] Some would say that the Qur'an must also be God if it is eternal. This would be similar to the way Christians speak of Jesus as being

---

65. Ibid., 95.
66. Sahas, *John of Damascus on Islam*, 113.
67. Ibid., 114n 2.
68. Ibid., 115.
69. DIS 5.10.
70. Sahas, *John of Damascus on Islam*, 114n4. In fact, according to Guillaume (referred by Sahas), John was the first non-Muslim to mention these Mu'tazilite arguments.
71. Le Coz, *Jean Damascene*, 160. Incidentally, Le Coz mentions that the use of the argument on the unity of God, or "al-tawhid," was often used in opposition to the Christian concept of the Trinity, which John shows awareness of in this dialogue.

the "uncreated Word of God" who is of the "same substance with the Father and Holy Spirit, existing before the ages."[72]

At that time, most of the Arabs believed that God controlled all men's actions.[73] The Umayyad government used this belief to claim that the administration, acting in the place of God, had the right to control their subjects as they wished, because it was the will of God. Those who said that the Word and the Spirit of God were not eternal, as the Mu'tazilites believed, were labeled "heretics," but it was their related belief in man's free will that was interpreted as undercutting the authority of the government. A number of Mu'tazilites were executed at that time for spreading this "heresy," such as Ja'd b. Birham (AD 743) and Ghayln (also in AD 743). Even the leader of the Jahmite group, Jahm b. Safwan, who was the first to teach on the createdness of the Qur'an,[74] was executed in AD 746 for his teachings.[75] These men were all contemporaries of John of Damascus.

Early in the Abbasid period, just decades later, the Mu'tazilite position became more popular, and in time it became the accepted view. This historical issue lends credibility to the acceptance of John of Damascus as the original writer of the *Disputation*, for the allusion to the Mu'tazilites does not appear in the later parallel text in Abu Qurra's *opusculum*, which may indicate that it was no longer considered heretical. Sahas even goes so far as to state that "this reference is a perfect example of the accuracy and the extent of the knowledge that John of Damascus had of Islam and the Muslim community of his days."[76]

Section 2b: The Word (λόγος) and the Words of God (λόγια, ῥήματα)—(Kotter 6)

> And if a *Saracen* asks you, "are the words[77] of God created or uncreated?" they pose this very difficult question to us in their effort to prove that the Word[78] of God is created, which is not true. If *you* answer they are "created," *he* will tell you, "behold you are affirming that the Word of God was created." But if *you*

---

72. OF 1.6, p. 174; 1.8, pp. 177–78.
73. Esposito, *Islam: The Straight Path*, 69–70.
74. Le Coz, *Jean Damascene*, 161.
75. Sahas, *John of Damascus on Islam*, 114n4. Le Coz places his death in 740.
76. Ibid., 115.
77. λόγια
78. λόγον

Analysis of the Disputation between a Christian and a Saracen 157

answer "they are uncreated," *he* will say, "Behold, all the words[79] of God that exist are uncreated, yet they are not gods. So, you agree with me that although Christ is the Word[80] of God, he is not God." For this reason, *answer* with neither "created" nor "uncreated," but, rather say, "I confess that there is only one hypostatic Word of God, who is uncreated, as you also acknowledge. Furthermore, I do not call my Scripture in its entirety 'words,'[81] but rather 'utterances'[82] of God."[83]

Most Saracens in the early eighth century believed the Qur'an, or the Word of God, had to be uncreated.[84] However, they would not allow this view to be ascribed to Jesus Christ as the Word of God, for they believed that he was created by God.[85] In this section, John tries to clarify the issue by pointing out that the word of God, the Logos (λόγος), or Christ, is necessarily always existent, but the words, or utterances (λόγια, ῥήματα), or Scriptures, are created. For John, this distinction was very important, but much of the significance was inconsequential for orthodox Saracens, because they accepted the Qur'an alone as the uncreated Word of God. Even the written words from the Qur'an were considered uncreated. For Christians, however, the concept of the Logos conveys the idea of the eternal mind of God represented to man through His utterances, which are the Scriptures. This distinction between the Word and utterances did not quite have a parallel in Muslim theology at that time. In fact, the Jahmites, who spread the belief that the Qur'an was created, also believed that any distinction between the Word (λόγος), and utterances (λόγια or ῥήματα), was meaningless, because for the Jahmites both λόγος and λόγια, "Word" and "words," were believed to be created.[86] It was not until the Mu'tazilites taught that the Qur'an had to be created, or else worshiped as another god, that the orthodox Saracens were challenged to consider the distinctions. Due to their emphasis on reason and the unity of God, a distinction began

79. λόγια
80. λόγος
81. λόγια
82. ῥήματα

83. DIS 6.1–11. Please note: the Saracen seems to be confusing λόγος with λόγια. Therefore, the Christian is seeking to make a distinction regarding λόγος as Christ, the hypostatic Word of God, and λόγια, which are merely the words communicated by God through Scripture, which are better understood as ῥήματα, or inspired utterances of God. See Lampe, 805.

84. Esposito, *Islam: The Straight Path*, 69–70.

85. Q. 19:34; 3:59.

86. Sahas, *John of Damascus on Islam*, 116.

to develop among the Mu'tazilites in which they said that while the Qur'an is the created word of God, the uncreated source of the utterances must be God Himself. This is very similar to John's explanation that the Logos is the uncreated source of the words or utterances found in the Christian Scriptures. Though Sahas says that it is difficult "to say that John of Damascus' distinction between "Word" and "words" (or utterances) finds an exact parallel in Muslim theology,"[87] it is possible that John was at least partially responsible for "pushing" this development in Muslim theology, since we see similar distinctions being developed by the Mu'tazilites around the time that John was writing.

Still, it was not until Al-Ash'ari, in the late ninth century, that a distinction was felt necessary, and the Sunni orthodox were able to fully embrace the belief that God's speech is eternal but the written Qur'an is just a representation of the eternal Qur'an in heaven.[88] Thus, under the challenge of the Jahmites and the Mu'tazilites, the orthodox Saracens developed a distinction between the eternal Qur'an and the written representation, and the Jahmites and Mu'tazilites, in turn, could have been challenged by John of Damascus to develop a distinction between the Word of God and the words of God.

We can illustrate this possibility in this section of the *Disputation,* for the Saracen portrayed here, according to Sahas,[89] may represent an early Jahmite position since he tries to "prove that the Word of God is created." However, he does not seem to recognize the distinction between the Word of God (λόγος), and the utterances of God (λόγια or ῥήματα), because in the example the Saracen alludes to in Psalm 11:7, where David writes the "words of the Lord are words that are pure," (τὰ λόγια κυρίου λόγια ἀγνα).[90] The Saracen does not understand why the psalmist uses λόγια instead of ῥήματα, since he apparently believes that λόγια should refer to the Word of God. Therefore, the author tries to clarify to the Saracen the distinction between the Word of God (Jesus Christ, the λόγος), the words of God

---

87. Ibid., 117.

88. Wensinck, *Muslim Creed,* 127. The early creed, Fikh Akbar, stated that the "pronouncing, writing, and reciting of the Kuran (sic.) is created, whereas the Kuran itself is uncreated."

89. Sahas, *John of Damascus on Islam,* 116. Sahas did not have the complete dialogue for this section and therefore may have concluded erroneously that the position represented throughout the section represented the Jahmite beliefs. Le Coz (*Jean Damascene,* 163), who worked from the critical text, disagrees with Sahas and regards the Saracen as orthodox since he considers the Qur'an to be uncreated. As in the previous section, however, the author of the Disputation seems to be introducing both types of responses from the Saracens in order to teach his students the proper way to answer the questions.

90. Ps 11:7 (LXX).

(λόγια), and the utterances of God (ῥήματα). The Word of God, of course, is the eternal Logos (λόγος), which is associated with Jesus Christ, while the words of God (λόγια), are the words that emanate from the Logos as specific revelation found in the Scriptures. The utterances of God (ῥήματα) then, would be the utterances, or words, in Scripture that were inspired by God but not necessarily direct revelation from the Logos.[91] The Christian also tries to explain that David is using a figurative sense of "word" rather than a literal sense. However, this distinction may have been confusing for the Saracen since he raises the question as to whether a prophet would ever use figurative language in the first place. There seems to be not only confusion between λόγος and λόγια, but also a lack of understanding of the fundamental difference between the figurative use of a word and a literal one. Could this dialogue represent actual conversations that John had with Saracens in his day? If John's intent for teaching this material was to train other Christians in their apologetic approach to the Saracen beliefs, it is very possible that he is reflecting the controversies prevalent in Muslim theology during that time.

It is interesting to note that Sahas, in his translation of this section of the *Disputation*, argues that the Greek word for "created" (κτίστα) must have been copied incorrectly by the editor since the word "uncreated" (ἄκτιστα) fits the context better; but again his conclusions are based on an incomplete manuscript.[92] In Kotter's critical edition, it is clear that the author first explains to his students what a Saracen would say if the Christian agrees that the words (λόγια) of God are "created"—they would cry out and claim that the Christian also believes that the Word of God is created, not realizing that there is a great distinction between the "words of God" (his utterances, meaning the Scriptures) and the Word of God (referring to Jesus Christ).[93] The author then deals with the issue of what the Saracen would say if the Christian replied that the words were "uncreated." They would claim that the Christians believed that the words were either all gods or that the Word, although uncreated, could not be God Himself. The Saracen would follow this up with the exclamation that even though Christians confessed Christ as the Word of God, they would have to recognize that he is not God. Therefore, the author encourages his students to say that the Word is neither "created" nor "uncreated," but rather that He is the one hypostatic Word of God,[94] who even the Saracens admit is uncreated. In other words,

---

91. Le Coz, *Jean Damascene*, 164–65.
92. Sahas, *John of Damascus on Islam*, 115n2 and Appendix II, 151.
93. DIS 6.4–5. This is the line that is missing in the text used by Sahas.
94. DIS 6.9.

the author is emphasizing that the Word of God refers to a "person" and not just to speech or mere "words."

Section 2c: The Communication of the Word to Men: The Incarnation (Kotter 7)

> And if a *Saracen* asks you, "How did God descend into the womb of a woman," *say* to him, "Let us use your Scripture and my Scripture. Your Scripture says that God purified the Virgin Mary above all other women and the Spirit of God and the Word descended into her;[95] and my Gospel says 'The Holy spirit will come upon you, and the power of the Most High will overshadow you.' Behold, both statements are saying the same thing."[96]

John points out that both the Saracen Scriptures[97] and the gospels testify that God's Spirit and Word were involved in the impregnation of Mary. The important distinction is that Christians would recognize the union of the divine Logos with humanity in the incarnation while the Saracens would only assent to a miraculous conception and birth of the human prophet, Jesus.

In his *De Fide Orthodoxa,* John developed the concept of the incarnation of God Himself, the Creator, being born from the womb of a woman who was a created being. John begins by stating that the Word, without leaving the presence of the Father,

> came to dwell uncircumscribed in the womb of the holy Virgin, without seed and without being contained, but after a manner known to Him, and in the very same Person as exists before the ages He made flesh subsist for Himself from the holy Virgin.
>
> Thus, He was in all things and above all things, and at the same time He was existing in the womb of the holy Mother of God, but He was there by the operation of the Incarnation. And so, He was made flesh and took from her the first-fruits of our clay, a body animated by a rational and intellectual soul, so that the very Person of God the Word was accounted to the flesh. And

---

95. Qur'an, 3:42. "Behold the angels said: O Mary Allah hath chosen thee and purified thee—chosen thee above the women of all nations."

96. DIS 7.1–7.

97. Since we do not know exactly what stage the Quranic text had reached during John's life, the term "Saracen Scriptures" will be used to refer to the writings of the Saracens/Ishmaelites known to John.

> the Person of the Word which formerly had been simple was made composite. Moreover, it was a composite from two perfect natures, divinity and humanity.[98]

The incarnation was an incomprehensible doctrine to the Saracens, but what they could comprehend about the idea of God becoming flesh was abhorrent to them and became the basis for what they considered to be the greatest sin, known as *"shirk*, which was the association of a created being with the uncreated God.[99] For the Mu'tazilites, the Christian belief in the incarnation threatened their view of the unity of God. For the orthodox Saracen, the incarnation would destroy their view of a God who is wholly transcendent and wholly "other." In fact, many of their objections centered on the difficulty of understanding how God could be transcendent and yet limited by a human body. John anticipated those objections and dealt with the two natures of Christ in his next section.

Section 2d: The Two Natures of Christ (Kotter 8)

> If, again, the *Saracen* asks you: "If Christ was God, how did he eat, drink, sleep, and so on?"[100] *tell* him that "The pre-eternal Word of God, the one who created all things, according to the testimony of my Scripture as well as yours; the one who became a perfect man from the flesh of the holy virgin Mary, possessing a soul and intelligence; this is the one who ate and drank and slept. In contrast, the Word of God did not eat, nor did he drink, nor did he sleep, nor was he crucified, nor is he dead, but it was the holy flesh that he received from the Blessed Virgin that was crucified. You should know also that Christ is said to have two natures but one hypostasis. For the pre-eternal Word of God is one, even after the reception of the flesh hypostatically, with

---

98. OF 3.7, p. 282.

99. Q. 5:72. "They do blaspheme who say: "Allah is Christ the son of Mary." But said Christ: "O Children of Israel! worship Allah, my Lord and your Lord." Whoever joins other gods with Allah—Allah will forbid him the Garden, and the fire will be his abode. There will for the wrongdoers be no one to help." See also Q. 9:31. "They take their priests and their anchorites to be their lords in derogation of Allah, and (they take as their Lord) Christ the son of Mary; yet they were commanded to worship but one Allah: there is no god but he. Praise and glory to him: (far is he) from having the partners they associate (with him)."

100. This could be a reference to the Q. 5:75—"Christ, the son of Mary, was no more than a Messenger; many were the Messengers that passed away before him. His mother was a woman of truth. They had both to eat their (daily) food. See how Allah doth make his Signs clear to them; yet see in what ways they are deluded away from the truth!"

respect to person and not nature, for indeed, a fourth person has not been added to the Trinity after the ineffable union with the flesh."[101]

John presses this distinction of the two natures of Christ by having the Saracen ask, "if Christ were God, then how could he 'eat, drink, sleep and so on?'"[102] From this point John is then able to explain that Christ had two natures in one hypostasis. Thus, in his human nature he could eat, drink, and sleep, but in his divine nature, as the eternal Logos, or Word of God, the second person of the Trinity, he could not die. The reference to the two natures, divine and human, and one hypostasis, God the Son, is critical at this point because it demonstrates one of the major differences between Christianity and Islam. Muslims view the Trinity as three separate entities added to one another, Father, Son and Holy Spirit, and therefore three and not one. John makes a point of stating that the incarnation did not mean that "there was added a fourth person"[103] to the Trinity, for that would be heresy and a refutation of the oneness of the Trinity. What he wants to do here is to distinguish between the eternal word of God and the perfect man who was born in the flesh to the Virgin Mary.

Again, it is interesting to note that this reference to a "fourth person of the Trinity" may be another link to John as the original writer of the *Disputation*, for in *Orthodox Faith* John develops the same argument:

> His two natures belong to the one Person and the one subsistence of the Word of God ... Thus, I do not add a fourth person to the Trinity—God Forbid!—but I do confess the Person of the word of God and of His flesh to be one. For, even after the incarnation of the word, the Trinity remained Trinity.[104]

It is also helpful to note what John says about the Incarnation and the two natures of Christ:

> Before the Incarnation, the Person of God the Word was simple and uncompounded, bodiless and uncreated. But when it had assumed flesh, it became person to the flesh also, and it became compounded of the divinity, which it always had, and the flesh, which it took on in addition. Being thus found in two natures,

---

101. DIS 8.1–12.
102. Ibid., 8.1–2.
103. Ibid., 8.11–12.
104. OF 3.8, p. 285. See also DIV 1.4, p. 22, where John writes, "I venerate together with the King and God the purple robe of his body, not as a garment, nor as a fourth person (God forbid!)."

Analysis of the Disputation between a Christian and a Saracen 163

it bears the properties of the two, so that the same one person is at once uncreated in its divinity and created in its humanity, both visible and invisible. Otherwise, we are obliged either to divide the one Christ and say that there are two persons, or to deny the difference of the natures and thus introduce change and mingling.[105]

In another part of his *Orthodox Faith* John explains the hypostatic union:

> Moreover, the Lord's natures are hypostatically united without confusion and they are divided without separation by reason and way of their difference. In so far as they are one, they have no number. For we do not say that Christ's natures are two Persons or that they are two according to Person. They are numbered, however, by way of their being divided without separation. For there are two natures by reason and way of their difference. Thus, being hypostatically one and mutually immanent, they are united without any confusion or transformation of one into the other and with each preserving its own natural difference for itself. For the created remained created and the uncreated, uncreated.[106]

It should be obvious by now that the Christians and the Saracens did not have the same concept of the Word of God or the nature of Christ. In many ways, it seems that Muslim theology in the eighth century developed, to a certain extent, as a reaction to the encounters that the Saracens had with Christian theologians such as John. For example, we may note in one of the Medinan Surahs, Al-Nisa', or one of last Surahs "revealed," a strong antipathy to the Trinity and the deity of Christ:

> O People of the Book! Commit no excesses in your religion: nor say of Allah aught but the truth. Christ Jesus the son of Mary was (no more than) a Messenger of Allah, and His Word, which He bestowed on Mary and a Spirit proceeding from Him: so believe in Allah and His Messengers. Say not "Trinity": desist: it will be better for you: for Allah is one God: glory be to him: (far exalted is He) above having a son.[107]

It should also be noted in reference to John's explanation of the hypostatic union above, that unless the Saracen understood the theological

---

105. Ibid., 4.5, 339–40.
106. Ibid., 285–86. See also See also DIV 1.21, p. 35.
107. Q. 4:171.

connotations in the specific Greek words used to explain concepts such as the hypostatic union of Christ or even the incarnation, he would probably be unable to fully grasp the ramifications of the terms or even the depth of the arguments themselves. After all, John was the recipient of almost 800 years of theological discussion and development, and much of it took place in the Greek language. Also, many of the theological terms had been coined in order to express concepts that were almost ineffable in themselves. Now, the language of the dialogue in the Disputation is not on the level of a theological treatise, but it still involves, and even necessitates, an understanding of a context that only Christianity could provide. Apparently, however, that was not important to the Saracens. They had rejected the incarnation of Christ, and therefore believed that it was blasphemy to associate a man with the one God, and that it was foolishness to believe that the one God could be a Trinity.

As we go on to the next section, the death of Theotokos, or the mother of God, we may assume that the Saracen had in mind the death of Christ, for the Christian would have just explained that God could not die, yet Jesus suffered and died on the cross. For the Saracen, however, if Jesus Christ is God and died on the cross, then God Himself must have died, and since God cannot die, then Christ could not have been God. For the Christian, however, the concept of the hypostatic union posited that since Christ was fully God and fully man, and both natures were "united without confusion" and "divided without separation,"[108] it was possible for Christ, in his human nature, to actually die on the cross; and yet for Christ, as God, He could not die.

Section 2e: The Death of Theotokos (Kotter 9)

> If the *Saracen* asks, "Did the *Theotokos*[109] [mother of God] die or live?"

> *Reply* to him, "We can say with confidence upon the evidence of the Scriptures that she did not die. The natural death of man came upon her, but she was not bound or subjected to it, as we are—far from it—but it was more like the sleep of the first man when his rib was removed."[110]

---

108. OF 3.8, p. 285.

109. Sahas did not have this word in his text, so he centered this conversation around the divinity of Jesus Christ and unfortunately missed the distinction between the death of Christ and the death of man.

110. DIS 9.1–6.

Analysis of the Disputation between a Christian and a Saracen 165

At first it seems strange for the Saracen to bring up the mother of Jesus at this time in the conversation, but actually it is a logical jump from the previous section since it still concerns the incarnation of Christ. Jesus not only ate, drank and died, but as God, His human body developed in the womb of Mary, who was not divine. As mentioned above, "the Word came to dwell uncircumscribed in the womb of the holy Virgin ... but after a manner known to Him."[111] Only God fully understands how the incarnation could place him "in the womb of the holy Mother of God," and yet, at the same time "He was in all things and above all things."[112] His mother, on the other hand, was subject to death, like all humans. However, the Christian softens death, at least for the mother of Jesus, to an open door that leads beyond life through "sleep."[113]

Section 2f: Secondary Causes after Creation (Kotter 10)

> If the *Saracen* asks you, "Suppose that I have been struck somewhere on my body, and the flesh, being wounded, formed a contusion and in the contusion a worm has formed. Who has created the worm?"
>
> *Tell* him that we have already answered that before.[114]

Perhaps this section would be better suited to follow section 1d on Creation and Generation since it also fits under the category of whether God can be blamed for the ills in the world since He created all life. The Christian answers as he did before and says basically that just as man was cursed by his rebellion, the rest of the world is now subject to pestilence as well. Thus, while God created the original world, and called it "good," man's sin has brought "thorns and thistles" into the fields and pesky worms to our bodies to remind us of our fallen nature.

Section 2g: Who is Greater? (Kotter 11)

> The *Saracen* asked the Christian another question, "According to you, who is greater, the one who sanctifies or the one who is sanctified?"

---

111. OF 3.7, p. 282.
112. Ibid.
113. ὕπνωσεν
114. DIS 10.1–4.

> The *Christian*, however, realizing the implication of the question replied, "I know what you want to say."
>
> The *Saracen*: "If you know, tell me."
>
> The *Christian* said, "If I tell you that the one who sanctifies is greater than the one who is sanctified, you will say to me, 'Go, then, and bow down before John the Baptist because he baptized and sanctified your Christ.'"
>
> And the *Saracen*: "That is what I wanted to say to you."[115]

In this last dialogue in the *Disputation*, the Saracen tries again to bring up a point that would demonstrate that Jesus could not be God, for if John the Baptist, who baptized Jesus, was greater, then it would be difficult for the Christian to argue that Jesus is divine. However, the Christian reminds the Saracen that when a servant helps his master bathe, this action does not give the servant greater status than the master for it is merely the duty of the servant to serve his master.[116] In the same way, John the Baptist was serving Jesus in the baptism and not making himself out to be superior. In fact, John at first refused to baptize Jesus since he did not even feel worthy of tying the shoe laces of his Lord. In the dialogue, the Christian also alludes to Jesus crushing the "heads of the evil demons who were lying in wait"[117] in the river during the baptism. In *De Fide Orthodoxa* John of Damascus also alludes to this demonstration of the power of Christ over Satan and his demons:

> Jesus was baptized not that He Himself stood in any need of purification but that by making my purification His own He might 'crush the heads of the dragons in the waters,'[118] wash away the sin and bury all of the old Adam in the water, sanctify the Baptist, fulfill the Law, reveal the mystery of the Trinity, and become for us a model and example for the reception of baptism.[119]

Indeed, through his baptism Jesus revealed his divine nature and demonstrated his sovereignty over the creation, over Satan and his demons, and over sin. Perhaps the Saracen realized the implication of Christ's divinity in the Christian's answer and was therefore "very much amazed and disturbed,

---

115. DIS 11.1–7.
116. Ibid., 11.7–12.
117. Ibid., 11.15–17.
118. Ps 74:13.
119. OF 4.9, p. 347.

Analysis of the Disputation between a Christian and a Saracen 167

and having nothing to reply to the long-suffering Christian, departed from him."[120]

It is interesting to note that this challenge by the Saracen may have been another one that John was familiar with since the Christian in the dialogue seems to know where the line of reasoning is leading. It may have been that the Saracens were already challenging the Christians with scriptural expressions of Jesus' subordination to the Father, which, for the Saracen, would reveal that Jesus could not be God himself because it shows that Jesus is separate from the Father, and therefore not divine. For example, they may have referred to John. 5:30, John 14:31, or Matthew 20:23, which state that Jesus did nothing on his own authority. Also, John 14:10 and John 8:28–29 affirm that Jesus did not speak on his own authority, while in Mark 14:32 and Luke 5:16, Jesus very clearly prayed to God. For Christians, however, this voluntary humiliation of the Son did not demonstrate an inferior position before the Father, but rather revealed that Jesus, in order to redeem us, "did not consider equality with God something to be grasped, but made himself nothing, taking the very nature of a servant," even though He was "in very nature God."[121]

The *Disputation* ends with this section when the Saracen leaves, but Lequien attaches to his transmission a section from Theodore Abu Qurrah's *opusculum 18*, which claims to be "διὰ φωνῆς Ἰωάννου Δαμασκηνοῦ" or "through the voice of John of Damascus."[122] As detailed in an earlier section,[123] this assertion not only supports the view that the *Disputation* was written by John of Damascus, but it also places it before the ninth century. What is more, the argument that is dealt with in this *opusculum* concerns a similar question of "greatness," but it is in regard to which prophet is greater, Moses, Jesus or Muhammad. The Saracen begins by getting the Christian, in this case Theodore Abu Qurrah, the bishop of Carae, to agree that Moses was responsible for developing Judaism, which was superior to idolatry. The Saracen then gets Theodore to agree that Christianity, which was brought about by Jesus, was superior to Judaism. He then tries to complete this development by getting the Christian to accept Muhammad and the religion of Hagarism[124] as the prophet and religion that supersede Christ and Chris-

120. DIS 11.18–19.

121. Phil 2:6,7.

122. PG 94:1585/1586. "Caeterum magnam ejus partem expiscari mihi licuit ex dialogis Theodori Abucarae, qui ut suum 18, quem subjiciemus, ita et alios διὰ φωνῆς, ex ore Joannis nostri excepit."

123. See chap. 7 on the authenticity of the *Disputation between a Christian and a Saracen*.

124. It is interesting to note that Theodore did not use the term "Muslim," which did

tianity, but Theodore would not accept the conclusion. When asked "why?" by the Saracen, Theodore answers that the conclusion would be false, "For, Muhammad was not as Moses and Christ, who proved worthy of being accepted because they preached and taught; but in order for Muhammad to also be believed for his preaching and teaching, listen to what makes each one of them worthy of being accepted."[125] Theodore then recounts the signs given to Moses in Egypt by God to prove the worthiness of his message, and he lists the miracles of Jesus to prove that He had come from God. However, when it comes to Muhammad, Theodore leaves the Saracen with the question, "Where, therefore, does your prophet fall?" since Muhammad did not do any miracles or signs.[126] Muslim apologists today, of course, would counter with the argument that Muhammad brought forth the greatest miracle of all in the form of the Qur'an, but this was not even alluded to by Abu Qurrah. It could mean that the Qur'an had not been completed at the end of the eighth century when Abu Qurrah used this dialogue, or at least during the middle of the eighth century if the dialogue were directly from John of Damascus. Or it could mean that, if the Qur'an had been completed by the time of Abu Qurrah, that it had not yet attained the miraculous status that it would later hold. Whatever the case, Theodore Abu Qurrah did not accept Muhammad as a true prophet, and certainly not greater than the Lord Jesus Christ.

CONCLUSION

What does this chapter reveal about John of Damascus and his association with the development of Islam? What is the significance of John's responses, as portrayed through the Christian in his dialogues? First of all, the comparison between John's theological work, *Orthodox Faith*, and the *Disputation between a Christian and a Saracen* confirms many similarities in style, content and word usage. This gives strong support to the view that the person who wrote the *Disputation between a Christian and a Saracen* also wrote *Orthodox Faith*. Secondly, the dialogues reveal that John of Damascus was an astute observer of the transformations that were taking place in his culture. More than that, he understood the polemical points of disagreement between accepted Christian doctrine and what he viewed as the aberrant theology of the Saracens. He gave an accurate analysis of mid-eighth-century Islamic theology, and his representation of Christian orthodox faith

---

not come into use until the late eighth century.

125. Translation of *opusculum* 18 found in Sahas, *John of Damascus on Islam*, 156–59.
126. Ibid.

Analysis of the Disputation between a Christian and a Saracen

became the standard for centuries to come. The tone of the dialogues also showed that he was more concerned with Christians understanding their own beliefs in contradistinction to what he called the heresies of the Saracens rather than reaching a point of reconciliation with his opponents. This was to become the precedent for centuries of apologists to come.

It is now time to focus on John's understanding of the Trinity. As we have seen in John's treatise, *Heresy of the Ishmaelites*, and also in his set of dialogues making up the *Disputation between a Christian and a Saracen*, the belief in a triune God was one of the main points of controversy between the Christians in Syria and their Islamic rulers. It is possible that the development of John's apologetic approach was based on his understanding of orthodox theology, and that both aspects of his work were in turn the result of his response to the growth of Islamic theology and hegemony. In order to explore these relationships, we will focus on his exposition of the doctrine of the Trinity and then his interaction with early Islamic theology regarding this doctrine.

9

The Trinitarian Beliefs of John of Damascus

INTRODUCTION

The doctrine of the Trinity, a central doctrine of the Christian church, was also one of the main doctrines countered by the early Muslim apologists. It is therefore important to explore exactly how this doctrine fits with John's overall approach to Islam. What does his explanation and defense of the Trinity reveal about the belief Christians had at that time? How did others understand it? Could John of Damascus' apologetic interaction with early Islamic theology have helped mold the way he presented the orthodox doctrine of the Trinity? John's apologetic approach was based on his understanding of orthodox theology. In turn, his writings in both of these areas may have been motivated by the growth of Islamic theology and hegemony. In order to pursue these points, it will be necessary to first study John of Damascus' understanding of the doctrine of the Trinity. The best place to begin is by examining his most famous work, *Orthodox Faith*.

THE TRINITARIAN BELIEFS OF JOHN OF DAMASCUS

John of Damascus' *Orthodox Faith* is the third part of his larger work, the *Fount of Knowledge* (Πηγὴ γνώσεως—Pēgē gnōseōs), which was written around AD 743.¹ It contains one hundred chapters divided into four books. The first book deals with God in unity and Trinity, the second book deals with God's creation, the third book focuses on Christology and the fourth book discusses a number of theological issues such as faith, baptism, the Eucharist and the resurrection. The topics seem to follow the order of the Nicene Creed, though John placed the discussion of the Holy Spirit in with the Trinity and he did not deal with the church at all.² John borrowed material from many writers, especially Greek theologians such as the three Cappadocians (Gregory of Nazianzus, Gregory of Nyssa and Basil the Great), to such an extent that some critics have faulted him for merely compiling ideas taken from others. However, Frederic Chase suggests that John had a genius for selecting appropriate material and that he was a master of synthesis rather than of mere compilation.³ At one point Chase writes that "the whole is a surprisingly successful synthesis of traditional Catholic teaching as handed down by the Greek Fathers and the ecumenical councils."⁴ Chase also adds that "there is nothing new or original in the matter of doctrine, but there is something original in the treatment and in the clarity of this treatment."⁵

In chapter 1 of book 1 of the *Orthodox Faith*, John follows the example of Gregory Nazianzen,⁶ as well as the words of the apostle John (John 1:18), in proclaiming that ultimately God is "ineffable and incomprehensible,"⁷ and therefore what is said about His nature is through revelation by the Son, the Holy Spirit and the creation. This knowledge is then passed down to us through the traditions in the Old Testament, the Law and the Prophets, and then through the New Testament, especially through "His only-begotten Son, our Lord and God and Savior, Jesus Christ."⁸ This appeal to what can be known about the nature of God and what cannot be known about the mysterious Trinity has led to various ways of distinguishing God's nature from his activities, or what He is not in contrast to what He is. This latter distinction categorizes the apophatic (ἀποφατικός), or negative, terms in contradistinction to the kataphatic (καταφατικός), or positive, words used in relation to God. Thus, the apophatic terms, using the alpha-privitive form

---

1. Chase, *St. John of Damascus: Writings*, xxv.
2. Ibid., xxxii.
3. Ibid., xxxv.
4. Ibid., xxxiii.
5. Ibid., xxxv.
6. Florovsky, *Byzantine Fathers*.
7. OF 1.1, p. 165.
8. Ibid., 1.1, p. 166.

in Greek (α-, not), would be represented by "not-finite," "not-created," "not-begotten," and would seek to reveal what God is not, while the kataphatic terms would relate what He is: "maker of all things," "provider of all," and "ruling over all."[9] Andrew Louth also points out another important distinction between the concepts *theologia* and *oikonomia*,

> Between knowledge of God in himself, which principally entails recognition of the divine being (including the mystery of the Trinity), and knowledge of God's revelation of himself through the *oikonomia*, his activity with regard to human kind in and through creation, including his presence among us in the Incarnation. This distinction corresponds largely to the distinction between God's unknowable being and his activity or energy, through which he makes himself known.[10]

In chapter 2, John elaborates on his view of the oikonomia (οἰκονομία) in order to demonstrate that there are some things about the Godhead that are capable of being expressed and there are also some things that can be known, especially through revelation through the Scriptures and through the Word, the λόγος, the Son of God.[11] He cautions the reader that even when we use words to describe God's nature, we need to be careful because God is beyond any words. Thus, when we engage language to describe the ineffable, we go from the familiar to the unfamiliar and then on to the transcendent. So, while we may, in speaking about God, "attribute to Him sleep, anger, indifference, hands and feet, and the alike,"[12] we need to realize that He is far beyond these human assignations. It is because God's nature is ultimately beyond the ability of man to capture his essence in words that often when we speak about God we use the apophatic, or negative form. John gives several instances of these terms referring to God, such as "without beginning and without end, everlasting and eternal, uncreated, unchangeable, inalterable."[13] He then balances the negative with the positive: "the maker of all created things, all-powerful, all-ruling, all-seeing, the provider, the sovereign, and the judge of all."[14] He lists these divine attributes at the beginning of a type of doctrinal "confession" as a way, perhaps, of linking his *summa theologica* with the creeds of the church and the theology of the

---

9. Ibid., 1.8, 176.; Louth, *St. John Damascene*, 91. See also Fortman, *The Triune God*, 222; and Pelikan, *Spirit of Eastern Christendom*, 264–65.

10. Louth, *St. John Damascene*, 91.

11. OF 1.2, pp. 166–67.

12. Ibid., 1.2, p. 167.

13. Ibid.

14. Ibid.

Church Fathers who preceded him. After his list of divine attributes, John confesses that "God is one, that is to say, one substance (οὐσία), and that He is both understood to be and is in three Persons (ὑπόστασεις)—I mean the Father and the Son and the Holy Spirit."[15] It is significant that John uses the words "οὐσία" and "ὑπόστασεις," not only because the use confirms his orthodox link to the Church and the Church Fathers, but also because, as the "summarizer of the Orthodox Faith," he is able to establish these terms as the way that the Church in the future will refer to the one God in three persons. It is also significant that in the midst of stating that God is ultimately ineffable, and that if we use words to try to describe His nature they must either show what He is *not* or else they can only be used as inadequate "referents" to something far greater, John establishes two words, *ousia* and *hypostasis*, as foundational words in describing the relationship between the one and the three. Of course, the two words themselves are the product of hundreds of years of refinement by both Western and Eastern theologians and are borrowed most heavily from the Cappadocians, but they still represent man's best attempt to capture the essence of the relationship that John continually claims is "unknown and beyond all understanding."[16] Indeed, John says that it is because we do not know "what the substance of God is, or how it is in all things,"[17] that we must be careful with our choice of words and make sure that what we ascertain about God does not go "beyond what has been divinely proclaimed to us, whether told or revealed, by the sacred declarations of the Old and New Testaments."[18] Thus, even the words that are used must conform to the parameters set in God's revealed nature through Scripture and the created world.

In chapter 3, John is concerned with demonstrating the existence of God, not through some elaborate philosophical argument, but rather through the testimony of those who have accepted His existence, such as the writers of the Old and New Testaments, most of the Greeks, and also by those who acknowledged God's existence through the testimony of nature. He also says that the apostles, through the power of God and the wisdom of the Holy Spirit, not only gave testimony to the existence of God, but brought enlightenment to all those who listened. He then credits the early "shepherds and teachers" with further enlightenment through the grace of the Spirit, and the conversion of those who were once in error. It is interesting to note that John apparently does not feel worthy enough to be counted as part

---

15. Ibid.
16. Ibid., 1.4, p. 170.
17. Ibid., 1.2, p. 168.
18. Ibid.

of that great company, as one who has "not received the gifts of miracles and teaching,"[19] but he does hope that with the aid of the "Father, Son and Holy Spirit" he would be able to discuss some of the wisdom handed down from the Apostles and teachers.[20] John then goes on to deal with the distinction between "all things [that] are created or uncreated"[21] which Andrew Louth claims "had become the fundamental ontological distinction for Christian metaphysics."[22] The argument is based on the distinction that created beings (men, angels, etc.) were changeable and uncreated beings (the three persons of the Trinity) were not. Changeable agents change by free choice, either positively, in a more God-like manner, or negatively, in a more corrupt manner. As a result, all changeable things must be created. Perhaps a simple syllogism will help illustrate the difference.

1. Only created things are changeable.
2. Man is changeable.
3. Man is created.

On the other hand,

1. All created things are changeable.
2. God is not changeable.
3. Therefore, God is uncreated.

Also, if God had been created, someone else would have had to have created Him, and so on until we get to the uncreated being, which is an ontological necessity. Even in today's world, we understand, through the 1st Law of Thermodynamics, that the world of physical matter had to have a beginning and a source greater than itself: something could not come from nothing, but rather it has to come from something, or Someone, greater and eternal. The created universe, like all created things, is an effect and therefore requires a cause to bring it into existence. God, on the other hand, is not an effect and therefore does not need a cause to bring Him into existence. Rather, God is the Uncaused Cause who brings all things, or effects, into existence. Moreover, John, through a series of questions regarding the formation of the heavens and the earth, postulates that there must have been an architect who not only formed them from prior material, but also brought them into being, into existence. He also reasons that it could

---

19. Ibid., 1.3, p. 169.
20. Ibid.
21. Ibid.
22. Louth, *St. John Damascene*, 93. See also Letham, *Holy Trinity*, 238.

not have occurred spontaneously or by chance, for the "very harmony of creation" speaks about the design that is apparent and requires a designer or supreme architect, better known as God.[23]

In chapter 4, John deals with the nature of God, especially that He is without a body, for "how could a body contain that which is limitless, boundless, formless, impalpable, invisible, simple, and uncompounded?"[24] It is important to note that God is without a body, but Christ, through the incarnation or the activity of the *oikonomia*, has to have a body that fully identifies him as human. Yet He is also fully God. Only by having two natures can Christ be fully identified with God, who has no body and does not change, and also fully with man, who has a body and is subject to change. At this point John focuses on the immutability of God because he wants to emphasize that with change comes conflict, and conflict is "the cause of separation, and separation the cause of dissolution—but dissolution is altogether foreign to God."[25] Since God is uncreated and unchangeable, He cannot be subject to change which ultimately brings dissolution of a body. On the contrary, it is because God is transcendent over all created beings and not contained in a body that He can be the prime mover of all things. "Only the Divinity is unmoved, and by His immovability He moves all things."[26] Again, the reason that this is important is that anything that can be made to move by another is subject to change and therefore less than perfect. By necessity there must be a starting point, an immovable being who moves everything that is moved. However, since that which is immovable cannot be locally contained, He cannot be contained in a body.[27]

This argument is another instance in which John is making the point that in regard to God's essence, which is "unbegotten, without beginning, immutable and incorruptible,"[28] it is much easier to explain what God is not rather than what He is. It is very difficult to discuss God's nature because He transcends all created nature with which we are familiar. In fact, as John explains, "He transcends all beings and being itself."[29] Because of this, ultimately God's true nature is "limitless and incomprehensible ... and

---

23. OF 1.3, p. 170.
24. Ibid., 1.4, p. 170.
25. Ibid., 1.4, pp. 170–71.
26. Ibid., 1.4, p. 171.
27. Christ may have been incarnated in a body, but he cannot be contained in that body.
28. OF 1.4, p. 171.
29. Ibid.

incomprehensibility is all that can be understood about Him."[30] Therefore, we are not able to describe His true nature, but only what "relates to His nature," such as His attributes.[31]

In chapter 5, John establishes the unity of God. This is important in that it will lay the groundwork for the next sections which seek to establish the distinctions of the three persons of the one God. Although John seems to rely on Gregory of Nyssa's Great Catechetical Oration, especially his prologue and chapters 1–4,[32] John's biblical exegesis establishing the unity of God, based primarily on the Old Testament, and some on the New Testament, seems to be his own emphasis.[33] Perhaps John wanted to contrast the biblical view in order to show Jews and, especially, Muslims, that Christians worship one God who also happens to be triune.[34] Since both Jews and Muslims worshipped only one God, John may be consciously trying to build a bridge from a common belief to a distinctive belief in the Trinity through the development of this idea of God's unity, especially from a scriptural standpoint. After John reminds the reader of the incomprehensible nature of God, he asserts that a believer would accept this premise and still understand God to be "one and not several."[35] He supports this unity by establishing that both the Old Testament and the New Testament affirm belief in one God. He first quotes from Exodus 20:2,3 (the Ten Commandments) and Deuteronomy 6:4 (the *Shema*: "Hear, O Israel: The LORD our God, the LORD is one") in order to show that the Law of God establishes belief in one God. This is followed by Isaiah 43:10 ("Before me there was no God and after me there shall be none, and beside me there is none"), which affirms this view of God's unity among the prophets. Then he uses John17:3 ("This is eternal life: that they may know thee, the only true God"), in order to let the apostle represent the testimony of the gospels and the early church's belief in one God. John then goes on to establish the logical nature of one God in apposition to several gods by stating that the one God has to be "perfect and without deficiency,"[36] for if there were several gods with differences between them, then they would be incomplete and therefore less than perfect. But the one God must be perfect in order to be the only God, "for where there is

---

30. Ibid., 1.4, p. 172.

31. Ibid.

32. Gregory of Nyssa, *The Catechetical Oration*, xli–xlii. See also Louth, *St. John Damascene*, 100; and Bobrinskoy, *The Mystery of The Trinity*, 286.

33. Louth, *St. John Damascene*, 100.

34. Ibid., 101.

35. OF 1.5, p. 172.

36. Ibid., 1.5, p. 173.

one there cannot be another."[37] Now John is ready to show that this one God is also found in three persons who exist in such a way that they are still one God, inseparably separate, a unity within a community.

In chapter 6, John follows Gregory of Nyssa's prologue in his Catechetical Discourse[38] and he concentrates on the Word of God. Not only is there one God (chap. 5), but the word of God, the λόγος, is "identical with God."[39] Continuing with the idea that in the perfection of God there is a unity, John now shows that in that unity there is a subsistent Word or λόγος that is distinct from the one in whom he has his subsistence. He first compares the non-subsistent (ἀνυπόστατος) word of a human, which is derived from the mind, with the Word of God or λόγος, which must be subsistent (ἐνυπόστατος) in order to be a separate hypostasis which generates from the Father but always "is distinct from Him from whom He has His subsistence."[40] The significance of the analogy, which others like Augustine used,[41] is to show that in a human, speech is first derived from a thought in the mind and therefore shares the nature or essence of that thought, but then the words are spoken and dissipate in the air and so are gone. While the mind remains, the words do not, and are therefore non-subsistent or not subsistent in themselves. In regard to the eternal λόγος, while He is generated from the Father, He does not pass out from Him but always remains "within Him."[42] However, the λόγος is fully distinct from the Father and yet has his subsistence within the Father. In fact, he fully shares in the essence of the Father. The only way that this can be explained is that the unity of the one God must exist in more than one hypostasis and yet remain perfect in his unity. Therefore, just as perfection is found in the Father, it is also found in the Word.[43]

In chapter 7 John extends his analogy to include the third person of the Trinity, the Holy Spirit. Like the Word, the Holy Spirit also is subsistent in the Godhead, but also fully God in his own hypostatic relationship. John begins by stating that just as humans need breath in order to express a word that originates in the mind, the Word must also have a Spirit (πνεῦμα). The analogy falls short, however, because the breath of a human is not of the

37. Ibid.
38. Ibid., 1.6, p. 174.
39. Ibid.
40. Ibid.
41. Augustine used, for example, the three faculties of memory, understanding, and will as an analogy for the relationship of the Father, Son and Holy Spirit.
42. OF 1.6, p. 174.
43. Ibid.

same substance as the mind that originates the thought or the word that expresses that thought, but rather the breath comes from outside of the body and is used to give vocalization to the word. In the Godhead, just as the Word has his own subsistence in the unity, the Spirit shares the same οὐσία and yet has his own subsistence in himself, just like the Word. The Spirit, then, should also be conceived of as "substantially subsisting, endowed with will and operation, and all-powerful."[44] While much in this chapter is a summary of Gregory of Nyssa's explanation,[45] John adds an interesting phrase that indicates a more precise understanding of the procession of the Spirit in relation to the Son. John says that the Spirit proceeds "from the Father, coming to rest in the Word and declaring Him, not separated from God in essence or from the Word with whom it is associated."[46] John will develop this thought further in chapter 8, but it intimates a far deeper theme that will be developed more fully in his concept of the perichoresis of God, in which the three persons of the one God merge mystically within each other. Regarding this relationship, Robert Letham explains that,

> Indeed, the Holy Spirit has the same order and nature toward the Son as the Son has toward the Father. The Son is in the Father, and the Father is in the Son, and so also is the Holy Spirit in the Son and the Son in the Holy Spirit. Thus, the Spirit cannot be divided from the Word. So also the Spirit is in God the Father and from the Father. As the Son comes in the name of the Father, so the Holy Spirit comes in the name of the Son. There is one efficacy and action of the Holy Trinity, for the Father makes all things through the Word by the Holy Spirit.[47]

Also, while Gregory used the word *anhypostatos* (ἀνυπόστατος), John incorporates the word *enhypostatos* (ἐνυπόστατος) or "inexists."[48] What he means by this is that the Holy Spirit, like the Word, proceeds from the Father and yet still exists in union with him. In regard to this concept of inexistence, Cyril of Alexandria adds that the Spirit is from the being of the Son as he is from the being of the Father, in such a way that the Spirit can be said to not only be sent from the Father *through* the Son, but also that he proceeds from the Father *and* the Son.[49] John does not go quite as far as

---

44. Ibid., 1.7, p. 175.
45. Louth, *St. John Damascene*, 101–2.
46. OF 1.7, p. 175.
47. Letham, *Holy Trinity*, 214.
48. Louth, *St. John Damascene*, 102. See also Macleod, *The Person of Christ*, 201–2.
49. Cyril of Alexandria, *De sancta et consubstantiali Trinitate, Dialogus II* (PG 75:721–23).

Cyril in his perichoretical concept of the Trinity, for John would not say that the Spirit could proceed from the Father *and* the Son. However, if the ninth-century church understood his concept of enhypostatos (ἐνυπόστατος) or inexistence, or the fuller development of the co-inherence of the three persons of the one God, developed in the concept of perichoresis, then perhaps they would not have been divided over the filioque controversy.

In the next part of chapter 7, John seems to return to Gregory's Catechetical Oration in order to confront the "narrow monotheism of Judaism and the polytheism of paganism" with the transcendent view of Christian Trinitarianism. For John, this triune monotheism transforms the two "heresies" by taking the positive Jewish view of the one nature of God and synthesizing it with the positive view of Greek teaching on the "unique distinction of the hypostasis"[50] in order to develop the transcendent view of the triune God who exists eternally in the form of one nature in three persons (ὑπόστασεις).[51] In his concession to the beliefs of the Jews and the Greeks, John may have developed his presentation of the theology of the Trinity by using the Word and the Spirit, concepts that would be understandable to his audience. However, John may be thinking much more directly about the Muslims who, on the one hand denounced the Trinity and the deity of Christ, but on the other hand recognized that Allah possesses both Word and Spirit.[52] Perhaps what prompted John to begin his *Orthodox Faith* with an explanation of the Trinity focusing on the Word and the Spirit was the realization that Islam, with its strong denunciation of anyone who would associate a man with God, and its vehement denial of a triune God, would at least agree on the terms of the disagreement. In other words, perhaps John was specifically, and secretly, addressing some of the main concerns that the Muslims had in their rejection of Christianity. To be sure, later Christian apologists, like Theodore Abu Qurra, extensively used the argument of the Word and the Spirit of Allah in the Qur'an in order to present what they considered to be the superior nature of Christian doctrine and beliefs. John's summative treatment of the theology of the earlier Church Fathers, especially the Cappadocians, would have served this later apologetic cause well.

Chapter 8 is the longest chapter in the *Orthodox Faith* and one of the most important chapters concerning the doctrine of the Trinity. Andrew Louth divides the chapter into four sections: section one deals with a restatement of the belief in one God, who is "ineffable and transcendent," as

50. OF 1.7, 176.

51. Louth, *St. John Damascene*, 102. See also Letham, *Holy Trinity*, 210, 238–39; and Meyendorff, *Byzantine Theology*, 183.

52. HER 69.

well as the relationship between the Father and the Son, especially in regard to the difference between "begetting" (or generation) and "creation." Section two explores the differences between the nature of divine generation and procession, as well as the differences between ἀγεννετός, or "unbegotten," and ἀγενετός, "unoriginated" or "uncreated." In section three John explores the nature of the procession of the Holy Spirit and the relationship between the Holy Spirit and the Son. Then, in section four, John introduces the term "perichoresis" ("coinherence") for the first time and develops the concept of the nature of the divine unity.[53]

In the first section of chapter 8, John begins by clearly stating that Christians believe in one God. Again, this relates back to the Old Testament teaching of one God as well as to the foundation for the three persons so carefully described in the New Testament. In order to emphasize the nature of the one God, John begins to list a number of divine attributes that set the one God apart from His creation. There are four groups of attributes. The first group describes what God is not, using the alpha-privative form[54] such as "without beginning" (ἄναρχον), "uncreated" (ἄκτιστον), and "unbegotten" (ἀγεννετόν).[55] Since God is ineffable, it is hard to find words that can adequately describe His attributes. In the second group John uses words that show what God *is* through a description of His actions, such as "maker of all things," "provider for all," and "ruling over all."[56] His use of the "πάντον" emphasizes the extent of God's rule—over *everything*. The third group of phrases describes how God is beyond all things that are conceived, such as "supersubstantial and surpassing all," to the degree that God is "above essence and life and speech and concept."[57] These phrases indicate that God is unlike anything in the world of man, which is an important distinction to make before he goes on to deal with the nature of the Godhead. The fourth group of divine attributes begins this transition in its reference to the oneness of God's nature: "one substance, one Godhead, one virtue, one will . . . one kingdom."[58] John then concludes this list with a type of confession that states that this one God, with all these attributes, is "known in three perfect persons . . . united without confusion and distinct without separation, which is beyond understanding."[59] John will later develop this

---

53. Louth, *St. John Damascene*, 103–4.
54. See Parry, *Depicting the Word*, 115–16.
55. OF 1.8, 176.
56. Ibid., 1.8, 176–77.
57. Ibid., 1.8, 177.
58. Ibid.
59. Ibid.

sense of God's intermingling of the one and the three in his concept of the perichoresis (περιχώρησις),[60] or the "circle dance" of God's triune nature.[61] John often cautions the reader that the true essence of God is beyond understanding, but his perichoretic model of the Trinity seeks to give shape to the ineffable by describing the relationship of the three persons of the one God. Moltmann captures John's description of the "circulatory character of the eternal divine life" when he writes that "In the perichoresis the very thing that divides them becomes that which binds them together. The 'circulation' of the eternal divine life becomes perfect through the fellowship and unity of the three different Persons in the eternal love."[62] This image of interpenetration without confusion is developed in more detail later on as is the concept that the Godhead is somehow always in motion, as in a dance, but a dance of begetting, proceeding and yet remaining unbegotten. John then continues with a reference to how these three persons, the Father, Son and Holy Spirit, could all be involved together in the act of baptism, a moving of the one God through the life of the believer.

As John continues the confession, he begins to describe the relationship of the three persons. The Father, who is "uncaused and unbegotten," is also the "principle cause of all things."[63] The Son, the Lord Jesus Christ, was "begotten of the Father," and the Father is also called the "emitter"[64] of the Holy Spirit. John uses a number of phrases from the Niceno-Constantinople creed, such as "light from light, true God from true God, begotten not made, consubstantial with the Father."[65] It is possible that John links back to the established creed in order to give greater acceptance to his development of the relationship of the three persons.

For John, the essential relationship between the Father and the Son is that the Father has "begotten" the Son without bringing about any change in the Father or the Son. If there were any change—for example, if the Son were brought from "nothing into being"—then His begetting would not be

---

60. In general, περιχώρησις refers to a recurrence or cyclical movement, such as in a "circle-dance." Christologically it refers to reciprocity in a relationship, and in regard to the Trinity there is a sense of the interpenetration of the three persons. See Lampe, 1077–78.

61. See O'Collins, *Tripersonal God*, 132; and Macleod, "Trinity in Scripture," 56–57.

62. Moltmann, *The Trinity and the Kingdom*, 174–75. See also Oliver, *Metaphysics, Theology, and Self*, 65–69; and Crisp, *Divinity and Humanity*, 1–34.

63. OF 1.8, p. 177.

64. The term "emitter," or προβολεύς, may come from Gregory Nazianzen, Sermon 29.2 (PG 36.76B).

65. OF 1.8, p. 177.

"outside of time and without a beginning."[66] This would mean, among other things, that before the Son came into being then the Father would not have been a Father. This would then imply that a change in status had taken place, once not a Father and then after begetting the Son, becoming a Father; and this in turn would indicate that God is not perfect because any change in his nature would indicate imperfection. This is what Arius implied when he said that there was [once] when the Son was not.[67] Not only would this strip Jesus of his deity, but it would also strip Fatherhood from God. Therefore, John had to emphasize that the Son "was not brought from nothing into being," but rather "He was always with the Father, being begotten of Him eternally and without beginning."[68] Also, the "Father and the Son begotten of Him exist together simultaneously,"[69] so that the Father has always been the Father and the Son has always been begotten as the Son. Otherwise we would be "introducing a change into the substance of the Father"[70] and that would put him on the same status as a created being in need of some other god for his existence. Therefore, the Father has always been the Father and the Son has always been the Son. Even more, the Father is always begetting the Son and the Son is always being begotten. Otherwise this would also indicate a change in their status and a limitation to the nature of God. "Neither does His unfathomable begetting have beginning or end. It is without beginning, because He is immutable."[71]

On the other hand, creation is outside of God and "was brought from nothing into being by His Will and power."[72] Also, since it is "not of the substance of God," it "does not involve any change in the nature of God."[73] Therefore, creation has a beginning point in time and it is subject to change. Jesus Christ, the Son, could never have been a created being or He, too, would have had a beginning to his existence and a change in his nature, from non-existence to existence, and therefore he could not be deity. Thus, John destroys the argument of Arius and emphasizes that Jesus, the eternal Son, has always existed with the Father. However, it is likely that John had in mind the Muslim belief that Jesus is not the Son of God and therefore not divine, rather than the waning heresy of Arius. Having lived and worked

66. Ibid., 1.8, p. 178.
67. Alexander of Alexandria, *Depositio Arii* 2, ANF 4:70.
68. OF 1.8, p. 178.
69. Ibid.
70. Ibid.
71. Ibid., 1.8, p. 179.
72. Ibid., 1.8, p. 178.
73. Ibid.

The Trinitarian Beliefs of John of Damascus 183

under the "heresy of the Ishmaelites," it seems like John would have been keen to provide a counter to their false beliefs.

In the next section, John develops the nature of divine generation and procession, especially in the relationship of the Father and the Son. He makes references to the teachings of the holy Catholic and Apostolic Church in a similar manner to his earlier use of a creedal structure in order to maintain the sense that his views flow out of the church, its creeds and the Scripture upon which both the church and the creeds were founded. This link to authority is an important step in establishing the subsequent authority of his own teaching, especially if he had his Islamic counterparts in mind. In the relationship of the Father and Son, John echoes the Cappadocians when he says that in all things the Son is "like the Father except in the Father's being unbegotten."[74] So the Father and Son exist simultaneously together "without time or change or passion,"[75] in relation to their shared nature, but they are still separate in that the Father is unbegotten while the Son is eternally begotten of the Father. John then attempts to illustrate what he acknowledges is "in a manner beyond understanding"[76] through the use of an analogy concerning fire and the light that is produced. The light and the fire exist simultaneously, and "just as the light is ever being begotten of the fire, is always in it, and is in no way separated from it, so also is the Son begotten of the Father without in any way being separated from Him, but always existing in Him."[77] The main difference, of course, is that the light has no existence outside of the fire and both are of a created and changeable order, while the Son "does have His own individual existence apart from that of the Father."[78] The important distinction that John is making is that when we understand the fullness of the distinction of the Son's begetting, we will better understand the nature of the Godhead. In order to clarify the distinction of begetting, John emphasizes the point that the Holy Spirit is not begotten of the Father, but rather "proceeds" from the Father. It may be important to note that John consistently refers to the procession of the Holy Spirit as *from* the Father *only*. The Holy Spirit may proceed "through" the Son and be found "in" the Son, but the procession of the Holy Spirit only takes place "from" the Father. In fact, John likes to refer to the three persons

---

74. Ibid., 1.8, p. 181.
75. Ibid., 1.8, p. 180.
76. Ibid.
77. Ibid.
78. Ibid.

(ὑπόστασεις) as the unbegotten (Father), the begotten (Son) and the One who proceeds (Holy Spirit).[79]

Since the terms "unbegotten" and "begotten" can also be used of created man, John explains that there is an important distinction in the use of these terms. While Adam was unbegotten, since he was created by God of unhuman substance, and Eve was also unbegotten, since she was created from a part of Adam and not through begetting, their son Seth *was* begotten since he was the product of his parents. Though all three were brought into existence through different means, they were still of the same human nature, and therefore "consubstantial," and though they all came into existence differently, they were different only "in the manner of their existence."[80] Thus, with humans, they can be consubstantial and differ only in their modes of existence. However, there is a crucial distinction between the manner of created existence and that of the Trinity. John employs the use of two Greek words to explain that distinction, ἀγενητόν and ἀγεννητόν (with the double "ν"). The former "means that which has not been created" and therefore can be applied to all three persons of the Trinity since they are "uncreated and of the same substance."[81] This use of the term cannot, however, be applied to humans since there was a time when they were created and came into existence. The first term, ἀγενητόν, also indicates that the essence of the Godhead is different from that of created beings since the former has no origin and the latter "is created, or originated."[82] In fact, the application can only be made in reference to God since all things, or effects, had their cause in God, the only uncaused Cause. On the other hand, the word ἀγεννητόν "means that which has not been begotten."[83] While this term, in reference to creatures, "does not imply any difference in essence,"[84] there is an important distinction in reference to the Father. In a technical sense, all created things were "unbegotten," but only because God first created them uniquely. Thereafter they were begotten of their same nature or essence. In regard to the Father, however, He is the same substance (οὐσία) of the Son, but "the Father alone is unbegotten in so far as He does not have His being from another person."[85] Therefore, the Father is both unoriginate and unbegotten. While the Son may also be unoriginate, without beginning and

79. Ibid., 1.8, p. 181.
80. Ibid.
81. Ibid., 1.8, p. 182.
82. Ibid., 1.8, p. 181.
83. Ibid.
84. Ibid.
85. Ibid., 1.8, p. 182.

independent of time, the Son is begotten of the substance of the Father. The problem here is that if "begotten" refers to a time when something did not exist, as with created things, how could the Son still be unoriginate with the Father while being begotten of Him, since the implication of the Father's unbegotten state is that "He does not have His being from another person."[86] The Son, however, does have his being from another person, the Father. In order to demonstrate that while the Son is begotten, He is also unoriginate, and therefore different in his essence than created things, John appeals to Scripture, to the concept of causality and to the analogy of the fire. After reminding his readers that ultimately the concept of begetting in reference to the Godhead is "beyond understanding," he also reminds them that the "terms 'paternity,' 'sonship,' and 'procession' . . . were handed down to us from Scripture."[87] He then attempts to settle the issue by an appeal to causality. In reference to created things, there is a Cause who brings them into existence, and therefore there is a change in their status from non-being to being. However, in the case of the Son there was never a time when He was not, for that would indicate a change in his being and therefore a refutation of his deity status. Thus, the Son has to be "begotten of the substance of the Father without beginning and independently of time."[88] This means that the Father does not come "before the Son either in time or in nature,"[89] but rather that the Father is "naturally the cause of the Son" in that "the Son is begotten of the Father, and not the Father of the Son."[90]

The Father causes the Son, not the other way around, much like the light from the fire is caused by the fire which is its source. The Father is the source of the Son, but unlike the fire and the light in the analogy, since the light is only a natural property of the fire and does not have a separate "hypostasis" from the fire, the Son does have a separate hypostasis (ὑπόστασις) while sharing the same substance (οὐσία) with the Father. Moreover, in this relationship the Father "does all things whatsoever through His only-begotten Son . . . as through a natural and distinctly subsistent force."[91] This description of the relationship, where each is in each since "the Son in a perfect individual substance inseparable from that of the Father"[92] alludes again to the perichoretical nature of the Father and Son in that there is con-

86. Ibid.
87. Ibid.
88. Ibid.
89. Ibid.
90. Ibid.
91. Ibid., 1.8, p. 183.
92. Ibid.

stant movement in the Father eternally begetting the Son who is eternally expressing the nature of the Father. There is, of course, a third person in this relationship, the Holy Spirit, and John now moves on to developing the one who "proceeds from the Father."[93]

Andrew Louth comments that in the third section in chapter 8, John "brings together refinements in the understanding of the procession of the Holy Spirit that have been determinative for later Orthodox theology."[94] Similar concepts, Louth continues, can be found in Athanasius and Didymos, especially in the way the Spirit "abides" in the Son, but John takes the concept further and "speaks of an eternal resting of the Spirit *in* the Son, manifest in the *oikonomia* (ὀικονομία) where the Spirit rests or abides *on* the Son. Similarly with the Spirit as the manifestation of the Son: this takes place in the *oikonomia*, but it depends on the eternal self-manifestation of the Son in the Spirit."[95] This concept of the Spirit abiding *on* the Son and the Son *in* the Spirit as the Father is *in* the Son gives us a richer description of the perichoretical relationship. The mutual indwelling of the Father and Son is extended so as to include the Holy Spirit in the same coinherence with the other hypostases. Earlier John presents the Holy Spirit as the companion of the Word, the One who makes the Word "manifest."[96] A little further on John presents the Holy Spirit as the bond between the first and second Persons: "He is the median of the unbegotten and the begotten (Father and Son) and He is joined with the Father through the Son."[97] There is a unity in the community that has no beginning and no end, just like a circle, in this "circle-dance" of the one God who is there.

In this section, John again utilizes the structure of a creed in order to legitimize the introduction of the Holy Spirit as fully God and as One who is "adored and glorified together with the Father and Son as consubstantial and co-eternal with them."[98] In regard to the Father, John has developed the idea of the hypostasis who is uncreated and unbegotten. In regard to the Son, John has explored the concept of the hypostasis who is uncreated and eternally begotten. Now he turns to the hypostasis who is uncreated and proceeds eternally *from* the Father *through* the Son. The prepositions are extremely important in all these cases, for the *filioque* controversy, which

---

93. Ibid.

94. Louth, *St. John Damascene*, 109.

95. Ibid., 109–10. See also Fortescue, *The Greek Fathers*, 225; and Bobrinskoy, *The Mystery of the Trinity*, 71.

96. OF 1.7, p. 175.

97. Ibid., 1.13, p. 200.

98. Ibid., 1.8, p. 183.

John seems to be unaware of at this time,[99] was based on the belief that the Holy Spirit proceeded *from both* the Father *and* the Son. John, on the other hand, is very careful to portray the procession of the Holy Spirit as coming *from* the Father only, who is the source, then, for both the Holy Spirit and the Son. If the Holy Spirit also proceeded from the Son, then how could there only be one source? John does seem to be aware of this problem and therefore emphasizes that while the Holy Spirit "abides" in the Son and is "communicated through the Son," His procession comes *from* the Father only.[100] Like the Son, the Holy Spirit is "distinctly subsistent and exists in His own Person" and has everything the Father and Son have "except the being unbegotten and the being begotten."[101] Thus, "whatsoever the Son has from the Father the Spirit also has, including His very being."[102] In this relationship, therefore, the only *essential* difference between the three persons is that the Father is unbegotten, the Son is eternally begotten and the Holy Spirit eternally proceeds. Although John admits that it is beyond comprehension to truly understand these differences, he does concede that they must be "one simple essence, eminently and antecedently perfect, in three Persons,"[103] without being compounded, since that would make them imperfect. The only way this "unity within a community" could exist, then, is for the three Persons to exist in one another, "uncompounded and without confusion."[104] Otherwise there would not be the eternal motion that is the still point of the turning world: The unbegotten Father eternally begetting the Son through whom the Holy Spirit is being communicated to the world; who in turn proceeds from the Father and glorifies the Son, and together, both the Son and the Holy Spirit bring glory to the Father, as the three are one and the one God is three in a unity of community that is the dance, the perichoresis, the motion that never ceases and yet is in all as each Person is in one another; and still there is only One, for, as John concludes, "God and His Word and His Spirit are really one God."[105]

---

99. Louth, *St. John Damascene*, 108.
100. OF 1.8, p. 184.
101. Ibid.
102. Ibid.
103. Ibid., 1.8, p. 185.
104. Ibid.
105. Ibid.

THE TRINITY IN HERESY OF THE ISHMAELITES

In this section, John's explanation of the Trinity in his theological masterpiece, *Orthodox Faith*, will be compared to his treatment of the Trinity in his polemical works on Islam. The main questions to be answered are, first, did his theological works develop from his apologetic works, or was it the reverse? Second, is it possible that both formats worked dialectically to express and develop each other? Third, could Islam have acted to motivate John to write his theological works as well as his apologetic treatises? In his main treatise against Islam, *Heresy of the Ishmaelites*, John addressed the Saracens' denial of the divinity of Christ and their absolute rejection of the Triune nature of God. The followers of Muhammad considered belief in a Trinity to be the greatest of all blasphemies, since in their view it associated a created being with the eternal God. They called this sin "shirk," and those who associated another with God were called "mushrikun." For example, the Qur'an states in 5:72–73 that, "They do blaspheme who say: 'Allah is Christ the son of Mary' . . . Whoever joins other gods with Allah—Allah will forbid him the Garden, and the fire will be his abode . . . They do blaspheme who say: Allah is one of three in a trinity: for there is no god except One God." Also in surah 9:31 we find that the Ishmaelites were "commanded to worship but one Allah: there is no god but he. Praise and glory to him: (far is he) from having the partners they associate (with him)." However, the Qur'an also acknowledges that Jesus Christ is known as both the "Word of God" and the "Spirit of God." In surah 4:171 we find the words: "O People of the Book! commit no excesses in your religion: nor say of Allah aught but the truth. Christ Jesus the son of Mary was (no more than) a Messenger of Allah, and His Word, which He bestowed on Mary and a Spirit proceeding from Him: so believe in Allah and His Messengers. Say not 'Trinity': desist: it will be better for you: for Allah is one God." These verses are found in portions of the Qur'an with which John seems to have been familiar,[106] and in his response John acknowledges that the Ishmaelites accepted Jesus Christ as God's Word and Spirit. He then raises a very important question: "Since you also say that Christ is Word and Spirit of God, why do you accuse us of being Associators?"[107] As John has so meticulously explained in his *Orthodox Faith*, he also argued in his treatise against the Ishmaelites that God's Word and Spirit must be inseparable from God. Moreover, if God's Word and Spirit are outside of God, as the Ishmaelites seemed to imply, then God must be without his Word and Spirit, and therefore, according to John, mu-

---

106. See the chapter on the *Heresy of the Ishmaelites*.
107. HER 69–70.

tilated or torn apart. Thus, while the Saracens accused Christians of being "associators" (*mushrikun*) because they associated Christ with God, John accused the Saracens of being "mutilators" (*koptas*) of God because they ripped God's Spirit and Word away from him. This argument became one of the most popular ones developed by John and was used for centuries as Christians confronted Muslims in the defense of the Trinity. Perhaps the reason for the success of John's argument is that it is based on his foundational theological explanations of the nature and roles of the three persons of the Trinity in his *Orthodox Faith*. This raises a very important question. Could John have written his *Orthodox Faith* as a defense of the faith in light of the hegemony of Islam? Is it possible that the development of John's apologetic approach was based on his understanding of orthodox theology, and that his doctrinal explanation developed as a response to the misunderstandings of the belief systems surrounding John, like Islam? Louth reminds us that, "Christological doctrine did not develop on its own, but as a response to a series of misunderstandings of what faith in Christ entailed."[108] If this occurred in relation to christological misunderstandings, surely it would have been present in regard to Trinitarian ones. This certainly seems to be the case when we examine John's polemical writings.

In *Orthodox Faith*, John takes great care to show that it was necessary that the Word had always existed in the Godhead: "For there never was a time when God the Word was not."[109] Also, unlike human speech, which dissipates in the air, the Word of God is always subsistent, "always existing in Him."[110] John makes it clear that the Word could not be "outside of 'god,'" but since the Word is always begotten of the Father, he "must be always existing, living, perfect, distinctly subsistent, and having all things that His Begetter has."[111] Thus, the argument found in John's *Heresy* seems to be reflected in *Orthodox Faith*, and the theological underpinning of the argument in *Heresy* is more developed in *Orthodox Faith*. They work in tandem with each other. We also see this same argument developed in John's *Disputation between a Christian and a Saracen*.

---

108. See Louth, *St. John Damascene*, 155–56.
109. OF 1.6, p. 174.
110. Ibid.
111. Ibid.

THE TRINITY IN DISPUTATION BETWEEN A CHRISTIAN AND A SARACEN

In his treatise, the *Disputation between a Christian and a Saracen*, John also raises the issue of Jesus being the Word and Spirit of God: "I will ask you this, 'Before God created the Spirit and the Word did he have neither Spirit nor Word?'"[112] This is the same issue he raised in *Heresy* and in *Orthodox Faith*, explaining that "God is not without a Word," and "there never was a time when God the Word was not."[113] A little further in his *Disputation*, when John is explaining the two natures of Christ, he writes that "the preeternal Word of God is one ... for indeed, a fourth person has not been added to the Trinity."[114] This reference to a "fourth person of the Trinity" is also mentioned in *Orthodox Faith*, where John writes, "His two natures belong to the one Person and the one subsistence of the Word of God ... Thus, I do not add a fourth person to the Trinity—God Forbid!"[115] Hence, in both John's *Orthodox Faith* and his *Disputation*, reference to the Word as a "fourth person" is vehemently denied.

These close comparisons found in different works by John provide strong evidence for the inter-developmental production of these ideas. We may say that one source, perhaps his theological writings, provided the foundation for his apologetic works, or perhaps his apologetic works were later refined and developed in his theological works, or perhaps they interacted with each other as different expressions of the same ideas. It is also feasible to infer that the theological controversies that inspired John to pen his polemical treatises against Islam could also have served as a catalyst for his polemical works on such similar subjects as the Jacobite faction or Manichaeism. Even though orthodox Christians had remonstrated for centuries before John concerning what they considered to be errors in the belief systems of Jacobites and Manicheans, the greater freedom and growth these heresies received under Islamic rule may have prompted John to not only re-engage with them polemically, but to also use them as proxy arguments against Islam. Thus, the common background to these works may have been the growth of Islam as it began to dominate both John's religious and political worlds.

For example, in his criticism of the Byzantine Church, Kenneth Scott Latourette suggested that one of the characteristics of the time of John of

---

112. DIS 5.18–20.
113. OF 1.6, p. 174.
114. DIS 8.10–12.
115. OF 3.8, p. 285.

Damascus was "the growing sterility in theological thought."[116] According to some scholars, even John seemed to have little to add to theological thought other than to summarize the orthodox views of his predecessors. As for the cause of this sterility, Latourette suggests that it may have been a result of the Byzantine realm's defensive posture against encroaching invaders from the Persian Empire and subsequently from the Arab world. In John's works, we can certainly trace these defensive themes in his specific writings against Islam. Is it possible that his treatises against the iconoclasts, Manichaeans, Monophysites, and Nestorians, as well as his popular treatise on doctrine, the *Fountain of Knowledge*, were also written in response to the growth of Islamic theology and hegemony? If this is the case, then we should notice the same themes and arguments in both his treatises against Islam as well as his writings against the pervading Christian heresies of his day. We should also find these common elements addressed in his doctrinal writings, such as his *Orthodox Faith*, since his theology should form the foundation of his apologetics. If a pattern is present linking these works together, then it is feasible to postulate that his common desire was to instruct Christians in the fundamentals of the Christian faith in order to defend their beliefs against their detractors and refute error. The Byzantines were too far away, the Manichaeans were too weak, and the christological heresies were no more than a nuisance. The real challenger was the continuing growth and dominance of Islam. Could this situation have met his view on every horizon and prompted his words in all his apologetic writings? Let us examine some of these arguments in order to determine the extent to which this view can be supported.

ICONOCLASM

Leo III, the Byzantine emperor, issued an edict in 726 banning the veneration of Christian icons in places of worship.[117] John responded strongly against Leo's edict in his three treatises *On the Divine Images*.[118] John argued that the incarnation of Christ provided a visible form of worship of the invisible God. Therefore, the veneration of icons, which focused a worshiper's adoration on the person of Christ, should be considered a viable form of worship in the church.[119] It is possible, however, that the destruction of im-

---

116. Latourette, *A History of Christianity*, 313.
117. Deanesly, *The History of the Medieval Church*, 75–76.
118. DIV (also Louth, *St. John Damascene*, xv).
119. DIV 12; 1.4, 22; 1.8, 24; for example, John states, "I do not venerate matter, I venerate the fashioner of matter, who became matter for my sake and accepted to dwell

ages in Palestine was the prior underlying source of John's motivation for writing his treatises against Byzantine iconoclasm. During that time, some Byzantines believed they had lost God's favor due to rampant idolatry and blamed themselves for the Islamic takeover. Thus, in the Byzantine Empire, iconoclasm became one of the measures enacted to restore the favor of God and prevent further encroachment by the Muslims. In Palestine, however, it may have been an edict enacted by Yazid II[120] in 721 that had a greater initial effect on John of Damascus. The edict of Yazid II called for the purging of any image in churches in the region:

> Every kind of pictorial representation, be it on boards or in wall-mosaics or on holy vessels or altar-cloths, or anything else of the sort that is found in all Christian churches, should be obliterated and entirely destroyed; not only these, but also all the effigies that are set up as decoration in the marketplaces of cities.[121]

Evidence for this purge of images in Muslim-dominated lands has recently been found in a number of eighth-century churches in the area. The strange thing, however, is that often only a portion of the mosaics were damaged. Robert Schick, an archaeologist studying the phenomenon, believes that the evidence demonstrates that while the call for the destruction of images in the churches was "probably inspired by Muslim laws prohibiting the depiction of any living being," the gentle re-arrangement of many of the mosaic tiles seems to suggest that it was the Christians themselves who "desecrated" the images.[122] Unlike the iconoclasts in Byzantium, who only destroyed sacred images, the Palestinian "re-arrangers" defaced many images of animals and ordinary people, which would suggest their attention to Muslim objections. Thus, John of Damascus could have been reacting to Yazid II's edict of 721 calling for the destruction of icons and images. Even the cross was desecrated. The Palestinian mosaics may have had only gentle defacement, but the reason for the action was directly due to the Muslims, not Leo III.

Louth, however, maintains that John's treatises are specifically against the Byzantine form of iconoclasm. Even though John lived his whole life within a Muslim context, he still identified himself as a Byzantine priest, loyal to the emperor in his civil duties (though adamantly opposed to the

---

in matter and through matter worked my salvation," 1.16, 29.

120. Yazid II was the ninth Umayyad caliph, serving from 720 to 724.
121. Schick, "The Image Destroyers," 5.
122. Ibid., 2.

emperor's usurpation of ecclesiastical matters).[123] It is true that John's main criticism seemed to be concentrated on the Byzantine form, which attacked sacred images only and not mere images of living beings. However, he was certainly aware of the type of iconoclasm taking place under the pressure of the Muslims. John's reaction could still have been initiated by the destruction he saw around him in his own country as a result of Muslim demands and their call for the destruction of icons as well as the removal of the cross.[124] Louth also maintains that John's writings were probably not distributed in the Byzantine Empire and therefore not well known in Byzantium before his death.[125] However, the anathema at Hieria in AD 754 seems to counter this view and indicates that his arguments were indeed well known and caused enough of a stir that he received a four-fold anathema:

> To Mansur of evil name, Saracen at heart, Anathema!
>
> To Mansur, the image-worshipper and writer of falsehoods, Anathema!
>
> To Mansur, who denied Christ and betrayed his sovereign, Anathema!
>
> To Mansur, the teacher of impious doctrine and the perverter of Holy Scripture, Anathema![126]

Thus, John may have targeted his writing against the Byzantine Empire, but he was probably also reacting to the local pressure from the Islamic form of iconoclasm.

MANICHAEISM

What about heretical beliefs that seemed to flourish again due to the relative freedom they enjoyed under the new regime? The practice of Manichaeism, for example, was largely dead in the Byzantine empire of the eighth century. However, the tolerance for "people of the book" in the Umayyad Empire may have encouraged a resurgence of Manichaeism in the region.[127] The danger of dualism, a good deity versus an evil deity, which was a core belief of the Manichaeans, was seen as a threat by Byzantine Christians. John of

---

123. Louth, *St. John Damascene*, 205.
124. DIV, 12. In fact, John expresses this concern in Her, 78–79.
125. Louth, *St. John Damascene*, 197.
126. Mansi, xiii, 356, in Fortescue, *The Greek Fathers*, 231.
127. Louth, *St. John Damascene*, 64. See also Chase, *St. John of Damascus: Writings*, xix; Le Coz, *Jean Damascene*, 136; and Zaman, *Religion and Politics*, 65–66.

Damascus may have engaged himself with the Manichaeans due to these concerns. In all, John wrote two works against the Manichaeans: the short section in his *Heresies* and a treatise titled *Dialogus contra Manichaeus* (a Dialogue against the Manichees),[128] as well as four chapters in his *Orthodox Faith*.[129] Islam, therefore, plays a secondary role in creating an atmosphere suitable for the re-kindling of Manichaean ideas and practices, which John apparently thought were dangerous enough to write against. Thus, the argument concerning the Trinity against the Manichaeans may have actually been aimed at Islam. Louth writes, "One wonders if the real intellectual context with which John is engaging here is not so much Manichee objections to Christianity, as Muslim objections."[130] For example, as John seeks to ridicule the Manichee position on the principle of beginnings, the Manichee counters him with a question regarding the Trinity: "You say that there are three hypostases, and how can you say that they must begin from a Monad?"[131] John goes on for several pages exploring how the Son and Spirit derive from the Father and yet remain one. This could have been a way for John to teach Christians how they could defend the Trinity against the objections of Islam without confronting Islam directly. This would especially be necessary if direct criticism of Islamic beliefs was becoming dangerous.

Louth also gives several reasons why the dialogue against the Manichees could have focused more on Islam. First, he says that the objections to the Trinity were similar and would have fit well with the objections of Islam. In the same way, Louth says that issues discussed by John "were also of interest to his contemporary Muslims, especially the topic of providence and creaturely free will, which was hotly disputed in Muslim circles under the Umayyads."[132] The theological problems raised fit well within a Muslim context. In fact, Louth conjectures that, "Given that these are issues that engaged his Muslim contemporaries, and the fact that John at one point seeks to respond to problems raised by the Christian doctrine of the Trinity, one might conjecture that this dialogue was indeed a rhetorical exercise, composed when John was in contact with Muslims, with his ears full of their debates and their taunts against Christianity."[133] This dialogue may have also been a way to present arguments against Islam "under cover" without rais-

---

128. Kotter IV, 351–98.

129. See OF 92–95, pp. 383–89.

130. Louth, *St. John Damascene*, 66. See also Thomas, *Syrian Christians under Islam*, 37.

131. *Manichaean* 4.1–2. Quoted in Louth, *St. John Damascene*, 66.

132. Louth, *St. John Damascene*, 70.

133. Ibid., 71.

ing undue attention to the writer. Louth writes, "if this work does belong to John's time in Damascus, we might see in it a safe way for John to think through arguments that were hotly contentious among Muslim thinkers, as well as work out a defense against Muslim objections to Christianity in a way that would not attract unwelcome attention."[134] Another way to present arguments against Islam without direct exposure may have been through proxy apologetic critiques of popular Christian heresies that revealed Islamic misunderstandings of core Christian doctrine.

MONOPHYSITISM AND NESTORIANISM

Andrew Louth has reminded us that Christology developed through correcting misunderstandings in the various views of Christ.[135] As chapter one of this book has indicated, this was also true of the development of the doctrine of the Trinity. Inaccurate and inadequate views of how the one God related to the three persons of the Trinity forced Christian theologians to develop more precise definitions and more logical explanations. The creeds served to crystallize these benchmarks of the faith, but continual outbreaks of heretical views forced those in the orthodox position to re-contextualize the new threats and re-assert orthodox beliefs, sometimes having to come up with new definitions or more precise interpretations. In the time of John, the resurgence of christological and Trinitarian heresies likely motivated John to compose his theological work (*OF*) as well as his apologetical treatises. Some of these were direct defenses of orthodox faith against Christian heresies, but even then it was often against the backdrop of Islamic hegemony.

One of those heresies was monophysitism,[136] or the belief of those who denied there was a distinction in the two natures of Christ. This view existed before John's time and was still prevalent in Arabia and the fringe regions of the Byzantine Empire, providing a constant theological threat to Chalcedonian Christianity. Monophysites taught that Christ essentially had one composite nature (the human nature was absorbed by the divine nature). This was sometimes thought to create a new third nature, or *tertium quid*.[137] The

---

134. Ibid.

135. Louth, *St. John Damascene*, 155–56. "Christological doctrine did not develop on its own, but as a response to a series of misunderstandings of what faith in Christ entailed."

136. John wrote three treatises against the monophysites: *Against the Jacobites, Letter on the Thrice-Holy Hymn*, and *On the Composite nature against the Acephali*.

137. House, *Charts of Christian Theology And Doctrine*, 54.

monophysites argued that it was absurd to distinguish between nature and hypostasis because then there would be the possibility of "nature without any concrete reality" or "essence without a person."[138] However, as John explained, in the incarnation it is possible to have nature, or essence, distinct from the person, or hypostasis because, though both are necessary, there is a distinction between the kind of thing that something is and the thing itself.[139] In other words, Jesus Christ was not a composite nature, but a composition of two natures joined hypostatically in one person. Thus, the incarnate Jesus is wholly divine in his divinity and wholly human in his humanity, yet still one person in reference to the Godhead. Since Muslims did not believe in the incarnation of Christ, John's arguments against the Monophysites could have provided Christians with another way to understand the proper beliefs concerning Christ's incarnation. This would have allowed Christians to better refute the Islamic denial of the incarnation itself.

On the opposite side of the spectrum was Nestorianism.[140] The Nestorians, also known as the "Church of the East,"[141] taught that Jesus Christ had two natures as well as two persons. John agreed with the Nestorians in their view of Christ's immutability (in reference to his divine nature). However, in their over-emphasis of this single attribute, they rejected the one hypostasis of Christ by separating his two natures in such a way that they ended up advocating two separate persons, or hypostases as well, one divine and one human. In John's *De Haeresibus*, he writes that

> The Nestorians hold that God the Word exists by Himself and separately, and that His humanity exists by itself. And the more humble of the Lord's actions during His sojourn among us they attribute to His humanity alone, whereas the more noble and those befitting the divinity they ascribe to God the Word alone. But they do not attribute the both to the same Person.[142]

Louth writes that John "argues that their failure to distinguish properly between hypostasis and nature renders their position open to all sorts of

---

138. Jacobitas 11.1–3. Εἰ γὰρ μὴ ἔστι φύσις ἀνυπόστατος, οὔτε μὴν οὐσία ἀπρόσωπος οὐδ' αὖ πάλιν ἀνούσιος ὑπόστασίς τε καὶ πρόσωπον οὐ γάρ ἐστιν, ἀλλ' οὐ ταὐτὸν οὐσία τε καὶ ὑπόστασις οὐδὲ φύσις καὶ πρόσωπον.

139. Louth, *St. John Damascene*, 159. See also Letham, *Holy Trinity*, 279.

140. John wrote two works against the Nestorians (or more accurately, one based on another): *Against the Nestorians* is a rendition of a dialogue, *On the Faith, Against the Nestorians*. See Louth, *St. John Damascene*, 173.

141. Baum and Winkler, *The Church of the East*, 7.

142. John of Damascus, *Heresy 81*, "The Nestorians," found in Chase, *Saint John of Damascus*, 138.

error."[143] John taught that the orthodox Chalcedonian view, which was his position, put forward a middle way between the Nestorians and the Monophysites. Instead of Christ having two natures and two hypostases, as the Nestorians believed, or a composite nature, which the Jacobites favored, the orthodox Chalcedonian formula taught that Christ had two distinct natures in one person, or hypostasis. Again, a proper understanding of the interaction between Christ's two natures and his one hypostasis would help Christian apologists better defend their beliefs in the face of Muslim challenges.

The ultimate concern for John in confronting these heresies was to inform Christians about the false views so that they would not be misled. He addressed these two heresies in his theological work (OF) as well as his polemical works. Whether he was speaking theologically or apologetically, his message to Christians was the same: know what you believe, be able to defend your beliefs, and be ready to confront and refute error. This admonition was true whether it was meant in response to iconoclastic errors, christological heresies or challenges from Islam. John's apologetics flowed out of his theology and he developed his theology in order to lay a foundation for his apologetics. Therefore, since Islam was involved through opening up the theological playing field for previously subdued christological heresies, as well as initiating iconoclastic events in Syria, and also challenging the core doctrines of Christianity, most, if not all, of John's writings reflected some type of influence from the religion that was increasingly dominating his world.

CONCLUSION

The doctrine of the Trinity is one of the uncompromising beliefs of Christianity. In John's treatment of this subject in his *Orthodox Faith*, he gleaned from the Church Fathers who had preceded him in order to produce a standard explanation of the Trinity for those who would follow. The first half of this chapter, therefore, summarizes John's explanation of the Trinity and analyzes key concepts of this crucial doctrine. It is important to understand John's theological understanding of this doctrine so that his treatment of the Trinity in his apologetic works can be compared.

In the latter half of this chapter, John's view of the Trinity, as represented in his theological work *Orthodox Faith*, was compared to his defense of the Trinity against Islam in the *Heresy of the Ishmaelites* and the *Disputation between a Christian and a Saracen*. Not only were common themes

---

143. Louth, *St. John Damascene*, 173. See also Pelikan, *The Spirit of Eastern Christendom*, 82.

detailed, but it was shown that similar wording was also employed. These same themes were also developed in John's polemical writings against non-Muslim beliefs such as Manichaeism, which was outside of Christianity, as well as the Monophysites and the Nestorians, who were considered to hold to christological heresies within Christianity. These "proxy arguments" may have enabled John to address the Muslim challenges while remaining under the cover of critiquing a local heresy or a general religious dispute. In addition, the overlapping themes suggest that John of Damascus' apologetic interaction with Islamic theology, as well as non-Muslim heretical views, molded the way he presented the orthodox doctrine of the Trinity, as is found in his *Orthodox Faith*. Throughout this process, both aspects of his work seem to have developed in response to the growth of Islamic theology and hegemony. To counter this expansion, John's apologetic model was developed in order to support his views that Christianity was the true faith and, therefore, superior to Islam. Later, John's successors, especially Theodore Abu Qurrah, carried his work a step farther by upgrading John's apologetic approach so that orthodox Christian theology, which had been standardized by John, could deal more specifically with the developing Islamic theology. It is now time to examine John's apologetic approach as well as the way his successors adopted and adapted this approach for their own apologetic ends.

10

The Development of John's Apologetic Approach

WHAT WAS THE REASON FOR WRITING AGAINST ISLAM?

At the end of the seventh century, as noted in chapter 3, a number of Christians, whether orthodox or heterodox, viewed the Muslim conquests of that century as a punishment for their sins and their lack of following Christ.[1] In the beginning, the Jews, Nestorians and Jacobites seemed to fare better under Saracen rule than under Byzantine rule, which favored the Melkites, but in time they realized that the new regime was becoming increasingly hostile and demanding to any form of belief system other than its own.[2] During the first centuries of Islamic rule, more and more Christians saw that the only opportunity for advancement in society was in converting to Islam. John recognized the need to stem this flow of Christians converting to Islam and constructed simple dialogues to illustrate how Christians could give reasonable responses to the theological issues raised by the Saracens. One of the difficulties in developing an adequate apologetic approach with Islam, however, was that there were so many irreducible differences between the two belief systems.[3] This problem was exacerbated in the time of

---

1. Kaegi, "Initial Byzantine Reactions to the Arab Conquest," 139–49. See also Saadi, "Nascent Islam," 219.

2. Lamoreaux, "Early Eastern Christian Responses to Islam," 3–31.

3. Daniel, *Islam and the West*, 335–36. Daniel writes that in regard to Christianity

John of Damascus because Christians rejected the teachings of the Saracens without really knowing what they were rejecting, and the Saracens often had misunderstandings of the Christian doctrine that they had rejected. Even after Christians had lived two centuries under Islamic rule, John Meyendorff writes that a scholar named Nicetas Byzantinos, a ninth-century resident of Constantinople and a follower of Photius, did not really seem to understand the religion of the Muslims, even though he had several translations of the Qur'an. Meyendorff concludes that, like many Byzantines of the time, his polemics "illustrate the permanent misunderstanding between the two cultures and the two religious mentalities."[4] How could John of Damascus, then, as a writer and an apologist in the first century of this controversy, develop a way so that Christians could understand the beliefs of their opponents, stand strong in the face of growing controversy, and always be prepared to give an answer?

The Need for Apologetics in the Time of John

During the first centuries of Islam, there was a difference in approach between Christians who lived within the Islamic world and those who lived outside. Outsiders were often quite polemical and caustic.[5] Within the Islamic world, however, more diplomacy and dialogue was carried out. This was true of John of Damascus as well, especially since he worked for the Caliph himself as the chief financial administrator. Although John considered Islam a heresy, Nazir-Ali concedes that he was concerned about being fair in his treatment of their scripture and theological positions.[6] John knew the views of the Saracen scriptures and used logic to argue that if Christ is the Word and Spirit of God then either they are all one God or else *shirk*[7] is committed since they would otherwise be associating partners with God. John's response also demonstrates that he is aware of how the Saracens related the attributes to the divine essence. Through his understanding, John was able to acknowledge commonality of beliefs, especially in the oneness of God. This was an important foundation from which dialogue could then

---

and Islam, "There are irreducible differences between non-negotiable doctrines... The Christian creeds and the Qur'an are simply incompatible and there is no possibility of reconciling the content of the two faiths, each of which is exclusive, as long as they retain their identities."

4. Meyendorff, "Byzantine Views of Islam," 122.

5 Ibid., 115–32.

6. Nazir-Ali, *Conviction and Conflict*, 72.

7. Shirk is considered the greatest "sin" in Islam and refers to associating others with God, or in this case, equating Jesus with God.

proceed. This approach was also practiced by John's successors. For example, Theodore Abu Qurrah (d. 820), the Bishop of Harran, explained the Trinity by appealing to the common source for all scripture revealed to the apostles and prophets, which he referred to as the "preserved tablet."[8] He also used arguments based on his knowledge of the Qur'an to argue for Christianity. Like John, Abu Qurrah utilized touchstone points with Islam in order to promote his specific Christian conclusions from a common understanding.[9] Timothy I, an eighth-century Nestorian Patriarch whose theological dialogue with the Caliph has survived,[10] showed courtesy to the Muslim leader, but there is no hint of compromise in what he says. Nazir-Ali says that "the dialogues are full, frank and fair."[11] Besides indicating that the Islamic government was still open to respectful theological discussion at this time, the dialogue shows that Timothy was aware of the Christology of the Qur'an and used this knowledge in his argument. These Christian leaders were concerned with the number of Christian believers converting to Islam, but they still maintained diplomacy and decorum in their interaction with the dominant Muslims and they favored dialogue as the mode for exchanging ideas. As we shall see, John of Damascus may have been the first one to develop a form of dialogical apologetics against Islam, and he not only "set the tone for medieval perceptions of Islam," but his views "continued to be a major factor until the end of the Renaissance."[12]

John's Influence

Alexander Golitzin notes that a number of scholars do not think that John of Damascus was very creative in his thinking or influential in his writing. His position as the last of the church fathers is often defined as "occupying the place of a relatively unoriginal—if highly intelligent—compiler of the prior tradition and thus also as a stepping stone to the newly creative age of [western] medieval scholasticism."[13] Yet, there were a number of areas where John was quite influential in the Byzantine world, which always remained

---

8. Nazir-Ali, *Conviction and Conflict*, 72.

9. See Griffith, "Muslims And Church Councils"; and Griffith, "John of Damascus and the Church In Syria In The Umayyad Era."

10. Hoyland, *Seeing Islam*, 472–75. See also Griffith, *Shadow*, 45–48.

11. Nazir-Ali, *Conviction and Conflict*, 73.

12. Lumbard, *Islam, Fundamentalism, and the Betrayal of Tradition*, 146.

13. Carey, *Biographical Dictionary of Christian Theologians*, 283. See also McGiffert, *A History of Christian Thought*, 308; and Meyendorff, *Byzantine Theology*, 4–5. Chase reminds us that John's Orthodox Faith "is not a mere compilation; it is a new synthesis." See Chase, *St. John of Damascus*, xxvi.

his "heartland," as well as the Islamic society, which became his "homeland." First of all, John influenced theology for centuries in the Eastern Orthodox tradition. His theological masterpiece, the *Orthodox Faith*, summarized the previous six centuries of orthodox beliefs and organized these views in the first *summa theologica*, which apparently had an influence on Thomas Aquinas' version centuries later.[14] His theological prowess is still respected in the Orthodox Church today and his theological clarification continues to bring edification and elucidation to many students and worshippers. Secondly, John greatly influenced the iconoclastic revolution which began in the early decades of the eighth century. His three treatises called *On the Divine Images*, in which he emphasized that the incarnation of Christ provided the model of using icons to aid in worship, reached extensively into the territory of the Byzantine Empire and led to a strong reaction against the iconoclastic theology, especially among the monks. He was anathemized for his position by a council in 754, but was finally vindicated by the 7th Ecumenical Council at Nicaea in 787 after iconoclastic influence was overturned. His third main area of influence was in the music and worship world, where his hymnody has still left its mark on the Orthodox Church. Even today he is considered one of the church's great hymnologists. While many of his works are sung in the Eastern tradition, some of his resurrection hymns are still popular during Easter throughout the Catholic and Protestant world. In regard to the developing Islamic world, John of Damascus is perhaps best known for his defense of Christianity against Islam.[15] Not only did his treatises on the *Heresy of the Ishmaelites* and the *Disputation between a Saracen and a Christian* help Christians prepare for the controversies they would encounter, but John was able to provide an apologetic model for dealing with Islam that was both emulated and further developed for at least the following three centuries. It is to his apologetic approach that we will now turn.

THREE ASPECTS OF JOHN'S APOLOGETIC APPROACH

David Chidester lists three aspects of John's apologetic approach. First of all, John viewed Islam as a Christian heresy. It is perhaps noteworthy that Christians did not consider Islam at that time to be distinct enough in its practices and beliefs to be considered a distinct religion. In fact, it would be over 100 years before a Christian writer first acknowledges Islam as a

---

14. Sahas, *John of Damascus on Islam*, 53. See also Ierodiakonou, *Byzantine Philosophy*, 67; and Carey, *Biographical Dictionary of Christian Theologians*, 283.

15. Hoyland, *Seeing Islam*, 488.

separate religion.[16] Due to John's perspective on the religion of the Ishmaelites as a heresy, he attacked it as an internal Christian problem. Secondly, John accuses the Saracens of reviving pagan idolatry centered on the worship of the goddess Aphrodite, whose image John believed was carved into the rock housed in the ka'ba. Thirdly, John attacked the prophet and accused Muhammad of creating a heresy in order to satisfy his own sexual desires. In regard to Muhammad, these attacks would escalate in the centuries to follow.[17]

While Chidester's list is helpful, he is unconvincing in his claim that John accused the Saracens of reviving paganism, especially in the form of worshiping Aphrodite.[18] Also, although John's treatise at one point deals with Muhammad's claim of special revelation to cover his lasciviousness, evidential and theological considerations have a much greater importance for John. Instead, John's apologetic approach can be categorized along the following three lines. First John states what the Ishmaelites believe. He then counters those beliefs with Christian Scripture and doctrine guided by reason. Finally, he refutes the Muslim beliefs and argues that they are inferior and irrational in comparison to Christian doctrine. In all these arguments John is either trying to show the superiority of Christianity or what he refers to as the "foolishness" of the religion of Muhammad, more for the sake of boosting belief in Christianity in the eyes of his Christian readers rather than offering detailed arguments against the new "heresy," though he is interested in countering what he sees as their false beliefs.

John's First Step: Understand (What Does John Know about Islam?)

Robert Hoyland contends that John is well informed about the "Islam" of his day, and comments on John's arguments in *Heresy of the Ishmaelites*:

> This composition exerted great influence upon the language, tone and content of a subsequent Byzantine polemic against

16. Chidester, *Christianity: A Global History*, 175. Chidester claims that before his death in 859 Eulogius in Spain discounted the prophet of Islam as a "demoniac full of lies" and "attacked the Islamic doctrine of God as a Christian heresy, like Arianism." In addition to calling Islam a Christian heresy, Chidester claims that Eulogius was the "first Christian to recognize Islam as a separate religion." In this context Eulogius called Islam a "manifestation of the supernatural forces of the world" and attributed its origin to the devil. He also viewed Muhammad as the Antichrist, something that John only reserved for the heresy itself.

17. Chidester, *Christianity: A Global History*, 173–74.

18. John was referring to pre-Islamic practices: see HER 7–10.

Islam. The subjects of Christology, Muhammad's prophethood and scripture, worship of the cross and Muslim licentiousness, as evidenced by the story of Zayd and the description of paradise were all to feature time and time again and to be presented in the same hostile fashion. But though unsympathetic, the author is well informed.[19]

Living and working among the Saracens as a respected civil servant would have given John privileged access to the leaders in the government as well as opportunities to engage the theologians in dialogue. It has already been mentioned that John was probably at least bilingual in Greek and Arabic, and it is almost certain that he would have used Syriac in his community and church.[20] Therefore, as an administrator and later as a theologian, John would have had first-hand knowledge of any written documents, such as the Qur'an, or major oral accounts of Muhammad, such as sira material (since Ibn Ishaq would have been collecting and writing his biography around the end of John's life), as well as some narratives that would later be written down in the hadith. Thus, the first step in his apologetic approach was to gather and learn as much as possible about the beliefs and traditions of the group that he is assessing.

From the *Heresy of the Ishmaelites*, we can learn a number of things that John knew about the developing religion. First of all, the Ishmaelites worshiped one God and claimed to be within the traditions of religions which looked back to Abraham. They believed that Muhammad was a prophet in the same tradition as Abraham, Moses and Jesus, and that he was chosen to reveal the final revelation from God. John is aware that this revelation supposedly came to Muhammad while he was asleep and without witnesses. Apparently John was familiar with written material since he refers to the "writings" (γραφή), and since they were most likely only in Arabic, he must have had a fairly good grasp of Arabic, because his references to the writings are very similar to the Qur'an as we have it today. While silence does not imply ignorance, it is significant to note that John only mentions material from Surahs 2–5, and perhaps Surahs 112 and 19. These are mostly said to be later Medinan Surahs and tend to deal with administrative, theological and legal matters. They do contain some narrative information about Mary, the mother of Jesus, as well as about Jesus himself. John understood that the Ishmaelites believed that Christ was created in the womb by God and born to a virgin, but he also recognized that they only believed Jesus to be a creature and servant to God and not divine himself. He is aware of the verse that

---

19. Hoyland, *Seeing Islam*, 488.
20. Lamoreaux, "Early Eastern Christian Responses to Islam," 7.

states that Jesus was not crucified, but rather he was taken to heaven where God asked Jesus whether he had ever said to the people that he was the "Son of God and God" (Q. 5:116–17). Of course, Jesus is said to deny ever saying such a thing since the Ishmaelites did not believe that Jesus was God.

John's strongest critique focuses on the passage of Islamic writing that deals with Jesus Christ as God's Word and Spirit (Q. 4:169, 171). The Ishmaelites were adamant that Jesus could not be God. This understanding may reflect the years of John's witness to his Saracen employers and their constant rejection of his beliefs.[21] For these points of departure from the orthodox view of Christianity, John considers this new belief system to be a heresy. He also accuses the Saracens of idolatry because of what he has heard in regard to the ka'ba and the stone that they kiss and venerate. He links this practice to the pre-Islamic worship of Aphrodite, and even had heard that the stone still bore the head of this goddess carved into its surface. John then makes a peculiar statement that may have significant ramifications. He mentions that Muhammad "composed many absurd stories and gave a title to each one."[22] John mentions four of these titles, the book on *The Woman*, the book of *The Table*, the book of *The Heifer*, and one that is not in the Qur'an, the book of *The Camel of God*. If they were still individual books, and not collected into one book known as the "Qur'an," then it is possible that the canonization process had not taken place and therefore the Qur'an was not yet finalized. At the least, this verifies that John was aware of scriptures of some sort and that they were in a written form. From the book on *The Woman* John recounts that there is legal provision for a man to take up to four wives and up to a thousand concubines. He is also aware of some of the relatively straightforward divorce and marriage procedures which would contrast greatly with Christian practices. He also recounts in detail the story of Muhammad falling in love with his adopted son's wife and then urging his adopted son, Zayd, to divorce his wife so that Muhammad could marry her, justifying his actions because Allah had commanded it.[23]

The next part of the *Heresy* is very interesting because the story of the *Camel of God* is not in the present Qur'an, except for a few references. This indicates that either John had access to faulty, incomplete documents, or that it was subsequently removed from the final Qur'an. After this narrative

---

21. Louth, *St. John Damascene*, 71. Louth states, "Given that these are issues that engaged his Muslim contemporaries, and the fact that John at one point seeks to respond to problems raised by the Christian doctrine of the Trinity, one might conjecture that this dialogue was indeed a rhetorical exercise, composed when John was in contact with Muslims, with his ears full of their debates and their taunts against Christianity."

22. HER 95–96.

23. HER 96–113.

account John seems to tire of the treatise and quickly mentions two other books and some practices of the Ishmaelites. In regard to the book on *The Table*, it is curious that John only mentions Christ asking for an incorruptible table from God and then receiving it. Could it be that in regard to this surah he was only familiar with the verse referring to the title of the book and the preceding verses referring to Jesus' dialogue in heaven (Q. 5:114–15, 116–19), for there are a number of other important issues in this long surah? He is also dismissive in regard to the book of *The Heifer* and merely says that it is full of "sayings worthy only of laughter"[24] and passes over it. He concludes with a list of practices that Muhammad apparently ordered his followers to do or not to do: circumcision for men and women, regulations on what to eat or not to eat, refraining from keeping the Sabbath and from being baptized, and forbidding the drinking of wine.[25] This is not a very extensive list, but it at least indicates that practices that were not part of Christianity were probably already widespread. These would have further distinguished the religion of the Ishmaelites as a heresy in the eyes of John and his readers. Taken altogether, John reveals that quite a bit was known about this new heresy, and, by his own example, he encourages his readers to understand enough about the beliefs of the Ishmaelites so that they will be able to counter them with logical refutations, as well as biblical ones.

John's Second Step: Defend (What is "Heretical"?)

The second step in John's apologetic approach is to counter, guided by reason, what he sees as erroneous beliefs with reference to Christian Scripture and doctrine. Since he is mainly writing to Christians in order to help them understand what he considers to be the heretical nature of this new belief system and to keep them from converting, John is selective in his choice of practices to critique and seeks to show what he considers to be contradictions and inconsistencies in order to bolster the truth of Christianity. It is a commendation to John that his arguments were widely disseminated through the next three centuries. John may have also believed that the only way to fully overcome the Ishmaelite beliefs was to put the Christian house in order, and therefore it was very important to deal strongly with the "errors" with which they were confronted.[26] In the *Heresy of the Ishmaelites*,

---

24. HER 152–53.
25. HER 153–56.
26. See Haldon, *Byzantium in the Seventh Century*, 354. This may also have been the reason that John wrote his *Orthodox Faith* in the first place—to give Christians the theological understanding they needed in order to combat what John believed to be the

The Development of John's Apologetic Approach   207

John first deals with the origin of the "heresy" and states that it is a forerunner of the Antichrist, developed by a false prophet named "Mamed," who misunderstood the truth of the Old and New Testaments and instead led his people astray with "heretical pronouncements . . . worthy of laughter."[27] His appeal to biblical themes such as the "Antichrist" and "false prophets" allows John to make comparisons between the teachings of Muhammad and the Bible. It also allows him to raise the status of the Bible in contrast to the writings of the Ishmaelites. In addition, the reference to the Antichrist may have alerted the Christians of his time to the dangers of these new beliefs, since there seemed to be a heightened interest in the end times, and apocalyptic teaching was widespread.[28] In this context, it was apparently very important for John to label Muhammad a false prophet so that John could identify Muhammad as the false prophet that Jesus said would appear and deceive the people during the last days (Matt. 24:11). The implication that Muhammad's understanding was also influenced by an Arian monk would have given John's readers an instant association with the teachings of an ancient heretic, but it would also explain some of the reasons for the interpretation of Jesus as a created being in the writings of Muhammad, both separate from God and subservient to Him. John's reference to God as the "creator of all things" would resonate with Christians, but the Saracen claim that God has "neither been begotten nor has begotten"[29] was for John a direct affront to the deity of Jesus. Moreover, it is curious that the phrase, evidently from surah 112, is reversed from the Qur'anic version which states "He begetteth not, nor is He begotten (Q. 112:3)." This may indicate that John was misquoting from memory, had a faulty copy or perhaps even had a variant of the accepted version. Whatever the case, the significance for the Christian would be that the Saracens could not accept the incarnation of God in the flesh, and the implication for the Saracens would be that even though they accepted the idea that "Christ is Word and Spirit of God,"[30] they could only view Jesus as "a creature and a servant."[31] For the Christian, the denial of the deity of Christ would be enough to judge the Ishmaelite beliefs to be a heresy. Perhaps this is why John's main critique of Muhammad's religion is centered on Christology.[32]

---

growing influence and power of the heresy all around them.

27. HER 10–16.
28. Berkey, *Formation of Islam*, 98.
29. HER 17–18.
30. HER 69–70.
31. HER 19.
32. Moffett, "Divided by Christ," 39–40. See also, Irwin and Sunquist, *History of the*

In the next section, detailing the birth of Jesus to Mary, John focuses on several events in the life of Jesus which the Saracens would say deny the incarnation of Jesus, especially if he were only a "prophet and servant of God."[33] Though the Saracens believed that Jesus was "born without seed from Mary," and during the process the "Word of God and the Spirit" entered into Mary, they still denied that Jesus could be the son of God.[34] It is interesting that while John mentions that Muhammad writes that Mary was the "sister of Moses and Aaron,"[35] which would be an anachronism, he merely states this error without any comment. It may have been merely outside the focus of his argument and therefore he did not feel the need to pursue it. It may also have been that John wanted to stimulate thoughtful reflection on the part of his Christian readers so that they would not only have a better understanding of the Ishmaelite heresy, but that they would also be able to respond to further errors that they would encounter in their defense of the faith.[36] John then points out to his readers that the Saracens not only deny the deity of Jesus, but that they also deny another central Christian tenet, the crucifixion of Jesus. Without the crucifixion of Jesus, and his subsequent resurrection, John believes that hope in an eternal life would be futile thinking for a Christian. Salvation centered on Christ dying for the sins of humanity on the cross. Yet, the Qur'an seemed to deny that Jesus was crucified by the Jews and even suggested that God instead raised Jesus into heaven without dying. John seems to be familiar with the surah that describes Jesus standing before God in heaven where he is asked by God whether he ever said, "Worship me and my mother as gods in derogation of Allah" (Q. 5:116)? Of course Jesus denies ever doing this, but it is interesting that John replaces the phrase above with God asking Jesus if he ever said, "I am the Son of God and God."[37] Is this another place where the version that John referenced was different, or is John changing the words for his own purposes? It is understandable that someone who rejected the nature of Jesus as God, as the Saracens did, would more easily connect the deity issue to Mary and her son rather than reflect a Christian perspective that Jesus is the incarnation of the only God? However, rather than address these views of the incarnation that were contrary to the Bible, John brushes

---

World Christian Movement, 280; and Beaumont, *Christology in Dialogue with Muslims*.

33. HER 21–22.
34. HER 18–22.
35. HER 19.
36. Scharer, "The Polemic of the Tractate of Saint John of Damascus," 10–11.
37. HER 26–27.

them off as some of the "absurd stories worthy of laughter"[38] in Muhammad's book and then goes on to the next point.

John now comes to the section in his argument where he simulates a dialogue with a "representative" Saracen.[39] It may be the result of many discussions he had with the Saracens he worked with through the years. Some of these topics were developed in more detail in his *Disputation between a Christian and a Saracen*, while other Christian apologists, like Abu Qurrah, carried on the use of dialogue and developed the format to a higher degree. In fact, these dialogues became John's trademark form of apologetics and were influential for hundreds of years.

The first question dealt with is when John asks a Saracen, "Who testified that God has given him a scripture?"[40] He follows that question with one that asks which prophet foretold the coming of Muhammad. To both of these questions the Saracen is at a loss to answer. This often seems to be the case in John's dialogues. Either the Christian asks a detailed question that his counterpart cannot answer, or the Saracen asks a question that the Christian not only answers in a brilliant fashion, but with such finality that the Saracen feels the need to escape from the conversation. Of course, these contrivances were set up by John to make the Christian position seem much stronger than the Saracen one, but, judging by how they were used by future apologists, they were also effective for giving the Christian reader courage to engage in similar dialogues and even ask some of the same questions. In regard to these particular questions, John resorts to history and the authority of the Bible to refute the prophethood of Muhammad. He demonstrates that the prophethood of Moses was publicly validated by God, and while Moses testified to the coming of Jesus, as had all the prophets from Moses on down, the same cannot be said for Muhammad. All the prophets in the Bible, John maintains, "foretold the coming of Christ. They also said that Christ is God, and that as the Son of God he will come by taking on flesh, and that he will be crucified, and die, and rise again, and that he will be the judge of the living and the dead."[41]

However, Muhammad instead denies the incarnation, the deity of Christ and the crucifixion as well. Therefore, John asks the Saracen how his prophet could be from God if his message contradicted the earlier prophecy. The Saracen, not having an answer, can only offer that "God does as he

---

38. HER 32–33.
39. Some believe that this is all fictional. See Küng, *Islam: Past, Present and Future*, 8.
40. HER 34–35.
41. HER 38–41.

pleases."[42] Through this circumvention, John hopes to relay to the Christian reader that the Saracen beliefs are unbiblical and must resort to pleas from authority rather than the authority of the Bible. John follows this up by asking the Saracen how his prophet received his book. When the Saracen admits that it was during his sleep, John ridicules the Saracen's acceptance of a revelation that should have been received through the most heightened of perceptions and instead was relegated to the realm of "dreams." More than likely, John merely wants to maintain that the comparison of Muhammad with prophets like Moses and others in the Bible is a futile effort, especially since the message of Muhammad is so contrary to the biblical one.

In the next section John bolsters his argument by questioning Muhammad's credentials. He points out that the coming of the Saracen prophet was not testified to in the Bible, nor was his testimony of receiving revelation from God witnessed by anyone. John presses this lack of witnesses by pointing out that in the Saracen scriptures other business transactions, like marriage and buying property, required the presence of witnesses. Surely something as important as the transmission of God's revelation would have required a greater witness to the messenger. In the face of this interrogation, however, the Saracen is "ashamed" and remains silent.[43]

John now comes to one of his strongest arguments against the Saracens. Christians were called "associators" (ἑταιριαστάς) by the Saracens because the Christians were said to associate Christ with God, which was an abominable thing for the Saracens. John counters this criticism by pointing out that the prophets and the Christian Scriptures taught that the Christ is the Son of God, so if the Saracens truly accepted that the earlier Scriptures came from God, then they would accept this teaching as well. Some objected and said that Christians misinterpreted the prophets, and others said that the Jews fraudulently made up stories to mislead the Christians. However, John addresses these objections by developing a logical argument that became one of the most popular arguments used by Christians in the centuries to follow. John asked that if the Saracens call Christ the Word and Spirit of God, then why do they accuse the Christians of being associators. The Word of God and the Spirit of God are inseparable from God, John maintains, and therefore the "Word of God is in God," and must be God. If the Word and the Spirit were outside of God, then "God is without Word and Spirit," and this would be impossible.[44] Consequently, John continues, the Saracens have mutilated God by tearing out his Word and Spirit, and

42. HER 46.
43. HER 54–60.
44. HER 71–73.

therefore John calls them "mutilators of God" (κόπτας).⁴⁵ John caps off his argument by saying that "it would be far better for you to say that He had a partner, rather than mutilate Him."⁴⁶ Tolan suggests that John developed this argument so that he could provide a catchy name to call the Saracens ("mutilators"/κόπτας),⁴⁷ for he does not seem to take the opportunity to support the truth of the Trinity or further his argument.

In regard to John's successors, this use of the Qur'an in order to argue for the supremacy of Christian doctrine would prove popular and effective, but mostly in building up the faith of Christian believers and not necessarily bringing about the conversion of Muslims. Still, this highlights one of the main purposes of apologetics, which is to raise the awareness of Christians so that they not only understand the beliefs of other religions, but that they have a much better understanding of their own beliefs. This certainly was one the main goals in John's writings and in his apologetic approach.

John's Third Step: Refute (What is Logical and Consistent?)

John now turns to combating the criticisms of idolatry and polytheism. Previously it was the Christian asking questions that the Saracen could not answer. Now John has the Saracen ask questions or even accuse the Christian of error in order to refute the Saracen through logic, common sense, and even Scripture. In this section, the Saracen accuses Christians of being idolaters because they venerate the cross. John counters this accusation by saying that the Saracens are the idolaters because they rub themselves against a stone in their ka'ba and kiss and embrace it.⁴⁸ John does not reveal any sources for these views, for they are not mentioned in the Qur'an, but it seems to have been common knowledge in his day, and he goes on to say that some Saracens even claim that the stone was used as a bed for Abraham and Hagar, or a place to tie up his camel when Abraham was going to sacrifice Isaac.⁴⁹ The logic that John uses to refute this claim and call it "nonsense" is more of a tangential argument rather than a direct refuta-

---

45. HER 77.
46. HER 74–75.
47. Tolan, *Saracens*, 53.
48. HER 79–80.
49. It may be important to note that John does not seem to reflect any controversy as to whether the son to be sacrificed was Isaac or Ishmael. This may be an indication that his critique was written before Muslims claimed that the one who was to be sacrificed was Ishmael and not Isaac. It is interesting to note that the Qur'an does not mention the name of Abraham's son in the sacrifice narrative, whereas the Bible does (Gen 22).

tion, though he does bring in scriptural information in order to support his case. He notes that the stone could not have been the place of Isaac's intended sacrifice because "that place"[50] was known to be barren of trees for gathering wood and devoid of donkeys, which were mentioned in the biblical rendition of the narrative. Therefore, it could not have been the location of the biblical event. John says that the accusers are embarrassed and cannot counter his arguments, but nonetheless they continue to claim that the stone is Abraham's. John then changes his tack and assumes, for the sake of argument, that the stone is Abraham's. He further ridicules his Saracen accuser by pointing out how foolish it is for them to kiss a stone on which Abraham may have had relations with a woman or to which he may have tied a camel. In contrast to the earthy veneration of the Saracen, John holds up the power of the cross of Christ "through which the power of the demons and the deception of the Devil have been destroyed."[51] If anything should be venerated, John seems to be saying, it should be the symbol of the victory over death, not groveling in the dust of death. John uses this contrast in order to argue that Christianity is superior to the Saracen beliefs because its object of worship is so much more worthy. John also uses ridicule in order to accentuate the contrast between the two belief systems. It is interesting to note that John seems to have a better understanding of the real nature of the stone than his accusers, for they enlarged the stone in their vision to the size of a bed or the shape of a camel hitch. However, John claims that it was the head of a statue of Aphrodite which was once used in pagan worship, and he even mentions that it still bears "traces of an engraved image ... visible to careful observers."[52] Was John privy to information that his accusers were not?

Just as with the charge of polytheism, from which John was able to develop his argument between "associators" and "mutilators" in regard to the Word of God and the Spirit of God, with the charge of idolatry John used logic and Scripture in order to argue that the writings of Muhammad fall short of the established word of God found in the Old and New Testaments. The Saracens knew enough about the Old Testament prophets to claim them as their own, and they knew enough about Christian belief in Jesus to strike at the incarnation and the sonship issues. They also understood well enough the Christian's veneration of the cross to accuse Christians of idolatry. However, instead of following logical arguments, John portrays them as

---

50. John does not mention Mecca or even Arabia.

51. HER 90–91.

52. HER 93–94. Had John ever witnessed the stone? Did he know of eyewitness accounts? Why did he not mention the location of the stone by name?

The Development of John's Apologetic Approach   213

hiding behind authority arguments and excusing unanswerable questions with the phrase "it is God's will." On the other hand, Christians are portrayed as skilled apologists who demand evidence and eyewitness accounts, rely on the OT prophecies and argue from the prophets, and know enough about Saracen writings to point out heretical statements.

In the next two sections, John relies on ridicule to argue that the Saracen Scriptures are inferior to the Bible. In the book *The Woman* he looks down on the practice of a man being able to have up to four wives and a thousand concubines, but he focuses on the narrative of Zayd's divorce of his wife and her subsequent marriage to Muhammad, all at the supposed command of God. Evidently John hopes that Muhammad's "convenient" use of God's revelation in order to serve himself will keep Christians from being drawn toward Muhammad and his teachings. It is interesting that John includes this story under the heading of the book *The Woman*, but the story is not found in surah four, which is the surah in the Qur'an called "The Women," but rather in surah thirty-three.[53] It may also be significant that while John refers to the man as Zayd, he does not seem to know that he is supposedly Muhammad's adopted son and that the command from God was supposed to be, in part, a removal of the barrier so that a father of an adopted son may marry his adopted son's wife after she is divorced properly (Q. 33:37). John calls Zayd Muhammad's "friend" or "companion" rather than his son, which seems to indicate that either John did not know this narrative well or that he was familiar with a different version of the story. It is also interesting that John's version is more detailed and accuses Muhammad of committing adultery with Zayd's wife before the command was given by God. It is also possible that since John only seemed to be familiar with Surahs two through five, and this account was related in surah thirty-three, that he may have just been familiar with an oral account as it had been told in his presence. Another option is that John was working from a different version, perhaps one of the Companion Codices, which went out of favor during the process of canonization. Whatever the case, John's purpose in relating the story is to cast aspersions on the character of Muhammad as well as bring ridicule on the practices taught.

At the end of this section there is a teaching that John references in order to illustrate Muhammad's view of women. This is the saying that the woman is the man's "tilth,"[54] or, in other words, she is his field for sexual

---

53. Not only does John have the title of the surah incorrect, The Woman instead of The Women, but he places the story of Zayd in what is now surah 4 instead of surah 33 where the story is actually recounted in the Qur'an. Was John confused or did the Qur'an have a different order at that time?

54. Q. 2:223

exploitation. John then alludes to other "obscene things" that he did,[55] apparently in order to leave his readers with distaste for Muhammad and his practices. This critique may well have been designed to prevent Christians from apostatizing and joining the ranks of the heretics.

After belittling Muhammad, John ridicules the Saracen Scriptures in his lengthy rendition of the *Camel of God*.[56] There is no book in the Qur'an called the book of the Camel of God. There are a few verses that allude to a she-camel, but they only supply a brief version in comparison to John's lengthy tale. The Qur'an mentions a she-camel that was used by God as a way of bringing judgment upon the Thamud tribe. The she-camel was to have rights to drink from the nearby river on alternate days from the people and they were not to harm her under the threat of punishment from God. However, they became jealous, hamstrung her and after three days destruction was brought upon them.[57] This was meant to illustrate the judgment of God, but John used it to illustrate the "absurd" teachings in the Saracen Scriptures. John relates that the camel from God infuriated the people because she drank the whole river and became so big that she could not pass between two mountains. To make amends, she agreed to supply milk to the men. However, they were cruel and killed her instead. Her calf, though, survived and called on God for help and was taken up into heaven. To accent what he deems the "foolish" nature of the story, John proceeds to ask the Saracens a series of questions that seek to add layer upon layer of absurd events. The first question, "where did it come from?" warrants an answer from the Saracen: "from God." The next question: "was there another camel coupled with this one?" gained the response of "no."[58] From that point on John does not wait for a response: "Was it begotten? Why didn't Muhammad find out more about the camel? Was it taken up to heaven? Did it drink up the river of water in heaven leaving only the river of milk and the river of wine?"[59] These and other questions seem to be designed to persuade his

---

55. HER 113.

56. Küng uses what he calls John's "silly passage about a surah said to be about a female camel" to illustrate his conclusion that John's "self-confident and often ironic remarks about Islam are full of misunderstandings and the Christian answers lack any self-critical reflection." See *Islam: Past, Present and Future*, 8. However, this assessment is contradicted by statements by Sahas, *John of Damascus on Islam*, 95, Hoyland, *Seeing Islam*, 488, and Louth, *St. John Damascene*, 80, who have determined that John was well informed about the "Islam" of his day.

57. See Q. 91: 13; 26:155–57; 54:27, 28; 17:59; 11:64–66; 7:73

58. HER 121–23.

59. HER 123–39. These questions are paraphrases of some of the questions John raises in this section.

readers that the rest of the religion is just as lacking in spiritual depth as this story, and therefore should be avoided.

John also relates that without the river of water, the men in paradise would have to drink pure wine instead of mixing it with water and in their intoxicated state would sleep and miss out on all the pleasures of heaven. He does not mention what those pleasures might be, however, so he may not be aware of the promise of the "black-eyed beauties" (Q. 44:54). Nor does he seem to be aware that the river of wine is not supposed to be intoxicating. John is also aware of only three rivers, while the Qur'an mentions four (water, milk, honey and wine—Q. 47:15).[60] Again, this may show that he knows little of these "books," since they contain many areas on which he could choose to comment. However, given what we know of his scholarly approach and thoroughness in his doctrinal works, as well as his apologetic treatises, it may also indicate that he is being selective in his choice of material in order to illustrate the weaknesses of Islam and to ridicule a belief system that challenges his own.

John has used questions with the Saracens in order to argue for the superiority of Christianity; he has refuted accusations in order to show the more logical beliefs of Christians, and he also uses ridicule to demonstrate how the Saracen beliefs are not worthy enough to follow. However, John reserves perhaps his harshest words for the conclusion of this section, in which he warns that those who believe in such folly will have a fate worse than if the camel had preceded the Saracen into the souls of donkeys. The Saracens involved in these teachings, John says, are like beasts destined to go to the darkness and everlasting punishment of hell.[61]

John briefly mentions the book of *The Table* where Christ asked God for a table and God granted his wish and gave him an incorruptible one. Some commentators today believe this refers to the Last Supper, but John makes no assessment, which may show that he knows little of this book, since surah five contains many areas on which he could choose to comment.

John mentions the book called *The Heifer*, but he does not seem interested in discussing any more and simply dismisses it all as containing a great number of "sayings worthy only of laughter."[62]

He closes by listing several practices of the Saracens which are mentioned in the traditions but not specifically in the present Qur'an. These are

60. John's lack of knowledge in these areas may indicate simple ignorance of these passages in the Qur'an or it may indicate that changes or corrections were still taking place. It may also indicate that John was working from one of the Companion Codices that went out of favor in the canonization process.
61. HER 145–48.
62. HER 153–54.

laws for circumcision of men and women, injunctions against keeping the Sabbath and being baptized (in essence prohibiting Saracens from becoming a Jew or Christian), as well as food regulations and forbidding them from drinking wine. The treatise ends abruptly without a real conclusion or final admonition. It is almost as if John has felt that he has provided enough material on what he calls the "absurd" beliefs and practices to persuade Christians to avoid the religion of the Ishmaelites. If his goal has been to create an aversion to the Saracen beliefs among his Christian readers through logical arguments as well as ridicule, then he seems to feel he has accomplished his purpose. However, if John's desire was to inform his Christian audience of the main teachings of the Saracen beliefs in order to prevent Christians from converting, then these aspirations were also served. Ultimately, John provided his readers with crucial information on the beliefs and practices of his opponents so that Christians would be able to defend their faith. This next section will outline some other components of John's apologetic approach.

JOHN'S APOLOGETIC APPROACH IN THE DISPUTATION BETWEEN A CHRISTIAN AND A SARACEN

In his dialogue with a Saracen, John focuses on two main themes in which Christians differ from the Saracens. The first is Free Will versus the Sovereignty of God and the second deals with various aspects of Christology. Concerning the first area of dispute, the Jabarite theologians in the early 700s believed that God was the author of both good and evil, for otherwise men would have the power to counter God's will, and this would be a limiting factor on God's power. Therefore, in order to preserve their view of an omnipotent God, they had to limit man's free will. The Qadarites, on the other hand, held that man still had power over his actions and therefore man was ultimately responsible for what he did. John favored the Qadarite position more highly, but explains that without the incarnation, where the goodness of God meets the justice of God, man's use of free will would never bring praise to God.[63]

In John's argument, as well as other areas of dispute in his dialogues, he demonstrates that he understands the teaching of their scriptures on this subject, and proceeds to use a logical approach in order to first illustrate

---

63. OF 3.1, pp. 268–69; 1.8, p. 176.

what he considers to be the fallacies of his opponents' views and then explains how the Christian position answers the dilemma more completely.

In the next section dealing with the nature of Jesus Christ as the Word of God, John employs a method that I will call "didactic apologetics." He again utilizes a dialogue format between a Christian and a Saracen, but this time it is more casual in the sense that the dialogue tags are dropped and the opening questions are in the subjunctive case. This allows John to develop his logic as a teacher would build his case point by point in a lecture. This didactic lesson format presents possible scenarios to the Christians so that they would be better able to answer their interlocutors. Again, John uses the knowledge of the Saracen Scriptures and their developing theology to make a common link, but then he demonstrates how the Christian view gives a much more elaborate understanding of Christ's nature and his relationship with the Father. For example, in the dialogue, the Christian displays his knowledge of the Saracen Scripture by pointing out that it affirms that Christ is the Word of God.[64] If this is so, and the Saracens believed that the Word of God must be uncreated, then Christ as the Word of God must also be uncreated, and therefore God himself, because only God is uncreated. If the Saracens argue in return that Christ could not have been uncreated, the Christian then replies that Christ must be uncreated, for if God created the Word, then how could he have had his Word before it was created?[65] In this exchange, the Saracens are portrayed to have a truncated, and sometimes heretical, view in contra-distinction to the orthodox position of the Christian. This afforded John the opportunity to teach from what he considered to be a position of intellectual strength rather than one based on theological inconsistencies and illogical arguments. This format was very helpful, as well as persuasive, for teaching his Christian readers how to best defend their faith against the contrary positions of the Saracens. While encouraging them to understand the theological ideas of the Saracens, it also provided them with the arguments so that they could question their opponents as well as provide superior answers to the questions that were asked of them. Thus, John not only gave them a way to defend themselves, but he also gave them the intellectual weapons by which they could advance their own doctrine. He taught them to first understand their opponents as well as understand their own doctrine. He then trained them to point out the weaknesses of the other side and promote the strengths of their own arguments.

---

64. DIS 5.1–8.
65. DIS 5.9–19.

THE WEAKNESSES OF JOHN'S APPROACH

On the other hand, what were some of the short-comings of John's apologetic approach? First of all, John did not seem to seek out common areas with the Saracens, or commend any positive beliefs or practices. It is not so much that he set up "straw-man" arguments in order to make Christianity appear superior, but rather that he portrayed the Saracen believer as a one-dimensional man who could only think along certain lines and was often at a loss when asked to give a reply (such as the time they were asked to supply the names of any prophets who foretold the coming of Muhammad). Of course, this portrayal of the Saracen apologists' limited ability to use reason and logic in their arguments served to bolster the reasonableness of the Christian Scriptures and the deity of Jesus Christ, but it sometimes hindered Christians from understanding the Saracen's position. John did not instruct the Christians in ways to reach out to the Saracens and witness to them, but rather tried to show how their religion was inferior to Christianity and unworthy of believing. Also, John did not seem to be interested in really engaging the Saracens in a true dialogue. Even though the major differences were brought up and possible answers given, John did not engage in a serious intellectual interchange of religious arguments. Again, he seemed more concerned with proving Christianity to be correct and superior to what he considered a "heresy" than with representing both sides as accurately as possible. To be fair to John, however, if his main purpose was to inform Christians of what he considered to be the false teachings of the Saracen's beliefs, then it was logical for him to criticize his opponents and defend the strengths of Christianity. A debate can be won by either revealing the weaknesses in an opponent's arguments or by persuading others of the superiority of one's own. In the end, John was able to do both successfully. Perhaps this is why his apologetic approach became the standard for such a long time.

11

The Apologetic Successors of John

INTRODUCTION

For Christians subject to Muslim rule in the eighth and ninth centuries, criticizing Muhammad in public could be dangerous. For example, in AD 742, Peter, the bishop of Damascus, who was also a friend of John of Damascus, apparently could not stand the imposed restrictions any longer and went out to the public square and brought anathemas down on Muhammad and his beliefs. He was punished by having his tongue cut out and being exiled from his home. While in exile he died from his wounds.[1] Still, though persecution of the Christians by their Muslim rulers occurred, there often seemed to be considerable freedom for Christians to defend their beliefs and engage in dialogue as well as debates with their Muslim counterparts when they were conducted with more sensitivity. Sidney Griffith, in his book, *The Church in the Shadow of the Mosque*, even documents that the development of Christian apologetics at that time was in tandem with the evolving theology of Islamic religious thought. He writes that,

> In this context, Christians sought to defend the reasonableness of their distinctive doctrines in terms of the same religious idiom as that employed by their Muslim interlocutors and

---

1. Hoyland, *Seeing Islam*, 354–360. See also Turtledove, *Chronicle of Theophanes*, 107–8.

counterparts, who, in accord with the teachings of the Qur'an, often rejected the central Christian doctrines.[2]

This apologetic approach was unique at the time because it used the scriptures and language of the Muslim religion.[3] Unlike the earlier Greek apologists, the Arab-speaking Christians constructed their arguments in the religious expressions of the Qur'an and the traditions of the prophet Muhammad, which they were familiar with. Griffith continues, "as a result, the discourse of the Christian apologists in Arabic presents a conceptual profile that cannot easily be mistaken for Christian theology in any other community of Christian discourse."[4] Even their apologetic approach involving the two main issues of the Trinity and the Incarnation was patterned after Muslim theological constructs. In regard to the Trinity, the "ontological status of the divine attributes" of God was argued, while the arguments for the Incarnation often focused on the "signs of authentic prophecy and the true religion."[5] These were both topics discussed by their Islamic counterparts. It is also of importance to recognize that all the principal genres of the apologetic approaches of that time were "dialogical in form and literary structure."[6]

It is not a coincidence that John of Damascus also used the dialogical format in some of his apologetic writings. While he may not have been the first one to use dialogue in his apologetic approach (the encounter of John I with the emir may have preceded him), his dialogues were popular and may have influenced the development of this genre down through the following centuries. In fact, Sidney Griffith even says that "In defense of the doctrine of the Trinity, most Christian apologists who wrote in Arabic adopted the strategy first encountered in the Greek works of St. John of Damascus."[7]

We can even trace this strategy through several Christian apologists who came after John and seemed to glean from both his apologetic style and his theological arguments. In this pursuit we will need to explore the styles of apologetics that were used by Arab Christians in the latter half of the eighth century and early ninth century. We need to not only identify the ones who followed John's lead, but we need to also understand how their

2. Griffith, *Shadow*, 75.
3. Griffith, "Apology of Abu Qurrah," 273.
4. Griffith, *Shadow*, 75.
5. Ibid., 76. See also Griffith, "*Apology of Abu Qurrah,*" 273–74. It is important to note that this format makes sense in the Middle East, but it is not very effective when "translated into the theological idioms of the West."
6. Ibid., 76.
7. Ibid., 95.

approach was similar to John's and how it differed. Through this exploration we should be able to gain a much better understanding of the nature of the theological arguments taking place as well as the unique ways that these Arab Christians took up John's mantle and further developed their own witness to the Muslims ruling over them.

GRIFFITH'S FOUR APOLOGETIC GENRES

In order to better understand John of Damascus' successors, it would be helpful to review four categories of apologetic genres used in the Abbasid period as assembled by Sidney Griffith. His first genre is called "the monk in the emir's majlis."[8] In these accounts, monks or bishops are summoned to appear before the Muslim leader and give a defense of their Christian beliefs. These were written in a dialectical format and were usually anonymous, even if the named figures were real.[9]

The topics covered by these dialogues followed a standard pattern and were contextualized so that the Qur'an and the traditions of Muhammad could be addressed in a way that was understandable for Muslims. The two main topics of controversy centered around the doctrine of the Trinity and the incarnation, but other topics dealt with the resurrection, the veneration of the cross and idols, the comparison of the status and verifiability of prophets, especially the nature of the prophet-hood of Muhammad, and the claims of the Qur'an as a new and final revelation from God.[10]

A good example of a letter recounting a dialogue dealing with these topics is the supposed debate between the Patriarch Timothy I and the caliph al-Mahdi held in 781. The conversation was probably conducted in Arabic,[11] but the letter was first consigned to Syriac, which was Timothy's

---

8. Griffith, *Shadow*, 77.

9. For example, the earliest dialogue, supposedly between the Patriarch John I and the Muslim emir, Umayr ibn Sa'ad al-Ansari, was probably not written until the first third of the eighth century even though the narrative, in the form of a letter, relates the events of an encounter that supposedly took place on Sunday, May 9, 644. Like most of the narratives in this genre, it was an apologetic text that sought to allay the fears of Christians by demonstrating that Christianity was the true religion and could provide good and reasonable answers to the questions raised by the new rulers.

10. Griffith, *Shadow*, 78.

11. Newman, *Early Christian-Muslim Dialogue*, 170. See also Griffith, "Disputes with Muslims In Syriac Christian Texts," 251–73. In his article, Griffith also writes that, while Christians spoke Arabic in the debates with Muslims, "one knows of no Muslims who learned Syriac for the purpose of arguing with Christians," 256. Also, Christians recorded the debates in Syriac, ostensibly because the treatises were for Christian eyes only. Perhaps this is why John of Damascus could write some fairly strong words

native tongue. He seems to be aware of the content of the Qur'an, especially the longer and later Surahs (similar to John of Damascus), though he does not call it by that name and seems to know verses orally rather than in a written format, though he does allude to "mysterious letters" found at the beginning of some Surahs, which would indicate some familiarity with a written text.[12] Sydney Griffith writes that in this popular narrative, "the reader is invited to observe the patriarch giving brilliantly satisfactory answers to the Islamic challenge to Christian teachings in a way that not only commended the veracity of the Christian doctrines and practices, but did so in a style of writing that subtly discounted the claims of Islam in seemingly inoffensive language as well."[13] We later see this popular format used to describe the debate between Theodore Abu Qurrah against the Caliph al-Mamun in 829, as well as the "Christian Bahira legend," which depicts an encounter between a Christian monk and Muhammad in which the monk supposedly teaches the future prophet all the good and true things that make their way into the Qur'an.[14] Whether factual or fictional, these narratives tried to present the superiority of Christianity in contrast to what Christians viewed as the inconsistent and often incoherent beliefs of the Muslims.

The second apologetic genre that Griffith describes is the "Master and his disciple," which is really a "question and answer" catechetical-like format designed to give Christians solid answers to questions that are often brought up by Muslims. Usually the "student" takes the role of the Muslim and asks the question, which is usually short, and then the "teacher" gives an elaborate answer that not only answers the question but tends to demonstrate the superiority of Christianity over all other religions. Often by the end, the Muslim is so impressed that he will make some statement suggesting that if community pressure and status were not an issue, he would convert to Christianity! In time this format became very popular, and Griffith suggests that the more literary and theological elements even contributed to the formation of the Islamic science of Kalam, or the philosophical system of inter-religious dialogue in Arabic.[15]

A good example of a ninth-century Nestorian apologist who used this genre of apologetic literature was Ammar al-Basri. In his "book of Questions and Answers," he organized his list of answers to questions under four

---

against Islam and Muhammad with seeming impunity for what he said. There may have been few Muslims who could read Greek.

12. Newman, *Early Christian-Muslim Dialogue*, 172.
13. Griffith, *Shadow*, 78.
14. Ibid., 80.
15. Ibid., 81–82.

categories, but instead of the conventional *erotapokiseis*[16] exchange, Griffith explains that al-Basri's construction is more along the lines of the Islamic Kalam texts which use the question as a *protasis* of a statement, "If someone says or asks this," and the answer as its *apodosis*, or "then we say this." In this way he is able to develop his defense of Christian doctrine along a more philosophical system that was designed, as Griffith puts it, "to thwart the views of his adversaries."[17] This is very similar to the technique used by John of Damascus in his *Disputation between a Christian and a Saracen*, written over fifty years earlier. In sections five through ten (according to Kotter's listing), John uses the *protasis/apodosis* formula, and in sections one to four and eleven he uses the *erotapokiseis* constructions. As discussed in chapter 7, these two divisions were probably written or transmitted at different times; hence the different formats. The significance, however, is that John, whose work was known and used by these later apologists may have been influential not only in popularizing the question/answer format, but due to his knowledge of the ideas being developed by the Saracens of his time and the theological nature of his arguments, he may have had a hand in the development of the Islamic Kalam.

Griffith's third category of Christian apologetic genre is the Epistolary Exchange. This was also a popular format which framed a theological exchange between a Muslim and a Christian within the literary device of a letter. Usually the Muslim would initiate the discussion with a short letter inviting the Christian to accept Islam and then follow the invitation with a brief overview of the five pillars of their faith. The Christian would then write a long letter, or series of letters, inviting the Muslim to embrace Christianity, and then he would defend his doctrines in detail and illustrate how Christianity is the true religion and superior to Islam.[18]

Among the examples of this letter format, Griffith lists the correspondence between the Byzantine emperor Leo III (r. 717–41) and the caliph 'Umar II (r. 717–20). Even though Hoyland concludes that the letter did not originate until the end of the eighth century,[19] and was probably enhanced by further iterations, it apparently contained some authentic examples of issues current in the mid-eighth century such as his "attack on the Ka'ba and its stone, the licentious nature of Muslim marriage, divorce and concubinage,

---

16. Referring to a question-answer format where one person asks and the second person answers. The speakers are usually identified by a name followed by a colon.

17. Griffith, *Shadow*, 84.

18. Ibid., 85.

19. Hoyland, *Seeing Islam*, 494.

and the carnal vision of paradise."[20] All of these topics are already found in the works of John of Damascus, so they may have come from knowledge of his writings or they could simply represent the theological issues of the times.

Another important apologetic work using the epistolary genre was the exchange between the Muslim character 'Abd Allah ibn Ismail al-Hashimi and the Christian character 'Abd al-Masih Ibn Ishaq al-Kindi. Though this was written anonymously and the debaters were probably fictional, it is likely that the author was Nestorian and writing in the 820s.[21] In this exchange, the Muslim gives a brief overview of the basic beliefs of Islam and then the Christian gives a long defense on the doctrines of Christianity. Though this was common, the boldness of the Christian position and its negative depiction of Islam, the Qur'an and Muhammad was somewhat inordinate for a document written within the Islamic empire at this time. However, the anonymity and the polemical style made it a popular work to copy, and it was distributed widely among the Nestorians as well as the Melkites and the Jacobites.[22]

The last apologetic genre covered by Griffith is what he calls the "Systematic Treatise." These were major apologetic tracts or treatises, often written by named theologians, who defended Christian doctrine by means of a dialogue format styled after the philosophical and religious discourses of the Muslims.[23] This Christian form of Kalam could be understood by the Muslims and it served to create a "bridge" between the very different doctrines by appealing to logic as well as biblical and Qur'anic exegesis.

The earliest treatise of this sort is by a now unnamed author and is called "On the Triune Nature of God."[24] According to Griffith, it was written in Arabic around AD 755, but Hoyland allows it to be as early as AD 737. There is a notation in the treatise that states, "If this religion were not truly

---

20. Ibid., 499.
21. Ibid., 472. Griffith, *Shadow*, 86–87.
22. Griffith, *Shadow*, 87.
23. Ibid., 89.
24. See Griffith, "Monks of Palestine," 21. of the earliest documentary Christian texts in Arabic, Griffith lists the Anonymous tract on The Triune Nature of God, (with some dating it around the 740s and some putting it in the 780s), an Arabic version of the "Fathers who were killed at Mount Sinai" (Sinai Arabic MS 542 and British Museum Oriental MS 5019), written around 772 AD, and a copy of the Pauline Epistles in Arabic, dated around 867. Of the text on The Triune Nature of God, which contains portions of the Arabic text of the Qur'an, Griffith notes that the early date presents an interesting anomaly: "The irony of this situation is that if the dating of the manuscript to the first half of the eighth century is secure, this Christian text is among the earliest surviving documents containing quotations from the Arabic text of the Qur'an."

from God, it would not have endured and stood for 746 years."[25] Griffith derives his date by adding the 746 years to the Alexandrian world era date of Christ's incarnation in AD 9 and therefore comes up with AD 755.[26] Hoyland advocates starting from the resurrection in the Alexandrian era, which would add 746 to AD 42 in order to produce the year 788. However, he also mentions that in the Melkite era the incarnation was reckoned at 9 BC and the resurrection around AD 25–26. Thus, the earliest possible time of writing would be AD 737 (or 746 years after the birth of Christ in 9 BC).[27] What makes this possibility interesting is that this early date would place it within the time span of John of Damascus. It has earlier been stated that all the writings of John of Damascus that we have were written in Greek. However, he would have also known Arabic in order to carry out his civil service position under the caliphs, especially Walid I (r. 705–15), who required the upper level civil servants to be able to do their work in Arabic. When we examine the words of this tract, which was probably written in Arabic in the original, we can see some parallels between John's own treatise on the Trinity, as well as his writings on Islam, and the ideas and phrases of this Arabic tract. Could it be that toward the last decade of his life John may have penned a work in Arabic defending one of the most important doctrines of the Christian faith? This is not the place to pursue this comparison, but it may be of interest for a future project.

Here is a paragraph from the beginning of the treatise:

> We do not say three Gods . . . but we say that God and His Word and His Spirit are one God and one Creator . . . We do not say that God begat his Word as any man begets—God forbid? Rather we say that the Father begat his Word as the sun begets rays, as the mind begets speech (al-kilma) and as the fire begets heat.[28]

The words are not quite the same as John's,[29] but the themes are very similar, and if John were writing for Muslims instead of Christians then it may be expected that he would probably choose a different style and vocabulary, especially if he were writing in Arabic instead of Greek. Of course, the resemblance may simply be that these metaphors had become widespread in the Christian culture of the time and would have been picked up by other writers besides John of Damascus.

25. Hoyland, *Seeing Islam*, 503.
26. Griffith, *Shadow*, 89–90.
27. Hoyland, *Seeing Islam*, 503n174.
28. Ibid., 502.
29. OF 1.8, 180

Griffith goes on to note three important treatises in this genre. The first is a letter-treatise written in Syriac by the Patriarch Timothy I to his friend Sergius detailing a debate Timothy conducted with the caliph al-Mahdi around the year 781 (mentioned earlier).[30] Hoyland says the debate was conducted in Arabic, but the letter was composed in Syriac and later translated into Arabic.[31] The topics were standard fare for the time: the Trinity, the incarnation and Christ's nature, the crucifixion, the veracity of the Bible versus the Qur'an, and the claims of prophet-hood by Muhammad.[32] Again, these were areas of dispute already dealt with by John of Damascus at least three decades before. The importance of Timothy's exchange is that it was conducted in Arabic and indicates that it was possible for Christians to have such discussions under Muslim rule.

The next writer mentioned, Theodore Abu Qurrah, was one of the most important Christian theologians to write in Arabic. His debate with the caliph al-Ma'mun in 829 has already been mentioned, but his dominant format was through the use of questions and answers systematized so that a more comprehensive understanding of Christian theology would be taught. Sidney Griffith adds that "his purpose was to explain the tenets of Melkite theology in the Arabic idiom of the contemporary discussions about religion among the Muslim *mutakallimun*, as well as to defend the proposition that Christianity is the true religion."[33]

Another writer of this period who developed arguments in favor of the Trinity and the Incarnation against the Muslims, as well as christological disputes between the Melkites and the Nestorians, was the Jacobite Habib ibn Khidmah Abu Ra'itah. He was a contemporary of Abu Qurrah, and even debated with him on differences with their christological views. He also debated with Muslims, especially in regard to Christology. In his *Letter on the Incarnation*, he supplied answers to forty-four questions posed by Muslims on the incarnation.[34]

The common goal in all of these apologetic genres was to promote Christian beliefs and refute Islamic ones. They were meant mostly for Christian audiences, so that the saints could be encouraged and trained to always be prepared to give an answer to everyone who asked them to give a reason for the hope that they had.

---

30. Griffith, *Shadow*, 90.
31. Hoyland, *Seeing Islam*, 473.
32. Ibid., 474.
33. Griffith, *Shadow*, 90.
34. Beaumont, *Christology in Dialogue with Muslims*, 45.

Before dealing more thoroughly with the way these apologists dealt with the Trinity, let us first review the distinctions of three different sects of Christianity as they attempted to explain their views on Christology to the Muslims.

CHRISTOLOGY AS REPRESENTED BY THE EARLY CHRISTIAN ARABIC APOLOGISTS

In his book, *Christology in Dialogue with Muslims*, Mark Beaumont argues that the ninth century was one of the most creative periods of Christian-Muslim dialogue, especially in regard to the area of Christology. Also, Beaumont's exploration of the various apologetic approaches presented by theologians of three different perspectives, Orthodox, Nestorian and Jacobite, has elucidated different objections that Muslims have had with the Christian belief that Jesus is God himself. It has also provided a touchstone for further development on the apologetics of the Trinity. The three ninth-century Christian theologians Beaumont highlighted were Abu Qurra, Abu Ra'ita and Ammar al-Basri. Abu Qurra was an Orthodox Melkite who believed that Christ existed in two natures, divine and human, in one hypostasis. Abu Ra'ita followed the Jacobites, or monophysites, who taught that the divine nature and human nature are one since the human nature was subsumed by the divine. The third, Ammar al-Basri, represented the Nestorian beliefs and argued that Christ had two natures and two hypostases. The Nestorians did not want either nature to be emphasized to the exclusion of the other. A comparison of these subtle differences not only points to their apologetic approach, but also their effectiveness in dialogue with Muslims. The challenge they all faced was how to best communicate the essential Christian truth of the divinity of Christ to those who accepted the human nature of Christ but rejected his divinity. While the earlier apologists, such as John of Damascus and Timothy I, endeavored to argue for errors in the Qur'an and Muslim teachings, the ninth-century apologists argued with Muslims on their own terms and tried to base Christian perspectives on Quranic teaching.[35] For example, John of Damascus referred to Muhammad as a "false prophet" and the religion that he started as a heresy and the "forerunner of the anti-Christ."[36] The ninth-century apologists pursued a more nuanced course that portrayed the Qur'an as an insufficient source for Christology compared to the Bible. As Beaumont writes, "rather than merely expound a received Christology composed from within a totally

---

35. Beaumont, *Christology in Dialogue with Muslims*, 200.
36. HER 2 and 11.

Christian environment, they entered into a Muslim framework of thought to show the validity of a Christian view of Christ in terms that Muslims might understand as credible."[37]

The ninth-century Christians believed in an ontological union of the human and divine in Christ, and therefore argued from a developed theology of the incarnation against the Muslim's refusal to accept the divinity of Christ. Abu Ra'ita represented the Word/flesh Alexandrian tradition which took the divine as the "operative principle in Christ," and humanity as a "passive receptacle for divine thought and action."[38] At the other extreme, Ammar al-Basri followed the Word/human Antiochene tradition, which saw the union of the separate natures of Christ in "active co-operation" with a genuine interplay in thought and action between the human and divine.[39] Abu Qurra upheld the Chalcedonian prescription of the "union of the Word with human nature" which taught that, while there were two distinct natures in Christ, they were in complete harmony in regard to all thoughts and actions.[40] Which of these views proved to be the most effective in dialogue with Muslims? Abu Ra'ita's Word/flesh tradition failed to allow for a truly human Christ since Christ's humanity is obscured, and therefore this view fails to produce a Christ that resonates with the Qur'an. Ammar believed in a fully human nature and divine nature of Christ in a "dialectical relationship" (there are real struggles between the two natures), but the "divinity is compromised by the humanity." In other words, the importance of the divine is swallowed up in the humanity. On the other hand, Abu Qurra's Chalcedonian view represents a stronger union between the two natures. The two minds are always in tune with each other and there is no struggle to carry out the will of God. As Beaumont explains, "Christ may suffer and die, but Christ at the same time does not suffer or die, since the two minds experience different realities simultaneously without cancelling the other out."[41] Thus, Abu Qurra's Christology is far more satisfactory "since his Christ is far more integrated in thought and action than Ammar's dialectical Christ, and far more human than Abu Ra'ita's one-dimensional Christ."[42]

As with the apologetic development in regard to the incarnation and the nature of Christ, the Arabic apologists succeeding John of Damascus realized that they would need to create new theological terms in Arabic to

---

37. Beaumont, *Christology in Dialogue with Muslims*, xix
38. Ibid., 204.
39. Ibid.
40. Ibid.
41. Ibid., 205.
42. Ibid., 206.

express their views, just as with Greek and Syriac beforehand. They also sought to give new meanings to Arabic words that had been developed by Muslim theologians to express Muslim theological concepts, but these were fraught with difficulty because of the existing connotations. This can be seen readily in the debates over the Trinity. Following the lead of John of Damascus, all the Christian apologists employed the "basic strategy of presenting the doctrine of the Trinity in the context of the Islamic discussion of the ontological status of the divine attributes."[43] Griffith goes on to say,

> Typically this involved the Christian claim that all of the attributes of essence and action, as both Christians and Muslims distinguished them, can reasonably be shown to presume the presence of three irreducible, substantial attributes: "existing" (mawjud), "living" (hay), and "speaking" (natiq), on which all the other attributes can then logically be argued to depend. The apologists then proposed that these three substantial attributes indicate the three persons or hypostases (qnome/aqanim) of the one God, who is one in ousia (jawhar) as the Christians teach, and three in the divine personae (parsope/wujuh, askhas), Father, Son, and Holy Spirit, of which, according to the Christians, the Bible so clearly speaks.[44]

As we continue with our overview of Christian Arabic apologists who succeeded John of Damascus, we will focus our survey on the arguments they developed in defense of the Trinity, noting the different emphases of two different Christian sects, the Orthodox and the Nestorian. We will also examine both the nature of their arguments and the method of apologetics used. These apologetic approaches will then be compared to the words of John of Damascus in order to support the view that these later approaches were influenced by his writings. The three main apologists that we will explore are Theodore Abu Qurrah, a Melchite, the Patriarch Timothy I, a Nestorian, and 'Abd al-Masih b. Ishaq al-Kindi, who was also a Nestorian.

THEODORE ABU QURRAH

Biographical Background

If it is hard to find solid evidence for the life of John of Damascus, it is even harder to find biographical material on Theodore Abu Qurrah. Little is known about his life except what was recorded in two Syriac chronicles,

---

43. Griffith, *Shadow*, 95.
44. Ibid.

references to some of his debates, and a few hagiographical allusions. In the *Chronicle of Michael the Syrian*, Abu Qurrah is mentioned as the bishop of Harran during the time that Patriarch Theodoret was in Antioch, which was from 785–99.[45] Sidney Griffith surmises that Abu Qurrah was probably the bishop of Harran between the years of 795 and 812.[46] The second chronicle to mention Abu Qurrah, *The Anonymous Chronicle of 1234*, recounts Abu Qurrah's involvement in a debate with the Caliph al-Ma'mun (813–33) in 829.[47] From the scant biographical evidence for his life, we can say that he was probably born in Edessa, Syria around AD 755 and died shortly after his debate with the caliph in AD 829. He followed the Melkite, or orthodox Chalcedonian doctrine, and, according to Sidney Griffith, he was probably a monk at the famous monastery at Mar Sabas.[48] However, John Lamoreaux believes that the hagiographical reference to a Theodore of Edessa, who once resided at the monastery at Mar Sabas, points to a different person and therefore concludes that Theodore Abu Qurrah was probably NOT a monk at Mar Sabas.[49] Lamoreaux also questions the evidence that Theodore debated the caliph al-Ma'mun in 829, since others attribute the debate to Simeon, the eighth-century Monophysite bishop of Harran, who was also known by the name Abu Qurrah.[50] Most early references to Theodore Abu Qurrah, however, do have him spending some time at Mar Sabas, acting as the Melkite bishop of Harran and debating the caliph al-Ma'mun before his death.[51] We know that he was a monk. We know that he was the bishop of Harran. We also know that he was involved in a number of debates against the Muslims. It is at least possible that he would have spent some time at Mar

---

45. Beaumont, *Christology in Dialogue with Muslims*, 28.
46. Griffith, "Monks of Palestine," 22–23.
47. Beaumont, *Christology in Dialogue with Muslims*, 28.
48. Griffith, "Monks of Palestine," 22–23.
49. Lamoreaux, *Theodore Abu Qurrah*, xii, xiii, xvii. Also, in Lamoreaux's essay, *The Biography of Theodore Abu Qurrah Revisited*, 33, 38–39, Lamoreaux argues that the only evidence that points to Abu Qurrah being at Mar Sabas is the hagiographical work called the *Passion of Michael the Sabaite*, which Lamoreaux claims does not fit with other facts that are known of the monastery and the inhabitants during that time. Lamoreaux also discredits the link to John of Damascus because he says that more recent evidence reveals that the famous "through the voice of John of Damascus," which prefaced Abu Qurrah's *opusculum* 18, really should read "through the voice of John the Deacon," who he claims was the real narrator of a debate between Abu Qurrah and a Muslim, which has come down to us as *opusculum* 18. This would take John of Damascus out of the picture, remove Abu Qurrah as the author of the dialogue and make it unlikely that Abu Qurrah ever lived at Mar Sabas. The evidence for this controversial claim is found in Khoury, *Johannes Daskenos und Theodor Abu Qurra*, 86.2.
50. Lamoreaux, "The Biography of Theodore Abu Qurrah Revisited," xii, xiii, xvii.
51. Griffith, "Monks of Palestine," 22–23.

Sabas and, before he died, debated with the caliph al-Ma'mun. If Lamoreaux is correct, however, all we have documentary evidence for is that Abu Qurrah was born in Edessa, Syria around the middle of the eighth century, was a Melkite bishop of Harran from 795 to 812, debated with the Muslims and died sometime in the first third of the ninth century. Fortunately, we do have a number of his writings, and to these we will now turn.

His mother tongue was probably Syriac, but he wrote many of his important works in Arabic. Some even considered him a "wonder" because he was able to engage in dialectics in Arabic.[52] Abu Qurrah probably knew Greek, since it was still present in much of the liturgy[53] and he was known for translating a Greek work for one of the caliph's generals, but it is likely that the Greek translations that we have of his written work were originally written in Arabic.[54] The fact that Abu Qurrah wrote in Arabic not only demonstrates that he was comfortable with the nuances of the language, especially the unique theological language that had to be created for the discussion of new theological ideas, but it also shows through the way he approached his arguments that he was familiar with the Muslim approach to philosophical and theological issues and therefore was able to develop his apologetic approach in accord with this understanding.[55] Lamoreaux, in his recognition that Abu Qurrah was one of the first to write a theological defense against Islam in Arabic, also says that he was "one of the most creative and imaginative Christian theologians of the early Middle Ages."[56]

Abu Qurrah's Three-Pronged Approach

In his apologetic writings, Abu Qurrah had a three-pronged approach as he addressed Christians, Jews and Muslims. For Christians, he defended the Chalcedonian definition of orthodoxy against those Christian sects opposed to it. For Jews, Abu Qurrah argued that Jesus is superior to Moses, especially because he initiated his own miracles in his own name and in his own power. For Muslims, Abu Qurrah wrote three treatises on Christology, meant to help Christians understand Islam better and also defend

---

52. Ibid.

53. Greek was replaced by Arabic as the ecclesiastical language in the first Abbasid century. See Griffith, "Monks of Palestine," 5.

54. Griffith, *Shadow*, 61.

55. Beaumont, *Christology in Dialogue with Muslims*, 29.

56. Lamoreaux, *Theodore Abu Qurrah*, xii.

Christianity philosophically and rationally against the Muslims.[57] Sidney Griffith writes that,

> Abu Qurrah's purposes were to answer the objections of the adversaries, and, perhaps most importantly, to make a clear statement of Christian faith in Arabic. The latter achievement is what put him in the vanguard of the movement toward a fully Arabophone Christianity in the caliphate, a movement which had its earliest life-giving roots in the monasteries of Palestine.[58]

Abu Qurrah also successfully used his knowledge of Islam, Muslims and the Qur'an to fashion his arguments in terms that would impact his readers. In regard to Abu Qurrah's use of his knowledge of Islam, Beaumont concludes that Abu Qurrah provided "arguments for Christological beliefs that were based on principles derived from Islamic teaching."[59] Due to this new approach, Abu Qurrah was able to fulfill his purposes of both training Christians to defend their beliefs, and also of reaching out to Muslims with a meaningful apologetic bridge.[60]

Abu Qurrah's Defense of the Trinity

One of these "bridges" involved the defense of the Trinity. Griffith says that Abu Qurrah expresses the Trinity "in terms of the current Islamic theories of divine attributes."[61] In fact, it seems that, like John of Damascus before him, almost everything that Abu Qurrah wrote dealt with countering either the Christian heresies being taught around him or the Islamic doctrines that were becoming so pervasive and constricting to what he believed to be at the heart of his theology, the nature of the true religion and the true church.[62] In regard to one of Abu Qurrah's main writings, "On Orthodoxy," Griffith explains how the presence and influence of the Muslims shaped much of what he wrote.[63]

---

57. Ibid., 28–29.
58. Griffith, "Monks of Palestine," 23.
59. Beaumont, *Christology in Dialogue with Muslims*, 30.
60. J. H. Crehan remarked that Abu Qurrah's use of reason "shows that Eastern Christians were at this time far ahead of the West in the depth and range of their apologetics." Quoted in Dulles, *A History of Apologetics*, 94.
61. Griffith, *Muslims and Church Councils*, 273.
62. Lamoreaux, *Theodore Abu Qurrah*, xxv.
63. This was also the case with John of Damascus even when writing against other belief systems. See Louth, *John Damascene*, 66, as well as chapter 10b of this book.

The ever-present background to Theodore Abu Qurrah's ecclesiology is the Islamic milieu within which he elaborated his views. The very structure of the essay 'On Orthodoxy,' as we shall see, is dictated by the kerygmatic posture of Islam. The essay is in every line a response to the call to Islam as well as an answer to Christian adversaries; it provides an Arabophone Christian's apology for his beliefs, in the face of what one Muslim controversialist of the ninth century called the 'silencing questions' to be put to Christians.[64]

A number of these "silencing questions" had to do with the Trinity, which Abu Qurrah defended against Islam, as well as against the Nestorians and the Jacobites, in a treatise entitled, appropriately enough, "On the Trinity."

Theodore Abu Qurrah's "On the Trinity"[65]

Abu Qurrah begins his treatise on the Trinity by stating that there are three kinds of people: those who will not believe, those who believe but will not examine their faith, and those who desire to understand that which they believe by faith. He contends that those who examine the world's beliefs will choose Christianity, since Christianity is the only religion that will appeal to those who "became believers through the action of their minds."[66] Other religions, he says, are accepted based on either deception or desire. Thus, Christianity is superior because it is followed not by desire or deception (or force), but by exercising humility and by following reason. This would even be true if someone is asked to believe in something that they do not understand, such as the Trinity. Thus, one of his goals in his treatise is to show that the Trinity is not only supported by Scripture, but that it is also supported by reason, and that together faith and reason will confirm belief in the Trinity.

The Subject of his Treatise

According to Abu Qurrah, the doctrine of the Trinity, which teaches that the Father, son, and Holy Spirit are three hypostases and one God, and "each of these hypostases is in itself fully God," may confuse people when they

---

64. Griffith, *Muslims and Church Councils*, 277.
65. Lamoreaux, *Theodore Abu Qurrah*, 175–93.
66. Ibid., 177.

hear about it.[67] These confused people want to say that it cannot be so and would rather argue falsely that when Christians reject the idea of one hypostasis, and therefore one God, and argue that there are three hypostases instead, then the Christians must also believe that there are three Gods. However, Abu Qurrah argues that the Scriptures affirm that the Father is God, the Son is God, and the Holy Spirit is God—and yet there is only one God. Therefore, these three hypostases must be one God.

Even though it may be beyond our understanding,[68] Abu Qurrah says that through faith the Scriptures are confirmed, and if they testify to the existence of three hypostases and one God, then this truth should be accepted.[69] Abu Qurrah also relates that the Holy Spirit will provide "persuasive arguments" to confirm this doctrine when a person accepts it through faith. Thus, both the testimony of Scripture and the testimony of reason are used by Abu Qurrah in order for him to make his case.

The Testimony of Reason

Abu Qurrah realizes that reason on its own cannot verify the doctrine of the Trinity, but when it is aligned with Scripture it can confirm and make reasonable the claims of Scripture, just as faith in what Scripture teaches can confirm the reliability of arguments from reason. In this section Abu Qurrah begins by reminding his reader that while man has a single nature, that of being "man," if you have three people, say Peter, James and John, these three people still only have the one nature, that of man. Their one nature cannot be misconstrued to be three natures. Abu Qurrah goes on to say, "In the same way, Father, Son, and Holy Spirit are three persons with one nature (that being God)."[70] He is not saying that one God is three gods, but rather the three persons are one God. He is also not saying that three persons are one person, but rather that three persons are one God. Therefore, "the Father is God, but God is not the Father." In the same way, "the son is God, but God is not the Son, and the Spirit is God, but God is not the Spirit."[71] It is important not to confuse the nature with the person or hypostases. Critics

67. Ibid., 178.

68. See Rom 10:17.

69. This is similar to John of Damascus declaring that while the essential nature of God is incomprehensible, what we can know about him is revealed to us through revelation. Both John and Theodore would argue that the Trinity is clearly revealed in Scripture.

70. Lamoreaux, *Theodore Abu Qurrah*, "On the Trinity," 183.

71. See Janosik, "Explaining the Trinity to a Muslim." See also Geisler and Saleeb, *Answering Islam*, 265.

may say that this statement does not make sense, but it is actually not illogical. Abu Qurrah illustrates this same point when he says that just as three pieces of pure gold are not three golds, but rather one gold (by nature), in the same way the Father, Son and Holy Spirit are, by nature, one God, not three gods.[72]

Conclusions on the Trinity

As Abu Qurrah started out addressing three types of people, he also concludes with a word for Jews, Muslims and Christians. To the Jews who accept the Torah, Abu Qurrah asks that if they accept the Old Testament Scripture that says that "Man and woman are one body," even though they have separate bodies, all the more should the Jews accept the Scripture that says that Father, Son and Holy Spirit are one God, especially since each person is fully God. How can the Jews accept the analogy between a man and a woman without accepting the deeper reality of the relationship between the Father, Son and Holy spirit, who are three persons and yet one God?

As for the Muslims, and others "who do not believe in the Christian's Old and New Testaments," Abu Qurrah challenges them to accept the rational arguments presented in his treatise on the Christian doctrine that the Father, Son and Holy Spirit are each fully God and that the three of them are one God since the arguments "compel them to have faith . . . and against which they have no defense."[73]

As for Christians, Abu Qurrah says that the testimony of Scripture should be enough to confirm for them the truth of the Trinity even if they cannot find "anything to confirm . . . this belief in a rational manner." For Abu Qurrah, the testimony of Christ and the believer's obedience to him, through faith, is enough confirmation, for he believes that in the end it is enough in itself to persuade others of the truth of the Trinity.

Similarities and Differences between John of Damascus and Theodore Abu Qurrah

In many ways Abu Qurrah's method of apologetics toward Muslims was very much like John's. First, Abu Qurrah was concerned that Christians

---

72. John of Damascus develops these intricate relationships between the three persons of the Trinity in chaps. 6–8 of his *Orthodox Faith*. Since it is likely that Abu Qurrah was familiar with John's writings, he may be reflecting some of John's ideas in his own work.

73. Lamoreaux, *Theodore Abu Qurrah*, 192.

would be able to understand the distinctions between their own Christian doctrines and the heretical views that they encountered in their discussions with Muslims. Second, he was concerned that Christians should be able to defend and explain their own faith to Muslims. Thus, there was the same "prepare and defend" approach that John utilized in his training.[74] Both also used a dialogical approach, such as when they developed a defense for the Trinity, but they were also known to be polemical—John in his sarcasm toward Muhammad and the Qur'an, and Theodore in his criticism toward Islam both for condoning violence in order to make converts and for promising sensual rewards in this life as well as the next.[75] By the time that Abu Qurrah was writing, however, the Islamic presence was much more deeply felt. Thus, Abu Qurrah would have had to explain the success of Islam over Christianity as he encouraged the believers to remain faithful to what they believed to be the truth. Also, while John portrayed Muslim theology as a heresy of Christianity, Theodore used Muslim theology in order to portray Christianity as the true religion.[76] In this regard John Tolan concludes that "Abu Qurrah attempts to justify Christianity through the vocabulary and ideas of the *mutakallimun* of Abbasid Baghdad. He calmly accepts the existence of Islam on the political and social level: we are all seekers of truth, he seems to be saying to Muslims; you just happen to be wrong."[77]

Did John of Damascus Influence Theodore Abu Qurrah?

Both John of Damascus and Theodore Abu Qurrah were known for their theological acumen and their dialogical apologetic styles, but is there any evidence that Abu Qurrah was familiar with the writings of John of Damascus? Even if Abu Qurrah had been born after John died and had never lived at the monastery at Mar Sabas, as Lamoreaux argues,[78] evidence supports the view that Abu Qurrah was familiar with John's work and patterned his own method of dialogical apologetics upon John's dialogues found in both the *Heresy* and the *Disputation*.[79] Louth even refers to Abu Qurrah as "John's intellectual heir." In addition, in relation to the iconoclastic controversies, Louth says that "all Theodore's arguments are found in John, or are developments of them." Louth then goes on to say later that "there can scarcely be

---

74. Beaumont, *Christology in Dialogue with Muslims*, 30.
75. Tolan. *Saracens*, 59.
76. Ibid., 58.
77. Ibid., 59.
78. Lamoreaux, *Theodore Abu Qurrah*, xii, xiii.
79. Louth, *St. John Damascene*, 220–22.

any doubt that Theodore knew John's treatises."[80] Therefore, the similarities in their writings would be understandable. Also, it is still likely that, given his theological interests, his ability to read Greek and his relatively close proximity to Jerusalem and the monastery, Abu Qurrah would have been familiar with the arguments and style used by John. It is perhaps telling that not only did the phrase "διὰ φωνῆς Ἰωάννου Δαμασκηνοῦ" become connected with the work of John of Damascus rather than John the deacon, but even one of the manuscript stems of John's *Disputation* ended up being attributed to Abu Qurrah.[81] These early connections and confusions may have been the result of an earlier known link that eludes us today. Whatever the case, we can still postulate possible sources of Abu Qurrah's writings in the thoughts and works of John. For example, in Abu Qurrah's treatise *On the Trinity*, there are at least five touch points back to John's works. Four are in the form of analogies or metaphors, which are found in the writings of both authors, and the fifth is a main theological point that cuts to the heart of the Muslim apologetic against the divinity of Christ. Of course, these similarities do not prove that Abu Qurrah received his ideas from John of Damascus, but Abu Qurrah's proximity to John's place of writing, the similarities in word choice, content and arguments, as well as the possibility of Abu Qurrah's own attribution to John's influence, all support the proposition that Abu Qurrah knew and used John's treatises as a basis for his own.

The first analogy of Abu Qurrah refers to the sun giving light to humans through its rays. In context, this is where Abu Qurrah is relating that God created the world *through* his Son just as the sun gives light to humans *through* its rays.[82] Just as the rays of the sun are contiguous with the sun, so is the Son with the Father. Likewise, in chapter 8 of book 1 of *Orthodox Faith*, John of Damascus discusses how the Holy Spirit is communicated to us through the Son. John writes, "It is just like the rays and brightness coming from the sun, for the sun is the source of its rays and brightness and the brightness is communicated to us through the rays, and that it is which lights us and is enjoyed by us."[83] Both use the analogy of the sun and its rays and both link the analogy to the operation of the Trinity.

A second analogy they both share also uses the medium of light. Abu Qurrah writes, "the Father, Son and Holy Spirit resemble, rather, three lamps in a dark house. The light of each is dispersed in the whole house,

---

80. Ibid., 220–22.

81. PG 97:1588–94, *Opuscula* 35–38. See also Lamoreaux, *Theodore Abu Qurrah*, 212–13.

82. Lamoreaux, *Theodore Abu Qurrah*, 186.

83. OF 1.8, p. 188.

and the eye cannot distinguish the light of one from the light of the others or the light of all from the light of one."[84] In similar fashion John writes, "The Godhead is undivided in things divided, just as in three suns joined together without any intervening interval there is one blending and the union of the light."[85]

A third analogy is a common one that St. Augustine also used, and that is the relationship of speech to the mind. As the mind produces the word through the operation of the voice, or breath, so the Father communicates his Word through the operation of the Spirit. Abu Qurrah alludes to this analogy,[86] as does John.[87]

A fourth analogy utilized by both John and Theodore relates how the arm and finger of a person is representative of the Son as the arm of God and the Spirit as the finger of God.[88] In John's disputation, section 5 of Kotter's system, John likens the Word of God to the "arm and power of God." He then relates the Word of God to Christ.[89] Abu Qurrah refers to a different verse, but the idea is the same.[90]

The most important comparison is when both John and Theodore refer to whether God has a Word or not. Abu Qurrah is countering those who deny that the Son and the Holy Spirit could be God, for they believe that there would then be three gods. Abu Qurrah responds, "Does God have a Word? If you say that he does not, you have both made him mute and made human beings better than him."[91] This is reminiscent of John's criticism in *Heresy of the Ishmaelite* when he accuses the Saracens of being "mutilators" for tearing apart the Trinity. In his *Disputation,* John argues that Christ must be the Word of God, and God's Word must have always existed because there could not be a time when God could not have had his Word. Both of John's references to the Word of God may have been in the background of Abu Qurrah's thoughts as he constructed his own arguments, especially if he were already intimately familiar with John's works.

---

84. Lamoreaux, *Theodore Abu Qurrah*, 184.

85. OF 1.8, p. 187. Even though it seems that John first lifted this metaphor from Gregory Nazianzen (sermon 31.14—PG 36:149A—see Chase, *St. John of Damascus*, 187n22), it is more likely, given the proximity and time period, that Abu Qurrah would have gotten the idea from John rather than Gregory.

86. Lamoreaux, *Theodore Abu Qurrah*, 186.

87. OF 1.13, p. 201.

88. Lamoreaux, *Theodore Abu Qurrah*, 191.

89. DIS 5.3–4.

90. Lamoreaux, *Theodore Abu Qurrah*, 191.

91. Ibid., 190.

The Apologetic Successors of John 239

For now, let us turn to another apologist who may have been influenced by John's style and theological arguments, the Nestorian Patriarch, Timothy I.

TIMOTHY I
Background Information

Sidney Griffith relates that during the lifetime of Abu Qurrah, especially through the latter half of the eighth century and early ninth, "Christian thinkers who lived among the Muslims were already doing theology with the challenges of Islam uppermost in their minds."[92] One of the most influential of these thinkers and apologists was the Nestorian Patriarch Timothy I, who lived from 727–823, and served as patriarch of the Eastern Church, first in Seleucia and later in Baghdad, for forty-three years (780–823).[93] He overlapped with the lives of both John of Damascus and Theodore Abu Qurrah, though there is no mention of him ever meeting with either of them. His administrative duties were spread over a vast area that extended eastward into Central Asia and southward into India, but it was for his scholarly acumen and celebrated debates, recorded in letters, that he was remembered best. One writer even states that Timothy's writings may have contributed to the apologetic formation of later "*summae theologiae* in Christian literature."[94] Also, in one of his letters recounting a discussion with a Muslim philosopher, Griffith says that Timothy's interplay with the theory of knowledge as he thinks through and answers the Muslim's objections "reveals Patriarch Timothy as a thinker on the order of John of Damascus or Theodore bar Koni, who realize that the challenge of Islam requires a return to the basics."[95] His theological works were mostly transmitted through "letter-treatises" that he addressed to fellow bishops and monks, and, perhaps, Muslim scholars. He wrote in Syriac, which was still the ecclesiastical language of his time, but Griffith says that "it is clear that he was competent in Greek and, of course, fluent in Arabic."[96]

The discourse that we will focus on took place as a debate between Timothy I and the caliph al-Mahdi over a period of two days in the year AD 781. While the debate itself was most likely conducted orally in Arabic,

---

92. Griffith, *Shadow*, 45.
93. Ibid.
94. Griffith, "Disputes with Muslims in Syriac Christian Texts," 264.
95. Ibid.
96. Griffith, *Shadow*, 45.

Timothy recorded the details several years later in a letter written down in Syriac and ostensibly sent to a friend.[97] Timothy was reluctant to write the letter, and even felt "repugnance" when he considered the "futility" of the outcome of his work, since he did not feel that his words would be very convincing to Muslims or serve as a restraint for Christians who were sliding over to the Muslim beliefs. However, this work became an "immediate success" in the Syriac-speaking Christian communities which were very familiar with the topics dealt with in the debate.[98] The format of the actual debate consisted of short questions from the caliph, which dealt with objections to Christian doctrine and practices, and long answers from the patriarch. In this way Timothy was able to provide detailed apologetic training for his extensive flock. The catechetical format was already a familiar didactic tool in the Syriac church,[99] but the patriarch took it to a new dimension as he not only sought to provide accurate and persuasive answers for the Muslims, but also to demonstrate how Christians living under Muslim rule could respond to their situation and defend their beliefs while retaining good rapport with their rulers and remaining good citizens in difficult circumstances. Throughout the long debate Timothy retained his composure and conducted himself with extreme civility and graciousness. One of the best illustrations of this was when he was asked by the caliph, "What do you say about Muhammad?" Just forty years earlier John of Damascus had referred to Muhammad as a "false prophet" who spread rumors and wrote scriptures that were worthy only of "laughter."[100] Timothy, on the other hand, continually referred to the caliph in reverential terms such as "our victorious king," "king of kings," or even our "God-loving lord." Thus, when asked about Muhammad, Timothy's reply was filled with graciousness and accolades for the esteemed prophet of the Muslims. He defers that Muhammad "walked in the path of prophets" because he "taught the doctrine of one God," "drove men away from bad works," "separated men from idolatry and polytheism, and attached them to God," and "taught about God, His Word and His

---

97. Samir, "The Prophet Muhammad as Seen by Timothy I," 91. See also Griffith, "Disputes with Muslims In Syriac Christian Texts," 262.

98. Mingana, "Patriarch Timothy I and The Caliph Mahdi," 174. See also Griffith, *Shadow*, 48. It is interesting to note that the editor of the Mingana text, N. A. Newman, writes that "neither Timothy nor Mahdi seem to have had a very good knowledge of each other's religion," and even that Timothy "does not display any familiarity with the hadith or Islamic history," Newman, trans., *Early Christian-Muslim Dialogue*, 165. However, in 781 there were probably few hadith circulating, and Ibn Ishaq's biography (d. 767) may not have been in circulation long, leaving only the Maghazi narratives for written historical information.

99. Griffith, "Disputes with Muslims in Syriac Christian Texts," 263.

100. HER 16.

Spirit."[101] However, Timothy stops short of saying that Muhammad was a true prophet, primarily because the Old Testament and the New Testament did not prophecy the coming of Muhammad and he had not performed any miracles. Trying to get around this obstacle, the caliph asks the patriarch, "Who then is the Paraclete?"[102] It seems that even at this early date the Muslims were already trying to associate Muhammad with the Paraclete mentioned in the Bible in order to substantiate the prophethood of Muhammad. This interpretation originates from the upper room discourse where Jesus is referring to the coming of the Holy Spirit, or the Comforter. Muslims were trying to make the Greek word παράκλητος (Paraclete) into περίκλητος (periclete), which refers to the "praised one" (one of the meanings of the term "ahmed," which makes up part of Muhammad's name), but the word is not used in the New Testament. After Timothy explains why Muhammad is not found in the Bible, the caliph goes on to say that the reason Muhammad is not in the present Bible is that it was corrupted, and all mentions of Muhammad were expunged from God's original revelation.[103] Timothy defends the Bible against the claims of corruption, saying that since the Jews and the Christians were at enmity with one another it would not serve either side to corrupt the Bible since the Christians relied on the prophecy of the Old Testament to validate Jesus and the Jews continued to reject Jesus even though their Scriptures were replete with prophecies concerning him. In regard to Muhammad not being mentioned in any of the prophecies, Timothy says that prophecy ended with Jesus Christ, for after the coming of Christ "there will be neither prophet nor prophecy."[104] He also warns that anyone who claims to be a prophet after Christ is fulfilling the Scripture that states "many false prophets will arise and deceive many."[105] Thus, he claims that Muhammad fulfills the prophecy of a false prophet.[106]

Timothy's Explanation of the Trinity

In regard to Timothy's beliefs and statements concerning the Trinity, there are a number of "echoes" back to the theological and apologetic works of John of Damascus, not only in the theological constructs used, but also in the ways that analogies were utilized. On the second day of the debates the

101. Mingana, "Patriarch Timothy I and the Caliph Mahdi," 218.
102. Ibid., 191.
103. Ibid., 193, 212–15.
104. Samir, "The Prophet Muhammad as Seen by Timothy I," 99.
105. Matt 24:11–12.
106. Samir, "The Prophet Muhammad as Seen by Timothy I," 101.

caliph asked Timothy about his belief in God. For Muslims there can only be one God. To associate another with God is considered *shirk*, or the greatest of all sins. Thus, when the caliph queried, "You believe in one God, as you said, but one in three," he was probing the deepest of their theological disputes. Timothy answered, "I do not deny that I believe in one God in three and three in one, but not in three different godheads, however, but in the persons of God's Word and His Spirit. I believe that these constitute one God, not in their person, but in their nature. I have shown how in my previous words."[107] Indeed, references to the Trinity were sprinkled throughout the debate. Earlier Timothy used three analogies to communicate the sense that there could be one object and yet three aspects of the one nature. For example, the sun is one but it produces light and heat, and while the light and heat are different attributes of the sun they carry the essential nature of the sun in the light they produce and the heat that is radiated. The same could be said about an apple which is known by its scent and by its taste. He also used the familiar analogy of the mind producing the thought that is communicated through the voice (breath).[108] This was formulated as far back as the time of St. Augustine, but it is also prominent in the work of John of Damascus.[109] Two of the ways that Timothy echoes John's ideas on the Trinity are in regard to the Word and Spirit not being separable from God and also in Timothy's explanation of how the three persons of the Trinity relate to one another, which hearkens back to John's perichoretical description of the Trinity's co-inherence with each person in a type of "circle dance." The first connection involves the relationship between God's Word and his Spirit. In *Heresies*, John accused the Saracens of being "mutilators" of God because they were attempting to tear apart the nature of the Trinity.

> Since you also say that Christ is Word and Spirit of God, why do you accuse us of being "ἑταιριαστάς" (Associators)? For the Word and the Spirit are inseparable from the one in whom they exist by nature. Therefore, if the Word of God is in God, then it is evident that he is God as well. If, however, the Word is outside of God, then, according to you, God is without Word and Spirit. Consequently, by avoiding the association of a partner with God, you have mutilated him.[110]

107. Mingana, "Patriarch Timothy I and The Caliph Mahdi," 219.

108. Ibid., 180–85.

109. Of course, Timothy could have simply picked up on the standard metaphors circulating in the Christian community of his day, as had John. However, the similarities between John's prior writings and Timothy's arguments at least provide circumstantial evidence of Timothy's knowledge of John's apologetic.

110. HER 69–74.

Timothy also has a problem with the way the caliph views the Trinity. When Mahdi asks, "Are the Word and the Spirit not separable from God," Timothy responds:

> No; never. As light and heat are not separable from the sun, so also (the Word) and Spirit of God are not separable from Him. If one separates from the sun its light and its heat, it will immediately become neither light-giver nor heat-producer, and consequently it will cease to be the sun. So also if one separates from God his Word and His Spirit, He will cease to be a rational and living God, because the one who has no reason is called irrational, and the one who has no spirit is dead. If one, therefore, ventures to say about God that there was a time in which He had no Word and no Spirit, such a one would blaspheme against God, because his saying would be equivalent to asserting that there was a time in which God had no reason and no life.[111]

Both John and Timothy respond to the Muslim by emphasizing the necessity of the Godhead always having the Word and the Spirit, for without the Word of God and the Spirit of God then God could not be God. Therefore the Word and the Spirit must also be God. There cannot be a time when God did not have his Word or his Spirit and, indeed, God cannot be God without having his Word and his Spirit.[112] Whether or not Timothy picked up this concept from reading John's works, the apologetic reasoning and the intent of the argument is the same.

In another response concerning the Trinity, Timothy seems to hearken back to John's perichoretical formulation. The caliph asked Timothy, "What is the difference between the Son and the Spirit, and how is it that the Son is not the Spirit, nor the Spirit the Son?" At first Timothy gives the caliph the standard answer that the relationship in the Trinity is that the Father is not begotten while the Son is begotten of the Father and the Spirit proceeds from the Father.[113] However, as he continues to explain the relationship, his description sounds as if it could be "through the voice" of John of Damascus.

> In this very way from the uncircumscribed Father the Son is begotten and the Spirit proceeds, in an uncircumscribed way: the eternal from the eternal, the uncreated from the uncreated, the spiritual from the spiritual. Since they are uncircumscribed, they are not separated from one another, and since they are not bodies, they are not mixed and confused with one another, but

---

111. Mingana, "Patriarch Timothy I and The Caliph Mahdi," 181.
112. See also OF 1.6, 174.
113. Mingana, "Patriarch Timothy I and The Caliph Mahdi," 183.

are separated in their persons in a united way, so to speak, and are united in their nature in a separate way. God is, therefore, one in nature with three personal attributes.[114]

In John's Orthodox Faith we find this similar statement:

> And so we speak of perfect individual substances to avoid giving any idea of composition in the divine nature. For composition is the cause of disintegration. And again, we say that the three Persons are in one another, so as not to introduce a whole swarm of gods. By the three Persons we understand that God is uncompounded and without confusion; by the consubstantiality of the Persons and their existence in one another and by the indivisibility of the identity of will, operation, virtue, power, and, so to speak, motion we understand that God is one. For God and His Word and His Spirit are really one God.[115]

Both Timothy and John recognized that the relationship between the Father, Son and Holy Spirit is a mystery, and yet they also recognized that the concept of the Trinity is not illogical. If they could at least convey the idea that God could be one and yet three, one in substance and three in persons, and those persons in one another without mixing or confusion, but united in their separate ways, then perhaps they would have accomplished as much as they were able. Their Christian readers would be further instructed and their Muslim objectors would have something more to ponder.

AL-KINDI

The Apology of 'Abd al-Masih b. Ishaq al-Kindi

This text claims to be a Muslim challenge by a cousin of a caliph in the Abbasid period to a Christian serving in the court with the family name of al-Kindi. The actual names were concealed in order to protect the security of the writers, who also claimed friendship. The actual names that have become attached to this debate are Abdullah Hashimi, a cousin of the caliph Ma'mun, and 'Abd al-Masih b. Ishaq al-Kindi, a Nestorian Christian apparently serving as a translator in the court of Ma'mun around the year AD 820. Sir William Muir believes that the surnames may be correct and the rest fictitious in order to protect the identities. A number of Western

---

114. Ibid., 184–85.
115. OF 1.8, 185.

The Apologetic Successors of John   245

scholars of Islam have come to doubt the authenticity of the text,[116] and some ascribe it to a fictitious account written centuries later, but Muir concludes that the internal evidence of the apology substantiates the claim that this correspondence is an "authentic production of the early ninth century."[117] The apology consists of a challenge from the Muslim for the Christian to accept the Muslim religion. This is followed by an explanation of the five pillars of the religion, with Jihad curiously listed as the fifth pillar instead of *zakat* (the giving of alms).[118]

While Timothy I and the caliph Mahdi apparently did not know much about each other's religions (AD 781),[119] by the time al-Kindi comes on the scene his Muslim protagonist not only has studied the Bible, but he also sprinkles his own anti-Christian apology with numerous Qur'anic injunctions. In the Muslim's summons, he says that he has spoken his mind "in the spirit of goodwill and sincere affection." However, he follows this up with a list of Qur'anic verses calling down "everlasting fire" on those who don't believe as he does.[120] Even when he challenges the Christian to think correctly about the nature of the oneness of God, he warns him that "he who worships more Gods than one lies against God with a grievous sin."[121] The Muslim claims that his faith is the "orthodox faith" and that he has spoken the true Word of God. In his challenge to the Christian concerning the Trinity, he cajoles him to renounce his folly:

> Away then with your present unbelief, which means error and misery and calamity. Will you any longer cleave to what you must admit is a mere medley? I mean your doctrine of Father, Son and Holy Ghost, and the worship of the cross? I have grave doubts on your behalf. What has one of your knowledge and reputation to do with so mean a conception of the divine?[122]

---

116. Newman, *Early Christian-Muslim Dialogue*, 356.

117. Muir, "The Apology of Al-Kindi," 365–80.

118. Newman, *Early Christian-Muslim Dialogue*, 389–91. "Then I summon you to wage war in the ways of God, i.e., to raid the hypocrites and to slay the unbelievers and idolater with the edge of the sword; to capture and plunder till they embrace the faith and witness that there is no god but God and that Muhammad is His servant and Apostle, or else pay the tribute and accept humiliation."

119. Ibid., 165.

120. Ibid., 401.

121. Ibid., 400 (Q. 4:51).

122. Ibid., 400.

Al-Kindi's Response Regarding the Trinity

Al-Kindi's response in regard to the Trinity follows a familiar pattern embraced by his apologist predecessors and is based on ideas and practices demonstrated by John of Damascus. He first deals with ontological issues of God's essence, then explains that God without his Word cannot be God, and finally concludes that the mystery of the Trinity can only be fully accepted through God's revelation. The Muslims at that time were strongly opposed to anyone who questioned the oneness of God, or the concept of *tawhid*. Therefore, when al-Kindi dealt with this issue, he emphasized that he not only accepted the oneness of God, but that without one accepting also the triune nature of God then there was only a deficient belief. As to God's essence, al-Kindi says that "we describe Him as One, perfect in essence, threefold in his personality."[123] He also says that "He is the Father of all existence in virtue of His essence, without mingling, merging or composition."[124] Again he says, "as to that which touches His essence, we believe that, co-essential and co-eternal with him are His Word and Spirit, alike transcendent, exalted above all attribute and predicate."[125] These are specific teachings of John of Damascus in his writings, reflected in the specific responses of the apologists succeeding John. However, al-Kindi then writes something that goes beyond John's words and brings a significant twist to this argument when he says that "the definition of God is only complete when both aspects are included." In other words, God's essence has to be allied to his personality in order to be fully understood (one *ousia* and three *hypostases*). He even chides that Muhammad contradicted himself due to his failure to understand this relationship. Muhammad continually said that God was one, but then he also referred to God's Word and God's Spirit, without realizing that only unity in Trinity could explain the relationship of the three persons in one God.[126]

Secondly, al-Kindi alludes to the Damascene argument that God without his Word could not be God.

> Now if it is said that God existed without any world until such time as He chose to create one, it might appear reasonable to say of Him in the same way, that He was without life, knowledge and wisdom till life, knowledge and wisdom came to birth within the Godhead, and were found in Him. But that were an

---

123. Ibid., 417.
124. Ibid.
125. Ibid., 419.
126. Ibid., 422.

abuse of terms. How could God for a single second be lacking in life or knowledge?[127]

Though he does not say it explicitly, the same would hold true for the Word of God. How could God be God without his Word? He then gives his definition of the one he worships: "We assert that God with His Word and Spirit, is one; three persons in the one substance or essence."[128] Ultimately, though, as he continues his explanation, he claims that this mystery of the Trinity can only fully be accepted and believed through revelation by God.[129]

Toward the end of his section on the Trinity, he asks his challenger a question: "Do you know any who say that God is the third of three?"[130] In other words, the Muslims accused the Christians of believing in three gods, but none of the sects, even the most heretical ones, ever claimed to worship three gods.[131] Thus, al-Kindi challenges his Muslim friend to cease from his error and embrace what al-Kindi has expounded, that "in the one God are the Word and Spirit; one yet three."[132]

CONCLUSION

As we analyze the statements of these three men on the Trinity, we recognize on the one hand that there are a number of similar ideas and practices that may have come through their knowledge of the writings of John of Damascus. Prominent among these views is that the Word and Spirit had to have been eternally with the Father; otherwise there would have been a time when God would not have had his Word and Spirit. The successors also made use of analogies for the Trinity, which are found in John's writings: the sun giving off heat and light; the arm of a man being likened to Christ being the arm of God; and the mind producing a thought that is communicated through the voice (breath). These analogies were commonly used before John, but in the scholastic isolation brought on by Islam, these

---

127. Ibid., 420.
128. Ibid., 421.
129. Ibid.
130. Ibid., 425.
131. Al-Kindi does mention that the Marcionites sometimes are interpreted as saying this: "I am sure you do not, unless you mean the sect known as Marcionites, who speak of three substances which they term divine yet distinct, one of which represents justice, the other mercy and the other for an evil principle. But these Marcionites are not Christians, nor are they known by that name." (Newman, *Early Christian-Muslim Dialogue*, 425)
132. Ibid.

Christian Arabic scholars may have had a better chance of receiving the application of these analogies from a theologian, John, who was local and familiar. There are also strong ties to John's explanation of the perichoretical relationship within the Trinity. Unless these men had read Gregory of Nyssa regarding these ideas, they most likely had their first introduction through John's writings. In conclusion, while John's apologetic approach was based on a Greek philosophical model and Chalcedonian beliefs, his successors took parts of John's method and further contextualized it for the Muslim mindset. They built their model on answering questions from the Qur'an rather than merely defending doctrine, and their reasoning was founded upon Kalam philosophical constructs. Still, both John and his successors had the same overarching goals in their respective apologetic approaches: to instruct Christians in doctrine, to prepare them to defend their beliefs, and to teach them how to refute error.

12

Concluding Thoughts

HISTORICAL CONSIDERATIONS

As one of the first major theologians to confront what he called a "heresy," John believed that it was his duty to protect believers from what he viewed as false beliefs.[1] Therefore, he took it upon himself to summarize the preceding seven centuries of orthodox Christian faith in order to provide a theological foundation for Christians living among the Muslims. He also developed two works, the *Heresy of the Ishmaelites* and the *Disputation between a Christian and a Saracen*, in order to warn Christians of the dangers of the new beliefs,[2] to demonstrate the rational basis of Christianity, and to provide a model for refuting the challenges of Islam. Through this study we gained a deeper appreciation of the historical and apologetical nature of one of the first arguments on the Trinity between a Christian theologian and his Muslim opponents.

The background on John's life helped to establish his key position as both a theologian and an apologist serving in an important civil servant role in the court of the caliph, which qualified him to give eyewitness testimony of the historical and theological developments of Islam. He knew the early developmental phases of Islamic politics and theology first-hand.

---

1. Louth, *St. John Damascene*, 77. Griffith points out that Anastasios in the 690s, like John at a later time, also considered Islam as a kind of Christian heresy: Griffith, *Shadow*, 31–32.

2. See Armour, *Islam, Christianity, and the West*, 41.

He knew Arabic. He held a position of authority and respect. He interacted with both the civil and religious spheres of his day, and he developed an apologetic approach to Islam that was copied and adapted for centuries after his death. The biographical material on John of Damascus may be minimal, but through the substantiated historical evidence, together with the logical conclusions based on the internal and external evidence of writings during that time, as well as the hagiographical information on John's life, education and accomplishments, we can establish that John was employed in a key position as chief financial officer in the Umayyad Empire, served as a priest and monk in the Melkite tradition, and was responsible for writing at least two treatises on Islam and other significant doctrinal and liturgical works for the church. Thus, John's position, intelligence and faith uniquely qualified him for his assessment of Islam.

The material on the Islamic context of John's time highlighted the historical controversies facing him. It is necessary to understand the historical and theological context of the first century of Islam in order to better evaluate the historicity of John's critique of the religion of Islam. Like John, early witnesses provided a window into the development of the "heresy of the Ishmaelites" as well as examples of the responses of the various Christian groups displaced by the conquest. These non-Muslim "voices" are very significant, not only in that they give us a literary connection back to the beginning of the conquest in the 630s, but also in that they provide an outsider's critical view of events and developments within the religion that has become Islam. Some of the conclusions from these accounts are very helpful in re-creating the social, religious and intellectual environment of John's time. For example, there were no written Islamic accounts in Arabic of Muhammad or the beliefs of the Muslims in the seventh century other than the words etched on the Dome of the Rock (AD 691) and some Arab coins (AD 686). From the testimony of the non-Muslims, references to a "prophet" were generalized and actually supported a renegade leader of a new monotheistic religion similar to the forms of heterodoxical Judaism and Christianity found in that area.

An overview of the Islamic development of theology aided in providing a theological context for John's defense of Christian doctrine against what he viewed as heresy. The early Muslims wrestled with issues regarding faith versus works, free will versus predestination, and the uncreated nature of the Qur'an. These doctrines were not hammered out in a vacuum, but rather in the midst of a predominantly Christian milieu. Just as apologetics was used to forge Christian doctrines such as the Trinity, evidence suggests it was also employed in the development of the early Islamic doctrines. As Christians and Jews critiqued the Qur'an and argued against Muslim theological viewpoints, Muslim scholars devised ways to counter their opponents' beliefs and strengthen their own views. Muslim theologians also had to suppress heretical ideas within their own fold. From this crucible of controversy, "orthodox" Muslim theology was forged and defended. These theological controversies challenged the existing religions in the area and forced Christian theologians like John of Damascus to re-contextualize doctrinal issues that were under fire, such as the Trinity and the deity of Christ.

WRITINGS OF JOHN OF DAMASCUS ON ISLAM

John's apologetic approach in his major works on Islam, the *Heresy of the Ishmaelites* and the *Disputation between a Christian and a Saracen* was analyzed in order to explore John's arguments against Islam's rejection of the deity of Christ and the doctrine of the Trinity. These treatises were also utilized to explore the writing of Christian theology in an Islamic context, especially the relationship between the expression of orthodox teaching on the Trinity and the apologetic process of defending, as well as commending, the Trinity to Muslims.

John's work in re-contextualizing the doctrine of the Trinity in his defense of Christianity against Islam was significant for his own time, and it also had far reaching effects on his successors. He summarized Christian doctrine systematically for his day based on prior work done by theologians who were also apologists. He was also the first major theologian to engage in a written apologetic with Islam through two works specifically crafted to defend Christianity against what he referred to as the "heresy of the Ishmaelites."[3] In this role, he modeled for us a way that the apologetic process engages doctrine. John's teaching on the Trinity revealed the standard of orthodoxy at this stage in the church's development. His contentions with Islam can therefore show the importance of how Trinitarian doctrine developed through the previous councils and theological writings up through the challenge of this new threat facing the church.

One of the significant conclusions reached in this book was that the evidence supported John as the author of the *Heresy of the Ishmaelites* and that it was probably written in the third or fourth decade of the eighth century. John had a clear, though limited, knowledge of the writings of the Saracens, as well as of Muhammad. He knew parts of the Qur'an (Surahs 2, 3, 4 and 5), and he made references to a "book" not present in the Qur'an, the supposed Surah on the *She-Camel*. He called Muhammad a "false prophet" and did not consider Muhammad a religious model to emulate. John also

---

3. Louth, *St. John Damascene*, 77. See also Saperstein, "Encounters with Islam."

understood that the core beliefs of Christianity, the doctrine of the Trinity and the deity of Christ, were strongly opposed by the Muslims. Throughout his dialogues, John raised very real questions and attempted to give real theological answers. John's concern was to equip his fellow Christians with an understanding of the Muslim belief system and provide a ready defense of the Christian faith.

The authenticity and authorship issues of the *Disputation between a Christian and a Saracen* helped determine the importance of this work in making appropriate assesments of the development of Islam at this time. Though Kotter does not believe firm authorship by John of Damascus can be assigned to the *Disputation* because of the number of variant forms, this book has found that the best explanation is that the various transmissions may have been assembled from a "composite" text derived from John's written and oral dialogues. A careful examination of the different formats suggests that the original order can be reconstructed, and it supports John's authorship as well. If this work is truly from John, then we have a description of what the theological arguments between the Christians and the Saracens consisted of in the middle of the eighth century.

The analysis of John's *Disputation between a Christian and a Saracen* also revealed several significant things about John's association with the development of Islam. First of all, the comparison between John's theological work, *Orthodox Faith*, and the *Disputation between a Christian and a Saracen* confirms many similarities in style, content and word usage. This gives strong support to the view that the person who wrote the *Disputation between a Christian and a Saracen* probably also wrote *Orthodox Faith*. Secondly, the dialogues reveal that John of Damascus was an astute observer of the transformations that were taking place in his culture. More than that, he understood the polemical points of disagreement between accepted Christian doctrine and what he viewed as the aberrant theology of the Saracens. He gave an accurate analysis of mid-eighth-century Islamic theology, and his representation of Christian orthodox faith became the standard for centuries to come. The tone of the dialogues also showed that he was more concerned with Christians understanding their own beliefs in contradistinction to what he called the heresies of the Saracens than with reaching a point of reconciliation with his opponents. This was to become the precedent for centuries of apologists to come.

The doctrines of the Trinity and the deity of Christ, found in John's major theological treatise, the *Orthodox Faith*, were specifically examined because these are crucial theological issues in Christianity, and they were the primary doctrines attacked by the theological pronouncements of Islam. These were also issues that were clearly dealt with in the Aplogetic writings of John of Damascus as well as his successors. As we have seen in John's treatise, *Heresy of the Ishmaelites*, and also in his set of dialogues making up the *Disputation between a Christian and a Saracen*, the belief in a triune God was one of the main points of controversy between the Christians in Syria and their Islamic rulers. It is possible that the development of John's apologetic approach was based on his understanding of orthodox theology, and that both of these aspects of his work were in turn the result of his response to the growth of Islamic theology and hegemony.

John's view of the Trinity, as represented in his theological work *Orthodox Faith*, was then compared to his defense of the Trinity against Islam in the *Heresy of the Ishmaelites* and the *Disputation between a Christian and a Saracen*. Not only were common themes detailed, but it was shown that similar wording was also employed. These same themes were also developed in John's polemical writings against non-Muslim beliefs such as Manichaeism, which was a Gnostic heresy, as well as Monophysitism and Nestorianism, which were considered to be christological heresies. These "proxy arguments" may have enabled John to address the Muslim challenges while remaining under the cover of critiquing a local heresy or a general religious dispute. In addition, the overlapping themes suggest that John of Damascus' apologetic interaction with Islamic theology, as well as non-Muslim heretical views, molded the way he presented the orthodox doctrine of the Trinity, as is found in his *Orthodox Faith*. In turn, his orthodox views on the Trinity, gained from a number of Christian theologians from the past, were further developed through the controversies facing Christians in the time of John, and in the end set the standard by which new heresies, such as the beliefs of the Ishmaelites, were judged. The apologetic approaches of those who followed John were used to critique new heresies by providing counter arguments based on the theological formulations developed by prior systematic theology, as is found in John's *Orthodox Faith*.

THE DEVELOPMENT OF JOHN'S APOLOGETIC APPROACH TO ISLAM

The development of John's apologetic approach was explored as an extension of his theology, first to instruct Christians in orthodox beliefs and, second, to provide a model for defending their beliefs and refuting the false doctrine of others. The focus on the tasks of apologetics involving preparation, defense and refutation was important because these areas were correlative with the development of the Trinity in the formative stages preceding John of Damascus. It is possible that the development of John's apologetic approach was based on his understanding of orthodox theology, and that both aspects of his work were in turn the result of his response to the growth of Islamic theology and hegemony. John's apologetic model was further developed as a way of supporting his views that Christianity was the true faith and, therefore, superior to what he believed was the heresy of Islam.

Finally, John's apologetic legacy was explored in order to reveal the success of his model through the further development of his ideas and methods by his successors. As the Trinitarian statements of three of John's successors were analyzed and then compared with John's writings, a number of similar ideas and practices that may have come through their knowledge of the writings of John of Damascus were highlighted. Prominent among these views is that the Word and Spirit had to have been eternally with the Father; otherwise there would have been a time when God would not have had his Word and Spirit. These successors also made use of analogies for the Trinity, which are found in John's writings. These patterns of thought and parallel arguments strongly suggest that, while John's apologetic approach was based on a Greek philosophical model and Chalcedonian beliefs, his successors took parts of John's method and further contextualized it for the Muslim mindset. They built their model on answering questions from the Qur'an rather than merely defending doctrine, and their reasoning was founded upon *Kalam* philosophical constructs. Still, both John and his successors shared the same overarching goals in their respective apologetic approaches: to instruct Christians in doctrine, to prepare them to defend their beliefs, and to teach them how to refute error.

Certainly, John of Damascus was one of the most important Christian voices in the discussions taking place during the first half of the eighth century between Christians and Muslims. In the end, this simple monk and priest provided a window into the development of Muslim theological ideas of this time. In addition, John's writings on Islam, especially his explanation and defense of the Trinity, provided a deeper appreciation of the historical and apologetical nature of the first arguments on the Trinity between a Christian theologian and the Muslims.

Appendix A
Substantiated Historical "Markers" in the Life of John of Damascus

1. John was born in Damascus, Syria around 675 AD. [1,2]
2. He was part of a prominent family in the civil administration of Syria. [3,4]
3. John's family was probably Semitic—"Syrian rather than Arabic" (Mansur most likely means "victorious," "ransomed," or "saved"). [5,6]
4. His grandfather, Mansur ibn Sarjun, surrendered the city of Damascus to the Muslims in 635 AD, but retained his position under the Caliphs.[7]
5. John's father, Sarjun ibn Mansur, succeeded John's grandfather as the General Logothete (treasurer).[8,9,10]

---

1. Sahas, *John of Damascus on Islam. Revisited*, 106.
2. Hoyland, *Seeing Islam as Others Saw It*, 482.
3. Ibid., 480.
4. Sahas, *John of Damascus on Islam*, 17–19, 29–30.
5. Ibid., 5.
6. Le Coz, *Jean Damascene*, 43.
7. Sahas, *John of Damascus on Islam*, 17–19, 26–27, see esp. n4.
8. Turtledove, trans., *The Chronicle of Theophanes*, 212 : "Originally, logothetes were accountants. As Byzantine bureaucracy evolved and many late-Roman offices disappeared during the crises of the seventh and eighth centuries, logothetes began to fill their functions, and the title came to mean 'minister.'"
9. Hoyland, *Seeing Islam as Others Saw It*, 480–81.
10. Sahas, *John of Damascus on Islam*, 26–29.

256 APPENDIX A

6. John's Arabic name, Mansur ibn Sarjun, was the same as his grandfather's (though in later life it was Yuhanna b. Mansur b. Sarjun. [11, 12]

7. His facility with Greek verse and prose demonstrates that he had some type of classical education. [13, 14]

8. John succeeded his father as the chief financial officer of the Umayyad Empire during the reign of Abd al-Malik (685–705). [15, 16]

9. John resigned from his post in the Umayyad government and retired to a monastery near Jerusalem, perhaps St. Sabas. [17, 18, 19, 20]

10. He took the monastic name of John. [21]

11. He never mentions St. Sabas in his writings, but it is assumed that his monastery was near Jerusalem since John mentioned being close to the patriarch of Jerusalem (presumably John V, 706–35) and often preached in the Church of the Holy Sepulcher in Jerusalem. [22, 23, 24, 25]

12. He was ordained as a priest. [26, 27, 28, 29]

13. He was of the Melkite order (a supporter of the Orthodoxy of the Byzantine king, which in Syrian is *malka*). [30]

11. Ibid., 26–29.
12. Louth, "St John Damascene: Preacher and Poet," 248.
13. Louth, *St. John Damascene*, 19.
14. Chase, *St. John of Damascus: Writings*, xv, xxviii.
15. Sahas, *John of Damascus on Islam*, 26–29, 42.
16. Sahas, "John of Damascus on Islam. Revisited," 106.
17. Ibid.
18. Louth, *St. John Damascene*, 6.
19. Le Coz, *Jean Damascene*, 54.
20 Chase, *St. John of Damascus: Writings*, xii.
21. Sahas, "John of Damascus on Islam. Revisited," 105.
22. Le Coz, *Jean Damascene*, 54.
23. Chase, *St. John of Damascus: Writings*, xii, xv.
24. Louth, *St. John Damascene*, 6.
25. Louth, "St John Damascene: Preacher and Poet," 247.
26. Turtledove, trans., *The Chronicle of Theophanes*, 100. "In Syrian Damascus the priest and monk John Chrysorrhoas (the son of Mansur), an excellent teacher, shone in his life and his words."
27. Florovsky, *Byzantine Fathers*, 254.
28. Chase, *St. John of Damascus: Writings*, xii.
29. Hoyland, *Seeing Islam as Others Saw It*, 484.
30. Louth, *St. John Damascene*, 12

Substantiated Historical "Markers" in the Life of John of Damascus 257

14. He was described as a Presbyter of the Holy resurrection of Christ our God. [31]

15. Eustratiades thought he was the 'sacred preacher of the Church of the Anastasis" (Church of the Holy Sepulcher). [32]

16. He may have written his liturgical poetry and homilies in this post. [33]

17. He was called John Chrysorrhoas ('flowing with gold') by Theophanes, apparently in regard to his oratory skills in his preaching. [34, 35]

18. He delivered a sermon in praise of Peter of Maiuma, who was martyred for blaspheming Muhammad. [36, 37]

19. He was condemned at the synod of Hieria (east of Chalcedon) in 754, apparently posthumously, and he was anathematized under the name of "Mansur" for his writings in favor of the use of icons. [38, 39]

20. He was exonerated by the 2nd Council of Nicaea (the Seventh Ecumenical Council of 787). [40]

21. John probably wrote most, if not all, of his theological works while in the monastery (though it is hard to construct a chronology of his works). [41]

22. John's works fall into three categories: "exposition and defense of Orthodoxy, sermons, and liturgical poetry." [42]

---

31. Turtledove, trans., *The Chronicle of Theophanes*, 100.
32. Louth, *St. John Damascene*, 6.
33. Ibid., 6.
34. PG 94:108.841A. Chase adds that the term "Chrysorrhoas" can be translated "golden-flowing" and probably refers to the name of the river that ran through Damascus (Chase, *St. John of Damascus: Writings*, xiv–xv). Louth gives a slightly different rendition of Theophanes's words relating that Theophanes called him "John Chrysorrhoas ('flowing with gold'), 'because of the golden gleam of spiritual grace that bloomed both in his discourse and in his life'" (Louth, *St. John Damascene*, 6).
35. Louth, "St John Damascene: Preacher and Poet," 249.
36. Turtledove, trans., *The Chronicle of Theophanes*, 107.
37. Louth, "St John Damascene: Preacher and Poet," 249.
38. Chase, *St. John of Damascus: Writings*, xiii–xiv.
39. Sahas, *John of Damascus on Islam*, 3–7.
40. Tsirpanlis, *Anthropology of Saint John of Damascus*, 11–12.
41. Sahas, *John of Damascus on Islam*, 51.
42. Louth, *St. John Damascene*, 9.

23. His work in theology, *De Fide Orthodoxa*, was the first *summa theologica* and has become a standard for the Eastern Orthodox Church. [43]

24. He was known as one of the "greatest liturgical poets." Some of his hymns are still used today, and his poetry still graces the pages of Orthodox liturgy.[44]

25. John lived to be an old man and used the phrase "in the winter of words" in reference to himself.[45]

26. He probably died around 750 AD (at the age of 75). [46, 47, 48, 49, 50, 51, 52]

---

43. Ibid., 13.
44. Ibid.
45. Ibid., 6.
46. Chase, *St. John of Damascus: Writings*, xviin32.
47. Simmons, *Fathers and Doctors of the Church*, 96.
48. Louth, *St. John Damascene*, 7.
49. Hoyland, *Seeing Islam as Others Saw It*, 482n95.
50. Sahas, "John of Damascus on Islam. Revisited," 107.
51. Sahas, *John of Damascus on Islam*, 48.
52. Florovsky, *Byzantine Fathers*, 254.

Appendix B
Theological Development Chart

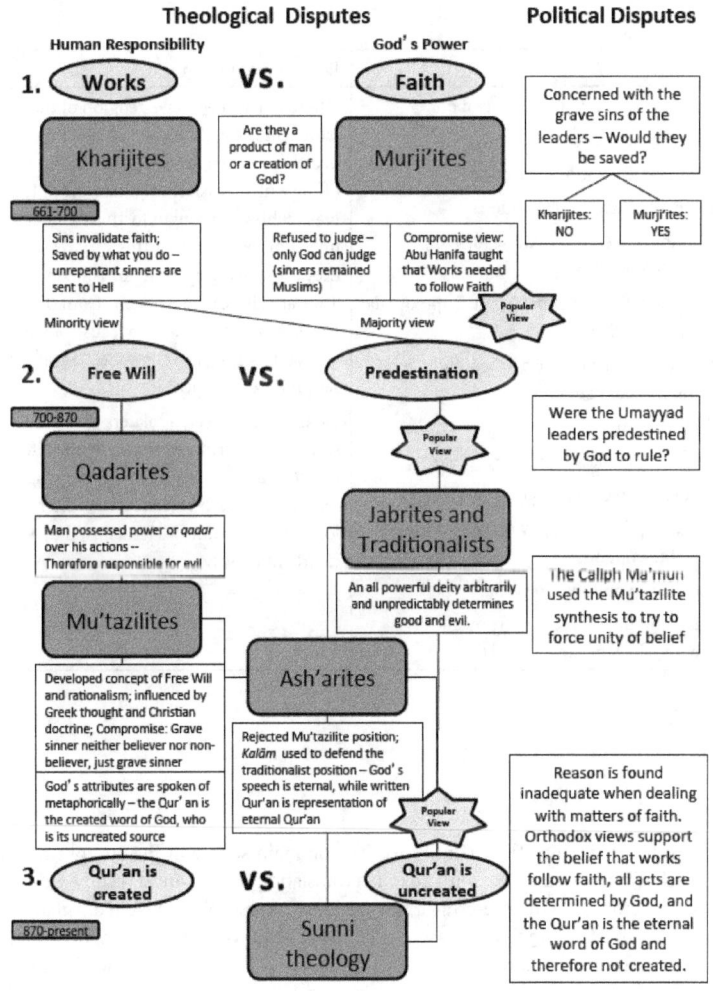

Appendix C
Heresy of the Ishmaelites (Translation from Kotter's text)[53]

Greek Text	English Translation
Ἔστι δὲ καὶ ἡ μέχρι τοῦ νῦν κρατοῦσα λαοπλανὴς θρησκεία τῶν Ἰσμαηλιτῶν πρόδρομος οὖσα τοῦ ἀντιχρίστου. Κατάγεται δὲ ἀπὸ τοῦ Ἰσμαὴλ τοῦ ἐκ τῆς Ἄγαρ τεχθέντος τῷ Ἀβραάμ· διόπερ Ἀγαρηνοὶ καὶ Ἰσμαηλῖται προσαγορεύονται. Σαρακηνοὺς δὲ αὐτοὺς καλοῦσιν ὡς ἐκ τῆς Σάρρας κενοὺς διὰ τὸ εἰρῆσθαι ὑπὸ τῆς Ἄγαρ τῷ ἀγγέλῳ· Σάρρα (5) κενήν με ἀπέλυσεν. Οὗτοι μὲν οὖν εἰδωλολατρήσαντες καὶ προσκυνήσαντες τῷ ἑωσφόρῳ ἄστρῳ καὶ τῇ Ἀφροδίτῃ, ἣν δὴ καὶ Χαβὰρ τῇ ἑαυτῶν ἐπωνόμασαν γλώσσῃ, ὅπερ σημαίνει μεγάλη. Ἕως μὲν οὖν τῶν Ἡρακλείου χρόνων προφανῶς εἰδωλολάτρουν, ἀφ' (10)	There is also a coercive religion of the Ishmaelites which prevails at this time and deceives the people, being the forerunner of the Anti-Christ. It originates from Ishmael, who was brought forth from Hagar unto Abraham, and for this very reason they are called Hagarenes or Ishmaelites. They are also called Saracens from the word "Σάρρας κενοὺς"[A] because of what was said by Hagar to the angel, "Sarah has sent me away empty." So then, these were idolaters and worshiped the morning star and Aphrodite, whom they also called in their language "Khabar,"[B] which means "great." Therefore, until the time of Heraclius, they were clearly idolaters,

---

53. Kotter IV, 60–67. This critical text was the main source of the author's translation, which was then compared with a French translation of the critical text, Le Coz, *Jean Damascene*, 210–27. Other pre-critical text translations were also consulted: *Sahas, John of Damascus on Islam,*, 132–41. Chase, *St. John of Damascus: Writings*, 153–60; Voorhis, "John of Damascus on the Moslem Heresy," 391–98; and Edgecomb, "Biblicalia Blog."

Heresy of the Ishmaelites (Translation from Kotter's text)

Greek Text	English Translation
οὗ χρόνου καὶ δεῦρο ψευδοπροφήτης αὐτοῖς ἀνεφύη Μάμεδ ἐπονομαζόμενος, ὃς τῇ τε παλαιᾷ καὶ νέᾳ διαθήκῃ περιτυχών, ὁμοίως ἀρειανῷ προσομιλήσας δῆθεν μοναχῷ ἰδίαν συνεστήσατο αἵρεσιν. Καὶ προφάσει τὸ δοκεῖν θεοσεβείας τὸ ἔθνος εἰσποιησάμενος, ἐξ οὐρανοῦ γραφὴν ὑπὸ θεοῦ κατενεχθῆναι ἐπ' αὐτὸν διαθρυλλεῖ. Τινὰ δὲ συντάγματα ἐν τῇ παρ' (15) αὐτοῦ βίβλῳ χαράξας γέλωτος ἄξια τὸ σέβας αὐτοῖς οὕτω παραδίδωσι.	and from that time until now, a false prophet, called Mamed, sprung up among them; who, after conversing with an Arian monk concerning the Old and New Testament, fabricated his own heresy. And after ingratiating himself and gaining favor from the people under a false pretense of piety, he spread rumors[C] that a book had been sent down to him from heaven by God. Thus, heretical pronouncements[D] inscribed in his book and worthy of laughter, were instead handed down to them as something to be revered.
Λέγει ἕνα θεὸν εἶναι ποιητὴν τῶν ὅλων, μήτε γεννηθέντα μήτε γεγεννηκότα. Λέγει τὸν Χριστὸν λόγον εἶναι τοῦ θεοῦ καὶ πνεῦμα αὐτοῦ, κτιστὸν δὲ καὶ δοῦλον, καὶ ὅτι ἐκ Μαρίας, τῆς ἀδελφῆς Μωσέως καὶ Ἀαρών, ἄνευ σπορᾶς ἐτέχθη. Ὁ γὰρ λόγος, φησί, τοῦ θεοῦ καὶ τὸ πνεῦμα εἰσῆλθεν (20)	He says there is one God, creator of all things, who has neither been begotten nor has begotten. He also says that Christ was the Word of God and his Spirit, but only a creature and a servant, and that he was born without seed from Mary, the sister of Moses and Aaron. For, he says, the Word of God and the Spirit entered
εἰς τὴν Μαρίαν, καὶ ἐγέννησε τὸν Ἰησοῦν προφήτην ὄντα καὶ δοῦλον τοῦ θεοῦ. Καὶ ὅτι οἱ Ἰουδαῖοι παρανομήσαντες ἠθέλησαν αὐτὸν σταυρῶσαι καὶ κρατήσαντες ἐσταύρωσαν τὴν σκιὰν αὐτοῦ, αὐτὸς δὲ ὁ Χριστὸς οὐκ ἐσταυρώθη, φησίν, οὔτε ἀπέθανεν· ὁ γὰρ θεὸς ἔλαβεν αὐτὸν πρὸς ἑαυτὸν εἰς τὸν οὐρανὸν διὰ τὸ φιλεῖν αὐτόν. Καὶ τοῦτο δὲ λέγει, ὅτι, τοῦ (25) Χριστοῦ ἀνελθόντος εἰς τοὺς οὐρανούς, ἐπηρώτησεν αὐτὸν ὁ θεὸς λέγων· Ὠ Ἰησοῦ, σὺ εἶπας, ὅτι υἱός εἰμι τοῦ θεοῦ καὶ θεός; Καὶ ἀπεκρίθη, φησίν, ὁ Ἰησοῦς· Ἵλεώς μοι, κύριε· σὺ οἶδας, ὅτι οὐκ εἶπον οὐδὲ ὑπερηφανῶ εἶναι δοῦλός σου· ἀλλ' οἱ ἄνθρωποι οἱ παραβάται ἔγραψαν, ὅτι εἶπον τὸν λόγον τοῦτον, καὶ ἐψεύσαντο κατ' ἐμοῦ, καί εἰσι πεπλανημένοι. Καὶ (30)	into Mary and she gave birth to Jesus, who was a prophet and servant of God. And he says that the Jews unlawfully wanted to crucify him, but after arresting him they only crucified his shadow; for, he says, the Christ was not crucified nor did he die, for God took him up to himself into heaven because he loved him. And this is what he says, that when Christ ascended into heaven, God questioned him, saying "O Jesus, did you say 'I am the Son of God and God?'" And Jesus answered, saying, "Be merciful to me, Lord. You know that I did not say (that), nor am I too proud to be your servant. Errant men have written that I have made this declaration, but they are lying about me and they are the ones in error." And,

Greek Text	English Translation
ἀπεκρίθη, φησίν, αὐτῷ ὁ θεός· Οἶδα, ὅτι σὺ οὐκ ἔλεγες τὸν λόγον τοῦτον. Καὶ ἄλλα πολλὰ τερατολογῶν ἐν τῇ τοιαύτῃ συγγραφῇ γέλωτος ἄξια, ταύτην πρὸς θεοῦ ἐπ' αὐτὸν κατενεχθῆναι φρυάττεται. Ἡμῶν δὲ λεγόντων· Καὶ τίς ἐστιν ὁ μαρτυρῶν, ὅτι γραφὴν αὐτῷ δέδωκεν ὁ θεός, ἢ τίς τῶν προφητῶν προεῖπεν, ὅτι τοιοῦτος ἀνίσταται προφήτης, καὶ δια (35) πορούντων αὐτοῖς, ὡς ὁ Μωσῆς τοῦ θεοῦ κατὰ τὸ Σινὰ ὄρος ἐπόψεσι παντὸς τοῦ λαοῦ, ἐν νεφέλῃ καὶ πυρὶ καὶ γνόφῳ καὶ θυέλλῃ φανέντος ἐδέξατο τὸν νόμον, καὶ ὅτι πάντες οἱ προφῆται ἀπὸ Μωσέως καὶ καθεξῆς περὶ τῆς τοῦ Χριστοῦ παρουσίας προηγόρευσαν καὶ ὅτι θεὸς ὁ Χριστὸς καὶ θεοῦ υἱὸς σαρκούμενος ἥξει καὶ σταυρωθησόμενος θνήσκων καὶ ἀναστη- (40)	according to them, God answered him, saying, "I know that you did not say these words." There are many other absurd stories[E] worthy of laughter recorded in this writing, which he insolently boasts[F] descended upon him from God. But when we ask, "and who testified that God has given him a scripture? And who among the prophets has announced that such a prophet would rise up?" they are at a loss. We then relate to them how Moses received the law from God who appeared on Mt. Sinai in the sight of all the people in a cloud and fire and darkness and a whirlwind. We also relate to them that all the prophets, beginning with Moses and in succession, foretold the coming of Christ. They also said that Christ is God, and that as the Son of God he will come by taking on flesh, and that he will be crucified, and die,
σόμενος καὶ ὅτι κριτὴς οὗτος ζώντων καὶ νεκρῶν, καὶ λεγόντων ἡμῶν, πῶς οὐχ οὕτως ἦλθεν ὁ προφήτης ὑμῶν, ἄλλων μαρτυρούντων περὶ αὐτοῦ, ἀλλ' οὐδὲ παρόντων ὑμῶν ὁ θεός, ὡς τῷ Μωσεῖ βλέποντος παντὸς τοῦ λαοῦ, καπνιζομένου τοῦ ὄρους δέδωκε τὸν νόμον, κἀκείνῳ τὴν γραφήν, ἣν φατε, παρέσχεν, ἵνα καὶ ὑμεῖς τὸ βέβαιον ἔχητε, ἀποκρίνονται, ὅτι ὁ (45) θεός, ὅσα θέλει, ποιεῖ. Τοῦτο καὶ ἡμεῖς, φαμέν, οἴδαμεν, ἀλλ' ὅπως ἡ γραφὴ κατῆλθεν εἰς τὸν προφήτην ὑμῶν, ἐρωτῶμεν. Καὶ ἀποκρίνονται, ὅτι, ἐν ὅσῳ κοιμᾶται, κατέβη ἡ γραφὴ ἐπάνω αὐτοῦ. Καὶ τὸ γελοιῶδες πρὸς αὐτοὺς λέγομεν ἡμεῖς, ὅτι λοιπόν, ἐπειδὴ κοιμώμενος ἐδέξατο τὴν γραφὴν καὶ οὐκ ᾔσθετο τῆς ἐνεργείας, εἰς αὐτὸν ἐπληρώθη τὸ τῆς δημώδους παροι- (50)	and rise again, and that he will be the judge of the living and the dead. We ask them, then, "how is it that your prophet did not come in this same way, with others witnessing about him? And how is it that God did not give him the scripture, of which you speak, while in your presence, as God gave the law to Moses on the smoking mountain while all the people were looking on, so that you may have assurance?" They reply that God does as he pleases. We tell them that we know this also. But, we ask, "In what manner was the writing revealed to your prophet?" They replied that while he was asleep the writing came down upon him. Then, in jest, we say to them that since he received the writing while sleeping and was not aware of the divine activity taking place, the popular proverb is fulfilled in him: ["you are spinning me dreams"].[G]

Heresy of the Ishmaelites (Translation from Kotter's text)

Greek Text	English Translation
μίας. Πάλιν ἡμῶν ἐρωτώντων· Πῶς αὐτοῦ ἐντειλαμένου ὑμῖν ἐν τῇ γραφῇ ὑμῶν μηδὲν ποιεῖν ἢ δέχεσθαι ἄνευ μαρτύρων, οὐκ ἠρωτήσατε αὐτόν, ὅτι πρῶτον αὐτὸς ἀπόδειξον διὰ μαρτύρων, ὅτι προφήτης εἶ καὶ ὅτι ἀπὸ θεοῦ ἐξῆλθες, καὶ ποία γραφὴ μαρτυρεῖ περὶ σοῦ, σιωπῶσιν αἰδούμενοι. Πρὸς οὓς εὐλόγως φαμέν· Ἐπειδὴ γυναῖκα γῆμαι οὐκ ἔξεστιν ὑμῖν ἄνευ (55) μαρτύρων οὐδὲ ἀγοράζειν οὐδὲ κτᾶσθαι, οὔτε δὲ ὑμεῖς αὐτοὶ καταδέχεσθε ὄνους ἢ κτῆνος ἀμάρτυρον ἔχειν, ἔχετε μὲν καὶ γυναῖκας καὶ κτήματα καὶ ὄνους καὶ τὰ λοιπὰ διὰ μαρτύρων, μόνην δὲ πίστιν καὶ γραφὴν ἀμάρτυρον ἔχετε· ὁ γὰρ ταύτην ὑμῖν παραδοὺς οὐδαμόθεν ἔχει τὸ βέβαιον οὐδέ τις προμάρτυς ἐκείνου γνωρίζεται, ἀλλὰ καὶ κοιμώμενος ἐδέξατο ταύτην. (60)	Again we ask, "How is it that when he commanded you in your scripture not to do or to receive anything without witnesses, you did not ask him 'first show us through witness that you are a prophet, and that you have come from God, and which scriptures testify about you.'" Ashamed, they remain silent. "With good reason we say this, for you are not allowed to marry a woman without witnesses, nor to do business, nor to acquire (property)—you do not even allow one to receive a donkey or any beast unwitnessed. On the one hand, you take wives and possess property and donkeys and everything else through witnesses; yet, on the other hand, you accept your faith and your scriptures unwitnessed. For the one who has handed down this scripture to you has no verification from any source, nor is there any prior witness to him known. Furthermore, he received this while asleep!"
Καλοῦσι δὲ ἡμᾶς ἑταιριαστάς, ὅτι, φησίν, ἑταῖρον τῷ θεῷ παρεισάγομεν λέγοντες εἶναι τὸν Χριστὸν υἱὸν θεοῦ καὶ θεόν. Πρὸς οὓς φαμεν, ὅτι τοῦτο οἱ προφῆται καὶ ἡ γραφὴ παραδέδωκεν· ὑμεῖς δέ, ὡς διισχυρίζεσθε, τοὺς προφήτας δέχεσθε. Εἰ οὖν κακῶς λέγομεν τὸν Χριστὸν θεοῦ υἱόν, ἐκεῖνοι ἐδίδαξαν καὶ παρέδωκαν ἡμῖν. Καί τινες μὲν αὐτῶν φασιν, ὅτι (65) ἡμεῖς τοὺς προφήτας ἀλληγορήσαντες τοιαῦτα προσεθείκαμεν, ἄλλοι δέ φασιν, ὅτι οἱ Ἑβραῖοι μισοῦντες ἡμᾶς ἐπλάνησαν ὡς ἀπὸ τῶν προφητῶν γράψαντες, ἵνα ἡμεῖς ἀπολώμεθα. Πάλιν δέ φαμεν πρὸς αὐτούς· Ὑμῶν λεγόντων, ὅτι ὁ Χριστὸς λόγος ἐστὶ τοῦ θεοῦ καὶ πνεῦμα, πῶς λοιδορεῖτε ἡμᾶς ὡς ἑταιριαστάς; Ὁ γὰρ (70)	Moreover, they call us "ἑταιριαστάς" (Associators) because, they say, we introduce in addition to God a partner when we declare that Christ is the son of God and God. We say to them in response: "This is what the prophets and the Scriptures have delivered to us. You insist that you also accept the prophets. If, therefore, we are wrong in saying Christ is the son of God, then so too are those who have taught this and handed it down to us." Some of them say that we have allegorized the prophets and added these things to what they have said, while others say that the Hebrews, out of hatred, have deceived us by writing those things as if they had been written by the prophets, so that we might be misled. Again we say to them, "Since you also say that Christ is Word and Spirit of God, why do you accuse us of being "ἑταιριαστάς" (Associators)?

Greek Text	English Translation
λόγος καὶ τὸ πνεῦμα ἀχώριστόν ἐστι τοῦ ἐν ᾧ πέφυκεν· εἰ οὖν ἐν τῷ θεῷ ἐστιν ὡς λόγος αὐτοῦ, δῆλον, ὅτι καὶ θεός ἐστιν. Εἰ δὲ ἐκτός ἐστι τοῦ θεοῦ, ἄλογός ἐστι καθ' ὑμᾶς ὁ θεὸς καὶ ἄπνους. Οὐκοῦν φεύγοντες ἑταιριάζειν τὸν θεὸν ἐκόψατε αὐτόν. Κρεῖσσον γὰρ ἦν λέγειν ὑμᾶς, ὅτι ἑταῖρον ἔχει, ἢ κόπτειν αὐτὸν καὶ ὡς λίθον ἢ ξύλον ἤ τι τῶν ἀναισθήτων παρεισ (75) ἄγειν. Ὥστε ὑμεῖς μὲν ἡμᾶς ψευδηγοροῦντες ἑταιριαστὰς καλεῖτε· ἡμεῖς δὲ κόπτας ὑμᾶς προσαγορεύομεν τοῦ θεοῦ. Διαβάλλουσι δὲ ἡμᾶς ὡς εἰδωλολάτρας προσκυνοῦντας τὸν σταυρόν, ὃν καὶ βδελύττονται. Καί φαμεν πρὸς αὐτούς· Πῶς οὖν ὑμεῖς λίθῳ προστρίβεσθε κατὰ τὸν Χαβαθὰν ὑμῶν καὶ φιλεῖτε τὸν λίθον ἀσπαζόμενοι; Καί (80)	For the Word and the Spirit are inseparable from the one in whom they exist by nature. Therefore, if the Word of God is in God, then it is evident that he is God as well. If, however, the Word is outside of God, then, according to you, God is without Word and Spirit. Consequently, by avoiding the association of a partner with God, you have mutilated him. It would be far better for you to say that he had a partner, rather than mutilate him and treat him like a stone, a piece of wood or some inanimate object. Thus, since you falsely call us "ἑταιριαστάς" (Associators), we will, in turn, call you "κόπτας" (Mutilators) of God. They also accuse us of idolatry because they say we worship the cross which they despise. So we say to them, "Why, therefore, do you rub yourselves[H] against the stone attached to your "Χαβαθὰν" (Ka'ba), and express your adoration for the stone by kissing it?
τινες αὐτῶν φασιν, ἐπάνω αὐτοῦ τὸν Ἀβραὰμ συνουσιάσαι τῇ Ἄγαρ, ἄλλοι δέ, ὅτι ἐπ' αὐτὸν προσέδησε τὴν κάμηλον μέλλων θύειν τὸν Ἰσαάκ. Καὶ πρὸς αὐτοὺς ἀποκρινόμεθα· Τῆς γραφῆς λεγούσης, ὅτι ὄρος ἦν ἀλσῶδες καὶ ξύλα, ἀφ' ὧν καὶ εἰς τὴν ὁλοκάρπωσιν σχίσας ὁ Ἀβραὰμ ἐπέθηκε τῷ Ἰσαάκ, καὶ ὅτι μετὰ τῶν παίδων τὰς ὄνους κατέλιπεν. Πόθεν οὖν (85) ὑμῖν τὸ ληρεῖν; Οὐ γὰρ ἐκεῖσε ξύλα δρυμώδη κεῖται οὔτε ὄνοι διοδεύουσιν. Αἰδοῦνται μέν, ὅμως φασὶν εἶναι τὸν λίθον τοῦ Ἀβραάμ. Εἶτα φαμεν· Ἔστω τοῦ Ἀβραάμ, ὡς ὑμεῖς ληρεῖτε· τοῦτον οὖν ἀσπαζόμενοι, ὅτι μόνον ὁ Ἀβραὰμ ἐπ' αὐτὸν συνουσίασε γυναικὶ ἢ ὅτι τὴν κάμηλον προσέδησεν, οὐκ αἰδεῖσθε, ἀλλ' ἡμᾶς εὐθύνετε, ὅτι τὸν σταυρὸν τοῦ Χριστοῦ (90)	Some say that it is because Abraham had sexual relations with Hagar upon it, and others that he tied his camel to it when he was about to sacrifice Isaac. And we reply to them, "The Scripture says that the mountain was wooded and had trees from which Abraham cut wood and laid it upon Isaac for the sacrifice of a whole burnt offering, and he left the donkeys with the servants. Therefore, why talk nonsense, for in that place there is neither wood from a forest or passage[I] for donkeys." They are indeed ashamed; nevertheless, they assert that the stone is of Abraham. Then we respond, "Suppose that it is of Abraham, as you foolishly maintain. Are you not ashamed for kissing this thing just because Abraham had sexual relations with a woman upon it, or that he tied a camel to it? Yet you convict us of venerating the cross of Christ,

Heresy of the Ishmaelites (Translation from Kotter's text)

Greek Text	English Translation
προσκυνοῦμεν, δι' οὗ δαιμόνων ἰσχὺς καὶ διαβόλου καταλέλυται πλάνη. Οὗτος δέ, ὅν φασι λίθον, κεφαλὴ τῆς Ἀφροδίτης ἐστίν, ἣ προσεκύνουν, ἣν δὴ καὶ Χαβὰρ προσηγόρευον, ἐφ' ὃν καὶ μέχρι νῦν ἐγγλυφίδος ἀποσκίασμα τοῖς ἀκριβῶς κατανοοῦσι φαίνεται. Οὗτος ὁ Μάμεδ πολλάς, ὡς εἴρηται, ληρωδίας συντάξας ἑκάστῃ τούτων (95) προσηγορίαν ἐπέθηκεν, οἷον ἡ γραφὴ "τῆς γυναικὸς" καὶ ἐν αὐτῇ τέσσαρας γυναῖκας προφανῶς λαμβάνειν νομοθετεῖ καὶ παλλακάς, ἐὰν δύνηται, χιλίας, ὅσας ἡ χεὶρ αὐτοῦ κατάσχῃ ὑποκειμένας ἐκ τῶν τεσσάρων γυναικῶν. Ἣν δ' ἂν βουληθῇ ἀπολύειν, ἣν ἐθελήσειε, καὶ κομίζεσθαι ἄλλην, ἐκ τοιαύτης αἰτίας νομοθετήσας. Σύμπονον ἔσχεν ὁ Μάμεδ Ζεῒδ προσαγο- (100)	through which the power of demons and the deception of the devil have been destroyed?" Moreover, this "stone," about which they speak, is the head of Aphrodite, whom they used to worship, and whom they also called *Kabar*. Even today, traces of an engraved image are visible to careful observers. This Mamed, as it has been related, composed many absurd stories[J] and gave a title to each one. For example, there is the writing *On Woman*, in which he clearly makes legal provision for taking four wives as well as a thousand concubines, if one is able—as many as his hand can possess and support beyond the four wives. He also made it legal for one to divorce whomever he pleases, or, if he wishes, to take up another, for the following reason: Mamed had a companion named Zayd.
ρευόμενον. Οὗτος γυναῖκα ὡραίαν ἔσχεν, ἧς ἠράσθη ὁ Μάμεδ. Καθημένων οὖν αὐτῶν φησιν ὁ Μάμεδ· Ὁ δεῖνα, ὁ θεὸς ἐνετείλατό μοι τὴν γυναῖκά σου λαβεῖν. Ὁ δὲ ἀπεκρίθη· Ἀπόστολος εἶ· ποίησον, ὥς σοιὸ θεὸς εἶπε· λάβε τὴν γυναῖκά μου. Μᾶλλον δέ, ἵνα ἄνωθεν εἴπωμεν, ἔφη πρὸς αὐτόν· Ὁ θεὸς ἐνετείλατό μοι, ἵνα ἀπολύσῃς τὴν γυναῖκά σου (105) Ὁ δὲ ἀπέλυσε. Καὶ μεθ' ἡμέρας ἄλλας φησίν· Ἵνα κἀγὼ αὐτὴν λάβω, ἐνετείλατο ὁ θεός. Εἶτα λαβὼν καὶ μοιχεύσας αὐτὴν τοιοῦτον ἔθηκε νόμον· Ὁ βουλόμενος ἀπολυέτω τὴν γυναῖκα αὐτοῦ. Ἐὰν δὲ μετὰ τὸ ἀπολῦσαι ἐπ' αὐτὴν ἀναστρέψῃ, γαμείτω αὐτὴν ἄλλος. Οὐ γὰρ ἔξεστι λαβεῖν αὐτήν, εἰ μὴ γαμηθῇ ὑφ' ἑτέρου. Ἐὰν δὲ καὶ ἀδελφὸς ἀπολύσῃ, γαμείτω αὐτὴν (110)	This man had a beautiful wife with whom Mamed fell in love. While they were sitting together, Mamed said, "Zayd,[K] God has commanded me to take away your wife." Zayd replied, "You are an apostle. Do as God has told you; take my wife." Or rather, that we may tell it more precisely from the beginning, he said to him, "God has commanded me (to tell you) that you should divorce your wife." And Zayd divorced her. After several days he said, "God has now commanded that I should also take her." Then, after having taken her and committed adultery with her, he made up this law: "Let him who desires it, divorce his wife. But if he should desire to return to her after having divorced, let someone else (first) marry her. For it is not lawful to take her unless she has been married by another. Furthermore, even if a brother divorces her, let his

Greek Text	English Translation
ἀδελφὸς αὐτοῦ ὁ βουλόμενος. Ἐν αὐτῇ δὲ τῇ γραφῇ τοιαῦτα παραγγέλλει· Ἔργασαι τὴν γῆν, ἣν ἔδωκέ σοι ὁ θεός, καὶ φιλοκάλησον αὐτήν, καὶ τόδε ποίησον καὶ τοιῶσδε, ἵνα μὴ πάντα λέγω ὡς ἐκεῖνος αἰσχρά. Πάλιν γραφὴ τῆς καμήλου τοῦ θεοῦ, περὶ ἧς λέγει, ὅτι ἦν κάμηλος ἐκ τοῦ θεοῦ καὶ ἔπινεν ὅλον τὸν ποταμὸν καὶ οὐ διήρχετο μεταξὺ δύο ὀρέων (115) διὰ τὸ μὴ χωρεῖσθαι. Λαὸς οὖν, φησίν, ἦν ἐν τῷ τόπῳ, καὶ τὴν μὲν μίαν ἡμέραν αὐτὸς ἔπινε τὸ ὕδωρ, ἡ δὲ κάμηλος τῇ ἑξῆς. Πίνουσα δὲ τὸ ὕδωρ ἔτρεφεν αὐτοὺς τὸ γάλα παρεχομένη ἀντὶ τοῦ ὕδατος. Ἀνέστησαν οὖν οἱ ἄνδρες ἐκεῖνοι, φησί, πονηροὶ ὄντες καὶ ἀπέκτειναν τὴν κάμηλον· τῆς δὲ γέννημα ὑπῆρχεν μικρὰ κάμηλος, ἥτις, φησί, τῆς μητρὸς ἀναιρεθεί- (120)	brother marry her, if he is willing." In this same scripture precepts are given such as: "Till the land which God has given you, and beautify it. And do this and in this manner"—not to say all the obscene things, as he did. Again, there is the writing of the *Camel of God*. On this subject he says that there was a camel from God, and she drank a whole river and could not pass between two mountains due to inadequate space. There were people in that place, he says, and on one day they would drink the water, while the camel would drink it on the next. Moreover, by drinking the water she nourished them because she provided them with milk instead of water. However, since these men were wicked, he says, they rose up and killed the camel. However, she had an offspring, a small camel, which, he says, when the mother had been destroyed,
σης ἀνεβόησε πρὸς τὸν θεόν, καὶ ἔλαβεν αὐτὴν πρὸς ἑαυτόν. Πρὸς οὕς φαμεν· Πόθεν ἡ κάμηλος ἐκείνη· Καὶ λέγουσιν, ὅτι ἐκ θεοῦ. Καὶ φαμεν· Συνεβιβάσθη ταύτῃ κάμηλος ἄλλη; Καὶ λέγουσιν· Οὐχί. Πόθεν οὖν, φαμέν, ἐγέννησεν; Ὁρῶμεν γὰρ τὴν κάμηλον ὑμῶν ἀπάτορα καὶ ἀμήτορα καὶ ἀγενεαλόγητον, γεννήσασα δὲ κακὸν ἔπαθεν. Ἀλλ' οὐδὲ ὁ βιβάσας (125) φαίνεται, καὶ ἡ μικρὰ κάμηλος ἀνελήφθη. Ὁ οὖν προφήτης ὑμῶν, ᾧ, καθὼς λέγετε, ἐλάλησεν ὁ θεός, διὰ τί περὶ τῆς καμήλου οὐκ ἔμαθε, ποῦ βόσκεται καὶ τίνες γαλεύονται ταύτην ἀμέλγοντες;"Ἢ καὶ αὐτὴ μὴ ποτε κακοῖς ὡς ἡ μήτηρ περιτυχοῦσα ἀνῃρέθη ἢ ἐν τῷ παραδείσῳ πρόδρομος ὑμῶν εἰσῆλθεν, ἀφ' ἧς ὁ ποταμὸς ὑμῖν ἔσται, ὃν ληρεῖτε, τοῦ γάλακτος; (130)	cried out to God; and he took it to himself. Then we say to them, Where was that camel from?" And they reply that it was from God. And we say, "Did any other camel couple with this one?" and they say, "No." Therefore, we say, "How then was it begotten? For we see that your camel was without father, without mother, and without genealogy, and the one who begat suffered evil. Yet there appears neither the one who coupled (with the mother), nor (where) the small camel was taken up. According to you, your prophet spoke from God. Why, then, did he not learn where the camel grazed and who got milk from milking it? Was she destroyed one day by evil men, as her mother had been? Or did she enter into Paradise as your forerunner so that you might have the river of milk that you so foolishly talk about?

Heresy of the Ishmaelites (Translation from Kotter's text)

Greek Text	English Translation
Τρεῖς γάρ φατε ποταμοὺς ὑμῖν ἐν τῷ παραδείσῳ ῥέειν· ὕδατος, οἴνου καὶ γάλακτος. Ἐὰν ἐκτός ἐστιν ἡ πρόδρομος ὑμῶν κάμηλος τοῦ παραδείσου, δῆλον, ὅτι ἀπεξηράνθη πείνῃ καὶ δίψῃ ἢ ἄλλοι τοῦ γάλακτος αὐτῆς ἀπολαύουσι, καὶ μάτην ὁ προφήτης ὑμῶν φρυάττεται ὡς ὁμιλήσας θεῷ· οὐ γὰρ τὸ μυστήριον αὐτῷ ἀπεκαλύφθη τῆς καμήλου. Εἰ δὲ ἐν τῷ (135) παραδείσῳ ἐστί, πάλιν πίνει τὸ ὕδωρ, καὶ ἀνυδρίᾳ ξηραίνεσθε ἐν μέσῳ τῆς τρυφῆς τοῦ παραδείσου. Κἂν οἶνον ἐκ τοῦ παροδεύοντος ἐπιθυμήσητε ποταμοῦ, μὴ παρόντος ὕδατος— ἀπέπιε γὰρ ὅλον ἡ κάμηλος— ἄκρατον πίνοντες ἐκκαίεσθε καὶ μέθῃ παραπαίετε καὶ καθεύδετε· καρηβαροῦντες δὲ καὶ μεθ' ὕπνον καὶ κεκραιπαληκότες ἐξ οἴνου τῶν ἡδέων ἐπιλαν- (140)	For you say that three rivers flow for you in Paradise: of water, wine and milk. If the camel, your forerunner, is outside of Paradise, it is evident that either she is dried up from hunger and thirst, or others are enjoying her milk. In vain, then, your prophet insolently boasts of having conversed with God, for the mystery of the camel has not been revealed to him. But, on the other hand, if she is in Paradise, she will again drink up the water, and for lack of water you will dry up in the midst of the delights of Paradise. Even if you desire to drink wine from the river flowing by, since there is no water to mix with your wine, for the camel drank it all, you will become inflamed, overcome with drunkenness and fall asleep. And because your head is heavy with a drunken sleep and you are intoxicated by wine, you will miss out on the
θάνεσθε τοῦ παραδείσου. Πῶς οὖν ὁ προφήτης ὑμῶν οὐκ ἐνενοήθη ταῦτα, μήποτε συμβῇ ὑμῖν ἐν τῷ παραδείσῳ τῆς τρυφῆς, οὐδὲ περὶ τῆς καμήλου πεφρόντικεν, ὅπου νῦν διάγει; Ἀλλ' οὐδὲ ὑμεῖς ἠρωτήσατε αὐτόν, ὡς ὑμῖν περὶ τῶν τριῶν διηγόρευσεν ὀνειροπολούμενος ποταμῶν. Ἀλλ' ἡμεῖς σαφῶς τὴν θαυμαστὴν ὑμῶν κάμηλον εἰς ψυχὰς ὄνων, ὅπου καὶ (145) ὑμεῖς μέλλετε διάγειν ὡς κτηνώδεις, προδραμοῦσαν ὑμῶν ἐπαγγελλόμεθα. Ἐκεῖσε δὲ σκότος ἐστὶ τὸ ἐξώτερον καὶ κόλασις ἀτελεύτητος, πῦρ ἠχοῦν, σκώληξ ἀκοίμητος καὶ ταρτάριοι δαίμονες. Πάλιν φησὶν ὁ Μάμεδ· ἡ γραφὴ "τῆς τραπέζης" λέγει δέ, ὅτι ὁ Χριστὸς ᾐτήσατο παρὰ τοῦ θεοῦ τράπεζαν, καὶ ἐδόθη αὐτῷ. Ὁ γὰρ θεός, φησίν, (150)	pleasures of Paradise. How is it, then, that your prophet did not think you might encounter these things in the Paradise of delights? Nor did he show any concern about where the camel now lives. But neither did you ask him (about the camel); instead, this dreamer was informing you about the three rivers. But we clearly profess to you that your wonderful camel has run before you into the souls of donkeys, where you also are destined to spend your life as beasts. But at that place are the outer darkness, eternal punishment, roaring fire, worms that never sleep, and the demons of Hell. Mamed speaks again in the writing on *The Table*. He says that Christ requested a table from God and it was given to him. For God, he says,

Greek Text	English Translation
εἶπεν αὐτῷ, ὅτι δέδωκά σοι καὶ τοῖς σοῖς τράπεζαν ἄφθαρτον.	said to him, "I have given to you and to yours an incorruptible table."
Πάλιν γραφὴν "βοιδίου" λέγει καὶ ἄλλα τινὰ ῥήματα γέλωτος ἄξια, ἃ διὰ τὸ πλῆθος παραδραμεῖν οἴομαι δεῖν. Τούτους περιτέμνεσθαι σὺν γυναιξὶ νομοθετήσας καὶ μήτε σαββατίζειν μήτε βαπτίζεσθαι προστάξας,τὰ μὲν τῶν ἐν τῷ νόμῳ ἀπηγορευμένων ἐσθίειν, τῶν δὲ ἀπέχεσθαι παραδούς· (155) οἰνοποσίαν δὲ παντελῶς ἀπηγόρευσεν.	Furthermore, I think I will pass over the writing on *The Cow* as well as other sayings worthy only of laughter because of their number. He legislated that they be circumcised, including their wives. He also gave a command not to keep the Sabbath and not to be baptized, as well as on the one hand, to eat what is forbidden in the law, and on the other hand, to abstain from other things that are permitted. He also absolutely prohibited the drinking of wine.

A. Σάρρας + κενοὺς = Saracens ("cast away empty by Sarah").

B. Χαβὰρ in Greek and كبر in Arabic.

C. Lampe, διαθρυλλεῖ, 348.

D. Lampe, συντάγματα, 1338.

E. Lampe, τερατολογῶν, 1388.

F. Lampe, φρυάττεται, 1492.

G. The proverb is not in the text, but Lequien suggests that it comes from Plato. See Sahas, *John of Damascus on Islam*, 135, n.1, and Chase, *St. John of Damascus: Writings*, 155, n. 106.

H. Lampe, βεσθε, 1168.

I. Since the Greek means simply to "travel through," this could mean "travel through so far," which may refer to the long passage from Palestine to Arabia. See Newman, *Early Christian-Muslim Dialogue*, 155, n. 39.

J. Lampe, ληρωδίας, 800.

K. Lampe, 335. Lampe writes that δεῖνα, translated as "such a one," can be "used to indicate that the name of a person is to be inserted by the reader or speaker."

Appendix D
Disputation between a Christian and a Saracen

(A translation of selected passages from Kotter's text)[54]

Greek Text	English Translation
Διάλεξις Χριστιανοῦ καὶ Σαρακηνοῦ Section 1 Ἐρωτηθεὶς ὁ Χριστιανὸς παρὰ Σαρακηνοῦ· Τίνα λέγεις αἴτιον καλοῦ καὶ κακοῦ; ὁ Χριστιανός· Πάντων τῶν ἀγαθῶν οὐδένα φαμὲν αἴτιον εἶναι εἰ μὴ τὸν θεόν, κακῶν δὲ οὔ. Καὶ ἀποκριθεὶς ὁ Σαρακηνὸς εἶπεν· Τίνα λέγεις αἴτιον τῶν κακῶν; Ὁ Χριστιανός· Τὸν ἀπὸ γνώμης ὄντα διάβολον δηλονότι καὶ ἡμᾶς τοὺς ἀνθρώπους. Ὁ Σαρακηνός· (5) Χάριν τίνος; Ὁ Χριστιανός· Διὰ τὸ αὐτεξούσιον.	Disputation between a Christian and a Saracen Section 1a: The omnipotence of God and the cause of evil (Kotter 1)[A] When the Christian was asked by the Saracen, "Who do you say is the cause of good as well as of evil?" The *Christian*: We say that God alone is the author of all that is good, but not of evil. The *Saracen* asked in response: "Who do you say is the cause of evil?" The *Christian*: Obviously the devil, who has perverted the truth by choice, and we humans. *Saracen*: Because of what? *Christian*: Because of our own free will.

54. Kotter IV, 427–38. This critical text was the main source of the author's translation, which was then compared to a French translation of the critical text, Le Coz, *Jean Damascene*, 210–27. PG 94:1336–48 and PG 96:1596–97 were consulted, as well as the pre-critical text translation found in Sahas, *John of Damascus on Islam*, 142–59.

Ὁ Σαρακηνός· (6) Τί οὖν· Αὐτεξούσιος εἶ καί, ὅσα θέλεις, δύνασαι ποιεῖν καὶ ποιεῖς; Ὁ Χριστιανός· Εἰς δύο μόνα πέπλασμαι ὑπὸ τοῦ θεοῦ αὐτεξούσιος. Ὁ Σαρακηνός· Ποῖα ταῦτα; Ὁ Χριστιανός· Κακοπραγεῖν καὶ ἀγαθοπραγεῖν, ὅ ἐστι καλὸν καὶ (10) κακόν. Χάριν τούτου κακὰ μὲν πράττων τιμωροῦμαι ὑπὸ νόμου τοῦ θεοῦ, ἀγαθὰ δὲ πράττων οὐ φοβοῦμαι τὸν νόμον, ἀλλὰ καὶ τιμῶμαι καὶ ἐλεοῦμαι ὑπὸ τοῦ θεοῦ. Ὁμοίως καὶ ὁ διάβολος πρὸ τῶν ἀνθρώπων αὐτεξούσιος πέπλασται ὑπὸ τοῦ θεοῦ καὶ ἡμάρτησεν, καὶ ὁ θεὸς τῆς ἰδίας τάξεως ἐξέωσεν αὐτόν. (15)	*Section 1b: Man's Power (Kotter 1)* **Saracen**: What then? Do you have free will to do anything you wish? **Christian**: God has created me free in regard to only two things. **Saracen**: What are they? **Christian**: Doing what is evil and doing what is good. Accordingly, if I do wrong, the law of God punishes me, but if I do what is good, I do not fear the law. Instead, I am rewarded by God and by his mercy. In the same way, before the first man, the devil had been created with his own free will by God, but he sinned, and God expelled him from his proper state.
ἐπεί, ὡς λέγεις σύ, καλὰ καὶ κακὰ ἐκ θεοῦ εἶναι, (20) εὑρεθήσεται ὁ θεὸς κατὰ σὲ ἄδικος, ὅπερ οὐκ ἔστιν· ἐπεὶ γὰρ ὁ θεὸς προσέταξεν, ὡς σὺ λέγεις, τὸν πόρνον πορνεύειν καὶ τὸν κλέπτην κλέπτειν καὶ τὸν ἀνδροφόνον ἀνδροφονεῖν, ἄξιοί εἰσιν τιμῆς· τὸ γὰρ θέλημα τοῦ θεοῦ ἐποίησαν. (24)	*Section 1c: Justice of God (Kotter 1)* **Christian**: If, as you say, good and evil come from God, then God is unfair; but he is not. Indeed, if God had commanded the adulterer to fornicate, the thief to steal and the murderer to kill, as you say, then these men deserve honor for their obedience to his will.

Ὁ δὲ Σαρακηνός· Τίς, φησί, πλάττει τὰ βρέφη ἐν κοιλίαις γυναικῶν; (28) Τοῦτο γὰρ προβάλλονται οἱ Σαρακηνοὶ πρὸς ἡμᾶς πρόβλημα δεινότατον θέλοντες ἀποδεῖξαι τὸν θεὸν αἴτιον τῶν κακῶν. Εἰ γὰρ ἀποκριθεὶς (30) λέγω, ὅτι ὁ θεὸς πλάττει τὰ βρέφη ἐν κοιλίαις γυναικῶν, ἐρεῖ ὁ Σαρακηνός· Ἰδοὺ ὁ θεὸς σύνεργός ἐστι τῷ πόρνῳ καὶ τῷ μοιχῷ. Ὁ Χριστιανὸς πρὸς ταῦτα ἀποκρίνεται· Οὐδαμῶς εὑρίσκομεν μετὰ τὴν πρώτην ἑβδομάδα τῆς κοσμοποιίας τὴν γραφὴν λέγουσαν πλάττειν τὸν θεὸν ἢ κτίζειν τι. (35) "ἐποίησεν ὁ θεὸς τὸν οὐρανὸν καὶ τὴν γῆν καὶ τὸν σύμπαντα (61) κόσμον ἐν ἓξ ἡμέραις καὶ τῇ ἑβδόμῃ κατέπαυσεν ἀπὸ πάντων τῶν ἔργων αὐτοῦ, ὧν ἤρξατο ποιεῖν," καθὼς καὶ ἡ γραφὴ μαρτυρεῖ μοι. (63)	*Section 1d: "Creation" and/or "generation," (Kotter 1)* And the *Saracen*: "Who," he says, "forms the infants in the wombs of the women?" (The Saracens present this difficult objection because they want to prove that God is the cause of evil. For if I reply by saying, "God forms the infants in the wombs of the women," the Saracen will say, "Behold, God is cooperating with the fornicator and the adulterer.") The *Christian* responds to this: "We find nowhere in Scripture where it says that God formed or created anything after the first week of the creation of the world. . . .. For God created the heavens and the earth and the universe in six days, and the seventh day he rested from all the work he had started doing, as the Scriptures witness to me."
Ὁ δὲ Σαρακηνός· Καὶ πῶς φησιν ὁ θεὸς πρὸς Ἰερεμίαν· "Πρὸ τοῦ (64) με πλάσαι σε ἐν κοιλίᾳ ἐπίσταμαί σε καὶ ἐκ μήτρας ἡγίακά σε;" Ὁ Χριστιανός· (65) Παντὸς ἀνδρὸς ἐν κοιλίᾳ ἔπλασεν ὁ θεὸς τὴν ἔμψυχον καὶ σπερματικὴν δύναμιν ἀπὸ Ἀδὰμ καὶ καθεξῆς. Ἀδὰμ γὰρ ἐν κοιλίᾳ ἔχων τὸν Σὴθ ἐγέννησεν, ὡς προεῖπον, καὶ Σὴθ τὸν Ἐνώς, καὶ ἕκαστος ἄνθρωπος προέχων ἐν τῇ κοιλίᾳ αὐτοῦ υἱὸν καὶ ὁ υἱὸς ἐγέννησε καὶ γεννᾷ μέχρι τοῦ παρόντος. (70)	*Section 1e: God's foreknowledge of man's destiny (Kotter 1)* And the *Saracen*: How is it that God said to Jeremiah, "Before I formed you in the womb I knew you, and while in the womb I sanctified you." The *Christian*: Since Adam onwards, God gave to every man the power to engender life in the womb. For Adam, having the power to engender life in the womb became the father of Seth, and Seth of Enosh, and every man engenders sons who in turn engender sons until this present time.

Section 2

Ὁ δὲ ἐναντίος· Καὶ ἦν πρὸ Χριστοῦ βάπτισμα; Ὁ γὰρ Ἱερεμίας (1) πρὸ Χριστοῦ γεννᾶται. Ὁ Χριστιανός· Ἦν κατὰ τὴν μαρτυρίαν τοῦ ἁγίου ἀποστόλου φάσκοντος, ὅτι οἱ μὲν διὰ νεφέλης, οἱ δὲ διὰ θαλάσσης ἐβαπτίσθησαν. Καὶ ὁ κύριος ἐν εὐαγγελίοις φησίν· "Ἐὰν μή τις γεννηθῇ δι' ὕδατος καὶ πνεύματος, οὐ μὴ εἰσέλθῃ εἰς τὴν βασιλείαν τῶν οὐρανῶν." (5) Ὥστε ὁ Ἀβραὰμ καὶ Ἰσαὰκ καὶ Ἰακὼβ καὶ οἱ λοιποὶ πρὸ Χριστοῦ ἅγιοι εἰσερχόμενοι εἰς τὴν βασιλείαν τῶν οὐρανῶν προεβαπτίσθησαν, ἐπεὶ κατὰ τὴν μαρτυρίαν τοῦ Χριστοῦ, εἰ μὴ ἐβαπτίσθησαν, οὐκ ἂν ἐσῴζοντο. Μαρτυρεῖ δὲ τὸ πνεῦμα τὸ ἅγιον λέγον· "Ἀπηλλοτριώθησαν οἱ ἁμαρτωλοὶ ἀπὸ μήτρας," τουτέστι τῆς τοῦ βαπτίσματος. Χάριν τούτου ὁμολογοῦμεν, (10) ὅτι πάντες οἱ σωθέντες καὶ οἱ σῳζόμενοι διὰ βαπτίσματος ἐσώθησαν καὶ σῴζονται χάριτι θεοῦ. (12)

Section 1f: Baptism and the will of God (Kotter 2)

And the *opponent*: "But was there baptism before Christ? For Jeremiah was born before Christ."

The *Christian*: "There was, according to the testimony of the holy apostle, some who were baptized in the cloud and others in the sea. And the Lord said in the gospels, "He who is not born of the water and the Spirit will not enter the kingdom of heaven." Therefore, Abraham, Isaac, Jacob, and all the other saints who preceded Christ and have entered the kingdom of heaven have been baptized before, since, according to the testimony of Christ, if they had not been baptized, they would not have been saved. ... Therefore, we proclaim that all who were and are saved through baptism, were or are saved by the grace of God.

Section 3

Ὁ Σαρακηνός· Τὸν ποιοῦντα τὸ θέλημα αὐτοῦ τοῦ θεοῦ καλὸν (1) εἶναι λέγεις ἢ κακόν; Γνοὺς δὲ τὴν πανουργίαν αὐτοῦ ὁ Χριστιανὸς ἔφη· Ὃ θέλεις εἰπεῖν, ἐπίσταμαι. Ὁ Σαρακηνός· Φανέρωσόν μοι αὐτό. Ὁ Χριστιανός· Εἰπεῖν θέλεις, ὅτι ὁ Χριστὸς θέλων ἔπαθεν ἢ μὴ θέλων; Καὶ ἐάν σοι εἴπω· Θέλων ἔπαθεν, ἵνα μοι εἴπῃς· Ἀπελθε λοιπόν, προσκύνησον (5) τοὺς Ἰουδαίους, διότι τὸ θέλημα τοῦ θεοῦ σου ἐποίησαν. Ὁ Σαρακηνός· Οὕτως, φησί, σοὶ ἤθελον εἰπεῖν· εἰ ἔστι σοι λόγος, ἀποκρίθητί μοι. Ὁ Χριστιανός· Ὃ τι σὺ λέγεις θέλημα εἶναι, ἐγὼ λέγω ἀνοχὴν καὶ μακροθυμίαν. Ὁ Σαρακηνός· Πόθεν δύνῃ τοῦτο παραστῆσαι; (9)

Section 1g: God's providential and permissive will (Kotter 3 and 4)

The *Saracen*: "In your opinion, is the one who does the will of his God good or evil?"

The *Christian*, however, sensing a trap, said: "I know what you are getting at."

The *Saracen*: "Explain it to me."

The *Christian*: You want to ask me: "Did Christ suffer willingly or unwillingly?" So that if I say to you, "He suffered willingly," then you will say to me, "go and bow down before the Jews, for they have done the will of your God."

The *Saracen* admits, "That is what I wanted to tell you. If you can answer me, do it."

The *Christian*: What you call "will," I call "tolerance" and "patience."

The *Saracen*: How can you demonstrate that?

Section 5

Ἐὰν ἐρωτηθῇς ὑπὸ Σαρακηνοῦ λέγοντος· Τί λέγεις εἶναι τὸν Χριστόν; (1)
εἰπὲ αὐτῷ· Λόγον θεοῦ, μηδὲν ἐν τούτῳ νομίζων ἁμαρτάνειν, ἐπεὶ
καὶ λόγος λέγεται παρὰ τῇ γραφῇ καὶ σοφία καὶ βραχίων καὶ δύναμις θεοῦ
καὶ ἄλλα πολλὰ τοιαῦτα· πολυώνυμος γάρ ἐστιν. Καὶ ἀντερώτησον αὐτὸν
καὶ σὺ λέγων· Τί λέγεται παρὰ τῇ γραφῇ σου ὁ Χριστός; Καὶ ἴσως θελήσει (5)
ἐρωτῆσαί σε ἐκεῖνος ἄλλο τι θέλων ἐκφυγεῖν σε·
μὴ ἀποκριθῇς αὐτῷ,
ἕως ἂν λύσῃ τὸ ἐρώτημά σου. Ἀνάγκη πᾶσα ἀποκριθήσεταί σοι λέγων·
Παρὰ τῇ γραφῇ μου πνεῦμα καὶ λόγος θεοῦ λέγεται ὁ Χριστός. Καὶ τότε
εἰπὲ αὐτῷ σὺ πάλιν· Τὸ πνεῦμα τοῦ θεοῦ καὶ ὁ λόγος παρὰ τῇ γραφῇ
σου ἄκτιστα λέγονται ἢ κτιστά; Καὶ ἐὰν εἴπῃ, ὅτι ἄκτιστα, εἰπὲ αὐτῷ· (10)
Ἰδοὺ ὁμοφωνεῖς μοι· καὶ γὰρ τὸ μὴ κτισθὲν ὑπό τινος, ἀλλὰ κτίζον θεός
ἐστιν. Εἰ δὲ ὅλως τολμήσει εἰπεῖν, ὅτι κτιστά εἰσιν, εἰπὲ αὐτῷ· Καὶ τίς ἔκτισε
τὸ πνεῦμα καὶ τὸν λόγον τοῦ θεοῦ;
Καὶ ἐὰν ἐξ ἀπορίας εἴπῃ,
ὅτι ὁ θεὸς αὐτὰ ἔκτισεν, εἰπὲ αὐτῷ· Πρὸ μικροῦ ἔλεγες, ἄκτιστα εἶναι,
καὶ ἀρτίως λέγεις, ὅτι ὁ θεὸς αὐτὰ ἔκτισε. Ἰδού, εἰ ἔλεγον ἐγὼ πρός σε (15)
τοιοῦτον, ἔλεγες ἂν πρός με, ὅτι· Ἠφάνισας τὴν μαρτυρίαν σου, καὶ
τοῦ λοιποῦ οὐ πιστεύω σοι, ὅσα ἂν εἴπῃς. Ὅμως οὖν καὶ τοῦτο ἐρωτῶ σε·
Πρὸ τοῦ κτίσαι ὁ θεὸς τὸ πνεῦμα καὶ τὸν λόγον οὐκ εἶχεν πνεῦμα
οὐδὲ λόγον; Καὶ φεύξεται ἀπὸ σοῦ μὴ ἔχων τι ἀποκριθῆναί σοι—
αἱρετικοὶ γάρ εἰσιν οἱ τοιοῦτοι κατὰ Σαρακηνοὺς καὶ πάνυ βδελυκτοὶ (20)
καὶ ἀπόβλητοι—καί, ἐὰν αὐτὸν θελήσῃς δημοσιεῦσαι τοῖς λοιποῖς
Σαρακηνοῖς, φοβηθήσεταί σε πολύ. (22)

Section 2a: Christ and the Word of God (Kotter 5)

If you will be asked by a *Saracen*, "What[B] do you say the Christ is?" *say* to him, "Word of God." And do not suppose that you commit a sin, because in the Scripture he is called Word and wisdom and arm and power of God and many other similar things, for he has many names. And *you* also return the question to him and ask "What is Christ called in your Scripture?" If he tries to avoid this question and wants to question you on another subject, do not answer him before he has answered your question. *He* will be compelled to answer you, "In my Scripture Christ is called Spirit and Word of God." And then *ask* him again, "According to your Scripture, are the Spirit of God and the Word said to be uncreated or created?" If *he* says they are uncreated, *tell* him: "Behold, you agree with me, for that which is not created by someone must be God who creates! If he is actually bold enough to say that they are created, say to him, "And who created the Spirit and the Word of God?" And if, out of perplexity, *he* tells you that God created them, *say* to him: "a little before you were saying that they are uncreated, and just now you are saying that God created them." Well, if I told you the same thing, *you* would have said to me, "You have destroyed your testimony, and whatever you say from now on, I will not believe you." Nevertheless, I will ask you this, "Before God created the Spirit and the Word did he have neither Spirit nor Word?" And *he* will flee from you, having nothing to say in answer to you. For those who say such things among the Saracens are regarded as heretics and are rejected and detested by other Saracens. And if you want to denounce him to other Saracens he will be very afraid of you.

Section 6 Καὶ ἐὰν ἐρωτήσῃ σε ὁ Σαρακηνὸς λέγων· Τὰ λόγια τοῦ θεοῦ κτιστά (1) εἰσιν ἢ ἄκτιστα; Τοῦτο γὰρ προβάλλονται πρὸς ἡμᾶς ἐρώτημα δεινότατον θέλοντες ἀποδεῖξαι κτιστὸν εἶναι τὸν λόγον τοῦ θεοῦ, ὅπερ οὐκ ἔστιν. Ἐὰν γὰρ εἴπῃς· Κτιστά εἰσιν, λέγει σοι, ὅτι ἰδοὺ λέγεις κτιστὸν τὸν λόγον τοῦ θεοῦ. Εἰ δὲ εἴπῃς· Ἄκτιστον, λέγει, ὅτι ἰδοὺ πάντα τὰ (5) λόγια τοῦ θεοῦ ὑπάρχοντα ἄκτιστα μέν εἰσι, θεοὶ δὲ οὔκ εἰσιν. Ἰδοὺ σὺ ὡμολόγησας, ὅτι ὁ Χριστὸς λόγος ὢν τοῦ θεοῦ οὐκ ἔστι θεός. Διὸ μηδὲ κτιστὰ μηδὲ ἄκτιστα ἀποκριθῇς αὐτῷ, ἀλλ' οὕτως ἀπόκριθητι αὐτῷ· Ἐγὼ ἕνα μόνον λόγον τοῦ θεοῦ ἐνυπόστατον ὁμολογῶ ἄκτιστον ὄντα, καθάπερ καὶ σὺ ὡμολόγησας, τὴν δὲ πᾶσαν γραφήν μου οὐ λέγω λόγια, (10) ἀλλὰ ῥήματα θεοῦ.	*Section 2b: The Word (λόγος) and the words of God (λόγια, ῥήματα). (Kotter 6)* And if a *Saracen* asks you, "the words of God, are they created or uncreated? They pose to us this very difficult question in their effort to prove that the Word of God is created, which is not true. If *you* answer they are "created," *he* will tell you, behold you are affirming that the Word of God was created. But if *you* answer "they are uncreated," *he* will say, "Behold, all the words of God that exist are uncreated, yet they are not gods. So, you agree with me that although Christ is the Word of God, he is not God." For this reason answer with neither "created" nor "uncreated," but, rather say, "I confess that there is only one hypostatic Word of God, who is uncreated, as you also acknowledge." On the other hand, I do not call my Scripture in its entirety "words," but rather "utterances" of God.[C]
Section 7 Καὶ ἐὰν σοι εἴπῃ ὁ Σαρακηνός· Πῶς κατῆλθεν ὁ θεὸς εἰς κοιλίαν (1) γυναικός; εἰπὲ αὐτῷ· Χρησώμεθα τῇ γραφῇ σου καὶ τῇ γραφῇ μου· ἡ γραφή σου λέγει, ὅτι προεκάθηρεν ὁ θεὸς τὴν παρθένον Μαρίαν ὑπὲρ πᾶσαν σάρκα γυναικός, καὶ κατέβη τὸ πνεῦμα τοῦ θεοῦ καὶ ὁ λόγος εἰς αὐτήν, καὶ τὸ εὐαγγέλιόν μου λέγει· "Πνεῦμα ἅγιον ἐπελεύσεται ἐπὶ (5) σέ, καὶ δύναμις ὑψίστου ἐπισκιάσει σοι." Ἰδοὺ μία φωνὴ ἀμφοτέρων τῶν λέξεων καὶ ἓν νόημα.	*Section 2c: The communication of the Word to men: The Incarnation (Kotter 7)* And if a Saracen asks you, "How did God descend into the womb of a woman," say to him, "Let us use your Scripture and my Scripture. Your Scripture says that God purified the Virgin Mary above all other women and the Spirit of God and the Word descended into her;[D] and my Gospel says "The Holy spirit will come upon you, and the power of the Most High will overshadow you." Behold, both statements are saying the same thing.

Section 8

Ἐὰν ἐρωτήσῃ σε ὁ Σαρακηνὸς λέγων· Καὶ εἰ θεὸς ἦν ὁ Χριστός, (1) πῶς ἔφαγεν καὶ ἔπιεν καὶ ὕπνωσεν καὶ τὰ ἑξῆς; εἰπὲ αὐτῷ, ὅτι ὁ προαιώνιος λόγος τοῦ θεοῦ ὁ κτίσας τὰ σύμπαντα, καθὼς μαρτυρεῖ ἡ γραφή μου καὶ ἡ γραφή σου, αὐτὸς ἔκτισεν ἐκ τῆς σαρκὸς τῆς ἁγίας παρθένου Μαρίας ἄνθρωπον τέλειον ἔμψυχον καὶ ἔννουν· ἐκεῖνος ἔφαγεν καὶ ἔπιεν (5) καὶ ὕπνωσεν, ὁ δὲ λόγος τοῦ θεοῦ οὐκ ἔφαγεν οὐδὲ ἔπιεν οὐδὲ ὕπνωσεν οὐδὲ ἐσταυρώθη οὐδὲ ἀπέθανεν, ἀλλ᾽ ἡ ἁγία σάρξ, ἣν ἔλαβεν ἐκ τῆς ἁγίας παρθένου, ἐκείνη ἐσταυρώθη. Γίνωσκε δέ, ὅτι ὁ Χριστὸς διπλοῦς μὲν λέγεται ταῖς φύσεσιν, εἷς δὲ τῇ ὑποστάσει. Εἷς γάρ ἐστιν ὁ προαιώνιος λόγος τοῦ θεοῦ καὶ μετὰ τὴν πρόσληψιν τῆς σαρκὸς ὑποστατικῶς ἤτοι (10) προσωπικῶς καὶ οὐ φυσικῶς· οὐ γὰρ προσετέθη τῇ τριάδι τέταρτον πρόσωπον μετὰ τὴν ἀπόρρητον ἕνωσιν τῆς σαρκός.

Section 2d: The Two Natures of Christ (Kotter 8)

If, again, the *Saracen* asks you: "If Christ was God, how did he eat, drink, sleep, and so on?"[E] *tell* him that "The pre-eternal Word of God, the one who created all things, according to the testimony of my Scripture as well as yours; the one who became a perfect man from the flesh of the holy virgin Mary, possessing a soul and intelligence; this is the one who ate and drank and slept. In contrast, the Word of God did not eat, nor did he drink, nor did he sleep, nor was he crucified, nor is he dead, but it was the holy flesh that he received from the Blessed Virgin that was crucified. You should know also that Christ is said to have two natures but one hypostasis. For the pre-eternal Word of God is one, even after he assumed the hypostatic body, personally but not physically, for a fourth person has not been added to the Trinity after the ineffable union with the flesh.

Section 9

Ἐάν σε ἐρωτήσῃ ὁ Σαρακηνός, ὅτι, ἣν λέγετε θεοτόκον, ἀπέθανεν (1) ἢ ζῇ; εἰπὲ αὐτῷ· Οὐκ ἀπέθανεν, θαρρῶν τῇ γραφικῇ ἀποδείξει. Λέγει γὰρ ἡ γραφὴ περὶ τούτου· "Ἦλθεν καὶ ἐπ᾽ αὐτὴν ὁ φυσικὸς τῶν ἀνθρώπων θάνατος, οὐ μὴν καθείρξας ἢ χειρωσάμενος ὡς ἐν ἡμῖν—ἄπαγε—, ἀλλ᾽ ὡς φέρε εἰπεῖν· Ὁ πρῶτος ἄνθρωπος ὕπνωσεν καὶ τὴν πλευρὰν (5) ἀφῃρέθη."

Section 2e: The Death of Theotokos (Kotter 9)

If the *Saracen* asks, "Did the *Theotokos*[F] [mother of God] die or live?" *Reply* to him, "We can say with confidence upon the evidence of the Scripture that she did not die. The natural death of man came upon her, but she was not bound or subjected to it, as we are — far from it — but it was more like the sleep of the first man when his rib was removed."

Section 10	Section 2f: Secondary causes after Creation (Kotter 10)
Ἐάν σοι εἴπῃ ὁ Σαρακηνός· Ἰδοὺ πέπληγμαι ἕν τινι τόπῳ τῆς (1) σαρκός μου, καὶ πληγεῖσα ἡ σὰρξ μώλωπα ἀπετέλεσεν, καὶ ἐν τῷ μώλωπι ἐγένετο σκώληξ. Τίς οὖν αὐτὸν ἔπλασεν; εἰπὲ αὐτῷ, ὡς προείπομεν,	If the *Saracen* asks you, "Suppose that I have been struck somewhere on my body, and the flesh, being wounded, formed a contusion and in the contusion a worm has formed. Who has created the worm?" *Tell* him that we have already answered that before.
Section 11	Section 2g: Who is greater? (Kotter 11)
Ὁ Σαρακηνὸς ἐρώτα τὸν Χριστιανὸν λοιπόν· Τίς ἐστι παρὰ σοὶ (1) μείζων, ὁ ἁγιάζων ἢ ὁ ἁγιαζόμενος; Γνοὺς δὲ ὁ Χριστιανὸς τὴν ἔνοπλον αὐτοῦ ἐρώτησιν εἶπεν· Ὃ θέλεις εἰπεῖν, γινώσκω. Ὁ Σαρακηνός· Καὶ εἰ οἶδας, ἀνάγγειλόν μοι. Ὁ Χριστιανὸς ἔφη, ὅτι· Ἐάν σοι εἴπω· Ὁ ἁγιάζων μείζων τοῦ ἁγιαζομένου, ἐρεῖς μοι· Ἄπελθε, προσκύνησον τὸν (5) βαπτιστὴν Ἰωάννην ὡς βαπτίσαντα καὶ ἁγιάσαντα τὸν Χριστόν σου. Ὁ δὲ Σαρακηνός· Οὕτως, φησί, σοὶ ἤθελον εἰπεῖν.	The *Saracen* asked the Christian another question, "According to you, who is greater, the one who sanctifies or the one who is sanctified?" The *Christian*, however, realizing the implication of the question replied, "I know what you want to say." The *Saracen*: "If you know, tell me." The *Christian* said, "If I tell you that the one who sanctifies is greater than the one who is sanctified, you will say to me, 'Go, then, and bow down before John the Baptist because he baptized and sanctified your Christ.'" And the *Saracen*: "That is what I wanted to say to you."

A. The titles used in this analysis are gleaned from Sahas and Le Coz, with some of my own additions and clarifications.

B. Sahas, John of Damascus on Islam, 113n1. Sahas notes that the use of the interrogative pronoun in the neutral gender, instead of the masculine "whom" do you say, indicates that the focus is on the nature of Christ as the "Word of God" rather than *the person of Christ*.

C. Please note: the Saracen seems to be confusing λόγος with λόγια. Therefore, the Christian is seeking to make a distinction regarding λόγος as Christ, the hypostatic Word of God, and λόγια, which are merely the words, or inspired utterances, communicated by God through Scripture. See Lampe, 805.

D. Qur'an, 3:42. "Behold the angels said: O Mary Allah hath chosen thee and purified thee—chosen thee above the women of all nations."

E. This could be a reference to the Qur'an 5:75: "Christ, the son of Mary, was no more than a Messenger; many were the Messengers that passed away before him. His mother was a woman of truth. They had both to eat their (daily) food. See how Allah doth make his Signs clear to them; yet see in what ways they are deluded away from the truth!"

F. Sahas did not have this word in his text, so he centered this conversation around the divinity of Jesus Christ and unfortunately missed the distinction between the death of Christ and the death of man.

Bibliography

PRIMARY SOURCES

al-Baladhuri. *The Origins of the Islamic State*. Translated by Philip Khuri Hitti. 1916. New York: AMS, 1968.

Al-Bukhari, Abu 'Abd Allah Muhammad ibn Isma'il. "The Translation of The Meanings of Sahih Al-Bukhari." 9 vols. Translated by Muhammad Muhsin Khan. Medina: Dar al-Fikr, 1981.

Alexander of Alexandria. *Depositio Arii*. NPNF² 4:69–72.

Ali, 'Abdullah Yusuf, trans. *The Meaning of the Holy Qur'an*. Beltsville, MD: Amana, 1999.

Al-Kindi. "Al-Kindi's Apology." In *The Early Christian-Muslim Dialogue: A Collection of Documents from the First Three Islamic Centuries (632–900 A.D.)*, 355–471. Hatfield, PA: Interdisciplinary Biblical Research Institute, 1993.

Al-Tabari. *The History of Al-Tabari*. Vol. 6. Translated by W. Montgomery Watt and M. V. McDonald. New York: SUNY Press, 1988.

Athanasius. *On the Incarnation of the Word*. NPNF² 4:36–67.

———. *Contra Arianos*. NPNF² 4:303–447.

Athenagoras, *A Plea for the Christians*, ANF 2:125–63.

Clement of Rome. *1 Clement*. ANF 1:1–23.

Cyril of Alexandria. *De sancta et consubstantiali Trinitate, Dialogus II* (PG 75: 721–23).

De Synodis. Councils of Ariminum and Seleucia. NPNF² 4:448–80.

Doctrina Jacobi (July 634). Translated by Robert Hoyland. In *Seeing Islam as Others Saw It: A Survey and Evaluation of Christian, Jewish, and Zoroastrian Writings on Early Islam*, by Robert Hoyland. Princeton, NJ: Darwin, 1997.

Eusebius. Translated by C. F. Cruse. *The Ecclesiastical History of Eusebius Pamphilus: Bishop of Cesarea, in Palestine*. Grand Rapids: Baker, 1990.

Fragment on the Arab Conquests [On the flyleaf of a 6th-century Syriac manuscript of the Gospels (post-636)]. Translated by Robert Hoyland. In *Seeing Islam as Others Saw It: A Survey and Evaluation of Christian, Jewish, and Zoroastrian Writings on Early Islam*, 116–17. Princeton, NJ: Darwin, 1997.

Gregory of Nazianzus. *Select Orations*. NPNF² 7:203–422.

Gregory of Nyssa. *The Catechetical Oration of Gregory of Nyssa*. Cambridge Patristic Texts. Cambridge: Cambridge University Press, 1903.

Hippolytus. *Against the Heresy of One Noetus*. ANF 5:223–31.
Ignatius. *Epistle to the Magnesians*. ANF 1:59–65.
Irenaeus. *Against Heresies*. ANF 1:309–567.
Ishaq, Ibn. *The Life of Muhammad: A Translation of Ibn Ishaq's Sirat Rasul Allah*. Translated by A. Guillaume. Oxford: Oxford University Press, 1955.
Jacob of Edessa. Translated by Sidney Griffith. In *The Church in the Shadow of the Mosque*, 31–32. Princeton: Princeton University Press, 2008.
John of Damascus. *Disputation between a Christian and a Saracen*. In Kotter IV, 419–38.
———. *Heresy of the Ishmaelites*. In Kotter IV, 60–67.
———. *On the Divine Images*. Translated by Andrew Louth. In DIV.
———. *Orthodox Faith*. Part 3 of *The Fount of Knowledge*. Translated by Frederic H. Chase. In *St. John of Damascus: Writings*, 165–406. Fathers of the Church 37. Washington, DC: Catholic University of America Press, 1958.
John of Nikiu: Chronicle. Translated by R. H. Charles. London: Williams & Norgate, 1916.
John I (Patriarch) and the Amir 'Amr b. al-'As. "Dialogue between the Patriarch John I and the Amir of the Hagarenes (639 A.D.)." In *The Early Christian-Muslim Dialogue: A Collection of Documents from the First Three Islamic Centuries (632–900 A.D.)*, 11–46. Hatfield, PA: Interdisciplinary Biblical Research Institute, 1993.
John bar Penkaye. *Seeing Islam As Others Saw It: A Survey and Evaluation of Christian, Jewish, and Zoroastrian Writings on Early Islam*. Translated by Robert Hoyland. Princeton, NJ: Darwin, 1997.
Justin Martyr. *First Apology*. ANF 1:159–87.
———. *Second Apology*. ANF 1:188–93.
Leo III. *Letter from Leo III to Umar II*. Translated by Yehuda Nevo. In *Crossroads to Islam: The Origins of the Arab Religion and the Arab State*, by Yehuda Nevo and Judith Koren, 239–41. Amherst, NH: Prometheus, 2003.
Chronique de Michel le Syrien, patriarche jacobite d'Antioche (1166–99). Translated by J. B. Chabot. 4 vols. Paris, Leroux, 1899.
Migne, J.-P., ed. *Patrologia Graeca*. 162 vols. Paris, 1857–1866.
Origen. *De Principiis*. ANF 4:239–384.
Polycarp. *The Martyrdom of Polycarp*. ANF 1:37–44.
Sebeos, Bishop of the Bagratunis.*The Armenian History according to Sebeos*. Translated by R. W. Thompson. Liverpool, UK: Liverpool University Press, 1999.
Sophronius, Patriarch of Jerusalem. *Sophronius' Christmas sermon for 634 C.E.* In *Crossroads to Islam: The Origins of the Arab Religion and the Arab State*, by Yehuda Nevo and Judith Koren, 115–121.. Amherst, NH: Prometheus, 2003. (Latin text, PG 87: col. 3201–12.)
———. *Holy Baptism*. Translated by Robert Hoyland. In *Seeing Islam As Others Saw It: A Survey and Evaluation of Christian, Jewish, and Zoroastrian Writings on Early Islam*, edited by by Robert Hoyland, 72–73. Princeton, NJ: Darwin, 1997.
———. *Pratum spiritual*. Translated by Robert Hoyland. In *Seeing Islam As Others Saw It: A Survey and Evaluation of Christian, Jewish, and Zoroastrian Writings on Early Islam*, edited by by Robert Hoyland, 63. Princeton, NJ: Darwin, 1997.
Tertullian. *Against Praxeas*. ANF 3:597–633.
Theodore Abu Qurrah. Translated by John Lamoreaux. Vol. 1. Library of the East. Provo, UT: Brigham Young University, 2005.

*The Chronicle of Theophanes.*Turtledove, Harry, Trans. Philadelphia: University of Pennsylvania Press, 1982.
Theophilus of Antioch. *Discourse to Autolycus.* ANF 2:85–123.
Thomas the Presbyter. *Chronicle.* Translated by Robert Hoyland. In *Seeing Islam As Others Saw It: A Survey and Evaluation of Christian, Jewish, and Zoroastrian Writings on Early Islam,* edited by by Robert Hoyland, 147. Princeton, NJ: Darwin, 1997.
Timothy I. "The Dialogue of Patriarch Timothy I with Caliph Mahdi." In *The Early Christian-Muslim Dialogue: A Collection of Documents from the First Three Islamic Centuries (632–900 A.D.),* edited and translated by N. A. Newman, 163–267. Hatfield, PA: Interdisciplinary Biblical Research Institute, 1993.
Pact of Umar. "Medieval Sourcebook." http://sourcebooks.fordham.edu/halsall/source/pact-umar.asp. Accessed August 15, 2016.

SECONDARY SOURCES

Adams, Isaac. *Persia By A Persian: Being, Personal Experiences, Manners, Customs, Habits.* London: Stock, 1906.
Aquilina, Mike. *The Fathers of the Church: An Introduction to the First Christian Teachers.* Huntington, IN: Our Sunday Visitor, 1999.
Armour, Rollin. *Islam, Christianity, and the West: A Troubled History.* New York: Orbis, 2002.
Armstrong, Karen. *Islam: A Short History.* New York: Modern Library, 2002.
Auzepy, Marie-France. "De La Palestine A Constantinople; Etienne Le Sabaite Et Jean Damascene." *Travaux Et Memoires* (Paris) 12 (1994) 183–218.
Bashir, Sulayman. *Arabs and Others in Early Islam.* Princeton, NJ: Darwin, 1997.
Bauer, Walter. *Orthodoxy and Heresy in Earliest Christianity.* Philadelphia: Fortress, 1971.
Baum, Wilhelm, and Dietmar Winkler. *The Church of the East: A Concise History.* New York: Rutledge-Curzon, 2003.
Beaumont, Mark. *Christology in Dialogue with Muslims: A Critical Analysis of Christian Presentations of Christ for Muslims from the Ninth and Twentieth Centuries.* Cumbria, CA: Paternoster, 2005.
———. "Early Christian Interpretation of the Qur'an." *Transformation* 22, no. 4 (2005) 195–203.
Beisner, E. Calvin. *God in Three Persons.* Eugene, OR: Wipf and Stock, 1984.
Bell, Richard. *The Origin of Islam in Its Christian Environment.* Gunning Lectures. Edinburgh: Edinburgh University Press, 1925.
Berkey, Jonathan P. *The Formation of Islam: Religion and Society in the Near East, 600–1800.* Cambridge: Cambridge University Press, 2003.
Boa, Kenneth, and Robert Bowman. *Faith Has Its Reasons: Integrative Approaches to Defending The Christian Faith.* 2nd ed. Paternoster, 2006.
Bobrinskoy, Boris. *The Mystery of the Trinity.* Crestwood, NY: St. Vladimir's Seminary Press, 1999.
Bogle, Emory C. *Islam: Origin & Belief.* Austin: University of Texas Press, 1998.
Bosworth, C. E., et al., ed. *The Encyclopedia of Islam.* 4 vols. 2nd ed. New York: Brill, 1993.

Bowering, Gerhard. "Recent Research on the Construction of the Qur'an." In *The Qur'an in its Historical Context*, edited by Gabriel Said Reynolds, 70–87. Routledge Studies in the Qur'an. London: Routledge, 2008.
Bright, Martin. "The Great Koran Con Trick." *New Statesman*, December 10, 2001, pp. 1–4.
Brown, Harold O. J. *Heresies*. Peabody, MA: Hendrickson, 1984.
Butin, Philip W. *The Trinity*. Louisville: Geneva, 2001.
Burton, John. *The Collection of the Qur'an*. Cambridge: Cambridge University Press, 1979.
Butler, Alban. *Lives of the Saints*. Collegeville, MN: Burns and Oates, 1999.
Cameron, Averil. "Jean Damascene: Ecrits Sur l'Islam." *Journal of Theological Studies* 46 (1995) 368–72.
Carey, Patrick W., and Joseph T. Lienhard. *Biographical Dictionary of Christian Theologians*. Westport, CT: Greenwood, 2000.
Chadwick, Henry. *The Early Church: The Story of Emergent Christianity from the Apostolic Age to the Foundation of the Church of Rome*. Pelican History of the Church 1. New York: Penguin, 1967.
Chapman, Colin. *Cross and Crescent: Responding to the Challenge of Islam*. Downers Grove, IL: IVP, 2003.
Chase, Frederic H., trans. *St. John of Damascus: Writings*. Fathers of the Church 37. Washington, DC: Catholic University of America Press, 1958.
Chidester, David. *Christianity: A Global History*. San Francisco: HarperCollins, 2000.
Cook, David. "New Testament Citations In The Hadith Literature And The Question Of Early Gospel Translations Into Arabic." In *The Encounter of Eastern Christianity with Early Islam*, edited by Emmanouela Grypeou, Mark Swanson, and David Thomas, 185–223. History of Christian-Muslim Relations 5. Leiden: Brill, 2006.
Cook, M. A. *Early Muslim Dogma: A Source-Critical Study*. Cambridge: Cambridge University Press, 1981.
———. "The Origins Of Kalam." *Bulletin of the School of Oriental and African Studies, University Of London* (Cambridge) 43, no. 1 (1980) 32–43.
Cragg, Kenneth. *The Event of the Qur'an: Islam in its Scripture*. Oxford: OneWorld, 1994.
Craig, William Lane. *Reasonable Faith: Christian Truth and Apologetics*. Wheaton, IL: Crossway, 1994.
Crisp, Oliver. *Divinity and Humanity: the Incarnation Reconsidered*. Cambridge: Cambridge University Press, 2007.
Crone, Patricia. *Meccan Trade and the Rise of Islam*. Princeton, NJ: Princeton University Press, 1987.
———. *Slaves on Horses: The Evolution of the Islamic Polity*. Cambridge: Cambridge University Press, 1980.
———. "What Do We Actually Know about Muhammad?" Open Democracy News Analysis, June 10, 2008, http://www.opendemocracy.net (first published August 31, 2006).
Crone, Patricia, and Martin Hinds. *God's Caliph: Religious Authority in the First Centuries of Islam*. Cambridge: Cambridge University Press, 1986.
Crone, Patricia, and Michael Cook. *Hagarism: The Making of the Islamic World*. Cambridge: Cambridge University Press, 1977.
Cross, F. L., ed. *The Oxford Dictionary of the Christian Church*. New York: Oxford University Press, 2005.

Daniel, Norman. *Islam and the West*. Oxford: OneWorld, 1993.
Deanesly, M. *The History of the Medieval Church 590–1500*. London: Methuen, 1925.
Donner, Fred. *Early Islamic Conquests*. Princeton, NJ: Princeton University Press, 1981.
———. *Muhammad and the Believers: At the Origins of Islam*. Cambridge, MA: Harvard University Press, 2010.
———. *Narratives of Islamic Origins: The Beginnings of Islamic Historical Writing*. Princeton, NJ: Darwin, 1998.
———. "The Qur'an in Recent Scholarship: Challenges and Diesiderata." In *The Qur'an in its Historical Context*, edited by Gabriel Said Reynolds, 29–50. Routledge Studies in the Qur'an. London: Routledge, 2008.
Dorman, Harry Gaylord. *Toward Understanding Islam; Contemporary Apologetic of Islam and Missionary Policy*. New York: Teachers College, Columbia University, 1948.
Drobner, Hubertus R. *The Fathers of the Church: A Comprehensive Introduction*. Peabody, MA: Hendrickson, 2007.
Duggan, G. H. *Beyond Reasonable Doubt*. Boston: Pauline, 1987.
Dulles, Avery Robert. *A History of Apologetics*. Vol. 2. San Francisco: Ignatius, 2005.
Edgar, Brian. *The Message of the Trinity*. Downer's Grove, IL: InterVarsity, 2004.
Edgecomb, Kevin P. Biblicalia (blog). http://www.bombaxo.com/blog/st-john-of-damascus-on-islam/. Accessed August 15, 2016.
Elton, G. R., and Richard Evans. *The Practice of History*. Oxford: Blackwell, 1967.
Erhman, Bart. *Lost Christianities: The Battles For Scripture And The Faiths We Never Knew*. New York: Oxford University Press, 2003.
Erickson, Millard J. *Making Sense of the Trinity*. Grand Rapids: Baker, 2000.
Esposito, John L. *Islam: The Straight Path*. Oxford: Oxford University Press, 1998.
Fakhry, Majid. "Philosophy And Theology: From the Eighth Century C.E. to the Present." In *The Oxford History of Islam*, edited by John Esposito, 287. Oxford: Oxford University Press, 1999.
———. *A Short Introduction to Islamic Philosophy, Theology and Mysticism*. Oxford: OneWorld, 1997.
Farah, Caesar E. *Islam: Beliefs and Observances*. Barron's Educational Series, 2003.
Fastiggi, Robert L. "The Incarnation: Muslim Objections and the Christian Response." *Thomist* 57 (1993) 457–93.
Feener, R. Michael. *Islam in World Cultures: Comparative Perspectives*. Oxford: ABC/CLIO, 2004.
Firestone, Reuven. *Journeys in Holy Lands: The Evolution of the Abraham-Ishmael Legends in Islamic Exegesis*. New York: State University of New York Press, 1990.
Florovsky, Georges. *The Byzantine Fathers of the Sixth to the Eighth Centuries*. Vol. 9. Vaduz, Switzerland: Büchervertriebsanstalt, 1987.
Fortescue, Adrian. *The Greek Fathers: Their Lives and Writings*. San Francisco: Ignatius Press, 2007.
Fortman, Edmund J. *The Triune God: A Historical Study of The Doctrine of The Trinity*. Eugene, OR: Wipf and Stock, 1982, 1999.
Frame, John. *Apologetics to the Glory of God: An Introduction*. Phillipsburg, NJ: P&R, 1994.
Gaudeul, Jean-Marie. *Encounters & Clashes: Islam and Christianity in History*. Rome: Pontificio Instituto di Studi Arabi e Islamici, 1990.
Geisler, Norman. *Christian Apologetics*. Grand Rapids: Baker, 1988.

Geisler, Norman, and Abdul Saleeb. *Answering Islam: The Crescent in Light of the Cross.* Grand Rapids: Baker, 2002.

George, Timothy. *God the Holy Trinity: Reflections on Christian Faith and Practice.* Grand Rapids: Baker Academic, 2006.

Gilchrist, John. *Jam' Al-Qur'an—The Codification of the Qur'an Text: A Comprehensive Study of the Original Collection of the Qur'an Text and the Early Surviving Qur'an Manuscripts.* Mondeor, South Africa: Muslim Evangelism Resource Center of Southern Africa, 1989.

———. *The Qur'an: The Scripture of Islam.* Mondeor, South Africa: Muslim Evangelism Resource Center of Southern Africa, 1995.

Gilliot, Claude. "Reconsidering the Authorship of the Qur'an: Is the Qur'an Partly the Fruit of a Progressive and Collective Work?" In *The Qur'an in its Historical Context*, edited by Gabriel Said Reynolds, 88–108. Routledge Studies in the Qur'an. London: Routledge, 2008.

Gimaret, D. "Mu'tazila." In *The Encyclopedia of Islam*, edited by C. E. Bosworth et al., 7:783–93. 2nd ed. Leiden: Brill, 1993.

Goldziher, Ignaz. *Introduction to Islamic Theology and Law.* Princeton: Princeton University Press, 1981.

Griffith, Sidney. "Christian Lore and the Arabic Qur'an: The 'Companions of the Cave' in Suraht Al-Kahf and in Syriac Christian Tradition." In *The Qur'an in its Historical Context*, edited by Gabriel Said Reynolds, 109–38. Routledge Studies in the Qur'an. London: Routledge, 2008.

———. *The Church in the Shadow of the Mosque.* Princeton: Princeton University Press, 2008.

———. "Disputes with Muslims in Syriac Christian Texts: From Patriarch John (D. 648) To Bar Hebraeus (D. 1286)." In *Religionsgesprache Im Mittelalter*, edited by Bernard Lewis and F. Niewohner, 251–73. Wolfenbutteler Mittelalter-Studien 4. Wiesbaden: Harrassowitz, 1992.

———. "Faith and Reason in Christian Kalam: Theodore Abu Qurrah on Discerning the True Religion." In *Christian Arabic Apologetics during the Abbasid Period, 750–1258*, edited by Samir Khalil Samir and Jorgen Nielsen, 1–56. Leiden: Brill, 1993.

———. "John of Damascus and the Church in Syria in the Umayyad Era: The Intellectual and Cultural Milieu of Orthodox Christians in the World of Islam." *Hugoye: Journal of Syriac Studies* 11, no. 2 (2008) 207–37.

———. "The Life of Theodore of Edessa: History, Hagiography, and Religious Apologetics in Mar Saba Monastery in Early Abbasid Times." In *The Sabaite Heritage in the Orthodox Church from the Fifth Century to the Present*, edited by Joseph Patrich, 147–69. Belgium: Peeters, 2001.

———. "A 'Melkite' Arabic Text from Sinai and the Doctrines of the Trinity and the Incarnation in 'Arab Orthodox' Apologetics." In *The Encounter of Eastern Christianity with Early Islam*, edited by Emmanouela Grypeou, Mark Swanson, and David Thomas, 277–310. History of Christian-Muslim Relations 5. Leiden: Brill, 2006.

———. "Melkites, Jacobites and the Christological Controversies." In *Under Islam: The First Thousand Years*, edited by David Thomas, 9–55. Leiden: Brill, 2001.

———. "The Monks of Palestine and the Growth of Christian Literature in Arabic." *Muslim World* 78, no. 1 (1988) 1–27.

———. "Muslims and Church Councils; The Apology of Abu Qurrah." In *The Beginnings of Christian Theology in Arabic*, 270-99. Aldershot, UK: Ashgate, 2002.

Grillmeier, Aloys. *Christ in Christian Tradition: Volume Two: From the Council of Chalcedon (451) to Gregory the Great (590-604): Part Two: The Church of Constantinople in the Sixth Century*. Louisville, KY: Westminster John Knox Press, 1995.

Grunebaum, G. E., von. *Classical Islam: A History 600-1258*. New York: Barnes and Noble, 1970.

Guillaume, Alfred. *The Life of Muhammad: a Translation of Ibn Ishaq's Sirat Rasul Allah*. New York: Oxford University Press, 1967.

Gunton, Colin E. *The One, the Three and the Many: God, Creation and the Culture of Modernity*. Cambridge: Cambridge Press, 1993.

Habermas, Gary. *The Historical Jesus: Ancient Evidence for the Life of Christ*. Joplin, MO: College, 1996.

Haldon, J. F. *Byzantium in the Seventh Century: The Transformation of a Culture*. Cambridge: Cambridge University Press, 1990.

Hall, Christopher A. *Learning Theology with the Church Fathers*. Downers Grove, IL: InterVarstity, 2002.

Hamidullah, Muhammad. *The Emergence of Islam: Lectures on the Development of Islamic World-View, Intellectual Tradition and Polity*. Publication no. 90. Islamabad: Islamic Research Institute, 1993.

Hawting, G. R. *The Idea of Idolatry and the Emergence of Islam: From Polemic to History*. Cambridge: Cambridge University Press, 2004.

Heinze, E. Charles. *Trinity & Triunity: Salvation and the Nature of the Godhead*. Dale City, VA: Epaphras, 1995.

House, Wayne. *Charts of Christian Theology and Doctrine*. Grand Rapids, MI: Zondervan, 1992.

Hoyland, Robert. "The Content and Context of Early Arabic Inscriptions." *Jerusalem Studies In Arabic & Islam* 21, no. 3 (1997) 77-102.

———. "The Earliest Christian Writings on Muhammad: An Appraisal." In *The Biography of Muhammad: The Issue of the Sources*, edited by Harald Motzki, 32:276-97. Leiden: Brill, 2000.

———. "Epigraphy and the Linguistic Background to the Qur'an." In *The Qur'an in its Historical Context*, edited by Gabriel Said Reynolds, 51-69. Routledge Studies in the Qur'an. London: Routledge, 2008.

———. "New Documentary Texts and the Early Islamic State." *Bulletin of SOAS* 69, no. 3 (2006) 395-416.

———. *Seeing Islam As Others Saw It: A Survey and Evaluation of Christian, Jewish, and Zoroastrian Writings on Early Islam*. Princeton: Darwin, 1997.

Hurtado, Larry. *How on Earth Did Jesus Become a God?* Grand Rapids: Eerdmans, 2005.

Ierodiakonou, Katerina. *Byzantine Philosophy and its Ancient Sources*. Oxford: Oxford University Press, 2002.

Irwin, Dale, and Scott Sunquist. *History of the World Christian Movement*. Vol. 1, *Earliest Christainity to 1453*. Edinburgh: T. & T. Clark, 2001.

Janosik, Daniel. "Explaining the Trinity to a Muslim." *Christian Apologetics Journal* 4, no. 2 (2005) 73-85.

Jeffery, Arthur. "Materials for the History of the Text of the Koran." In *The Origins of the Koran: Classic Essays on Islam's Holy Book*, Ibn Warraq, 114-24. New York: Prometheus, 1998.

———. "The Orthography of the Samarqand Qur'an Codex." *Journal of the American Oriental Society* 62 (1942) 175-95.

Jenson, Robert W. "Jesus in the Trinity." *Pro Ecclesia* 8, no. 3 (1999) 308-18.

———. "Three Identities of One Action." *Scottish Journal of Theology* 28, no. 1 (1975) 1-15.

———. *The Triune Identity: God according to the Gospel*. Eugene, OR: Wipf and Stock, 2002.

Johns, Jeremy. "Archaeology and the History of Early Islam: The First Seventy Years." *Journal of the Economic and Social History of the Orient* 46, no. 4 (2003) 411-36.

Jugie, Martin. "St. Jean Damascene." In *Dictionnaire de Theologie Catholique*, 8:693-751. Paris: Letouzey et Ane, 1924.

Kaegi, Walter Emil. "Initial Byzantine Reactions to the Arab Conquest." *Church History* 38, no. 2 (1969) 139-49.

Kelly, J. N. D. *Early Christian Doctrines*. Peabody, MA: HarperCollins, 2004.

Kerr, David A. "Christian Mission and Islamic Studies: Beyond Antithesis." *International Bulletin of Missionary Research* 26, no. 1 (2002) 8-10, 12-15.

Khoury, Adel-Theodore. *Les theologiens byzantius et l'Islam: Textes et auteurs (VIIIe-XIIIe S.)*. 2nd ed. Louvain: Nauwelaerts, 1969.

Khoury, Paul. "Jean Damascene Et l'Islam." *Religionswissenschaftliche Studien* 33 (1994) 1-76.

Kotter, Bonifatius. *Die Schriften Des Johannes Von Damaskos*. Vol. 2. New York: de Gruyter, 1973.

———. *Die Schriften Des Johannes Von Damaskos*. Vol. 4. New York: de Gruyter, 1981.

Kreeft, Peter, and Ronald Tacelli. *Handbook of Christian Apologetics*. Downer's Grove, IL: InterVarsity, 1994.

Kroes, R. "Zendeling, Dilettant of Visionair? Een Recensie Van Ch. Luxenberg: Die Syro-Aramäische Lesart Des Qur'an." *Dialoog* 4 (2004) 18-35.

Küng, Hans. *Islam: Past, Present and Future*. Oxford: One World, 2007.

Küng, Hans, and Jurgen Moltmann. *Islam: A Challenge for Christianity*. London: Orbis, 1994.

Lamoreaux, John. "The Biography of Theodore Abu Qurrah Revisited." *Dumbarton Oaks Papers* 56 (2002) 25-40.

———. "Early Eastern Christian Responses to Islam." In *Medieval Christian Perceptions of Islam: A Book of Essays*, edited by John Tolan, 3-31. New York: Garland, 1996.

Lampe, G.W.H. *A Patristic Greek Lexicon*. Oxford: Clarendon, 1961.

Lane, Tony. "Heresy in the Early Church: Did You Know?" *Christian History* 15, no. 3 (1996) 2-3.

———. *The Lion Concise Book of Christian Thought*. Oxford: Lion, 1984.

Le Coz, Raymond. *Jean Damascene: Ecrits Sur L'Islam*. Sources Chretiennes 383. Paris: Cerf, 1992.

Leites, Adrien. "Sira and the Question of Tradition." In *the Biography of Muhammad: The Issue of the Sources*, edited by Harald Motzki, 49-66. Leiden: Brill, 2000.

Lester, Toby. "What is the Koran?" In *What the Koran Really Says: Language, Text, And Commentary*, edited by Ibn Warraq, 107-28. New York: Prometheus, 2002.

Letham, Robert. *The Holy Trinity: In Scripture, History, Theology, and Worship*. Phillipsburg, NJ: P & R, 2004.

———. "The Trinity—Yesterday, Today and the Future." *Themelios* 28, no. 1 (2002) 26–36.

Louth, Andrew. "John of Damascus and the Making of the Byzantine Theological Synthesis." In *the Sabaite Heritage in the Orthodox Church from the Fifth Century to the Present*, edited by Joseph Patrich, 301–16. Leuven: Peeters, 2001.

———. *St. John Damascene: Tradition and Originality in Byzantine Theology*. Oxford: Oxford University Press, 2002.

———. "St John Damascene: Preacher and Poet." In *Preacher and Audience: Studies in Early Christian and Byzantine Homiletics*, Mary Cunningham, 247–66. Leiden: Brill, 1998.

Louth, Andrew, trans. *Three Treatises on the Divine Images*. Crestwood, NY: St. Vladimir's Seminary Press, 2003.

Lumbard, Joseph, ed. *Islam, Fundamentalism, and the Betrayal of Tradition: Essays by Western Muslim Scholars*. Perennial Philosophy. Bloomington, IN: World Wisdom, 2004.

Lupton, J. H. *St. John of Damascus*. London: SPCK, 1882.

Luxenberg, Christoph. *The Syro-Aramaic Reading of the Koran: A Contribution to the Decoding of the Language of the Koran*. Berlin: Schiler, 2007.

Macdonald, Duncan B. *Development of Muslim Theology, Jurisprudence and Constitutional Theory*. New York: Scribner, 1903.

Marshall, David. "Christianity and the Qur'an." In *Islamic Interpretation of Christianity*, edited by Lloyd Ridgeon, 3–29. New York: St. Martin's, 2001.

Mayers, Ronald. *Balanced Apologetics: Using Evidences and Presuppositions in Defense of the Faith*. Grand Rapids: Kregel, 1984.

McEnhill, Peter, and George Newlands. *Fifty Key Christian Thinkers*. London: Routledge, 2004.

McGiffert, Arthur. *A History of Christian Thought*. Vol. 1, *Early and Eastern: From Jesus to John of Damascus*. New York: Scribner's, 1960.

McGinn, Bernard. *The Doctors of the Church*. New York: Crossroads, 1999.

McGrath, Alister E. *Heresy: A History of Defending the Truth*. New York: HarperCollins, 2009.

———. *Understanding the Trinity*. Grand Rapids: Academie, 1988.

Merrill, John Ernest. "Of the Tractate of John of Damascus on Islam." *Muslim World* 41, no. 2 (1954) 88–97.

Meyendorff, John. *Byzantine Theology: Historical Trends & Doctrinal Themes*. New York: Fordham University Press, 1974.

———. "Byzantine Views of Islam." *Dumbarton Oaks Papers* 18 (1964) 113–32.

Mingana, A. "Patriarch Timothy I and the Caliph Mahdi." In *The Early Christian-Muslim Dialogue: A Collection of Documents from the First Three Islamic Centuries (632–900 A.D.)*, translated by N. A. Newman, 169–267. Hatfield, PA: Interdisciplinary Biblical Research Institute, 1993.

Moffett, Samuel Hugh. "Divided by Christ." *Christian History* 74 (2002) 39–40.

Moltmann, Jürgen. *The Trinity and the Kingdom*. Translated by Margaret Kohl. Minneapolis: Fortress, 1993.

Montes, Adolfo Gonzalez. "The Challenge of Islamic Monotheism: A Christian View." In *Islam: A Challenge for Christianity*, edited by Hans Küng and Jürgen Moltmann, 66–75. London: Orbis, 1994.

Moorhead, John. "The Earliest Christian Theological Response to Islam." *Religion* (London) 11 (1981) 265–74.

Muir, William. "The Apology of Al-Kindi: An Essay on Its Age and Authorship." In *The Early Christian-Muslim Dialogue: A Collection of Documents from the First Three Islamic Centuries (632–900 A.D.)*, translated by N. A. Newman, 365–80. Hatfield, PA: Interdisciplinary Biblical Research Institute, 1993.

Nasrallah, Joseph. *Saint Jean De Damas: Son Epoque, Sa Vie, Son Oeuvre*. Paris: Office des Editions Universitaires, 1950.

Nazir-Ali, Michael. *Conviction and Conflict: Islam, Christianity and World Order*. London: Continuum, 2006.

Neuwirth, Angelika. "Qur'an and History—A Disputed Relationship. Some Reflections on Qur'anic History and History in the Qur'an." *Journal of Qur'anic Studies* 5, no. 1 (2003) 1–18.

———. *Studien Zur Komposition Der Mekkanischen Suren: Die Literarische Form Des Koran—Ein Zeugnis Seiner Historizitaet?* 2nd ed. Berlin: de Gruyter, 2007.

Nevo, Yehuda, and Judith Koren. *Crossroads to Islam: The Origins of the Arab Religion and the Arab State*. Amherst, NH: Prometheus, 2003.

Newman, N. A., ed. and trans. *The Early Christian-Muslim Dialogue: A Collection of Documents from the First Three Islamic Centuries (632–900 A.D.)*. Hatfield, PA: Interdisciplinary Biblical Research Institute, 1993.

Noldeke, Theodor. "The Koran." In *The Origins of the Koran: Classic Essays on Islam's Holy Book*, edited by Ibn Warraq, 36–66. New York: Prometheus, 1998.

O'Collins, Gerald. *The Tripersonal God: Understanding and Interpreting the Trinity*. New York: Paulist, 1999.

Ohlig, Karl-Heinz, and Gerd-R. Puin, eds. *The Hidden Origins of Islam*. New York: Prometheus, 2010.

Oliver, Harold H. *Metaphysics, Theology, and Self: Relational Essays*. Macon, GA: Mercer University Press, 2006.

Olson, Roger. "Trinity and Eschatology: The Historical Being of God in Jurgen Moltmann and Wolfhart Pannenberg." *Scottish Journal of Theology* 36, no. 2 (1983) 213–27.

Olson, Roger E., and Christopher A. Hall. *The Trinity*. Grand Rapids: Eerdmans, 2002.

Pagels, Elaine. *The Gnostic Gospels*. New York: Random House, 1979.

Pannenberg, Wolfhart. "Father Son Spirit: Problems of a Trinitarian Doctrine of God." *Dialog* 26, no. 4 (1987) 250–57.

Parry, Kenneth. *Depicting the Word: Byzantine Iconophile Thought of the Eighth and Ninth Centuries*. Leiden: Brill, 1996.

Patrich, Joseph. *Sabas, Leader of Palestinian Monasticism: A Comparative Study in Eastern Monasticism, Fourth to Seventh Centuries*. Washington, DC: Dumbarton Oaks, 1995.

Pelikan, Jaroslav. *The Emergence of the Catholic Tradition (100–600)*. Vol. 1, *The Christian Tradition: A History of the Development of Doctrine*. Chicago: University of Chicago Press, 1971.

———. *The Spirit of Eastern Christendom (600–1700)*. Vol. 2, *The Christian Tradition: A History of the Development of Doctrine*. Chicago: University of Chicago Press, 1974.

Peristeris, Aristarchos. "Literary and Scribal Activities at the Monastery of St. Sabas." In *The Sabaite Heritage in the Orthodox Church from the Fifth Century to the Present*, edited by Joseph Patrich, 171–94. Belgium: Peeters, 2001.

Peters, F. E. *A Reader on Classical Islam*. Princeton: Princeton University Press, 1994.

Phenix, Robert, Jr., and Cornelia B. Horn. Review of *Die Syro-Aramaeische Lesart Des Koran; Ein Beitrag Zur Entschlusselung Der Qur'ansprache* by Christoph Luxenberg. *Hugoye: Journal of Syriac Studies* 6, no. 1 (2003) 1–39.

Pines, Shlomo. "Some Traits of Christian Theological Writing In Relation To Moslem Kalam And To Jewish Thought." In *Studies in the History of Arabic Philosophy*, edited by Sarah Stroumsa, 3:79–99. Jerusalem: Magnes, 1996.

Plantinga, Jr., Cornelius. "Social Trinity and Tritheism." In *Trinity, Incarnation, and Atonement: Philosophical and Theological Essays*, edited by Ronald Feenstra and Cornelius Plantinga, 21–47. Library of Religious Philosophy Book 1. Notre Dame: University of Notre Dame Press, 1990.

Pratt, Douglas. *The Challenge of Islam: Encounters in Interfaith Dialogue*. Burlington, VT: Ashgate, 2005.

Puin, Gerd. "Observations on Early Qur'an Manuscripts in San'a." In *What the Koran Really Says*, edited by Ibn Warraq, 739–44. New York: Prometheus, 2002.

Puin, Gerd, and Karl-Heinz Ohlig. *Hidden Origins Of Islam: New Research into its Early History*. New York: Prometheus, 2009.

Rahman, Fazlur. *Islam*. 2nd ed. Chicago: University of Chicago Press, 1979.

Rahman, H. U. *A Chronology of Islamic History*. Boston: Hall, 1989.

Reilly, Robert R. *The Closing of the Muslim Mind: How Intellectual Suicide Created the Modern Islamist Crisis*. Wilmington, DE: ISI, 2010.

Reynolds, Gabriel Said. *A Muslim Theologian in a Sectarian Milieu: 'Abd Al-Jabbar And The Critique of Christian Origins*. Leiden: Brill, 2004.

Reynolds, Gabriel Said, ed. *The Qur'an in its Historical Context*. Routledge Studies in the Qur'an. London: Routledge, 2008.

Riddell, Peter. *Christians and Muslims: Pressures and Potential in a Post-9/11 World*. Leicester, UK: InterVarsity, 2004.

Ridgeon, Lloyd, ed. *Islamic Interpretation of Christianity*. New York: St. Martin's, 2001.

Rippin, Andrew. "Syriac In the Qur'an: Classical Muslim Theories." In *The Qur'an in its Historical Context*, edited by Gabriel Said Reynolds, 249–61. Routledge Studies in the Qur'an. London: Routledge, 2008.

Robinson, Francis, and Ira Lapidus. *The Cambridge Illustrated History of the Islamic World*. London: Cambridge University Press, 1996.

Robinson, Neal. *Christ in Islam and Christianity*. Albany: State University of New York, 1991.

Saadi, Abdul-Massih. "Nascent Islam in the Seventh Century Syriac Sources." In *The Qur'an in its Historical Context*, edited by Gabriel Said Reynolds, 217–22. Routledge Studies in the Qur'an. London: Routledge, 2008.

Saeed, Abdullah. *The Qur'an: An Introduction*. New York: Routledge, 2008.

Sahas, Daniel. "The Arab Character of the Christian Disputation with Islam: The Case of John Of Damascus." In *Religionsgesprache Im Mittelalter*, edited by Bernard

Lewis and Friedrich Niewohner, 185–205. Wolfenbutteler Mittelalter-Studien 4. Wiesbaden: Harrassowitz, 1992.

———. *John of Damascus on Islam*. Leiden: Brill, 1972.

———. "John of Damascus. Revisited." *Abr-Nahvain* 23 (1984) 104–18.

Said, Edward W. *Orientalism*. New York: Pantheon, 1978.

Samir, Samir Khalil. "The Prophet Muhammad as Seen by Timothy I and Other Arab Christian Authors." In *Syrian Christians under Islam: The First Thousand Years*, edited by David Thomas, 75–106. Leiden: Brill, 2001.

———. "The Theological Christian Influence on the Qur'an: A Reflection." In *The Qur'an in its Historical Context*, 141–62. Routledge Studies in the Qur'an. London: Routledge, 2008.

Saperstein, Andrew. "Encounters with Islam." *Christian History & Biography* 94 (2007) 32.

Schacht, Joseph. *The Origins of Muhammadan Jurisprudence*. Oxford: Clarendon, 1950.

Schaff, Philip. *The Creeds of Christendom with a History and Critical Notes*, 4th ed. Grand Rapids: Baker, 1966.

———. *History of the Christian Church*. Vol. 4. Grand Rapids: Eerdmans, 1910.

Scharer, Dorothy. "The Polemic of the Tractate of Saint John of Damascus and Apology of Al-Kindy Regarding Islam, Muhammad and the Qur'an." Annual meeting of the Evangelical Theological Society. Portland, OR, 2003.

Schick, Robert. "The Image Destroyers: Only Non-Sacred Images Were Destroyed in Eighth-Century Palestine." *Archaeology Odyssey* 2, no. 5 (1999) 1–9.

Schlager, Patricius. "Andrea Gallandi." *The Catholic Encyclopedia*. Vol. 6. New York: Appleton, 1909. http://www.newadvent.org/cathen/06349c.htm. Accessed 16 Aug. 2016.

Schleiermacher, Friedrich. *Brief Outline of the Study of Theology: drawn up to serve as the basis of Introductory Lectures*. Edinburgh: T. & T. Clark, 1850.

Seale, Morris. *Muslim Theology: A Study of Origins with Reference to the Church Fathers*. London: Luzac, 1964.

Shboul, Ahmad M. H. "Arab Islamic Perceptions of Byzantine Religion and Culture." In *Muslim Perceptions of Other Religions: A Historical Survey*, edited by Jacques Waardenburg, 122–35. Oxford: Oxford University Press, 1999.

Siddiqui, Habib. "An Analysis of Anti-Islamic Polemics." May 8, 2006. http://usa.mediamonitors.net/headlines/an_analysis_of_anti_islamic_polemics.

Simmons, Ernest. *The Fathers and Doctors of the Church*. Milwaukee: Bruce, 1959.

Smith, Jane I. "Islam and Christendom: Historical, Cultural, and Religious Interaction from the Seventh to the Fifteenth Centuries." In *The Oxford History of Islam*, edited by John L. Esposito, 305–35. Oxford: Oxford University Press, 1999.

Stewart, Devin. "Notes on Medieval and Modern Emendations of the Qur'an." In *The Qur'an in its Historical Context*, edited by Gabriel Said Reynolds, 225–48. Routledge Studies in the Qur'an. London: Routledge, 2008.

Stewart, P. J. *Unfolding Islam*. Reading, PA: Garnet, 1994.

Studer, Basil. *Trinity and Incarnation: The Faith of the Early Church*. Collegeville, MN: Liturgical, 1993.

Swanson, Mark N. "Folly to the Junafa: The Crucifixion in Early Christian-Muslim Controversy." In *the Encounter of Eastern Christianity with Early Islam*, edited by Emmanouela Grypeou, 237–56. History of Christian-Muslim Relations 5. Leiden: Brill, 2006.

Sweetman, J. W. *Islam and Christian Theology: A Study of the Interpretation of Theological Ideas in the Two Religions*. Part 1, vol. 1. London: Lutterworth, 1955.

Thomas, David. "Christian Theologians and New Questions." In *The Encounter of Eastern Christianity with Early Islam*, edited by Emmanouela Grypeou, 257–75. History of Christian-Muslim Relations 5. Leiden: Brill, 2006.

———. "The Doctrine of the Trinity in the Early Abbasid Era." In *Islamic Interpretation of Christianity*, edited by Lloyd Ridgeon, 78–98. New York: St. Martin's, 2001.

———. *Syrian Christians under Islam: The First Thousand Years*. Leiden: Brill, 2001.

Tisdall, William St. Clair. *The Sources of Islam*. 1901. Reprint, New Delhi: Amarko Book Agency, 1973.

Tolan, John. *Medieval Christian Perceptions of Islam: A Book of Essays*. New York: Garland, 1996.

———. *Saracens: Islam in the Medieval European Imagination*. New York: Columbia University Press, 2002.

Torrance, Thomas. *Trinitarian Perspectives: Toward Doctrinal Agreement*. Edinburgh: T. & T. Clark, 1994.

Tritton, A. S. *Muslim Theology*. London: Luzac, 1947.

Tsirpanlis, Constantine. *The Anthropology of Saint John of Damascus*. Athens, Greece: 1969. Reprint, New York: EO, 1980.

Turtledove, Harry, trans. *The Chronicle of Theophanes*. Philadelphia: University of Penssylvania Press, 1982.

Valkenberg, Pim. *Sharing Lights on the Way to God: Muslim-Christian Dialogue and Theology in the Context of Abrahamic Partnership*. Amsterdam: Rodopi, 2006.

Van Bladel, Kevin. "The Alexander Legend in the Qur'an 18:83–102." In *The Qur'an in its Historical Context*, 175–203. Routledge Studies in the Qur'an. London: Routledge, 2008.

Van Ess, J. "Kadariyya." In *The Encyclopedia of Islam*, edited by C. E. Bosworth, 4:667–68, Leiden: Brill, 1993.

Volf, Miroslav. *After Our Likeness: The Church as the Image of the Trinity*. Grand Rapids: Eerdmans, 1998.

———. "'The Trinity Is Our Social Program': The Doctrine of the Trinity and the Shape of Social Engagement." *Modern Theology* 14, no. 3 (1998) 401–23.

Voorhis, John W. "John of Damascus on the Moslem Heresy." *Muslim World* 24, no. 4 (1934) 391–98.

Wansbrough, John. *Quranic Studies: Sources and Methods of Scriptural Interpretation*. New York: Prometheus, 2004.

Warraq, Ibn. "Introduction." In *The Origins of the Koran: Classic Essays on Islam's Holy Book*, edited by Ibn Warraq, 9–35. New York: Prometheus, 1998.

———. "Koranic Criticism: 700 C.E. to 825 C.E." *New English Review*, October 2007, http://www.newenglishreview.org/custpage.cfm/frm/11036/sec_id/11036 (accessed July 21, 2016).

———. *What the Koran Really Says: Language, Text, and Commentary*. New York: Prometheus, 2002.

Watt, W. Montgomery. *Early Islam: Collected Articles*. Edinburgh: Edinburgh University Press, 1990.

———. *Islamic Philosophy and Theology*. Edinburgh: Edinburgh University Press, 1962.

———. *Muslim-Christian Encounters: Perceptions and Misperceptions.* New York: Routledge, 1991.

Wensinck, A. J. *The Muslim Creed: Its Genesis and Historical Development.* Cambridge: Cambridge University Press, 1932.

White, James R. *The Forgotten Trinity: Recovering the Heart of Christian Belief.* Minneapolis: Bethany House, 1998.

Wolf, Kenneth Baxter. "Christian Views of Islam in Early Medieval Spain." In *Medieval Christian Perceptions of Islam: A Book of Essays*, edited by John Tolan, 85–108. New York: Garland, 1996.

Wolfson, Harry. *The Philosophy of the Kalam.* Cambridge, MA: Harvard University Press, 1976.

Work, Telford. "Sharpening the Doctrine Of God: Theology Between Orthodox Christianity and Early Islam." Orthodox Theology Group, American Academy of Religion, November 25, 2002, unpublished manuscript.

Zaman, Muhammad Qasim. *Religion and Politics under the Early 'Abbasids: the Emergence of the Proto-Sunni Elite.* Leiden: Brill, 1997.

Index

A

Abbasid, 48, 85, 156, 221, 231, 236, 244
Abd al-Malik, 25, 26, 28, 29, 31, 39, 41, 54, 62, 63, 67, 69, 70–77, 84
abu Bakr, 59, 75
abu-Qurra(h), Theodore, 116–38, 167, 168, 179, 198, 201, 209, 220, 222, 226–39
abu-Ra'ita, 227, 228
al-Ansari, 221
al-Ash'ari, 80, 88, 89, 158
al-Baghdadi, 89
al-Baladhuri, 45
al-Basri, 84, 222, 227, 228
al-Bukha'ri, 45
al-Ghazali, 89
al-Hanafiyyah, 69, 70
al-Hashimi, 224
al-Juhani, 83, 84, 144
al-Juwayni, 89
al-Kindi, 224, 229, 244, 245, 246, 247
Allah, 68, 72, 75, 77, 101, 102, 107, 109, 146, 160, 161, 163, 179, 188, 205, 208
    Kalam Allah, 86
    Daughters of Allah, 99, 106
Allat, 99
al-Mahdi, 221, 226, 239
al-Ma'idah, 106
al-Ma'mun, 88, 222, 226, 230, 231
al-Shahrastani, 89
al-Tabari, 29, 45
al-Uzza, al-Uzzah, 99, 106
al-Walid, 25, 30, 31
al-Zubayr, 75, 76
amir, 75
Anastasias, Anastasios, 1, 56, 62, 249
Apologetic(s), 2–5, 18, 19, 62, 79, 89–91, 102, 115, 116, 126, 133, 179, 188, 190, 191, 195, 197, 200, 201, 209, 211, 215, 217, 219–50, 253
    Apologetical, 91, 249
    apologetic approach, 20, 69, 93, 114, 116, 130, 159, 169, 170, 189, 198, 199, 202, 203, 204, 206, 211, 216, 218, 220, 227, 229, 231, 248, 250, 251, 253, 254
    apologetic genre, 221, 222, 223, 224, 226
    Apologetic Successors of John Griffith's four Apologetic genres, 221–26
    Christology and the early Christian Arabic Apologists, 227–29
    Theodore Abu Qurrah, 229–38
    Timothy I, 239–44
    al-Kindi, 244–47
apologetic treatises, tracts, 3, 19, 188, 215, 224
apologetic work(s), 89, 188, 190, 197, 224, 241
apologetic writings, 191, 220, 231
apologist(s), 8, 10, 13, 14, 15, 91, 93, 117, 154, 168, 169, 170, 179, 197, 200, 209, 213, 218, 220, 222, 223, 227, 228, 229, 239, 246, 249, 251, 252
Aquinas, Thomas, 202

Index

Arabization, 30
archaeological, 51, 52, 53, 54, 65, 70, 73, 76, 78
archaeologist, 53, 129, 192
Arian beliefs, heresy, position, 11, 17, 18, 71, 100
Arianism, 9, 15, 18, 69, 100, 203
Arian monk, 57, 96, 98, 99, 207
Arians, 9, 10, 14, 16, 17, 18
Arius, 4, 9, 15, 16, 17, 182
Armstrong, Karen, 46
Ash'arite(s), 81, 86, 88, 89
Athanasius, 4, 15–17, 186
Athenagoras, 12
Augustine, 2, 18, 177, 238, 242

B

Bahira, 96, 100, 113, 222
Bauer, Walter, 3
Beaumont, Mark, 105, 126, 208, 226, 227, 228, 230, 231, 232, 236
black-eyed beauties, 215
Bonifatius Kotter. *See* Kotter, Bonifatius.
Byzantines, 59, 62, 191, 192, 200

C

Caliphate, 22, 25, 26, 29, 30, 42, 80, 88, 232
caliph(s), 21–30, 39, 41–43, 53, 63, 69, 75, 77, 81–85, 88, 111, 113, 144, 192, 200, 201, 221–26, 230, 231, 239–45, 249
   caliph abd al-Malik, 69
   caliph al-Mahdi, 88, 221, 226, 230, 231, 239
   caliph Ma'mun, 85, 222, 244
   caliph Yazid I, 23
   caliph 'Umar II, 223
Cappadocian(s), 9, 17, 18, 171, 173, 179, 183
Christology, 112, 141, 171, 195, 201, 204, 207, 216, 226–28, 231
Chrysorrhoas, 27, 28, 31, 35
Circle-dance. *See also* perichoresis, 181, 186;
codex, codices, 38, 213, 215
Constantine, 15, 17, 36

contradictions, 47, 206
controversial, 3, 54, 129, 133, 230
controversies, 5, 20, 21, 80, 89, 140, 146, 155, 159, 190, 202, 236, 250, 251, 253
controversy, 17, 22, 39, 42, 62, 79, 81, 151, 169, 179, 186, 200, 211, 221, 251, 253
counter-argument, 102, 103
Crone, Patricia, 50, 51, 53, 54, 58, 59, 63, 66–68, 70, 74, 113

D

Dance. *See also* circle dance, perichoresis, 181, 187, 242;
Daniel Sahas. *See* Sahas, Daniel.
debate(s), 2, 13, 16, 20, 82, 83, 93, 117, 126, 144, 147, 155, 194, 205, 218, 219, 221, 222, 226, 229, 230, 239, 240, 241, 242, 244
defend, 5, 19, 40, 71, 74, 80, 91, 116, 191, 194, 197, 206, 216, 217, 218, 219, 223, 226, 231, 232, 236, 240, 248, 251, 254
defending, 5, 17, 91, 225, 248, 251, 253, 254
defense, 3, 5, 11, 13, 18, 19, 35, 36, 43, 50, 85, 91, 170, 189, 195, 197, 202, 208, 220, 221, 223, 224, 229, 231, 232, 235, 236, 250, 251, 252, 253, 254
deity, 4, 9, 11, 13, 14, 16, 50, 71, 80, 89, 102, 103, 114, 122, 155, 163, 179, 182, 185, 193, 207, 208, 209, 218, 251, 252
   deity of Christ, 4, 16, 50, 71, 80, 89, 114, 155, 163, 179, 207, 209, 251, 252
   deity of Jesus, 13, 102, 207, 208, 218
Development of John's Apologetic Approach
   The need for apologetics, 200–201
   John's influence, 201–2
   Three aspects of John's Apologetic approach, 202–3
   John's first step: Understand, 203–6
   John's second step: Defend, 206–11
   John's third step: Refute, 211–16

John's Apologetic approach in the Disputation between a Christian and a Saracen, 216–17
Development of the Trinity through Controversy, 5–18
Early Church, 6
Apostolic Fathers, 7
Ignatius, 7
Polycarp, 7
Clement of Rome, 8
Second and Third-Century Apologists, 8
Justin Martyr, 10
Irenaeus, 11–12
Tertullian, 13
Origen, 14
Arianism, 15
Nicene Creed, 16
Augustine, 18
Disputation between a Christian and a Saracen, Authenticity, 115–40
Authenticity and Transmission, 115–26
Disputes on the dating of the Disputation, 126–27
Disputes on the authorship of the Disputation, 128–39
Disputation between a Christian and a Saracen, Analysis, 141–68
The omnipotence of God and the cause of evil, 141–43
Man's power, 143–44
Justice of God, 145–46
"Creation" and/or "Generation," 146–47
God's foreknowledge of man's destiny, 148–49
Baptism and the will of God, 149–50
God's providential and permissive will, 150–51
Christ and the Word of God, 152–56
The Word and the Words of God, 156–59
The communication of the Word to men, 160–61
The two natures of Christ, 161–64

The death of Theotokos, 164–65
Secondary causes after creation, 165
Who is better, the one who sanctifies or the one who is sanctified?, 165–68
Donner, Fred, 20, 46–53, 59, 76
Donner's four categories, 46
Donner's four views, 51

E

Early Formation of Islam
Early formation according to the neo-Revisionists, 68–71
The formation of Intermediate Monotheism, 71–78
epigraphic, 51–54, 65, 77, 78
Esposito, John, 46, 81, 84, 85, 87, 88, 89, 156, 157
eyewitness, eyewitnesses, 51, 52, 54, 55, 56, 57, 59, 78, 93, 212, 213, 249
eyewitness account(s), reports, 51, 54, 56, 57, 59, 78, 93, 212, 213
eyewitness testimony, 249

F

Fakhry, Majid, 81, 82, 84, 86, 89, 144, 146
Firestone, Reuven, 49, 52, 73
Florovsky, Georges, 21, 25, 34, 35, 171
fly-leaf fragment, 59
Foederati, 66
forensic, 51, 52, 65, 78
Fred Donner. See Donner, Fred.
Furqan, 63

G

Galland(i), 118–26, 128, 136, 138
Goddess, goddesses, 99, 106, 203, 205
Griffith, Sidney, 1, 30, 32, 33, 52, 59, 62, 63, 126, 201, 219, 220–226, 229–33, 239, 240, 249
Grosseteste, 118, 122, 125, 127

H

Habermas, Gary, 51

Index

hadith(s), 45, 47, 48, 49, 50, 51, 53, 87, 93, 98, 100, 204, 240
Hagarene(s), 56, 67, 98, 137
Heifer, 106, 205, 206, 215
Heraclius, 30, 73, 99
heresies, 2–18, 57, 90–98, 128, 169, 179, 190–98, 232, 242, 252, 253
heresy, 1–19, 55, 57, 62, 65, 69, 71, 76, 79, 87, 89–100, 106, 110–12, 115, 116, 127, 128, 131–35, 154, 156, 162, 169, 182, 183, 188–90, 196–98, 200–208, 218, 227, 236, 238, 249–54
Heresy of the Ishmaelites, Analysis, 93–111
    Authorship and Authenticity, 93–97
    Origins of the Saracen religion, 97–99
    Muhammad as a "false prophet," 99–101
    Muhammad's teachings on Christ, 101–3
    John's critique of Muhammad's teaching, 104–6
    The Qur'an and the Surahs used, 106–10
    Practices of the Saracens, 110–11
Heresy of the Ishmaelites, 1, 55, 57, 62, 79, 87, 89, 90–98, 110–16, 128, 131–35, 154, 169, 183, 188, 197, 202–6, 238, 249–53
heretic(s), 3, 4, 10, 12, 14, 87, 97, 152–56, 207, 214
heretical, 2, 3, 4, 9, 14, 15, 17, 71, 78, 79, 83, 88, 97, 102, 115, 133, 155, 156, 193, 195, 198, 206, 207, 213, 217, 236, 247, 251, 253
heterodox, 3, 5, 14, 90, 199
heterodoxical, 6, 19, 250
heteroousions, heteroousios, 16, 17
Hijrah, 66, 67, 74
Hippolytus, 12
homoiousia, homoousios, 15, 16, 17
Homoiousian(s), Homoiousions, 16, 17
Hoyland, Robert, 21, 23–25, 28, 29, 31–33, 37, 38, 42, 45, 46, 52–63, 66–77, 93, 96, 97, 112, 118, 129, 201–4, 214, 219, 223–26
hypostases, 10, 17, 186, 194, 196, 197, 227, 229, 233, 234, 246
hypostasis, 16, 17, 133, 161, 162, 173, 177, 179, 185, 186, 196, 197, 227

I

ibn-Hisham, 53, 69, 96, 101
ibn-Ishaq, 45, 53, 67, 69, 96, 100, 101, 107, 204, 224, 229, 240, 244
ibn-Khaldun, 86
ibn-Warraq. See Warraq, ibn.
iconoclasm, 36, 38, 191–93
iconoclast, 36
iconoclastic, 22, 24, 36, 42, 55, 197, 202, 236
iconoclasts, 31, 35, 37, 43, 92, 95, 191, 192
incarnate, 10, 196
incarnation, 11, 16, 120, 134, 160–65, 172, 175, 191, 196, 202, 207–9, 212, 216, 220, 221, 225, 226, 228
indwelling, 12, 186
Intermediate Monotheism, 65, 71, 72, 74, 75, 77
Irenaeus, 11, 12
Ishmael, 98, 99, 113, 211
Ishmaelite(s), 20, 47, 56–62, 67–69, 76, 79, 89, 96–98, 105, 106, 110, 111, 113, 135, 160, 183, 188, 203–8, 216, 238
isnads, 48, 49

J

Jabarite(s), Jabrites, 80, 143–47, 151, 216
jabr, 83, 84
Jacobite(s), 190, 195, 197, 199, 224, 226, 227, 233
Jahmite 86, 154–58
John Esposito. See Esposito, John.
Johns, Jeremy, 52, 53, 68, 75, 76, 77
John of Damascus, 22–42
    Birth and death, 22–25
    Prominence of his family, 25–29
    Retirement from Public Office, 30–31

Index   295

Monastery Life and Writings, 31–37
Traditional biographical information on John, 37–40
The high quality of his education, 41–42
John's Islamic Context, 46–65
Donner's four categories, 46–50
An alternative view of the development of Islam, 51–52
The Neo-Revisionist view, 52–54
Literature that may convey history, 54–55
Testimony of the non-Muslim sources, 56–65
Justinian, 26, 29, 134

K

ka'ba, 55, 105, 203, 205, 211, 223
Kharijite(s), 80–83, 143
koptae, 105
Kotter, Bonifatius, 1, 23, 95, 96, 116–29, 131, 133–36, 138, 141, 143, 145, 146, 148–52, 156, 160, 161, 164, 165, 194, 252

L

Letham, Robert, 6, 12–18, 174, 178, 179, 196
logothetes, 26
Luxenberg, Christophe, 49, 52

M

magaritai, 67
maghazi, 74, 240
Mahdi, 69, 240–245
Mahgraye, 63, 67, 68
Mahmed, 96
Manichaean(s), 133, 142, 143, 191–94
Manichaeism, 98, 142, 190, 193, 198, 253
Mansur ibn Sarjun, 25–29, 31, 36, 74, 193
Marcion, 4, 10, 11, 13
Marcionism, 10, 11
Mark Beaumont. See Beaumont, Mark.

Mar Sabas, 21, 23, 30, 31, 32, 34, 39, 40, 42, 43, 44, 230, 231, 236
Martyr, Justin, 10, 53
Marwan, 25, 69
Ma'mun, 85, 244
Melkite(s), 33–35, 44, 199, 224–31, 250
mhaggare, 68
mhaggraye, 67
mhmd, 62
modalism, 8, 13, 14
monad, 9, 194
Monarchian(s), Monarchianism, 13, 15
Monophysite(s), 56, 71, 133, 191, 195–98, 227, 230
Monotheism, monotheistic. See also Intermediate Monotheism, 8, 55, 56, 61, 63–66, 71–76, 179, 250
Muawiyah, Mu'awiyah, 23, 25, 62, 75, 76, 81
mu'minun, 54, 56, 67, 75, 76
Mu'tazila, 84, 85
Mu'tazilite(s), 80, 84–89, 146, 147, 154–58, 161

N

Nazianzus, Gregory, 12, 17, 171
Nyssa, Gregory, 14, 17, 171, 176, 177, 178, 248
Neo-Revisionists, 52, 65, 68, 69, 71, 72, 75, 77, 78, 114
Nestorianism, 195, 196, 253
Nestorian(s), 191, 196, 197, 198, 199, 233, 224, 226, 227
Nevo, Yehuda, 46, 49, 52–75, 77, 107–10, 129
numismatic, 51–54, 65, 69, 78

O

Origen, 2, 14, 18, 53
ousia, 10, 11, 17, 173, 229, 246

P

Pact of Umar, 27
papyrus, papyri, 66, 67, 71
Patricia Crone. See Crone, Patricia.

perichoresis, 12, 178, 179, 180, 181, 187
perichoretic, perichoretical. *See* also circle dance, 179, 181,185, 186, 242, 243, 248
polemical, 48, 49, 50, 57, 93, 98, 168, 188, 189, 190, 197, 198, 200, 224, 236, 252, 253
polemically, 110, 190
polemicist(s), 8, 116
polemics, 20, 47, 200
Polycarp, 7, 8, 11
protasis, 223

Q
qadar, 83
Qadarites, 80–85, 143–47, 151, 216
qadr, 84, 143, 144, 145

R
Ra'ita. *See* abu-Ra'ita.
refutation, 19, 142, 162, 185, 253
refute, 5, 10, 91, 110, 191, 196, 197, 209, 211, 226, 248, 254
revisionist(s), 49–52
Robert Hoyland. *See* Hoyland, Robert.

S
Sahas, Daniel. *See* also Daniel Sahas, 21–38, 92–100, 112–22, 125, 130–33, 136, 141, 143–47, 149, 151–59, 164, 168, 202, 214
Sana'a, 45
Saracen, 2, 19, 36, 55, 61, 64, 67, 68, 87, 93, 97, 101, 103, 110, 111, 114, 115, 123–68, 169, 189, 190, 193, 197, 199, 200, 202, 205, 207, 209–18, 223, 249, 251–53
Sargun, Sarjun b. Mansur – John's father, 23, 25, 26, 74
Sergius, also Sargun, 23, 26, 27, 226
She-camel, 106, 108, 214, 251
shirk, 103, 105, 161, 188, 200, 242
Shi'ites, 80
Sidney Griffith. *See* Griffith, Sidney.
Sophronius, 56, 57, 58, 60, 68, 93
source-critical, 46, 47, 48, 50

source-criticism, 47
subordination, 14, 15, 72, 167
subordinationism, 11, 14, 15
Sunni, 89, 151, 158
Syriac, 47, 49, 59, 63, 67, 73, 204, 221, 226, 229, 231, 239, 240
Syriac Christian, 49, 221, 239, 240
Syriacized, 67

T
Table, the, 106, 108, 205, 206, 215
Targums, 73
tayyaye, 59, 68
Tertullian, 12, 13
Theological Development of Islam, 80–89
  Early development of Islamic Theology, 80–81
  Faith versus Works, 81–82
  Predestination versus Free Will, 82–84
  Rise of the Mu'tazilites, 84–85
  Created Word (Qur'an) versus Uncreated Word, 85–87
  Fall of the Mu'tazilites and the rise of the Ash'arites, 88–89
Theodore, brother of John of Damascus, 24–25
Theodore of Edessa, 32–33
Theodore abu-Qurra(h). *See* abu-Qurrah, Theodore.
Theophanes, 23, 24, 26–37, 43, 219
Thomas Aquinas. *See* Aquinas, Thomas.
traditional account(s), 22, 46, 53, 58, 60, 67, 70
traditional biographical, 22, 37
traditional-critical, 46, 48, 50
traditional dates, 23, 31
traditionalism, 80
traditionalist(s), 75, 80, 86–89, 147
traditional view, 32, 45, 46, 73
Traditionists, 80, 87
Trinitarian, 10, 12, 13, 16, 17, 90, 91, 170, 189, 195, 251, 254
Trinitarian doctrine, 91, 251
Trinitarian heresies, 16, 90, 195

Trinitarian Beliefs of John of Damascus, 170–87
Fount of Knowledge and *Orthodox Faith*, 170–71
God is "ineffable and incomprehensible," 171
Apophatic and Kataphatic, 171–72
The use of "ousia" and "hypostasis," 173
Demonstrating the existence of God, 173–74
The nature and essence of God, 175
The unity of God, 176
The Word of God, the Logos, 177
The Holy Spirit, 177
The procession of the Spirit from the Father only, 178
Perichoresis, the circle dance and "inexists," 178
The triune monotheism in contrast to polytheism and the monotheism of Judaism, 179
The God who is "ineffable and transcendent," 180–82
The difference between the nature of divine generation and procession, 183–85
The nature of the procession of the Holy Spirit, 186
The nature of the relationship between the Holy Spirit and the Son, 186
Perichoresis ("coinherence") and the nature of the divine unity, 186–87

The Trinity in Heresy of the Ishmaelites, 188–89
The Trinity in Disputation between a Christian and a Saracen, 190–91
Iconoclasm, 191–93
Manichaeism, 193–95
Monophysitism and Nestorianism, 195–97
Trinity, 1–18, 36, 37, 50, 71, 79, 80, 89, 90, 91, 101–4, 114, 134, 155, 162, 163, 164, 166, 169–79, 181, 184, 186, 188–98, 201, 205, 211, 220–254
tritheism, 8, 9, 10, 14, 17

U

Umar, 25, 27, 30, 31, 43, 63, 75, 223
Umayyad, 21, 25, 28, 29, 30, 44, 71, 78, 81, 82, 83, 84, 99, 140, 156, 192, 193, 201, 250
Umayyad caliph(s), 25, 83, 192
Umayyad empire, 21, 28, 29, 44, 140, 193, 250
Umayyad era, 201
Umayyads, 82, 194
Uthman, 59, 75, 81

W

Wansbrough, John, 68, 72
Warraq, ibn, 25, 67, 70, 71, 72

Y

Yehuda Nevo *See* Nevo, Yehuda.